Teachers at Work

TEACHERS AT WORK

Achieving Success in Our Schools

SUSAN MOORE JOHNSON

BasicBooks
A Division of HarperCollins*Publishers*

Although *Teachers at Work* is factually accurate, the names and identifying details of individuals and institutions portrayed in the book have been changed.

Library of Congress Cataloging-in-Publication Data
Johnson, Susan Moore.
Teachers at work: achieving success in our schools / Susan Moore Johnson.
p. cm.
Includes bibliographical references.
ISBN 0-465-08362-5 (cloth)
ISBN 0-465-08363-3 (paper)
1. Teachers—United States—Case studies. 2. Teaching—Case studies. 3. Classroom environment—United States—Case studies. 4. Public schools—United States—Case studies. I. Title.
LB1775.J546 1990
371.11'02—dc20 89-49694
CIP

Printed in the United States of America
Designed by Linda Dingler
91 92 93 94 AT/HC 9 8 7 6 5 4 3 2 1

To My Parents
Teachers both, in their own places

Contents

Acknowledgments

I decided to write this book while returning from a meeting on the west coast, doing the kind of thinking that, for me, occurs only on airplanes. I felt the heady excitement of a new project conceived in solitude, uncomplicated by reality. I was certain that I could carry it off. That was the last heroic, self-sufficient moment of the effort. Since then, I have been dependent upon, beholden to, and grateful for the kindness and efforts of many generous people who have helped me to move that early idea out into the schools and eventually to these printed pages. It is well past time to acknowledge my debts.

Like many researchers who study schools, I am first and foremost grateful to the many teachers and administrators who participated in the research. Principals took the time to recommend staff, and teachers were kind enough to set aside their skepticism about researchers and speak candidly about matters of great personal and professional importance. I have tried earnestly to represent their views fully and fairly. I wish that I could thank each of them individually, but they must remain unnamed as promised.

I am grateful to the Spencer Foundation and the National Academy of Education for their support. As a Spencer Fellow of the Academy, which is headed by Patricia Albjerg Graham and administered by Gail Keeley, I was given a precious year for thinking and writing.

ACKNOWLEDGMENTS

I have taught a course about the school as a workplace for several years at Harvard. The class, composed largely of experienced teachers and principals, explored and debated the issues of this study. From this distance, I cannot recall the origins of all the ideas in this book, but many grew out of discussions with these students.

A small group of graduate students worked closely with me on the project, scheduling and conducting interviews with more care and attention than I thought possible. I am truly indebted to Sheryl Boris-Schacter, Tony Cipollone, Ada Beth Cutler, Paula Hajar, and Jeff Young for their skillful interviewing and analytic insights.

Over the course of four years, Gerry Basteri, Susan Thomas, Martha Metzler, and Linda Corey ably kept clerical order—preparing letters, cataloging responses, and printing chapter drafts. Paula Hajar and Molly Schen spent countless hours transcribing interview tapes, laboring to catch even the faintest aside when those less dedicated to the cause of improving education would have given up.

I am grateful as well to colleagues and reviewers who generously read and commented on earlier drafts of the manuscript. Kitty Boles, Ada Beth Cutler, Paula Hajar, Lesley Iura, Ann Lieberman, Gene Maeroff, Leticia Peña, and Blake Rodman offered encouragement and provided valuable critical assistance.

My friend and colleague, Helen Featherstone, kindly helped me find my way to Martin Kessler of Basic Books. Susan Arellano, my editor there, offered sound advice and provided continuing encouragement for the book. Stephanie Hoppe edited the manuscript with care and Cheryl Friedman skillfully supervised the book's production.

I have often been sustained or revived during the difficult periods of this project by friends who listened, laughed, offered encouragement and advice. They have commented on drafts, debated key points, dreamed up titles, suggested alternative explanations, and kept me believing that I was up to the task. Lori Berry, Kitty Boles, Kay Merseth, Barbara Neufeld, Peggy

O'Brien, John Ritchie, and Jane Roessner have been there for me and I thank them.

My children, Krister and Erika, came of age during the course of this project and followed its progress enthusiastically. Their pride often carried me along. Their stories of school regularly reminded me how teachers do change lives. Watching them grow and sharing their company has brought me great joy. My husband, Glenn, has compensated for my own uncertainties with unswerving confidence in me and my work. He has read drafts, helped me think in new ways, rescued me from technological disasters, and listened sympathetically to woeful tales of research and writing gone awry. Without my family's love and companionship, my own workplace would have been a desolate one.

Introduction

For over a decade those concerned about the well-being of the United States have monitored the vital signs of the public schools. Some school critics claim that American public education is already in its death throes, while others warn that the current school reform movement presents the last chance for resuscitation. Even those loyalists who contend that public schools now educate a greater proportion of youth than ever before acknowledge that serious problems persist. In some large cities 40 to 50 percent of the students never complete high school, and some who do cannot read or divide.[1] Those students who master basic skills often cannot solve problems requiring more sophisticated reasoning,[2] and international comparisons of test scores reveal that U.S. students no longer command the worldwide academic lead they once had. Leaders from business and industry charge that graduates are not prepared to do the jobs that must be done, and as a result, Japan and West Germany are fast becoming the United States' economic betters.[3]

Individuals may differ in estimating the severity of this educational crisis, but most agree that it exists, and that ultimately school improvement depends on good teachers being ready and able to do good work. Who teaches matters. If teachers are only minimally qualified or pedestrian in their approach to instruction, they will not likely inform or inspire their students. If they are intelligent, skilled, and creative in the classroom, students are likely to respond with hard work and academic progress.

Good teachers are in short supply. The most academically talented candidates never enter the classroom, and the best leave after only a short tenure.[4] When Louis Harris asked former teachers why they had quit teaching, they said that they were disappointed with working conditions that interfered with instruction, discouraged by low pay, and demoralized by their lack of professional prestige.[5] As workplaces, schools fell far short of their expectations. In some cases, those who left the classroom were probably not cut out to be teachers; they were not loving, versatile, patient, insightful, or tireless enough. In too many cases, though, successful and committed teachers have left the profession because their workplaces were inferior, confining, disheartening environments that prohibited them from doing the work they set out to do and that most people believe they should do.

The world has long assumed that teachers, like preachers, should serve with selfless disregard for the circumstances of their work; that they should ignore the leaks in school roofs; tolerate salaries that fail to cover their bills; cope with lockstep schedules, large classes, and inadequate supplies; gracefully accept their lack of influence in school policy and disregard the absence of opportunities to learn, grow, and advance in their work. However, teachers, like surgeons, engineers, or architects, do take stock of their workplaces; and when prospective teachers ask whether schools are well-equipped, hospitable organizations that support good teaching and good teachers, they seldom are reassured by the answer.

Three decades ago, women aspiring to professional work were restricted largely to careers in nursing or teaching. They had few choices and were obliged to accept whatever working conditions were available. Now that women routinely consider alternate careers in business, law, medicine, or engineering, the character and quality of the workplace matter much more. Public education no longer can rely on what has been called the hidden subsidy of women's work. If outstanding candidates reject teaching because of the workplace, if talented teachers abandon the classroom because schools as they are now organized discourage good teaching, public education certainly will not improve, and the society will continue to pay the price of an uneducated citizenry.

Many regions of the United States can expect to encounter severe teacher shortages during the next decade as student populations grow and large numbers of teachers reach retirement age.[6] In California and Florida, new immigrant populations have already swelled student numbers and created substantial teacher shortages.[7] Who will fill those vacancies? We know from past experience that school districts will manage to find an adult to stand at the front of every class; immediate demands for custodial care, safety, and social order will ensure that. But we also know that teachers hired in a state of urgency are likely to be marginally qualified and only minimally able. Some will lack the basic skills that they are expected to teach. Some will discourage serious inquiry in favor of rote learning. Some will not enjoy children.

Amid these discouraging prospects is reason for modest optimism. Evidence in 1988 that the qualifications of prospective teachers were on the rise suggests that a new generation of capable students is responding to the call for service.[8] The recruits are still few—the supply falls far short of the projected demand—but they offer a note of hope. Given the well-publicized shortcomings of today's schools, will these talented candidates actually enter and remain in teaching? And if they do, will they be able to do their best work and sustain their initial commitment? It seems likely that public schools ultimately will get the teachers they deserve; unfortunately, the students may not.

APPROACHES TO IMPROVING TEACHING

When *A Nation at Risk* raised the alarm about the threat to the nation posed by inferior schools,[9] states and local school districts responded with an array of regulations and prescriptions designed to upgrade teachers' qualifications and improve their performance—licensing exams, mandated curricula, competency tests for students. Teachers were to be directed like laborers, their productivity measured with tests. A large urban school district in Texas prescribed a proficiency-based curriculum and standardized tests to monitor teachers' performance, while the state mandated evaluation practices that tied jobs and pay to teachers' compliance.[10] School officials in Philadelphia who sought to control teachers' work prepared a standardized curriculum for each subject and grade along with a pacing schedule that dictated how much time teachers should spend on each topic. They established uniform grading and promotion standards based on a new series of standardized tests developed to match the curriculum.[11] Implicit in such regulatory measures was the assumption that teachers could be made more productive with standardized training, explicit directions, and close supervision.

Meanwhile other states, such as Florida and Tennessee, experimented with merit pay and bonuses for exemplary teachers. Although proponents of these incentive plans contended that rewarding outstanding practice would motivate better performance by all teachers, critics suggested that distinguishing a select few would undermine collegiality and actively discourage teachers from serving those students who offered less opportunity to the teacher but stood in the greatest need.[12]

Efforts to regulate teaching practice and institute merit pay encountered enormous opposition from teachers and achieved only modest, some would say short-lived, success in schools. Prescriptive policies often met passive resistance from staff and sometimes backfired. For example, one researcher found that only 11 percent of the Philadelphia teachers she interviewed implemented all aspects of the curriculum policy, only 10 percent used the pacing schedule, and 4 percent complied with the grading guidelines.[13] Eight magnet-school teachers in one Texas district were so discouraged by the constraints of packaged curricula that they resigned, taking with them their innovative ideas and their passion for teaching.[14]

As it became clear that these regulatory reforms not only evoked anger and resistance among teachers but also failed to increase test scores, policy analysts tendered a new explanation of the schooling problem, one that also centered on teachers and their work.[15] Schools were disabled, they said, by bureaucratic structures that kept teachers from doing their best work. Ironically, some of the constraints these analysts pointed to were the very ones that had been imposed and elaborated by the earlier reformers. According to the new analysis, if only teachers gained greater influence and authority in their careers and their schools, they would find greater satisfaction in their work, and students would benefit. The Holmes Group, for example, proposed differentiating teaching roles and staging careers to enhance the professional stature of teaching. The Carnegie Forum on Education and the Economy promoted a national certification program for master teachers and suggested that schools could be governed by executive committees of lead teachers who might hire their own principals. The strategy of these so-called second wave reformers was to transfer authority for educational design to teachers, making them the agents rather than the objects of school reform.

These policy analysts, like the architects of earlier changes, approached the problem as a political one, the issue being who was to have power over the direction of schooling. Where the early reformers placed control in the hands of state and local politicians and administrators, these proponents of greater professional control of schools contended that teachers were best suited and positioned to improve public education. This second strategy has met with greater favor among teachers and seems more consistent with what is known about teachers' need for control over their work, but it begs the question of how schools should be organized for better teaching and learning. What structures, standards, norms, and practices enable and encourage teachers to do their best work? We know little yet about how teachers themselves would systematically improve their work in schools if they were given the power to do so.

THE SCHOOL AS WORKPLACE

The school as workplace is composed of a constellation of features, each of which contributes to or detracts from teachers' satisfaction and productivity. For example, teachers not only pay attention to the *physical* components of their workplaces, considering whether they are safe, functional, comfortable, well maintained, and well equipped, but they are also concerned with *organizational structures,* including teaching loads, the demands and flexibility of the schedule, and the amount of discretion they are expected or allowed to exercise in their teaching. They take stock of their workplaces from a *sociological* perspective, considering their roles as teachers and their consequent relationships with colleagues, superiors, students, and parents. Teachers also assess the *political* character of their schools, noting whether they can influence policy decisions, such as how educational dollars are spent, who is hired, or which textbooks are ordered. They are watchful of *economic* conditions, including job security, salaries, and access to the incentives and rewards that matter to them. They respond to their schools' *cultures,* noting the presence or absence of positive norms, rich histories, and compelling traditions that engage students, peers, administrators, and parents in a shared set of constructive purposes. Finally, teachers assess the *psychological* dimensions of work in schools, considering whether the meaning of teaching is enhanced or diminished by their workplace, whether the personal and professional stresses of teaching are tolerable, and whether teaching provides sufficient opportunity for their own learning and growth.

Although an initial decision to enter teaching may involve only some of these workplace features, current teachers are influenced by the full array in deciding whether to continue in teaching. Deficits in some areas may drive good teachers away from schools, even if there are strengths in others. Sleek and efficient facilities may not compensate for inflexible schedules or excessive paperwork. Small classes will not guarantee good teaching if the school fails to encourage productive home/school relationships. Attractive opportunities for personal growth may be outweighed by discontent over salaries that fall short of expenses, obliging teachers to take second jobs. No single element will suffice to attract or retain good teachers; the overall balance of workplace features determines who staffs the schools.

Schools as workplaces not only influence teachers' career choices, they affect current teachers' attitudes toward their work. Workplace deficiencies are demoralizing; they constrain and inhibit good teachers from doing their best work. Teachers burdened with bureaucratic obligations, lacking a say in what and how they teach, having no time for discussions with their colleagues, and distanced from parents cannot forever rise above these conditions. Unappreciated staff withdraw to the isolation of their classrooms and withhold their energy and pedagogical wisdom from the larger organization. As Theodore Sizer observed, "Teachers are often treated like hired hands. Not surprisingly, they often act like hired hands."[16] Festering over time, such dissatisfaction is likely to reduce teachers' efforts, may even compromise their commitment to students, and ultimately will diminish the quality of schooling.

Even those teachers who retain their commitment may find their success limited. A chemistry teacher without a lab cannot successfully train aspiring scientists. An elementary-school teacher lacking clerical support must spend precious time collecting lunch money or duplicating work sheets. A social studies teacher who is required to comply with a prescribed curriculum cannot pursue timely topics of compelling interest to her and her students. A middle-school teacher who works amid unethical colleagues will have difficulty convincing students that responsible behavior is important in school or in life. Obviously, the character of the school as a workplace determines not only who teaches, but also how they teach.

INTRODUCTION

THE STUDY OF THE SCHOOL AS WORKPLACE

Few studies of schooling address the context of teaching, focusing instead on the act of teaching or the interaction of teachers and students. The school as workplace appears only as background for discussions of curricula, discipline, or instructional techniques. However, those who study schools have begun to acknowledge what has long been commonplace knowledge in other fields—that the workplace profoundly affects the work.

This study takes a new look at the instructional scene, bringing into sharper focus what is usually the background of inquiry. Rather than examining teaching objectives, assignments, or instructional strategies, this study centers on the context of teaching as it is experienced by teachers—physical setting and resources; organizational structures; relationships among colleagues, clients, and superiors; influence in governance; cultural norms and traditions; opportunities for learning and growth; and the role of pay and incentives. By shifting our perspective we may come to a better understanding of what it means to work in schools, an understanding that will enable us to explore the interaction of the workplace and instruction, and to recommend changes in the school as a workplace that will promote good teaching and better schooling. Of necessity the study is exploratory, given the methodological problems of defining such intangibles as good teaching or measuring with any certainty the degree to which features of the workplace contribute to or detract from the quality of schooling.

When most of us think about teachers, we call to mind individuals from our past who amused, bored, coerced, or inspired us—a third-grade teacher who was accomplished in the Palmer method of handwriting; a geometry teacher who could barely explain the proofs; a senior English teacher who was astute, literate, and spoke to us as adults. We may also think of our children's teachers whose classrooms are alive with gerbils and snakes, whose science lessons promote dinner-table discussions about acid rain and aerodynamics, or whose straight-from-the-book lectures imply that all knowledge has been codified, printed, and bound.

Particular teachers shape our expectations and responses to teachers as a group. Although we may acknowledge that teachers are not a homogeneous lot, we continue to generalize from the individuals we have known when we judge teachers' capabilities and their commitment to self or schooling. Such judgments, in turn, influence the design of policies intended to improve schools. Policy makers who regard teachers favorably tend to structure reforms for the best of them, proposing changes that increase teachers' authority and expand their instructional resources.[17] Those who judge teachers less favorably are more likely to consider reform as an opportunity to regulate the performance of the least able and advance proposals that prescribe and monitor minimum standards.[18]

Before we can contemplate school reform, we must clarify our stance toward teachers and our expectations for change. Will we direct reforms toward those teachers who are learned, thoughtful, and generous? Or base our designs on recalcitrant, illiterate, or selfish individuals? Should we move toward collegial governance for schools or continue management by nonteaching administrators? Should teachers be encouraged to innovate? To work from their own strengths and preferences? Or should they comply with formal curricula and meet fixed standards of productivity? Although most would say that these can never be either/or decisions, the school reforms of the 1980s typically featured one or the other approach, rather than a differentiated plan that addresses the needs of diverse teaching ranks.

The present study emerges from my own sympathetic and optimistic stance toward teachers. Many of my teachers were not particularly engaging, but the best of them changed my life. My children's teachers are not uniformly superb, but many are, and I have seen the difference that they make. In nine years of teaching, I came to understand how difficult it is to teach well and constructively influence all students' lives. A few of my colleagues were simply putting in time, but most worked very hard and often achieved remarkable results. I begin, therefore, not blind to the existence of mediocre or incompetent teachers, but committed to promoting policies and practices that will encourage better work by good people rather than simply ensure minimal compliance by weak ones. I believe that reform in schooling must look to the long term in attracting and sustaining able teachers.

I have chosen to examine work in schools from the perspectives of teachers whose work is valued, whose teaching has been judged by their principals to be "very good," and who are said to make positive contributions to their schools. I have sought to learn from them how they experience their schools as workplaces, what particular features they think support or compromise their best teaching, and what changes they believe might enable them to be better teachers. I began with the assumption that before embarking on further reform policy makers, school officials, and teachers themselves must better understand how exemplary teachers experience teaching.

My sample is intentionally drawn from above-average teachers. I believe it is worth carefully studying this group of teachers, because it is they, rather than those who are merely satisfactory, whose numbers should be increased. It is they who are likely to determine the course of school improvement. It is they who, under current working conditions, are most likely to leave teaching after several years. It is they for whom new roles as mentors and lead teachers are being fashioned. Finally, it is these valued teachers whose continued presence in the profession is likely to attract others like them into teaching. They represent the strength of the profession. If we care about our schools, we must attend to their views and be informed by their insights.

Readers may object that we should direct school reforms toward those "average" teachers, who are presumably less able or motivated, but greater in number. A better idea would be to tailor policies to diverse groups of teachers; proposals for lead teachers and career ladders do just that. However, in order for the education profession to attract and retain exemplary teachers, schools must become exemplary workplaces. They must attract individuals who seek responsibility and influence, who want to learn and grow, who expect to make a difference in children's lives and in society, and who believe that in their schools they can. Moreover, schools must be organized to ensure that all teachers of whatever abilities are encouraged and supported in doing their best work. Workplaces that inhibit and disable the best staff are unlikely to improve the performance of those who are only average. By contrast, schools that promote productive teaching by very good staff are likely to encourage less able teachers to improve or assume their share of responsibility for the larger organization. Schools should not be governed by a set of minimum standards that tolerate or encourage mediocrity. They should not isolate teachers in ways that spawn either insecurity or complacency. They should, in short, contribute to improved performance by all.

My approach is inductive. I have not tried to explain what the term "very good" meant to the principals who nominated respondents; their explanations would vary from individual to individual and school to school.[19] I sought only to know who such "valued" teachers were and to ask them how they experienced their schools as workplaces. Then, in the interviews, we probed the extent to which the teachers' perspectives, values, and insights were similar. The sample of 115 teachers includes 75 from public schools, 20 from independent schools, and 20 from church-related schools. (See appendix for details and methodology.) In fact, the responses were remarkably consistent; where they differed, it was possible and enlightening to account for those differences.

The past decade has seen an intense, somewhat frantic search for a single remedy for the widely perceived failings in U.S. schooling. Policy analysts have shifted their hopes rapidly from one attractive remedy to another—the formula for effective schools, standardized curricula and testing, professional governance, and, most recently, parental choice. Too often, reformers champion policies and initiatives that address the problems piecemeal. A legislature votes to increase pay, a union organizes to augment teachers' roles in decision making, or a principal makes a personal effort to acknowledge teachers' contributions with notes of thanks. Where such initiatives are complementary, it is more often by chance than design. Those who try to make schools better usually introduce only one or two initiatives, hoping that teachers will be buoyed by a new set of textbooks, a revised schedule, or classes with two fewer students. School work is not so simple. Thoughtful persons can hardly be surprised to learn that those sporadic and isolated initiatives have had little observable effect on teachers' satisfaction or students' performance.

There is no magic bullet, and those who would improve schooling must approach their task with respect for its complexity. This study suggests that improving the school as a workplace will involve many persons on many fronts—legislators to influence salaries; leaders from private industry to enrich school resources and opportunities for professional development; union leaders to encourage teachers to assume greater responsibility for their profession; administrators to make the central office a resource center rather than a control center; and parents, teachers, and principals to collaborate and ensure that their schools are responsive to students' needs. Responsibility for change is shared by all with a stake in public education. Reform must be instituted in many different places and then carefully tended and sustained over time. This strategy for reform is not only less linear than the regulatory interventions designed to control teachers, it is based on far more complex understandings of schools and teaching. If schools were restored and refashioned to attract and retain strong staff by making teaching both satisfying and productive work, student performance would likely improve as well. For good teachers want above all else to teach, and good schools ensure that they can.

Some changes that are called for, such as higher wages or renovated facilities, will be costly and will require political action at both the state and local levels. Much that is needed, however, can be done at little or no expense by those already working in schools. A principal can schedule teachers' nonteaching periods so that colleagues who need to work together can do so. A school can use community events and in-school tutors to build more open exchange with parents. Joint committees of teachers and administrators can ensure that in-service training goes beyond marginal matters of management to address issues of serious professional concern to teachers. Central-office administrators can grant teachers real authority in designing curricula and selecting textbooks. Union leaders can negotiate transfer policies that minimize disruption and maximize staff stability. Such reforms depend more on initiative than dollars and can be instituted by local communities without legislative intervention.

My inquiry centers on public schools, where the most serious educational challenges exist, and is designed to illuminate and ultimately improve practices there. The sample of teachers interviewed, including individuals from both private and public schools, permits comparisons between the experience of teaching in the public and private sectors, comparisons that have proved to be revealing. For example, teachers in nonpublic schools frequently reported that the smaller size of their student bodies and faculties, the opportunities for professional growth, and the strong bonds of norms and traditions over time supported their efforts as teachers, making school work more satisfying and productive. There were also costs associated with private schools' selectivity and independence. Salaries were generally lower than in the public sector, programs were less specialized, and student bodies were less diverse. There are lessons for all in these teachers' accounts, and in the end, the findings of this study may be as useful for those who are concerned about private education as for those intent on improving public schools.

The story of these teachers and their workplaces is a complicated one. We begin in chapter 1 with a broad look at work and workplaces, identifying the many factors that comprise any workplace, and reviewing the prominent features of work in schools. Those who are interested in exploring the relationship of teaching to other types of work and considering the similarities of schools to other workplaces should begin here. Those who prefer to meet the valued teachers of this study may move on to chapter 2, which introduces the respondents, investigates their reasons for entering the profession, and asks how satisfied they are with their schools and whether they plan to remain in teaching. Chapter 3 demonstrates the ways in which inadequate and inequitable school spaces and supplies impede valued teachers in their work. Chapter 4 examines the importance of close home/school relationships in teachers' work and suggests how schools can build bridges to the families they serve. Chapter 5 considers the bureaucratic structures of public schooling—large classes, preprogrammed curricula, standardized testing, block schedules—and their unsuitability for the task of teaching. Chapter 6 looks at teachers' isolation and considers ways in which collegiality can be promoted. Chapter 7 investigates why teachers have so little say in school governance and suggests how they might become more influential in determining policy and practice. Chapter 8 examines the lessons that private schools can offer about the importance of building communities and nurturing values, traditions, and norms. Chapter 9 asks why schools, which are in the business of educating children, do little to promote the learning and growth of the adults who work there. Chapter 10 considers the low salaries that make teaching unaffordable work for some and make it difficult for others to achieve the intrinsic rewards that are most important to teachers. The concluding chapter 11 discusses school reform in light of these findings, outlining the features of a model workplace, proposing policies that would permit its development, and analyzing the changes in attitudes and roles that would be required to bring it about.

Teachers at Work

CHAPTER ONE

On Work and Workplaces

We usually think about work in its place—journalism in news offices, glassblowing near furnaces, geriatric care in nursing homes, and teaching in schools. To be a lawyer is not just to think in lawyerly ways, but to do so within a lawyerly setting, one that is paneled in wood, furnished with leather, and peopled with impartial judges, combative peers, and skilled but subordinate clerks; one that is equipped with tools of the legal trade, such as long yellow pads, volumes of statutes, and sophisticated data bases storing arguments and precedents.

A workplace is more than a physical setting: it is also the context that defines how work is divided and done, how it is scheduled, supervised, compensated, and regarded by others. Lawyers practice their profession as specialists in estate law, labor law, corporate law, or criminal law. Their workdays are long and varied, often requiring overtime in the library but permitting lengthy lunches with clients and colleagues. Although flexible, lawyers' time is accounted for meticulously. Clients are billed for each minute of legal assistance, and lawyers enjoy the status that such exacting rates imply.

Contrast the context for practicing law with that of building cars on assembly lines where humans work beside robots, and the labor of both is regulated by the pace of a relentless conveyor belt. Rather than being masters of many skills, auto workers repeat narrowly prescribed tasks such as welding chassis and assembling window mechanisms in routinized fashion, under close, often critical, supervision. Except for short breaks, assembly-line auto workers are confined to their workstations. They, too, are paid for their time, but in eight-hour shifts rather than high-priced minutes.

To contemplate an occupation is not only to consider the kind of work it involves—sales, service, construction or design—but to reflect on its context as well. Is the workplace safe or hazardous? Do peers work together or alone? Cooperatively or competitively? Is the work challenging or demoralizing? Does the worker have a say in governance? Who controls the use of time? Who decides how the work will be done and judges whether it has been done properly? How secure are jobs and what is the rate of pay?

SIMILAR WORK, SIMILAR WORKPLACES

What accounts for the particular constellation of features that define a workplace? Why, for example, is the context of journalism so different from that of dentistry? Newspaper offices are predictably fast-paced, competitive, and highly interactive environments where journalists respond to the moment, pursue the unexpected, and rush to meet deadlines. By contrast, dentists' offices are controlled and efficient settings, where licensed professionals methodically and independently execute prescribed and practiced techniques. The particular character of any workplace is shaped, first, by the tasks and technologies of the work itself, what is to be done and what tools and techniques are used to do it. Preparing news stories and filling teeth are fundamentally different kinds of tasks. Journalism is interpersonal and adaptive work that calls for a range of abilities from spotting a good story to collecting accurate, telling data to recreating the event in parsimonious, compelling prose. Dentistry is more technical than interpersonal, requiring the execution of specified procedures on the teeth of patients who, ideally, cooperate passively and silently. The circumscribed workplace of the dentist—a few office rooms with mechanized chairs, x-ray machines, and laboratory equipment—is far more certain and controlled than the expansive, unpredictable work world of the journalist. The technology of journalism—asking questions, following leads, writing accounts—is varied and, compared with the explicit procedures of dentistry, only approximately specified.

Not only does the character of the workplace derive from the work itself, but it is also the product of historical and social conventions. Dentists have achieved professional status in our society largely by virtue of their association with physicians. Although the technical work of dentistry could conceivably be standardized and supervised much as car maintenance is, it has remained autonomous, discretionary work. Dentists are trained, licensed, and left largely to the oversight of their own professional consciences. By contrast, journalists come from a variety of educational backgrounds and are free of regulatory licenses. Although they may exercise considerable autonomy in pursuing stories, their written accounts of those stories are closely scrutinized by editors and eventually subjected to the standards of a large, anonymous public. Journalists may achieve respect, even renown, for their work, but they are not accorded regard simply by virtue of their occupation, as dentists routinely are. Fixing decayed teeth seems, in itself, no more lofty work than reporting the news, and it certainly might be argued that it is no more socially valuable, but over time, our society has come to grant it higher status.

Teachers' workplaces are easily distinguished from those of dentists or journalists. Schools are complex, busy institutions where licensed workers are responsible for batch processing the education of large groups of clients for several months at a time. Teachers need not generate work; it comes to them. Their time, but not necessarily their performance, is closely watched by principals whose administrative span of control is large and who assume many and varied managerial responsibilities, from monitoring instruction to monitoring buses. As with journalism and dentistry, the distinctive features of teaching can be traced to the task and technology of the work as well as its unique set of social and historical conventions.

Teaching is necessarily interactive and people centered. Imparting skills, conveying subject content and theoretical concepts, promoting personal development, and building social conscience and responsibility are complex and gradual endeavors requiring regular, close contact between teachers and students. Teaching is not a remote or disengaged activity.

Students, the clients with whom teachers work, are varied and unpredictable. Some students can read when they enter grade one, while others cannot read when they finish grade seven. Their brains work differently and they have different styles of learning. They have been nurtured by different families and bring to schools different attitudes toward formal education.

Further, the technology of teaching is neither well defined nor widely accepted. Compared with the explicit technology of building a bridge or flying an airplane, the most effective methods for teaching biology or history are elusive and in dispute. Despite years of effort, researchers still have only tentative notions about how children learn and, therefore, how they should be taught.[1] Although individual teachers frequently have complicated and detailed strategies for their work—phonics for teaching reading, science experiments for teaching inductive reasoning—there are no proven, standardized procedures that all teachers agree constitute good practice.[2] The goals of teaching are also multiple and sometimes conflicting. Different communities place different values on literacy, patriotism, critical thinking, creative expression, mastery of basic skills, and personal development, but teachers are seldom told how to achieve these goals in their work or how to reconcile conflicting expectations. They are expected to diagnose complex problems and address individual differences with an array of responses while simultaneously responding to competing sets of expectations. Little wonder Dan Lortie concluded: "Uncertainty is the lot of those who teach."[3]

The process of education is not only uncertain, but unfolds

over years rather than hours or days. Teachers must take their students as they find them and move them what distance they can along the course of their education and development. No one teacher begins or completes a student's education, and consequently, no single teacher can legitimately claim full credit nor be assigned full blame for what results. Over time, teachers' contributions are interdependent, and they must rely on their colleagues for long-term success in their work. However, at any one moment, they are likely to be on their own, focused on their interactions with their students, with little time to attend to their interdependencies with colleagues.

These characteristics of the task and technology of teaching determine some basic features of work in schools. Because teachers work with people, who are varied and complex, rather than with simple and uniform widgets, their activities are only partially specialized. They teach first grade, physical education, or social studies rather than right-brain learners or deductive reasoners. They must cope with the intellectual, physical, social, and psychological complexity of the whole child. As a result of both the variety of students and teaching's relatively unspecified technology, teachers must exercise discretion in their work. Autonomy, whether intentionally granted by superiors or necessarily seized by teachers behind the classroom door, is a central feature of their work.

Another consequence of teaching's unspecified technology is the difficulty of maintaining effective oversight. The supervision and evaluation of teaching are notoriously weak despite sustained and costly efforts to improve the practice. Given the minimal agreement about what teachers should do, supervising their work is inevitably problematic. Teachers can seldom be held accountable for a core set of purposes, because such purposes are intentionally left unspecified. No one teacher can legitimately be praised or blamed for students' test scores, since each taught (or failed to teach) only part of what students know (or do not know). The character of teaching has made work in schools a predominantly unspecialized yet interdependent enterprise which requires autonomy for teachers and defies close oversight and assessment by superiors.

Other features of teaching derive more from history and social conventions than from the character of the work itself. Because it is an outgrowth of child care, teaching has historically been women's work.[4] Since women and children are granted little respect or power in our society, teaching remains low in status, with teachers being paid far less than workers with similar years of training who hold more socially valued jobs. Schools are often shabby, barely adequate facilities, with broken windows, unpainted walls, and substandard equipment, reflecting the society's low regard for teachers' work and children's learning. Even in wealthy and prestigious school districts, teachers usually lack offices, phones, and computers. Moreover, teachers are explicitly subordinate to school administrators, who are usually male, and who often are removed from classrooms, attending to managerial rather than instructional matters. For those who teach, there are few opportunities for formal professional advancement, and most are called "classroom teachers" from the first to the last days of their careers. Given the low status that the physical condition of their work sites implies and the low compensation that their paychecks deliver, teachers must rely primarily on the intrinsic rather than the extrinsic rewards of their work.

A second legacy of educational history is the structure of school buildings themselves, what Dan Lortie has called their "cellular pattern of organization."[5] Originally schools housed only one classroom, but as they grew, they cloned colonies of separate classrooms, headed by isolated teachers. The segmented structure of schools has changed little since the 1800s. Even the open-space schools that were built in the 1960s have been transformed over time into traditionally structured facilities with partitions, doors, and intercoms. For the most part, teachers have chosen to work between high walls and behind closed doors. The isolation of their work is striking given the interdependent nature of education, and it is not clear whether teachers choose to work in isolation because of the highly personal character of teaching, the practical need for quiet and control, or the fear of being judged by others. Perhaps they are influenced by this historical evolution of school structures. Certainly history plays a role.

A third historical factor that shaped the organization of teaching was the movement to bureaucratize public education that began during the early 1900s. David Tyack recounts that the factory became the model for good management, while "efficiency, rationality, continuity, precision, [and] impartiality became watchwords" of those intent on reform.[6] Raymond Callahan has masterfully documented how U.S. educators took heart in the promises of "scientific management" and the prospect of ensuring the highest possible levels of educational productivity.[7] Prominent educators of the time, such as Ellwood P. Cubberly, expounded on the promise of "scientific efficiency" for schooling, and throughout the country, large school districts created so-called efficiency bureaus to assess the productivity of current practices and prescribe more rational and efficient means for educating students.[8] They gave currency to the industrial model of schooling, in which, as Cubberly explained, schools were like

> factories in which the raw products (children) are to be shaped and fashioned into products to meet the various demands of life. The specifications for manufacturing come from the demands of twentieth-century civilization, and it is the business of the school to build its pupils according to specifications laid down.[9]

In today's schools, we see the lasting influence of these beliefs and values in the bureaucratized structures of central offices; the rationing of instructional time; and the emphasis on testing and accountability, departmental structures, heavy teaching loads, and formalized teacher ratings.

The difficulty of specializing or supervising instruction, teachers' need for autonomy, reliance on intrinsic rewards to sustain teachers in their work, and the obstacles to accurately assessing performance derive primarily from the nature of teaching itself and might be expected to be prominent features of work in schools everywhere. Other dimensions of the school as a workplace that emerge more from history and convention than from the character of teaching or its technology, such as physical setting, low status, unstaged careers, poorly maintained facilities, isolation, limited authority, and unrealistic demands for efficiency, seem more likely to vary from workplace to workplace, and ultimately to be more amenable to change.

SIMILAR WORK, DIFFERENT WORKPLACES

Although similar work usually occurs in similar workplaces, sites can differ in important ways, as was dramatically portrayed during the 1970s, when the film and television series, "M.A.S.H.," changed the public's view of what it meant to be a surgeon. Before "M.A.S.H.," the popular image of surgery was imparted by the likes of Dr. Kildare and Ben Casey: it was exacting, well-paid, high-status work conducted alongside skilled attendants in spotless operating rooms equipped with sophisticated electronic monitors and diagnostic equipment. "M.A.S.H." made it clear that surgery in a war zone was a different kind of occupation. Although the task itself was much the same—cutting and sewing—the practice was different, and the differences extended well beyond facilities and setting. The surgeon on the battlefield was forced to be a generalist rather than a specialist. Supplies were limited and primitive, as were the support of learned colleagues and sophisticated information systems. Surgeons could neither regulate the flow of work nor share it with others; of necessity they improvised.

The comparison is extreme, but it illustrates the fact that just as the character of work determines certain features of the workplace, so the character of the workplace determines certain features of the work. For example, let us consider the work of psychotherapists. The various contexts in which psychotherapy is practiced are similar in that they all provide for intense, interactive relationships with clients, they permit the therapist to adapt treatment to the client's diagnosed needs, they rely on licensing rather than direct oversight for supervision, and they divide the workday into client hours. However, there are important differences between practicing psychotherapy in a state hospital, in a health maintenance organization, in a university health service, or in private practice. The particular circumstances of these different workplaces influence the type of client served, the extent of specialization possible, the importance of bureaucratic rules and professional norms, rates of pay, and the amount of isolation or interdependence that a therapist experiences in his or her work. For example, psychologists working in private practice are not bound by the fee scale, time schedule, or diagnostic categories of a health maintenance organization. They need not conclude a client's therapy within a fixed number of sessions in the interests of cost-effectiveness. They can specialize in family therapy or treat only adolescents. They have no formal supervisor. However, with autonomy come constraints such as the isolation of self-employment, the uncertainty of client demand, the absence of a supportive organizational culture, and the practical obligations of tending an office.

What is most important about these differences among workplaces is that they have profound implications not only for the worker but for the work that is done and for the service that is rendered. Workplaces are not inert boxes that house practice. Rather, they are complex sets of features that interact with practice. They convey information about what is expected. They influence what is possible. They determine what is likely. Social workers employed by state agencies find that their workplaces shape and limit the service that they can provide to their clients. The institutional settings, large client loads, tight budgets, bureaucratic hierarchies that discourage innovation, and the standardized procedures that structure their interactions often combine to make client care minimal and impersonal. One can imagine tending better to the needs of clients under different conditions—in comfortable settings; with small client loads and encouragement for creative solutions, respect for clients, and empathy for their needs.

Although schools are remarkably similar from site to site, we have come to recognize that there are important differences among them as well. Some schools are safe, hospitable workplaces where teachers enjoy the respect of the community, work cooperatively with colleagues, and take an active role in shaping organizational goals and influencing governance. For example, Joan Lipsitz describes the Samuel V. Noe Middle School in Louisville, Kentucky, where

> teachers are being acknowledged as professional adults who have the capacity to make decisions about curriculum, allocation of time, grouping of students, and student choice. One teacher comments: "We are given professional courtesies. We are professional people." Second, teachers are not alone. They discuss ideas together, reach group consensus, and have the support of the team for the humdrum and the adventuresome in the school day. Teaching is not a lonely profession at Noe.[10]

Other schools are worn and wearing environments that feature oppressive hierarchies, restrict teachers' authority, and discourage personal growth and advancement. Gertrude McPherson described her work in a school where "contact with one's peers usually occurred during 'stolen' time," primary and intermediate teachers were separated temporally and physically, "Old Guard" teachers excluded others, parent/teacher relationships were strained, and the principal was a remote and ineffectual "boss."[11]

It comes as no surprise to learn that teachers are happier working in some schools and districts than in others. Pleasant surroundings, cooperative relationships, manageable workloads, and ample resources promote greater satisfaction than do dreary buildings, hostile social climates, excessive demands and inadequate resources. But what is often overlooked or discounted by those who want good schools is that the character of the school as a workplace affects not only the satisfaction of faculty, but the work that even the most talented, highly motivated, well-intentioned teachers can do there.

THE CONCEPT OF THE WORKPLACE

As these various examples suggest, the workplace can usefully be conceived of very broadly, as spanning much more than the physical setting of work. Researchers studying job satisfaction and the quality of working life in diverse settings have proposed different lists of criteria by which to assess the character of the workplace,[12] citing factors such as alienation, health and safety, economic security, self-esteem, self-actualization, congruence with organizational goals, and extent of control and influence. John Robinson, summarizing work in this field, considered whether these lists of workplace variables were "equally applicable or equally meaningful to each occupational group," that is, whether assembly-line workers and clerical workers were concerned about the same kinds of things. He concluded that, in fact, they were.[13]

What, then, are the important variables of working life? What features of the work environments influence workers' satisfaction and productivity? Some researchers have approached that question empirically, surveying workers and generating lists of factors that they reported as significant.[14] Other researchers have relied on their own observations and subjective judgments about what matters to workers.[15] I originally wanted to examine work in schools against a range of occupations and work settings, but I found the lists of variables generated by other researchers to be insufficiently complete and conceptually too scattered for comparison. I therefore developed a model of the workplace inductively, beginning with the texts of monologues, interviews, and individuals' written descriptions of their work, its goals and procedures, demands and rewards, promises and constraints. The subjects included industrial, clerical, business, and professional workers.[16] My analysis of the varied accounts confirmed that, although people work in very different settings, they are attentive to a similar constellation of workplace variables. Accounts by secretaries, veterinarians, steelworkers, lawyers, and others reveal that whatever their work and workplaces, they are similarly influenced by the array of physical, organizational, sociological, economic, political, cultural, and psychological features.

Physical Features

The physical attributes of a workplace are those noticed most quickly by an observer, and because of their prominence they are often very influential in initial job choices. A worker contemplating employment in a particular company or office will consider: Is this a secure and comfortable place in which to work? Is there enough space? Are there adequate resources to do the job?

Safety and comfort. Workplaces vary from the dilapidated and hazardous to secure, even posh, havens. Physical dangers of workplaces lurk in unsafe spaces such as underground mines; in treacherous equipment, such as farming combines; or in perilous materials or by-products, such as asbestos, welding compounds, or carbon monoxide. For example, a steelworker interviewed by Studs Terkel compared his workplace to that of nonlaborers: "I say workin' in the steel mill is not like workin' in an air-conditioned office, where politicians and bankers sit on their fannies. There you have to eat all that dust and smoke, you can't work hard and live a long life."[17]

Space and resources. Some workers must cope with inadequate space or make do with insufficient resources. Nurses and doctors may be expected to squeeze too many patients into too few hospital rooms. Farmers may be unable to afford modern, efficient equipment. Public defenders may be required to share desks. Insufficient space and meager supplies are inconvenient and unsettling for workers and may inhibit their labors.

Features of Organizational Structure

Workers in a variety of settings wonder about the less visible and tangible elements of their workplaces: Who is in charge? How is work assigned? Will I do one task or many? How much will I be required to produce? Can I decide how to do the job, or will I be told? Will I work alone or with others? Who will decide if my work is well done? The answers to such questions can usually be found by examining what organizational theorists call the structural features of the organization.[18] These features determine how authority is distributed, to what extent tasks are specialized, what the work load is, how much discretion workers can exercise, how performance is assessed, the extent to which workers interact, and the interdependence of responsibilities.

Authority. Formal organization charts may tell only part of the story about how authority is distributed in an organization; workers learn to pay careful attention to hierarchy—who gives orders and who is obliged to comply. In some organizations authority is centralized, concentrated at the top in the hands of executive officers and delegated sparingly to those at lower levels. In less centralized organizations, authority is vested in many workers.

Workload. Individuals' accounts of their work often center on how much they are required to produce or how fast they are expected to work. Workers may complain about inhumane hours, unrealistic quotas, or an unrelenting pace. For example, an airline steward told Terkel about being on duty for thirteen hours at a time and having "fifty-five minutes to serve one hundred one coach passengers, a cocktail and full-meal service."[19] A felter in a luggage factory explained that she must complete "ten steps every forty seconds about eight hundred times a day."[20] By contrast, some bureaucratic workers regretted that little was expected of them and yearned for real work.

Specialization. In describing their work, people frequently discuss the extent to which they are expected to be specialists or generalists on the job; whether, for example, as supermarket employees, they only packed groceries or ran the registers and stocked shelves as well.[21] Although the repetition of carefully defined tasks may improve particular skills and increase efficiency, workers with narrowly defined assignments often complain of monotonous, demoralizing routine. Those with a range of responsibilities revel in the challenges of varied work. In contrast to an assembly-line worker whom Barbara Garson described as being distressed by the repetition of "stacking the ping-pong paddles into piles of fifty,"[22] a utility man at an automobile plant spoke enthusiastically about the variety of his job: "I'm what you call a trouble shooter. We got seventeen operations in the section and I can do all of it."[23]

Autonomy. Whether workers can exercise discretion in completing their assignments is a factor that seems to have substantial influence on their satisfaction. For example, a journalist for a corporate newspaper bemoaned the constraints of writing for a paper that "mustn't contain the smallest hint of controversy or present any idea that is not pleasing and soothing. . . ."[24] A W. T. Grant store manager, on the other hand, was said by Rush Loving to feel "like the captain of a ship—in charge of just about everything that went on. . . . He could raise or lower prices at will to beat the competition, and he had the power to concoct special promotions, even drawing up his own newspaper and radio ads."[25]

Supervision. A worker's autonomy often depends on the way work is supervised. In general, workers report that they resent being monitored closely and welcome arrangements that encourage them to think for themselves. Their accounts suggest that the former is common, the latter rare. A steelworker interviewed by Terkel warned: "Stay out of my way, that's all. . . .

I would rather work my ass off for eight hours a day with nobody watching me than five minutes with a guy watching me."[26]

Interdependence and interaction. How work is organized usually determines how often workers interact on the job as well as whether they need fellow employees to get their jobs done. Some jobs, such as playing professional football, are both interactive and interdependent.[27] However, interdependent work is not necessarily interactive. For example, labor on an assembly line can be personally isolating when a job is subdivided and workers perform partial tasks in separate locations.

Sociological Features

From a sociological perspective, workers ask how others expect them to behave: Should they be authoritarian or submissive, caring or demanding, competitive or cooperative? Will their clients and peers come from backgrounds similar to or different from their own? What difference will that make? As participants in particular workplaces, will they enjoy positions of high or low status?

Roles. Work roles, whether they be those of the office secretary, IRS auditor, or juvenile probation officer, shape the behaviors of those who hold them and, consequently, the work that they do. The secretary is expected to be deferential to, and protective of, the boss. The IRS auditor is likely to be authoritative, skeptical, and unflappable. The juvenile probation officer is supposed to be supportive, savvy, and firm. People often report that the roles they assume define how they behave, shaping their responsibilities and approaches to work and, ultimately, what they accomplish and how they feel about it.

Characteristics of clients and peers. Workers care about the kinds of people they work with and for. Gender, race, ethnic background, and socioeconomic status all influence how workers experience their jobs and what they do in them. A cocktail waitress described to James Spradley and Brenda Mann the indignities of serving sexist customers.[28] Some workers, such as airline attendants, enjoyed encountering celebrities on the job;[29] others, such as lawyers defending the interests of the indigent, derived satisfaction from helping people of less means and influence.[30]

Status. Workers care intensely about the social status that others ascribe to their work, both within their immediate organization and in the larger society. Often status derives from the kind of work they do. In other instances, social status derives from the roles that people assume within an industry or organization. An occupational therapist described the effect of hierarchy in her hospital where

> the nurses, the doctors, the medical students are set up on a rigid status kind of system. . . . The resident doesn't strike back at the attending man when he has a bad day. He strikes out at the nurse. The nurse strikes out at the hospital aide or the cleaning lady. . . .[31]

Workers' accounts suggest that high status can effectively counteract the indignities of low pay or the demands of heavy work loads, while low status may undermine satisfaction with more tangible features of their work.

Economic Features

Not surprisingly, workers carefully calculate how much and how often they will be paid. Are the benefits good? Are there financial incentives for greater productivity? Can I count on holding this job over time? These economic features of workplaces are crucial for many workers.

Pay and benefits. Pay and benefits influence workers' choices of industries, companies within industries, and positions within companies. The advantage of high pay and a generous benefits package can counteract disadvantageous factors, such as low status. Being in "the TOP THIRD income group in the nation" compensated many auto workers for remaining in the "very heart of the work class [where] life is dull, brutish, weary, stuporous."[32] Workers attend not only to starting pay levels, but also to anticipated wages over the course of a career. Typically, business and professional workers said that they could expect their incomes to grow, while industrial and service employees anticipated only modest, gradual increases over time.

Incentives and rewards. Workers are influenced by an array of incentives and rewards; some, such as window offices and letters of commendation, are non-monetary, while others, such as piece-rate pay and financial bonuses, are monetary. Although the security and predictability of a guaranteed paycheck enables some workers to attend more fully to the substance of their work, other workers seek the chance to earn more and thrive on opportunities for overtime or incentive pay.

Job security. The certainty of continued employment also enhances workers' satisfaction and confidence in carrying out their responsibilities. An industrial worker whose plant might be judged obsolete and closed, an airline attendant subject to sudden layoff when the company's profits sag, or a computer specialist whose future depends on the market success of a new product all attend to issues of job security.

Political Features

Workers also assess their workplaces politically. Will they have influence and a say in how their organizations are run? What are the competing interests among employees, and how is power distributed? Are workers treated fairly and equitably, or are some groups unduly favored and given unfair advantage? The distribution of formal authority can be seen in the official structure of the organization, but the exercise of power relative to that authority is usually described politically.

Voice in governance. Individual workers often speak about the extent to which their opinions are solicited, recognized, or ignored by those in charge of their workplaces. An airline-cargo handler interviewed by Patrick Fenton complained that his employer did not value workers' views and that, in his organization, "the worst thing a man could ever do is to make suggestions about building a better airplane."[33] Other organizations were said to be more responsive to employees. The president of a worker-managed insurance company described to Daniel Zwerdling the employees' power to change the organization in fundamental ways, a situation which he characterized as nothing "short of a total revolution."[34]

In most industrial organizations, it is the union that exercises workers' collective power in negotiating wages, hours, and working conditions with management and serving as watchdog for employee interests. In other workplaces, cooperative quality control circles and workers' councils provide employees with a formal voice in governance. Many employees, such as migrant farm workers, lack both individual and group representation.

Equity. Whether workers are treated fairly and given an evenhanded opportunity to succeed and advance in the workplace is of particular concern to women and minorities, who frequently report that they encounter discrimination on the job in the distribution of pay, promotions, or assignments. Instances of inequity are far more likely to draw comment than are conditions of equity.

Cultural Features

Well before notions of "corporate culture"[35] gained popular currency, workers were describing the ethos of their factories, offices, and shops. Their accounts suggest that they are strongly influenced by the norms, traditions, and rituals of their workplaces, factors that shape an understanding of, and commitment to, their tasks.

Recent analyses of corporate workplaces suggest that workers attend to the culture of the larger organization; studies document the enthusiasm and commitment of workers who are inspired by slogans, heroes, and rituals.[36] Most interviews reviewed for this research, however, emphasized workers' responses to the culture of their immediate work situation—the office rather than the company, the department rather than the university, the school rather than the district.

Strength of culture. In workplaces with strong cultures, workers can expect to find explicit goals and purposes that give meaning and purpose to their individual efforts and clearly define behavioral norms and shared expectations among coworkers. By contrast, workplaces with weak cultures are more likely to tolerate disengagement, self-interest, and apathy.

Supportiveness of culture. The culture of a workplace can be strong without being positive or supportive. Some organizations with strong cultures make workers feel like menial laborers rather than entitled members. Some encourage workers to compete mercilessly rather than attend to each other's needs. Some promote compliance and drudgery rather than play and celebration. Some engender humiliation rather than pride. For example, a utility man working in auto assembly described the intense supervision and exacting standards on the line, where humans were treated like machines and were berated and intimidated for anything short of full compliance with the company's standards: "They tear a man down and threaten 'im. . . ."[37]

Psychological Features

Finally, there are features of the workplace that can be productively considered from a psychological perspective. Is there some larger meaning in the work that I do? Will there be opportunities for learning and growth? How much stress will there be in difficult or dangerous assignments? Will this job enable me to meet responsibilities to my family?

Meaningfulness of work. Obviously, the meaningfulness of work depends highly on an individual's prior experience and personal values; work that is meaningful to an architect may not seem worthwhile to a veterinarian. Although the workplace cannot be responsible for ensuring that workers find meaning in what they do, it is instrumental in preserving and augmenting the meaning that workers typically associate with their jobs. Robert Coles writes that working people often ask him: "What am I doing that *really matters?* What is the point to it all?—not life, as some philosophers say, but the specific, tangible things I do or make?"[38] Workers are critical of workplaces that systematically extract meaning from their work by subdividing tasks, discouraging ingenuity, or preventing them from admiring the final product of their efforts.

A steelworker whose work site was located far from the final destination of the steel he made observed: "You can't take pride any more. . . . You're mass producing things and you never see the end result of it."[39] By contrast, a crane operator described his satisfaction in seeing the products of his labors:

> You drive down the road and you say, "I worked on this road." If there's a bridge, you say, "I worked on this bridge." Or you drive by a building and you say, "I worked on this building." Maybe it don't mean anything to anybody else, but there's a certain pride knowing you did your bit.[40]

The meaningfulness of work was an issue for industrial, bureaucratic, and professional workers. A staff writer for a company publishing health-care literature contended that

> jobs are not big enough for people. It's not just the assembly-line worker whose job is too small for his spirit, you know? A job like mine, if you really put your spirit into it, you would sabotage immediately. You don't dare. There's nothing I would enjoy more than a job that was so meaningful to me that I brought it home.[41]

Opportunities for learning and growth. Workers often wonder whether their jobs will lead them to new ideas, skills, and opportunties.[42] The airline-cargo handler who anticipated that his job would "never change" lamented "weary work" that made him feel "used up and worn out."[43] A spot welder looked forward to a different future in industrial relations: "It's the difference between a job and a career. This is not a career."[44]

Stress. Some workplaces create more physical and psychological stress than others. For example, a crane operator described the effects of tension in his workplace:

> The average age of the workingman, regular, is seventy-two. The average crane operator lives to be fifty-five years old. They don't live the best sort of life. There's a lot of tension. We've had an awful lot of people have had heart attacks.[45]

Some jobs accommodate workers' personal obligations to children, spouses, and parents; others ignore them. The opportunity for flexible hours or part-time work, the provision of child-rearing leaves, and access to good day-care facilities are still rare in the United States, but where they exist workers—particularly women—value them. In their absence, workers often experience the strain of conflicting obligations.

The Interaction of Variables

This constellation of workplace features, summarized in figure 1, influences workers in all settings, but certain variables tend to be more prominent in one line of work than another. For example, supervision may be a more salient feature in banking than in farming, but farmers are also aware of, and grateful for, the right to be responsible to themselves, sometimes rankling under the constraints of governmental oversight. Specialization is likely to present greater problems for workers who assemble products than for those who serve people, but human service workers may deliberately choose jobs that offer the

Figure 1
The Constellation of Workplace Variables

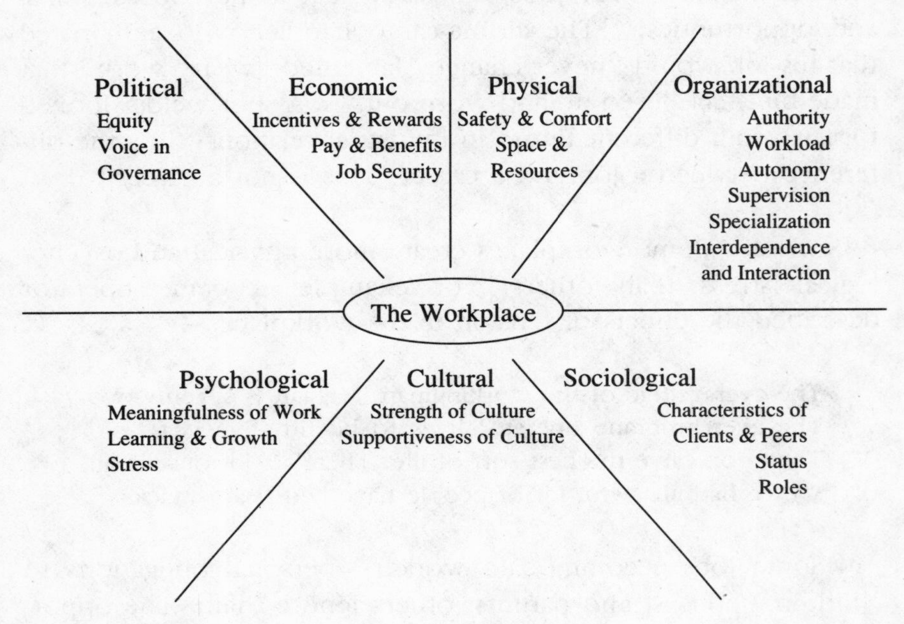

chance for holistic work. Status may be an obvious concern for women or minorities in semiprofessional work such as nursing, but status is also a central, if politely unstated, feature of professional work such as corporate law or orthopedic surgery. The fact that a worker does not complain about one of these variables does not mean that it is unimportant.

The categories used here to group and consider these workplace variables are intended to suggest only how people conventionally think about them, not to imply that any single discipline has full claim on any particular variable. Although job security is *primarily* an economic matter, it is not *exclusively* so, for the precariousness of some workers' positions can be explained sociologically. Similarly, specialization is a matter of organizational structure that has psychological consequences. Workers who are able to execute a variety of procedures may well become dispirited by changes in the production process that restrict their efforts to only one or two. Considering each of these variables from multiple perspectives can be illuminating.

Moreover, the elements of any workplace interact. For example, workers often organize politically in response to restrictive organizational structures that discourage their collective voice in governance. The structure is logically prior to the political activity that goes on in and around it, but subsequent political action by a union may alter that organizational structure. Understanding such interaction is central to understanding the character of any particular workplace.

Workers' accounts suggest that as they assess their workplaces, they informally weigh the advantages and disadvantages of the full array of variables. The presence of certain attractive features, such as high pay or status, may counterbalance the drawbacks of other unattractive ones, such as repetitive tasks or psychological stress. It is this informal balancing and tallying of workplace variables that ultimately determines workers' job satisfaction.

DOES SATISFACTION IMPROVE PRODUCTIVITY?

Workers reveal in interviews that they care deeply about the conditions and context of their work. Indeed, their satisfaction with the workplace is hard to distinguish from their satisfaction with the work itself.

We know from studies of the auto industry that worker satisfaction has important consequences for productivity. Assembly-line workers at the General Motors plant in Lordstown, Ohio, during the 1960s went on strike and sabotaged production in response to boring, routinized assignments and the intrusive oversight of foremen.[46] By contrast, Volvo workers who shared responsibility for building and inspecting major sections of cars and trucks not only found their work more satisfying but also produced greater profits for the company.[47]

The relationship between satisfaction and productivity has

been the focus of much research and policy debate over two decades.[48] Given similar types of work, what is to be gained or lost from making workplaces more satisfying? Are happy, well-cared-for workers more productive, or do they simply feel more entitled and become more recalcitrant? The relationship between job satisfaction and organizational productivity remains elusive, and efforts to document it have yielded only equivocal results.[49] Such research is difficult both because workers' assessments of their work settings are individual and subjective[50] and because few jobs provide any straightforward outcome measures of productivity.[51]

Measuring school productivity presents special challenges, given the contradictory and conflicting expectations of output. Some would have schools prepare students for jobs, others for college entrance, others for lifelong learning, and yet others for citizenship in the local community. Even when school officials narrow their sights and agree to work toward a measurable outcome such as improved test scores in reading or mathematics, they encounter difficulty assessing the results. Like patients who enter surgery in different states of health, students enter schools with varying abilities and experiences. Analysts who seek to quantitatively assess the productivity of schools often do so by accounting for student differences, usually adjusting their expectations to socioeconomic status and parental education, measures which do not adequately account for variations among student populations.[52]

Faced with the difficulty of showing that satisfied workers are more productive workers, advocates for reform of the workplace often find themselves on the defensive, championing changes that may be costly, that may challenge conventional assumptions about how work should be done, or that may disrupt current institutional procedures. Experiments during the 1970s with practices such as flextime, profit sharing, job enlargement, and job enhancement generated considerable interest among employees, but yielded mixed evidence about their effects on productivity.[53] Some argue persuasively that all workers deserve safe, clean, democratic workplaces with meaningful work and encouragement for personal growth and development, but the interests of the individual and the organization may not coincide, and what is best for the worker may not be best for the company. In the absence of a clear causal link between the quality of working life and organizational productivity, decisions about the character of the workplace often become political matters settled in legislatures or at bargaining tables.

What, then, about schools and their reform? Is there a causal relationship between the quality of schools as workplaces and their effectiveness? Many who set out to improve schooling in the 1980's believe that there is, and their prescriptions for change reflect two distinct and opposing sets of assumptions about the character of that relationship. These alternative approaches illustrate the two sides of the satisfaction/productivity debate in education.

After publication of *A Nation at Risk,*[54] states and local school districts devised an array of regulatory, prescriptive approaches to improve schooling, including mandated curricula, licensing exams for teachers, and competency tests for students. These measures, many of which were defended as good business practice, emerged from the tradition of scientific management in the early 1900s, which promised to maximize productivity by determining the most efficient methods for completing any task, from the movement of pig iron to the education of children.[55] Reforms advanced during the early 1980s were based on the assumption that teachers would become more productive (and schools more effective) with standardized training, explicit directions, and close supervision. Teachers' satisfaction was not treated as an important factor in school success.

Following three years of disappointment with experiments designed to regulate teachers' work, other reformers proposed a different set of approaches, intended to satisfy teachers and promote, rather than prescribe, effective practice. The Carnegie Forum on Education and the Economy and the Holmes Group proposed to improve the conditions of teaching and to professionalize schools by differentiating assignments, granting teachers greater roles in governance, and creating career ladders for professional advancement. Policy analysts sought to redesign work in schools and in turn, to remake schools.[56] Although the second round of school reforms is generally seen to be more consistent with what we know of schools as organizations and certainly is more attractive to teachers, these policy proposals are not explicitly based on research findings.[57] Those who contend that such changes would improve schooling once again confront the difficulties of relating satisfaction to productivity and measuring the effectiveness of the reforms in meaningful ways.

In *A Place Called School,* John Goodlad acknowledged the difficulty of establishing "a pattern of relationships between environmental problems and satisfaction and, in turn, between teachers' satisfaction and a criterion of productivity such as student achievement,"[58] but he argued that establishing such scientific relationships should not be necessary "to accept the proposition that teachers, like other humans, are entitled to a satisfying workplace."[59] Goodlad's research, however, does offer modest evidence that job satisfaction and school effectiveness are related. He found that the schools which teachers judged to be "more satisfying" or "less satisfying" workplaces were the same ones judged positively or negatively by students, parents, and teachers, leading him to hypothesize that

> schools staffed by teachers who are less than satisfied are likely to be schools perceived by teachers, parents, and students as having a greater array of serious problems. Conversely, schools in which teachers are more satisfied with their careers and teaching circumstances are relatively unlikely to be perceived by teachers, parents, and students as having serious problems. Happily, these are likely also to be the schools most frequently perceived by students as giving them a good education.[60]

Goodlad's work suggests that we should take seriously teachers' judgments about their schools as workplaces. However, even if we do accept his assertion that better workplaces are also better schools, we have only a general understanding about what matters to teachers in their schools, and we know even less about how to translate their judgments into policies and practices that work. What is the particular combination of features that constitutes a supportive and effective work environment for teachers? If, as industrial and corporate research suggests, the character of the workplace not only determines worker satisfaction but also shapes the character of work—both what is possible and what is likely—then school reformers must attend carefully to the effects of the changes that they introduce not only on workers' satisfaction but also on the kind of teaching and schooling that they promote.

How can policy makers anticipate the effects of proposals for such reforms as career ladders, peer evaluation, increased roles in governance, or merit pay? Past experiments suggest where some such innovations may lead,[61] but it is no simple matter to predict how an organizational change such as differentiated staffing will adapt to and affect the rest of the organization. Those who embark on school reform need to better understand not only how any single reform, such as school-site management, will affect teachers' satisfaction and their work, but also how that change is likely to interact with other features of the workplace, such as job security, autonomy, or opportunity for voice and influence.

There are those who argue that schools have already become imprudently responsive to teachers' preferences as a result of collective bargaining, that teachers' well-being rather than students' well-being is already driving educational policy in the United States, and that schools are suffering as a result.[62] The case for improving schools as workplaces is based on more than benevolent attitudes toward teachers or even beliefs that better workplaces promote better work. Predictions of modest to severe teacher shortages during the 1990s[63] suggest that, if schools are to attract and retain able teachers, they must become satisfying and supportive workplaces. Lacking a surplus of eager and able aspirants, policy analysts and school officials can no longer disregard teachers' dissatisfaction with their workplaces. As education is increasingly forced to compete with law, business, medicine, and technology in recruiting talented and committed individuals, the attractiveness and sufficiency of schools as workplaces will become more and more important. No longer will guarantees of job security and meaningful work compensate for heavy workloads, subordinate roles, lack of influence, and low pay. The full array of workplace variables will come into play. Moreover, if teachers are to succeed in meeting the many social and academic needs of their students, they must work in schools that make good teaching not just possible, but likely.

CHAPTER TWO

Teaching—The Privilege and the Price

Anna Capello, who teaches all the foods and nutrition courses offered by her inner-city high school, admires her students for being "gutsy" despite the fact that they are among the poorest and most troubled in the city. Drop-out rates are very high; student pregnancy is common; drugs and violence unceasingly threaten to disrupt the modicum of order that does exist. Over her sixteen years as a teacher in the district, Capello has won many grants and developed innovative programs, including two student-run restaurants. She is committed to culinary arts and in the evenings teaches chefs at a private school. She is even more committed to her high-school students, shepherding some into careers as chefs while she hopes others will lead safer and healthier lives because of their studies with her.

Richard Sand's suburban middle school is organized into clusters where 5 teachers provide the instruction and supervision for 125 students. Sand, who is the science teacher on his team, loves working with young adolescents because they are "fun," "eager," and "resilient." He likes the cluster system because each student can find one teacher with whom to work closely. Sand's students are economically well off and their parents are ardent advocates for their children's education, factors that contribute to the children's academic success. Sand believes that much of the credit for his school's good record belongs to his principal, recently a teacher himself, who treats the staff with respect and encourages them to experiment in their work. Sand does not feel hemmed in by the district's curriculum because he participated in writing it and knows that it is continuously revised.

Gary Stein, who teaches second grade in a suburban district, is the only male full-time teacher in his school, which is located in a traditional middle-class community. Stein says that his is a "production-oriented building," with strong norms that support serious work. The curriculum is carefully structured, and accountability is a major administrative preoccupation, with teachers being periodically required to submit student math tests and expository writing samples for review. Stein says that, although the staff expect their colleagues to work hard and "care for kids," he's never felt a strong sense of community within the school, "never anything that would pull us together."

Allen Rondo teaches in one of the oldest and most prestigious private schools in the country. With a faculty of 26 and a student body of 260, the school prepares boys in grades eight through twelve for elite colleges and influential careers. The school's large endowment permits it to attract and support a racially and ethnically diverse student body, and because admissions are intensely competitive, students who enroll are prepared to uphold the high academic and ethical standards that the school espouses. Having been at the school for half of his twelve-year career, Rondo teaches chemistry and oversees the school newspaper and yearbook. He is looking forward to becoming the school's director of studies during the coming year, a position that will permit him to continue teaching while pursuing his interest in administration.

Janice Gagne is the sole sixth-grade teacher in a Catholic elementary school which includes kindergarten through eighth grade. Of the staff of 9 teachers, 3 are nuns who preserve and perpetuate many of the school's traditional values. Parents, who Gagne says will "take nothing less than the best," are attracted to the school because of the structure it offers and because graduates typically go on to independent or church-affiliated high schools. Students study religion daily and are held to strict standards of courtesy, for example answering "Yes, Sister," rather than simply "Yes," to a nun. Although the school is located in an urban area, Gagne says there are few "problem families" and not many minority students. The small staff and principal know every child in the school and are expected to correct any student using profane language, punching another student, or running down the stairs.

These 5 teachers' varied backgrounds and assignments illustrate the diversity of this study's 115 respondents, which includes teachers committed to experiential learning and teachers convinced that structured classrooms are best, teachers who love to spend extra hours in extracurricular activities and teachers who devote all their extra time to classroom preparation, teachers who are active in their unions and teachers who oppose collective bargaining for professionals. Given this diversity, it would be impossible to select representative or typical teachers. One consistent feature, however, is these teachers' love for teaching. Virtually all would, if they could, make teaching their life's work, and in fact most have. Many of these teachers are survivors who have persisted in teaching through difficult times, who have returned to teaching after layoffs, and who have watched respected colleagues leave the teaching ranks either by necessity or choice. Some critics of the schools might infer that these teachers' endurance is a mark of their inferiority, that anyone who could have escaped the troubled schools of the past two decades would have. But there are others who see in these teachers' long tenure evidence of a determined commitment to children and the social purposes of schooling.

Despite their passion for teaching, most of these teachers regularly encounter frustrations, disappointments, and obstacles that compromise their best efforts and threaten to drive some of them out of the classroom. The contrast between their initial earnest hopes for teaching and the reluctant compromises that many of them must routinely make deserves careful attention, for it is this sizeable gap between what might be and what is that we must investigate in order to understand how the quality of the school as a workplace determines who teaches and how they teach.

WHY DID THEY ENTER TEACHING?

It is commonly believed that choosing to teach is a conservative decision, that those who enter teaching do so because they can do little else ("Those who can't, teach"), because they seek the security of tenure in a public-service job, because they never considered other possibilities, or because they were women accepting society's definition of an appropriate role. In 1963, when Dan Lortie asked 94 teachers what had attracted them to teaching, respondents emphasized the importance of working with people, serving others, remaining in settings that they knew and enjoyed, receiving the material benefits of jobs in teaching, and working according to the school schedule and calendar.[1] Over two decades have passed since Lortie collected his data, a period when women's employment patterns and the character of schooling in many districts have changed profoundly. John Goodlad's more recent survey of 1,350 teachers found:

> a large portion (57%) of the prime reasons for entering teaching chosen by these teachers clustered around the nature of teaching itself; the desire to teach in general or to teach a subject in particular (22%); the idea of teaching as a good and worthy profession (18%) and a desire to be of service to others (17%).[2]

Goodlad's respondents did not say that they were "full of love for children and dedicated above all else to serving them." Instead, he reports, "Liking the children was not, for the most in our group, the major reason for entering teaching."[3]

The responses of the valued teachers in this study resemble, in part, those of the broader samples surveyed by Lortie and Goodlad. Like Lortie's respondents, these teachers said that they had wanted to work with people and valued the way school schedules could accommodate other demands and interests in their lives. Like Goodlad's respondents, many of these teachers recalled having had an interest in subject matter or pedagogy. They stated that they had deliberately chosen teaching for the opportunity it provided to work with people, but unlike Goodlad's respondents they emphasized their interest in children. Many had believed that teaching would provide the opportunity to achieve social or religious purposes. The words and phrases that they chose in describing their decisions to teach were so similar that one might easily mistake them for answers to multiple-choice survey questions rather than spontaneous responses to the open-ended query, "Why did you enter teaching?" Few teachers gave only one reason for choosing to teach, making it impossible to rank-order their responses. However, the five prevailing reasons that teachers offered warrant further discussion.

Working with People (or Children)

Not only did many teachers observe that they liked to work with children—"I love kids" was a frequent comment—a number also said that they "needed" to work with people. In this regard they were similar to Lortie's respondents, whose explanations featured an "interpersonal theme," and differed from those whom Goodlad said did not cite "liking the children" as a major factor in their choice. An elementary-school teacher who observed, "I'm not just working with children; I work also with the parents," said also that although she had shown promise as a mechanical engineer and was "very good with computers," she chose teaching because she "needed to work with people—adults and children."

Many of those we interviewed said that they had decided on teaching at an early age. "I never wanted to be anything else" and "I always wanted to teach" appear again and again in the transcripts. Many developed their early interest in teaching by working as baby-sitters, camp counselors, or YMCA/YWCA instructors; when they began classroom teaching, it was not new or unfamiliar work, but a continuation of activities they had enjoyed since early adolescence.

Some respondents pursued other occupations before realizing how much they valued work with children. Gary Stein began studying criminal justice, but became intrigued with teaching when the woman he eventually married volunteered in a school. He, too, offered his services as a volunteer, and after a year and a half, transferred to an education program for formal training because of the pleasures he found in working with children:

> The way that you could just look into a kid's eyes, the sparkle when you showed them something that they didn't know or that they couldn't understand. . . . There was an energy there that was quite gratifying. It made me want to keep coming back.

Similarly, an urban middle-school teacher said that she had majored in economics and initially considered that field for work. However,

> there was something that always attracted me to teaching. I just feel like this is my profession. My bottom line is that I love kids. I get energy from them. I just think they're the brightest people on earth.

The public-school teachers' theme of working with children was echoed by teachers from the private sector. Janice Gagne recalled, "I just always wanted to do it. I wanted to work with children. I wanted to teach." A kindergarten teacher in an independent school said, "I've always worked with kids; I've always liked being with kids, with young children at the YMCA and camps." An art teacher at a Jewish day school reported that she had initially worked in an art museum, but found that she missed "the dynamic aspect of working with people directly. Whenever the children were missing, there was something absent" for her, and she left museum work for full-time teaching.

Pedagogy

A second common theme was the teachers' interest in pedagogy. For some that interest was grounded in an understanding of intellectual processes. A suburban kindergarten teacher who "wanted to do speech and language work" discovered that she "liked the idea of figuring out kids' language development, and what made that work, how the brain worked." An urban middle-school teacher, who spoke of her enjoyment in "working with the kids, seeing them achieve, helping them achieve the best," emphasized, "I love to watch the brains."

Some public-school teachers recalled an early interest in the challenges of becoming a good teacher. One told of attending a competitive public high school and deciding in his senior year that he would teach mathematics:

> You can blame it on some of the teachers. . . . There were some sharp teachers. They were sharp in that they knew their material, but whether they could get it across to students was another thing.

Similarly, a high-school physics teacher reported that she had made her decision in response to the teaching she had encountered as a student:

> These people definitely did a good job and were well organized. I really learned a lot those years. I just felt that I could do as well as those two teachers. I could do better than the poor teachers.

Although some teachers recalled an early interest in instruction, others discovered the excitement of pedagogy only after several years in the classroom. A suburban high-school English teacher initially entered the profession because he liked his subject, but "once I got into it, I discovered that there is something to enjoy in the actual imparting."

Again, the interests of teachers in independent and church-related schools paralleled those of public-school teachers. An English teacher in a prestigious private high school recalled, "As long as I can remember, I always wanted to be a teacher. . . . Back as far as third or fourth grade, I would picture myself—What would I do if I were running this class?" Allen Rondo explained that he had always respected his teachers and been intrigued by their work: "There's just something about the profession and the way they do it that's always fascinated me." A career counselor tried to discourage him from entering teaching when tests showed that he lacked "the missionary spirit." The counselor suggested that he might better become a dentist or a printer. Although this raised doubts for him, he persevered and eventually pursued the teaching career he had planned.

Subject Matter

Many of the secondary teachers in this sample chose teaching as a career because it permitted them to continue studying and learning or enabled them to make use of a subject they knew and enjoyed. A middle-school teacher said that she had entered teaching for

> no special reason. I was interested in language. I guess that would be the reason. I started off in Spanish. I thought that teaching would be the best way to make use of what I was studying, because I enjoyed it.

Similarly, a suburban high-school teacher recalled his decision to teach English: "What does one do with English in order to share that love? You go out there and teach it." I asked a high-school mathematics teacher whether he was initially more interested in the opportunity to focus on subject matter or students, and he responded, "Subject matter. I always liked mathematics. Anything I did, I'd have been pretty sure that it would have been math-related." A high-school physics teacher recalled that when he began teaching, "high-school teachers [were] always saying, 'I teach children, not biology.' I thought, 'No. I teach physics, and I teach it to some very interesting children.' "

Social or Religious Purposes

Many of those who began their careers in the late 1960s chose teaching for its larger social or religious purposes, a theme that was prominent in the responses of both Lortie's and Goodlad's teachers. An urban middle-school teacher explained, "It's my contribution to society—helping somebody else be the best that they can." Another recalled that her goals on entering teaching were "to make a difference. I always felt that one person can make a difference." A vocational-school English teacher recalled, "I went into education because it was, well, my mission." A suburban social studies teacher returned from military service and was "going to save the world. . . . It was one of those 'impact' decisions."

Spiritual explanations were central to some teachers' accounts of why they chose to teach. A first-grade public-school teacher explained:

> I feel that God has given all of us a gift to do something. Everybody has a strength. I really believe this strongly, that I can give children education, make them feel good about themselves, let them learn to like to read, let them look at school as "Wow! This is wonderful."

A secondary-school English teacher remembered that he first entered teaching "because I felt that I had somehow been touched by God. I really did." A first-grade independent-school teacher said that he had once been interested in the ministry but discovered that teaching "was [my] ministry." Not surprisingly, explanations of spiritual motivation were voiced most often by teachers in church-related schools. Several who were members of religious orders became teachers by virtue of choosing to join a particular convent. One said, "I entered teaching to serve God." Another explained, "I entered religious life, and [teaching] was [the convent's] ministry."

Schedule

Teachers' formal obligations in public schools typically begin at 8:00 A.M. and end at 3:30 P.M., September through June.

Of course, most teachers put in considerable additional time grading papers, preparing for classes, and writing curricula, but such work is under their own control and can be done at home after hours. Much has been made of the schedule of schooling and its importance to teachers, some arguing that it makes teaching appear to be unprofessional, part-time work. Reformers have advocated lengthening teachers' working hours and work year to bolster their public image and justify higher salaries.

However, for many of the valued teachers in this study, the schedule of schooling was a contributing factor in their decision to teach.[4] For many women, as for Janice Gagne, the correspondence of their work schedules and their children's school schedules made it possible for them to teach and to be with their children after school. Teaching is, as more than one teacher observed, "a career you can combine with family." For many, being at home with their children after school and during the summer was a matter of choice rather than necessity. A teaching father of five adolescents whose wife also teaches explained that the school schedule permits him and his wife "to really be around and know what's going on" during the school year and the family to travel together during the summer. "The teaching schedule permits me to do what I want. It fits in with my family values."

The freedom to pursue other interests during the summer, after ten months of intensive work, was also valued by teachers without children. One spent her summers reading, taking courses, and renovating her house. Many respondents traveled. Some suggested that they had deliberately sought, as one independent-school teacher said, "the life of a teacher," meaning not, as some might assume, short hours and minimal obligations but rather a balance of intense work and personal development—"that feeling of beginning in September anew . . . and being able to do something different in the summers."

None of those interviewed for this study chose to teach solely because of the schedule. Rather, the coincidence of that schedule with the opportunity for meaningful work made teaching both attractive and possible.

Decision by Default

There were 9 teachers in the sample who began to teach more by default than deliberate choice. An elementary-school teacher who had

> a couple of teachers in the family . . . went into teaching because—I hate to say it—it was probably the easiest course in college and I didn't know what else I wanted to do.

He came to enjoy the work and respond to its challenges.

Several women entered teaching because they had few other options or because their families expected them to become teachers. A middle-school teacher explained, "That's what was open to us at the time. It was either that you became a teacher or you became a nurse. I chose this way of life." Another recalled, "When I was in high school, my mother told me that teaching is a good profession for a girl to fall back on. I don't think I really gave it any thought at all." An elementary-school teacher who observed, "I don't think young people were as independent about their choices as they are today," said that her mother had emphasized that she would

> always have a job. It was a wonderful profession for a woman, something you could continue if you decided to marry, and certainly if you had children. Luckily it turned out well for me. I love teaching. It could have been a disaster to choose in that manner.

Another who had entered teaching because it was appropriate women's work recalled thinking, "This is what I can do and I have no choice." Now, she said, "education tops my list."

Finally, there were those who entered teaching because a job was there. Anna Capello had planned to study social work but learned from a friend that there was a demand for home-economics teachers in the city to which she had recently moved:

> It was 1970, and they were in need of teachers and it was the third week in August. They were actually desperate for a teacher in this position. I was thrilled to get the job. They asked me hardly any questions about my background. They were just happy that someone would take it. It was a very difficult position.

Another teacher in an urban school, who explained that at one time she "did not want to teach, absolutely, under no circumstances," accepted an unsolicited job offer because she was bored with secretarial work. A third, who had planned to become a dental hygienist, switched to teaching when she heard there were no jobs in the field of her choice.

For a large majority of those in this sample, the decision to teach was a deliberate one, motivated by deep convictions about the importance of the work and their capacity to do that work well. For a few, the decision to teach was a conservative, self-protective act, but even they reported that they eventually came to find that teaching offered work that suited them well.

WERE THEIR GOALS FULFILLED?

Given the high expectations and noble purposes that many of these teachers espoused, it was important to ask whether their goals were fulfilled. Has teaching been the career that they once anticipated? The answer to this very important question was an ambiguous "Yes, but." *Yes,* teachers experience tremendous satisfaction in their work with children and believe that their contributions have been meaningful, *but* their teaching careers have also been frustrating and disappointing, and they have not been nearly as effective in their work as they had once hoped. Both themes in this story of simultaneous elation and disappointment call for exploration.

Yes

It was reassuring to hear these teachers speak of the rewards they experience in teaching. Richard Sand said that he is proud to be a teacher, even if society fails to recognize his work, and he is proud that he "can reach a few kids every now and then that, for whatever reason, can't work with somebody else." Allen Rondo described the rewards of working with a variety of students:

> The job centers around a fascination with kids. And for all the kids I've taught, I can hardly think of two who are really alike. It's just mind-boggling how much, even over the years, you'll see patterns, but you don't see the same bird. Year after year. So, if you don't get tired of them, you really don't get tired of the job.

There is an undeniable rapture in other respondents' remarks as they describe what matters to them, what moves them:

> I like the way five-year-old minds work. There's a joy in listening to what they say. The curiosity that they have. The way they like to discover. And I like teaching them that way. So I guess that's why I've stayed.

> There are certain aspects of teaching I love. I love instructing. I love working with kids. I think having been a convert at a later age, my enthusiasm is still there.

> I love the give and take; I love to see the minds grow, I love to see them do what they think they can't do. It's just a challenge.

> I really like the feeling of sitting down with a small stack of papers at my desk late at night. . . . There's the feeling that I'm doing what it is that I do. You know, the knife cuts the bread, and the sun shines and the teacher corrects with his red pen. I feel a real personal commitment to my kids to give them the best that I can give them. It's very, very important to me.

This enthusiasm was by no means confined to teachers in wealthy and prestigious school districts. In fact, teachers of urban students seemed to speak with a special zeal about the rewards of working with their students. As Anna Capello explained, she is most proud of her "rapport with the students. Knowing them. Understanding them. Wanting to teach them. . . . They're really needy. I've learned how to teach them."

It seemed, however, that teachers of younger children were more confident about their achievements than were those in secondary schools, and several observed that teaching in the early grades afforded them a special opportunity to make a difference. One said, "I can see a lot of changes in them. I thought it was important to get in at the bottom level where you meet children one-on-one." Another, who found it rewarding "to know that you have helped a lot of people become literate," said that she got "a lot of satisfaction quickly, because you see it at the end of the year. I think you see it more in the lower grades than you can in the higher grades." Middle- and high-school teachers expressed less confidence that they had reached and influenced their students as they had hoped.

But

Despite the teachers' successes with children and their satisfactions with a school schedule that made it possible for many of them to work, they reported frustration and disappointment originating primarily in their workplaces. Throughout the interviews, teachers from both the public and private sectors characterized this unsteady balance between assets and deficits. One public-elementary-school teacher said:

> I get satisfaction, I get a lot of love from the kids I teach. I really feel that I have the possibility to make a difference in somebody's life, which to me is worth more than money, I guess. I mean, certainly you're not in it for the money. And you're not in it for the prestige. And you're not in it for the sense of autonomy you have, because you don't have much autonomy, in terms of what you want to do. But for what you get from the one-on-one with the kids, I don't think anyone could replace that feeling for me personally.

There was considerable agreement among those interviewed about the kinds of dissatisfactions they experienced in their work. They spoke of having few rewards beyond those directly gained from children. Pay was low, respect wanting, and opportunities for growth and development scarce. In addition to these personal disappointments, teachers spoke with annoyance about the many factors that distracted them and compromised the quality of their teaching, such as lax discipline standards, classroom disruptions, unnecessary bureaucratic demands, poorly maintained buildings, nonteaching duties, too much or too little parental involvement, scant interaction with colleagues, constraints on their instructional autonomy, administrative disregard or preoccupation with politics, and a failure to involve teachers in decisions of educational policy and practice. We will consider these disappointments in detail.

The personal price. Teachers repeatedly cited low salaries as one of the most frustrating features of their workplace. Some spoke with resignation:

> I'm not real happy about the money, but on the other hand, I couldn't be happy no matter how much money I was getting if I wasn't doing something like this.

Others spoke with resentment and dismay. An urban middle-school teacher, who admitted that there are "days when I'm honestly angry that I've chosen this," explained that "a lot of it has to do with money." She said that she could not comprehend why the society hands its children—"the most prized asset in the universe"—to teachers without caring about their qualifications or paying them well for their work.

Some respondents who reported that they had been willing to accept the trade-off of rewarding work for low pay early in their careers were less patient as their own children approached college age and they faced tuition bills. Richard Sand told of his daughter, who is ranked second in her high-school class, but will probably attend a state college for lack of money:

> Right now pay is critical. We've always been able to live. We were able to buy a house. We drive small, foreign, inexpensive cars. Most of the clothes come off the rack at Zayre's. At Christmastime, we can usually give the kids something that they've wanted. We have taken three family vacations. That I can live with. But I have a hard time living with the fact that this kid—who's not brilliant, she's not a genius, but she works her butt off—probably is not going to be able to go to the college she would like to go to, that would be right for her, because I can't afford it.

Teachers also voiced their disappointment with a profession that offered classroom teachers no opportunities for formal advancement. Anna Capello felt particularly disheartened with the undifferentiated nature of her career:

> There's no milestone. I look back, and essentially, even though maybe I've changed my style of teaching, or maybe the type of student I have has changed, nothing else has really changed. Some things have gotten better, but then, some things have gotten worse.

Although only a few teachers mentioned the absence of opportunities for formal advancement among their dissatisfactions with teaching, many noted the lack of status and respect that they receive as members of their profession. One urban teacher said that her parents and friends persist in asking, "Why are you still there? Why are you wasting your time? How can you possibly teach?" She observed that although she is "almost embarrassed to say, 'I'm a teacher,' " most of those who "criticize what I do would not last five minutes in the classroom."

Teachers also complained that little beyond their own interests and efforts encouraged them or assisted them in becoming better teachers. One observed:

> Nobody really inspires you to really put forth your best effort in the classroom. And nobody really comes down and says, "Gee, that's a great [reading] series; why don't you try that series?"

Respondents were disparaging of in-service training and staff development programs designed by administrators on noninstructional issues. Although it seems obvious that continuous learning is essential for good teaching, public schools were said to be in the business of promoting learning for students, not staff.

Many teachers made it clear that they were well aware of the personal price they paid for the privilege to teach—low pay, low status, little structured opportunity for personal growth. This group of teachers tolerated the costs but recalled many of their able colleagues who had considered the price too high and left education for other work.

Barriers to teaching. Respondents were less tolerant of conditions in their workplaces that interfered with teaching and undermined the potential of their schools—items such as substandard buildings, scarce resources, lax discipline, uncommitted students, large workloads, exhausting schedules, frequent disruptions of instructional time, misguided administrative decisions, isolation from their peers, constraints on their autonomy, and disregard for their views on matters of policy and practice. One urban high-school respondent recalled a recent television documentary in which a teacher said plaintively, "I want to teach. Why don't they let me teach?" She described her own disappointing but quiet compromise with the system:

> You want so badly to be able to make a change—to change the system, to change the quality. And yet you really feel powerless. What I've gotten down to this year is trying to make a difference on a very small, one-to-one basis.

Some teachers complained about schools that had low expectations for student behavior. Others were troubled by pull-out programs and special events that disrupted their classrooms and splintered the coherence of their teaching. An elementary-school teacher explained that students are removed from his class at arbitrary times for remedial reading, speech and hearing therapy, occupational therapy, physical therapy, and special-needs gym: "This frustrates the daylights out of me."

Most teachers were generally satisfied with the amount of autonomy they had in their teaching, but some worked in districts with centrally prescribed curricula that violated their professional judgment. A high-school mathematics teacher criticized the curriculum and testing program that he was obliged to follow:

> It's mind-boggling what they expect you to cover in a year with the type of students you have. They want us to cover trig and algebra II all in one year. We've told them that we could cover algebra II and then trig in another year. For two years we fought the same battle. We kept recommending this, and they kept coming back with the same curriculum.

In the face of these demands, this teacher had chosen to pace his teaching according to his students' abilities—to exert the discretion of the street-level bureaucrat:[5] "You can't really cover the whole curriculum. You've got to make a decision on what you think is the best."

Teachers complained of heavy workloads—five courses and 125 students for most secondary teachers—but few public-school respondents voiced strong objections about class size. Few taught more than 25 students at a time, and although they would have preferred smaller classes, they didn't imagine that it was economically possible. Several teachers did describe the difficulties of having classes with 30 or more students, many of whom presented special learning problems. Some middle-school teachers complained about rigid, departmentalized schedules that interfered with creative curricula and team teaching. Others criticized administrators' decisions to place students in classes beyond their capabilities. One English teacher who was assigned 350 students in a vocational school recounted how her teaching had been undermined by the principal's decision to create a rotating schedule enabling her to meet with her students only on alternate weeks. The new schedule had so compromised her chances for success with students who needed close attention that she had decided to leave teaching.

Many teachers expressed dismay over the increasing disrespect they perceived among young people for formal education, a concern by no means confined to those working with low-income students. As one suburban foreign language teacher said,

> I think there once was a time when education in itself was a valuable thing. . . . Now I get the impression sometimes that . . . it's like, "Okay, what have you got to teach me today? How are you going to motivate me today?"

In the face of such contempt, an urban high-school counselor had begun to question herself:

> Recently I've questioned whether I'm really helping young people. I used to feel that I was. But lately I don't know if I'm getting to really help them. There was a time when I could say something to a group of students and I would know that they were listening. I don't get the feedback like I used to. It just seems a little harder lately to motivate students.

Teachers often blamed parents for students who were "not ready to learn" and argued that parents should be more attentive to their children's education and support the schools' efforts more fully. Ironically, other parents, particularly those in wealthy districts or whose children attended independent schools, were said to be too demanding and to intrude on the professional domain of teachers. Richard Sand, for example, was distressed by the demands of certain pushy parents:

> There are too many parents seeking negative ways of getting what they believe is right for their son or daughter, without concern for other people's kids. It's not a majority, but it's enough to make life difficult and to force you to overlook the good parents, the ones who really are supportive.

In general, teachers hoped to work cooperatively, and in many cases closely, with parents, but few public schools systematically encouraged or facilitated productive home/school relationships.

Some teachers spoke of feeling deterred by excessive demands of nonteaching duties. Sand mentioned "paperwork up to the eyeballs" and long lines at the photocopier. Others objected to patrolling the cafeteria or supervising recess. Excessive and unproductive committee work consumed the precious after-school time of a few public-school teachers.

Teachers spoke of the isolation they experienced with lock-step schedules that left no time to talk with colleagues, segmented facilities that separated individuals and that segregated departments, and norms of self-sufficiency that superceded norms of interdependence. One high-school teacher said, "We're not only departmentalized, but compartmentalized." Another, who blamed the lack of collegial interaction on a rigid schedule and heavy demands, complained, "There are some people that I see on the first day of school and maybe five times throughout the year. And we work in the same building." Gary Stein explained that, although teachers in his elementary school are scheduled for one and one-half hours of preparation time each week, the time is not deliberately scheduled to promote meetings among colleagues who share similar responsibilities:

> If so, it's through dumb luck. Nothing is coordinated. There is nothing to take care of a need for you to be with and talk to other colleagues.

Although many teachers believed that greater interaction with their colleagues would be productive, few knew where to find the time or how to make it happen.

Teachers were also distressed about some administrators' seeming disregard for instructional matters, and they faulted both principals and central-office administrators for being preoccupied with bureaucratic irrelevancies. One urban elementary-school teacher said that he was unhappy over the lack of support he received "financially and philosophically" from the central administration and his principal. A suburban middle-school teacher faulted her superintendent for not being "an educator" and for disregarding pressing curricular problems in her school.

Speaking about their supervisors, teachers often distinguished between what they called educational and administrative values. Although they praised some principals and superintendents for their educational orientation to their jobs, more were described as absorbed in administrative concerns. As one urban high-school teacher explained,

> There is a radical—and I'm choosing that word carefully—radical dichotomy between the goals, aims, and objectives, educationally speaking, of a competent or better classroom teacher and the successful school administrator.

Such administrators were said to be more concerned with politics than curriculum, more responsive to pressure than information, more attentive to appearances than realities. They were seldom seen in classrooms and rarely offered educational leadership to the teaching staff. Teachers reported that they could continue to teach, sometimes very effectively, without administrative intervention, but they believed that their work would have been more productive and their schools more successful if there had been greater administrative support for the core task of their enterprise.

Finally, teachers faulted administrators for taking little account of faculty views when policies were drawn up or practices prescribed. Remarkably few teachers were active in formal school governance, and many were cynical about participating on advisory committees that held no formal authority. A middle-school teacher echoed many respondents' sentiments when she spoke about "upper administration":

> One of the things that happens a lot in the schools is that decisions made at that level are made without any input from us. I think if we had a lot more to say about what is done systemwide, everybody here would feel a whole lot better

> about being here. It just seems as though things are done by edict. Very often they are things that we are the experts on, and they're not. Not that I expect them to allow us to make the decisions without them, but consulting us would be really nice.

Many features of most teachers' workplaces fell short of their expectations, interfering with their teaching, and compromising their best efforts; many teachers reported failing to obtain sufficient respect, recognition, and recompense. However, of the 75 public-school teachers, 5 reported that they were very satisfied with their schools as workplaces. Notably, these included teachers in three urban and two suburban schools. One emphasized that she was "fortunate enough to find a school system that is helping me fulfill what I wanted to do in the profession. . . . If I had not found a school like the one I'm working in, I probably would have had to go into something else." An urban school teacher, whose only reservation about her work was the salary, said enthusiastically,

> I like my job very much. The people that I work with are like a second family to me. It's very comfortable. . . . The situation here, really, is close to perfect. I can't see that anything would make it more appealing than it is.

Such enthusiasm, though rare, suggests that teachers are not beyond being satisfied.

In this regard, it is also interesting to consider how teachers in independent and church-related schools viewed their workplaces. Did they share the complaints of their public-school counterparts or was their perspective on the school as a workplace unique? In general, teachers in the private sector also experienced the sting of low professional status. However, because their schools were more selective and their students' membership conditional, they generally enjoyed higher status than public-school teachers and commanded more respect from clients. Student discipline and parental disregard were less troubling in the private than in the public sector; parents were more frequently faulted for meddling than for not caring.

Probably because independent and church-related schools are typically smaller and less complex and cumbersome organizations than public schools, isolation and bureaucratic demands were rarely reported as problems. Schools were more often described as inclusive communities. Teachers such as Janice Gagne and Allen Rondo commented that they knew their colleagues well, although the relationships rarely extended to a familiarity with their classroom teaching. Teachers in independent schools reported having considerable autonomy in their work, but like public-school teachers, many Catholic-school teachers said that they were constrained in their instructional decisions. The principal of Gagne's school monitored whether students completed their workbooks and kept close track of what went on in each classroom, even though she didn't observe there directly.

In general, teachers in both independent and church-related schools seemed to be less distracted from their teaching by politics, bureaucratic demands, and administrative agendas than their public-school counterparts. However, independent-school teachers frequently said that heavy coaching responsibilities after school and on weekends compromised the quality of their classroom teaching. They typically were required to spend more time with their students than public-school teachers in coaching and extracurricular activities, leaving less time for instructional preparation than they would have liked.

A number of private-sector teachers were particularly troubled by low salaries, sometimes more than ten thousand dollars a year less than public-school wages for teachers with comparable experience. There was, however, considerable variation. Allen Rondo, whose school had a sizeable endowment, reported with some satisfaction that salaries there came within the top 10 percent for private schools and benefits were excellent. By contrast, Janice Gagne earned only 10,500 dollars after six years in the same Catholic school, a situation she endured because she could "come and go" with her own children who attended the same school. Some of those interviewed had reconciled themselves to low pay, but several had decided to move to the public sector in pursuit of higher wages. Gagne argued that, although she had decided to forgo an offer of twice her salary in the public schools because of the convenience that her job provided, others would not: "Something does have to be done if they want quality people. Something is going to have to be done."

In the chapters that follow, comparisons among teachers from the various sectors will show that they share many of the same hopes for their work: safe, clean, and well-equipped facilities; students who are willing and ready to learn; productive relationships with parents; manageable workloads and undisrupted teaching time; a reasonable degree of autonomy; fair treatment by administrators; principals, headmasters, and superintendents who promote strong positive norms about teaching and learning; a role in setting policies that affect their classrooms; and opportunities to work cooperatively with colleagues and to grow and develop as professionals.

PLANS FOR THE FUTURE

Given the many reservations that the teachers expressed about work in their schools, what are their plans for the future? Will they continue to teach? Of the 75 public-school teachers, 9 have decided to leave teaching and 18 others remain undecided. Some of those who leave classroom teaching will work in teacher training or administration, while others intend to quit the field of education altogether.

Four of the 20 teachers from church-related schools and 2 of the teachers from independent schools said that they will eventually move to full-time administrative positions or teacher training. Several teachers in church-related schools also said that they would likely move to the public sector in search of higher salaries, although they were reluctant to enter what they regarded as more taxing, less communal work settings. The prospective loss comprises over 13 percent of the talented teachers of the sample, which seems particularly noteworthy because those teachers are only part of a larger exodus of valued teachers who have left education in the past decade. The reasons that teachers offered for leaving included wages that fell short of family expenses; lack of respect from students, parents, and the public; poor discipline; weak, misguided, or punitive administrators; norms and practices that discourage serious teaching; overwhelming work loads; and professional isolation.

Janice Gagne plans to continue teaching, although she may move to a school that pays more when her children leave the Catholic school where she works. She has decided that nothing will lure her away for some years yet: "I enjoy teaching, and that is what I am allowed to do here."

Anna Capello remains undecided but will likely leave teaching if her school is closed and she is reassigned to a middle school. She feels frustrated by large classes, by frequent interruptions, by administrators who are careless about educational matters, by the scarcity of supplies, and by a society that is contemptuous of teachers:

> I'm torn. I've had other opportunities. I think that I'll leave. I might go back. I think that at this point I need to try something else.

She misses the support of respected colleagues who have left teaching:

> One of my best friends left. We were teaching side by side and she came in three years ago and said, "I can't take this anymore." I considered her one of the best and most talented teachers. She walked upstairs, filled out some forms, and walked out in one day.

Capello has thought hard about the benefits and costs of making such a move:

> People I've talked to all say that once you get out you realize how bad it was. I don't know if that's being too dramatic or if that just applies to city schools, which are not very positive work environments. But they look back at you as if you're the ones left behind on the refugee boat. You didn't make it across.

Richard Sand will probably remain in teaching, although at the time of the interview, he was leaning in the direction of taking a better-paying job in order to pay his daughter's college tuition.

> If I could find something right now that would pay me what I needed, that was not a routine-type job—an office job, sitting in an office and doing routine-type things—I would probably take it.

Few teachers were attracted by administrative careers, except for the greater financial rewards that such work offered. Gary Stein plans soon to leave teaching because of the energy drain, the nonteaching responsibilities, and above all the pay—the failure to

> pay someone a fair wage commensurate with their experience and their responsibilities. If I could be able to take care of my family as I might in industry or as I might in some other plane of education, then I'd do that. I'd be tickled pink. I think this is the most exciting and wonderful kind of job. That is why I'm looking now towards being an elementary principal, which I've done before. I'm looking to return to that primarily for the money.

Although Stein and 6 other of the 75 public-school teachers expressed a positive interest in administrative work, most rejected that option, saying that they would miss teaching or that administration was thankless or irrelevant work. As one high-school teacher explained, "I just don't see people in administration boasting about the same kinds of goals that I have. I see them as people who are interested primarily in organization and in accountability. . . ."

Many of the teachers in the sample had already struggled with decisions about whether to continue teaching, and most had chosen to remain. Some did so with enthusiasm. A math teacher who had worked for a time in business said, "Gee, what do I really want? I think all the things I've been telling you are what I really want. I'll teach." Allen Rondo said that he had experienced a crisis after six years of teaching, when the "novelty wore off" and he began to wonder, "Is teaching the thing?" Looking back, he realizes:

> At the time I was just very frustrated and I was ready to leave teaching because I'd had a bad year for myself and I needed to clear the air, and I decided [I'd try] one more school. This was conscious. One more school would make it clear whether teaching was the thing or not.

Changing schools did make a difference, and Rondo now says that he is "very much at peace with the issue of teaching." He looks forward to an assignment as the director of studies that will combine classroom teaching with administrative responsibilities.

Teachers often said that they could not conceive of being satisfied with any other kind of work, although many could easily envision more supportive workplaces. One who said that she "can't imagine doing anything else" explained: "It's the thing I do best, and the thing I like to do best." Others described feelings of ambivalence. An elementary-school teacher acknowledged that he is "always thinking about leaving"; still others, like this English teacher, see themselves holding out despite many factors that interfere with their work: "If I have absolutely nothing to redeem my efforts, if I feel that every constructive avenue has been closed, if there is nothing to inspire me, I wouldn't hesitate to leave. But I have never gotten to that point."

One high-school teacher told of a period when he had doubted his decision to stay:

> I was supremely naive up to that time. I really believed that the teachers were there to teach, and the parents were there to parent, and the politicians were there to see that the teachers could teach, and the students could learn, and parents could parent.

He described his discovery that "not everybody associated with the school system shares my idealism and my goals . . . not every parent shares my attitudes about what is best for young people, and . . . not every politician tells the truth." He told of disputes about academic freedom, "political leverage to maneuver grades," and administrators' "questioning the validity of a teacher's standards in the classroom." He said, "I really questioned whether or not I had sacrificed far too much for far too little recognition." Finally, he decided that he would be sustained by his own sense of accomplishment:

> It's like the tree falling in the forest. It does make a sound. I don't care if anyone's around to hear it or not. I make a sound—hell, I make a big boom, I think. So I'm going to go back to knocking over trees.

WHO WILL STAFF THE SCHOOLS?

Although many of the teachers will continue in their work, it is clear that they do so with misgivings and that they would be more productive and effective in work settings that support good teaching rather than the many that currently subvert it. Policy makers have proposed an array of reforms designed to improve work in schools and to retain the kind of teachers who participated in this study. These teachers' accounts suggest, however, that any plan to improve the school as a workplace must be comprehensive if it is to be effective. These teachers would welcome the higher salaries, greater roles in governance, and opportunities for career advancement that some policy analysts and politicians have recommended. However, such changes would not compensate for other features that compromise teachers' satisfaction and effectiveness, such as professional isolation, large and impersonal schools, unproductive home/school relationships, trivial in-service training, and scarce recognition for good work. These are matters that require serious, ongoing attention, school by school and district by district.

Careful attention must be paid as well to aspiring and beginning teachers, for they will be much needed in the coming decade. The majority of the teachers in this study began their careers before 1970, when few women had easy access to careers in business, law, medicine, or higher education. New recruits will be weighing the advantages and disadvantages of teaching against the benefits and costs of other work. Potential teachers are likely to be more attentive to salary, to the prospects for professional advancement, to the physical conditions of schools, and to the status of teaching than their seasoned colleagues were when they chose to enter the profession. Beginning teachers are likely to be less tolerant than their predecessors of inflexible schedules, large classes, impersonal bureaucracies, and inadequate supplies. Their standards for teaching will undoubtedly become more exacting as they compare their schools with other workplaces in which they might commence their careers.

CHAPTER THREE

The Politics of Space and Supplies

No one would ever surmise that teachers' work is crucial to the future of the country from the physical features of their workplaces, the condition of the buildings that house instruction and the supplies that support it. The facilities, textbooks, and materials of teaching may seem too mundane to warrant close consideration. The media have so often documented the shabby structures and scarce supplies of inner-city schools that they are no longer startling. The public, who presumably care very much about the education of their children, seem to assume that schooling can proceed in any setting, with no more than chalk and chairs. However, the physical features of schools affect both the circumstances and the substance of schooling—what it is like to teach and learn as well as what can be taught and learned.

The quality of school space and supplies affects not only teachers' satisfaction with their work but also their productivity. If we set aside the conventional image of the long-suffering public servant who, in earlier days, stoked the stove of a one-room schoolhouse and focus instead on the professional person with limited time to do important work, we can easily see that teachers who work in unsound or dirty buildings and lack adequate up-to-date supplies are like manufacturers whose plants are poorly ventilated, dentists whose drills are dull, lawyers whose casebooks are dated, architects without pencils, or physicians who can secure only enough polio vaccine to inoculate one-third of their patients. Deficits in space and supplies are not only indignities and inconveniences; they compromise the efforts and efficacy of even, and perhaps especially, the best teachers.

Although some schools are spacious, functional, well maintained, and safe, many others are cramped, decrepit, and dangerous. In some schools and programs, teachers work with modern equipment and sumptuous supplies, selecting their own materials and initiating new units and lessons with the support of discretionary funds and photocopiers that work. In too many schools, supplies are worn or scarce and teachers' enthusiasm for innovation is dampened by excessively bureaucratic ordering procedures, administrative mismanagement, and obsolete equipment such as manual typewriters lacking keys and ribbons.

Good teachers thrive when they work in good spaces with sufficient supplies. When buildings are antiquated and supplies scarce, they still try to cope by painting and sweeping their own classrooms, scavenging recyclable materials, and financing both essentials and extras from their own pocketbooks. Their efforts are laudable, but their accounts leave no doubt that these physical features of work in schools influence not only how they feel about their teaching but also how well they perform it.

This study tells a story about rich schools and poor schools, the latter figuring more prominently in the accounts of urban public-school teachers than those of suburban or private-school teachers.[1] The story talks also of good management and poor management, of fairness and favoritism, of trust and distrust. The teachers described districts with abundant books and materials, managed by central office bureaucrats who neither knew nor seemed to care about the needs of students, teachers, or schools. They told of school boards and district administrators who favored some schools with timely repairs while ignoring the maintenance of others. There were accounts of schools where teachers could order what they needed and purchase special items as the year proceeded, and others where teachers had to take what was delivered, where they remained beholden to custodians or secretaries who guarded supplies under lock and key.

The lessons of spaces and supplies are not only about adequate funding but also about good management, professional judgment, and equity.

SPACES

When asked about the buildings in which they worked, teachers from both the public and private sectors described the instructional and professional opportunities that the buildings provided; they spoke about maintenance, cleanliness, and security. Some said that their schools were well designed for the number of students and kinds of instruction. A junior-high-school art teacher in a suburban school proudly guided us through his well-equipped and well-lit studio. A kindergarten teacher in an independent elementary school said that she valued having a classroom "right off the courtyard" where students could build beaver dams and "physical environments for dinosaurs." Many other respondents said that instructional spaces were adequate, if not ideal.

Others spoke of schools that were poorly designed and inadequate. One middle-school history teacher called his building

> very, very undesirable. So much more could be done at this age level with a new structure. . . . It's very old and very, very inflexible. You know, straight off the corridor with boxes on either side. That's just about it—an inadequate auditorium, inadequate gym facilities.

An urban teacher whose school had just become a center for kindergarten education listed its shortcomings:

> There is no storage. That's intolerable for me. We need things at hand when we work with young children. . . . The school is really not built for kindergarten children. It's very big;

> things are far away. The bathrooms are far away. . . . There are smaller schools in the city that they could use.

A suburban high-school teacher, who said that the absence of windows in her classroom reminded her of a bomb shelter, contended that "architects should be forced to live in the schools that they build." Another suburban high-school teacher called his building "a disaster from point zero":

> There is one corridor that runs the entire length of the building, with lockers that are way up to the top so that you can't see what's going on behind them. . . . Some rooms are triangular. Some rooms are so small that you couldn't put half a class in them. . . . You can't find people in the building. You can't find kids in the building. There are thousands of places to hide. . . . I could go on forever on this.

A number of teachers spoke of overcrowding that forced them to travel from classroom to classroom or surrender their rooms to colleagues during nonteaching time. A middle-school English teacher who was obliged to share his room with a math teacher explained: "It's hard to leave things on the board, because if I leave my vocabulary on the board and she comes in, she needs the board space." By contrast, a bilingual teacher in a burgeoning urban high school said she was fortunate to have her own classroom:

> I've been lucky enough that I have the same room. I don't have to travel. If you spoke to another teacher, you might get a very different response. They have to go from room to room. I am in one room all day. I have materials, cabinet space. I am very fortunate. Some have to travel and lug books. I remember when I had to do that in my early days of teaching. That's exhausting.

Although a handful of schools provided professional work spaces for all teachers, most did not, a situation that contrasts markedly with that of professionals in other lines of work, who are routinely equipped with offices, phones, and computers. Elementary-school teachers could prepare lessons in their classrooms if they were not displaced by specialists. High-school teachers often perched at shared tables in faculty rooms during their preparation periods. Teachers in suburban and independent schools were more likely to have desks or cubbies they could call their own, but there was no guarantee, even in elite schools. One independent-school teacher complained, "I don't have an area that is mine, unencroached-upon." By contrast, Anna Capello, described unusually adequate facilities in her urban high school:

> I feel very fortunate that I have a classroom as well as a kitchen to myself. This is the saving grace: We have an office for the three of us and you can leave the classroom and go into the office and do your work in the office. And there's a phone there that's actually a link to the outside world, which I've never had in another school. We even have a bathroom. I remember in some schools that I would not use the bathroom all day because we had to use student bathrooms, which were filthy. These might seem unimportant, but they're not. We even have a typewriter.

Repeatedly, teachers said that faculty workrooms and lounges were small and furnished with cast-offs. One called hers "horrendous, filthy." Another said that the staff's refrigerator, to which they were entitled by contract, froze their lunches. She called the furniture "ratty" and complained that the school district had failed to provide the fundamental features of a workplace that teachers deserve:

> It's this feeling that I think does unite the faculty, that the people out there don't think we are deserving of these basic little things that they expect in their own lives and their own offices.

For her and others, the unspoken messages of small, dilapidated, ill-equipped faculty offices and lounges were as troubling as the annoyances and inconveniences caused by the spaces themselves.

Respondents also interpreted building maintenance as a practical matter carrying a political message. After a decade of tight budgets, schools in all sectors were said to have problems with poorly maintained facilities.[2] In some schools, where routine maintenance had been deferred repeatedly, the problems were severe. An urban teacher's school had "nice big rooms, high ceilings, and wood," but the window frames "had rotted away." A glazier replaced the broken glass, but it fell out within a month because the frames and sashes had not been repaired. Another teacher whose classroom also had broken windows complained about a leaky roof:

> The building is in terrible disrepair. We've needed a new roof for six years. They keep patching it, and it keeps leaking. They patch it more and it keeps leaking. . . . My room—it rains in my room. I have buckets all over the room. Some of it is coming through an electrical outlet, which I think is extremely dangerous. . . .

She went on to describe the helplessness that teachers come to feel:

> As teachers, we really have no control, no way of getting these repairs done. I also have a broken window, and it has been broken for two years. So, we usually will report it to the janitors or the principal. They'll fill out a form. It'll go to the administration. Then, somewhere it gets lost in the shuffle. This year they're saying there isn't enough money to fix it at this time, or right now it's the wrong season to repair a roof. But you see money being spent elsewhere. . . .

She noted that her superintendent's office, located in the same building, "has air-conditioning and wall-to-wall carpeting." Although the administrators work nearby, "you can't get through to them that they would not work in these conditions. They would be very upset if their rooms were leaking and they had to keep moving the barrels around." An elementary-school teacher in another urban district described similar problems:

> We need new rugs. We need new drapes. It needs to be painted. The ceilings in the bathrooms are falling down. It rains inside the learning center where I am. I don't plug in the computers while it's raining. Ever. Because I'm afraid of an electrical fire.

Stories of deferred maintenance and shoddy repairs were common—unpainted classrooms, vandalized doors, boarded windows, exposed asbestos, dry water-fountains, and inadequate heating or faulty air-conditioning systems. Teachers said that disrepair affected morale, health, and safety. One suburban teacher, who had joined her colleagues in filing a grievance over the faulty heating system, said that staff could not stay after school in the winter because it was "very cold, very unpleasant." An urban teacher blamed the defective air-conditioning system in her school for health problems:

> The building was supposedly built as a climate-controlled building—perfect in the summer, perfect in the winter, perfect in-between. And so we cannot open the windows; they are sealed. So no fresh air circulates, and it has been our contention as a faculty that a lot of illness, both of teachers and students, has been due to the poor circulation system.

Many teachers who complained of poor maintenance said that their districts did not deal even-handedly with the schools. A teacher whose school roof was scheduled for "desperately needed" repairs felt demoralized by her school's failure to capture its fair share of resources within the district. Other schools were getting computers "and we're getting a roof. . . . Sometimes you feel, 'What about us here?' "

Some said that low-income students were particularly vulnerable to the negative effects of substandard facilities. One explained, "A lot of us feel that many of the kids we have are coming from conditions that look like this and we ought to be offering something a little different." Another concurred: "I've heard this said, that kids leave broken-down, ransacked houses in the projects and they come to broken-down, ransacked schools. . . . It's true, I think."

By contrast, facilities in the private sector were generally adequate and sometimes sumptuous. Several independent-school teachers emphasized how much they valued a functional, comfortable setting that encouraged concentration rather than distraction. One said, "It's beautiful. I look forward to coming here." In Allen Rondo's independent school, officials deliberately downplayed the physical environment: "It doesn't have to be fancy. This school is not fancy, and it's got its ragged spots." Although faculty and students in this elite school may have learned that there is far more to education than facilities, they had not been relegated to dysfunctional, substandard spaces.

Even when public-school buildings were in decent repair, they were often dirty. Unswept and unwashed floors, filthy trash barrels, blackboards thick with chalk dust, and smelly corridors were surprisingly common concerns among teachers from both urban and suburban districts. Some attributed the problems to reductions in custodial budgets, while others said that they resulted from poor supervision of custodians. A teacher from a suburban high school said that the custodial staff there had been cut by "I don't know how many in order to save teachers and programs, which, of course, sounds very good, but it's awful. And I would say it's the biggest complaint that people here have." Another explained that after the introduction of Proposition 2½, the tax limitation law in Massachusetts, "almost all the janitors in the school were laid off, and it became filthy, absolutely filthy." A third respondent said the "custodial staff works hard, but I think the problem is too big . . . there are one hundred rooms in the school."

Teachers in Catholic schools also blamed budget cuts for dirty buildings. One teacher said, "Our budget is limited. We just let go of one of our two custodians. So it's hard." Janice Gagne said that there was not even one custodian assigned to clean her building, that teachers were expected to wash the floors of their classrooms, and that "the nuns will be out there at seven o'clock in the morning, before school, washing the windows."

More often, however, teachers attributed dirty buildings to the custodians' lack of commitment or the principal's inability to monitor custodial work. One teacher's account illustrates the importance of custodians' meeting their obligations:

> For the past few years we had an old janitor who was about to retire, and he did absolutely nothing. The floors were never washed; the floors were never swept. In my classroom, the kids sweep the floor—it's part of their duty because we have to eat lunch in the classroom. I used to do exercise routines on the floor with them. But it got to the point where the kids were saying, "Teacher, the floor smells, I can't!" So then I said to the janitor, "Could we get the floor mopped?" That was in May and he had not washed the floor since September. He said to me, "Well, there's only six weeks of school left. I'm not washing any floors."

When this teacher finally complained to the principal, he was able to insist that the work be done. The next year a new custodian was appointed, "an unbelievably super-duper janitor who has really cleaned up the place."

Another teacher, who complained that her classroom "is never swept unless I sweep it," blamed the custodians union:

> You might wonder why my room is not clean. It all goes back to the custodians union in which the principal has no say. He cannot tell the custodians what to do or reprimand them. There is an outside person who is in charge, who is the administrator for the custodians. So there are very few things that the principal can do. Consequently, as I said, in my school, there are several custodians, and if you happen to be on the right floor with a good one, you're fine. With one exception, I've always been on the outs.

Other respondents, who were very pleased with the cleanliness of their schools, praised custodians. A suburban elementary-school teacher said, "I think they're wonderful. If they weren't here, we couldn't do what we do. I really believe it." Another elementary-school teacher, who described his school as "immaculate," emphasized that custodians and teachers work closely together: "Our custodians are just marvelous people. We consider them part of the staff. They're not laborers. They are part of us."

Teachers generally agreed that well-maintained, clean schools promote higher morale among teachers and better behavior among students. Several teachers reported students' behavior improving when schools were repaired and cleaned. For example, a teacher from an inner-city high school said that students and faculty had better attitudes after employees from a local computer company painted the inside of their old and very worn building:

> They really have made a tremendous contribution. It has helped the school spirit, teacher morale. And the very fact that the walls have not been defaced says that the students appreciate that.

Teachers cope with the difficulties of unrepaired and unswept facilities as best they can. As one middle-school teacher observed, "We all do what we have to do." For many, that meant sweeping their own classrooms, washing desks, organizing student work details, and even painting their rooms. An urban middle-school teacher said that she had painted four different classrooms: "It's very important to me. I feel so strongly about it, and I know that someone else will not do it, that I have to do it." Such commitment deserves recognition, but it also seems clear that the time teachers devote to painting classrooms, sweeping floors, and washing blackboards must be stolen from other responsibilities such as planning classes or meeting with students. One can only wonder what the responses of lawyers or physicians might be if they were expected to repair their offices or ask clients to assist in cleaning them.

SUPPLIES

Although the heart of instruction is the personal interaction between teachers and students, that interaction is frequently mediated by the equipment, materials, and supplies of teaching—the chalk, books, computers, microscopes, blocks, and tempura paint. Some teachers may have their teaching needs met with minimal supplies, while others require more. A mathematics teacher argued, "I don't really use a whole lot other than blackboard and chalk. I occasionally use an overhead projector, but there's no need for it." However, he went on to explain that science teachers require more resources for good teaching and "they don't have all the equipment they need. No, they don't. They should have a whole lot more."

Many teachers have learned to make do with little, to cope with limited resources. When we asked Richard Sand whether he had sufficient materials for his work, he responded:

> Sufficient, as in enough to get by? Yes. Sufficient, as in enough to do what I'd like to do? No way. I have fewer dollars—actual money in my hand—fewer dollars per student than I had in 1972. When you realize that the inflation rate since then has been about three hundred fifty percent, I should have three and one-half times the money. I have less.

A shortage of sufficient and appropriate supplies impedes instruction. The lack of computers in writing classes and of oscilloscopes in physics labs limits what can be taught, and in some cases, what teachers bother to undertake.

The adequacy of supplies, like the assurance of building maintenance, is often a matter of wealth and an issue of equity. Independent-school teachers routinely said that their classrooms were well equipped. Moreover, their students could be expected to purchase books and materials. Likewise, suburban teachers from prosperous districts usually reported having adequate, sometimes abundant, supplies: "We are not wanting, absolutely not"; "We're in pretty good shape. If anything, sometimes I think we've got too much''; ''We're very well equipped. . . . I'd like my own VCR, but we do pretty well.'' By contrast, there were repeated accounts by urban teachers of lacking such basics as books, paper, and chalk, although those who worked in externally funded programs sometimes said that they could not make good use of all the funds available to them. A bilingual teacher in an economically depressed city told of having ''tons of materials. . . . I can get almost anything I want.'' A Chapter I teacher of economically deprived children spoke of having a virtually unlimited budget. A special-education teacher told of not being able to spend all the money that was available. However, this state of plenty in categorical programs was a new, and most respondents suspected, temporary situation. One middle-school teacher in a very poor district had just been told that

> teachers could order whatever we wanted in textbooks, and that the orders would be filled. The city received an enormous amount of money from federal and state aid, and so this is the year, if you are lacking materials, this is the year to order it.

Within school districts, there were accounts of inequities resulting from preferential treatment by the central office toward particular schools or principals. One teacher at a vocational school said,

> My situation is excellent. I get anything I want. Really. It's a vocational school. The superintendent's and the mayor's cars are regularly in getting bodywork, engine work, anything else they want. Our students are constantly out in the city doing other favors for other people. Consequently, the director of my school has no problem with his budget. I don't think my situation is typical in that regard.

Some principals granted teachers a say in setting priorities for the schools' supplies budgets while others did not. Very rarely did individuals or groups of public-school teachers decide how scarce dollars would be spent. Far more often, principals prepared their budgets with informal advice from only a few staff members. This situation stands in distinct contrast to independent schools, where teachers were granted considerable discretion in equipping their classrooms from the funds that were available.

The bureaucratic rules regulating the purchase of supplies in public schools, coupled with administrators' reported penchant for controlling expenditures, greatly diminished teachers' influence over the supplies and equipment of their trade. Most said that they could ask their principals or department heads to order new supplies, but that their influence usually ended there. Some principals treated such requests lightly, while others respected teachers' preferences and did their best to see that they were honored by the central office. One middle-school science teacher described having unusual influence in ordering supplies for her classes:

> All of my money is discretionary. That's only because of the principal. In the fall, a couple of months ago, I had to give him a budget. I had to state basically what I wanted to buy. However, I'm budgeting two years ahead. This money won't be available until next fall, and I won't finish spending it—because I use expendable products—until a year from June. So it's almost two years ahead. He's reasonable enough, and will fight anybody who says otherwise, to leave the money there, so I can spend it as I see fit.

Even when school-site administrators submitted teachers' requests to the central office, there was often no assurance that the administrators "downtown" would honor them. An urban middle-school teacher argued that, although she and her colleagues had plenty of materials, they were not the right items. "If we went down to the main office, to the superintendent, he would say that that's not true—that we're provided with everything we need. But it's what *they* see as need." A bilingual teacher explained that when her program received a grant to buy supplementary materials, district administrators had decided to buy computer equipment:

> I understand that there is going to be a computer and a printer in my classroom, although I really don't believe the kids will use the computer in the classroom. I made that clear. I really don't think I need it, but I'm getting it anyway.

Budgeting, purchasing, and delivery procedures further diminish public-school teachers' influence and control over their instructional supplies. A high-school teacher, who called the budget process "very cumbersome," argued that school districts squeeze the spontaneity out of teachers by requiring months of lead time for orders. A middle-school social studies teacher voiced a similar concern:

> Orders are put in at a certain point—usually almost a half-year in advance. So things are purchased and encumbered by the purchase orders. But what happens is that in the course of actually teaching from September to June, you see stuff that would be nice to have. You try to get it for the next year. But I don't want it next year. I want it now.

Other teachers were more tolerant of such time constraints; a suburban teacher explained:

> You make a preliminary budget plan way in advance, a year in advance, and then they come up with a figure that you're allowed to use, and then you're restricted to those figures. But as long as you tell them a year in advance that "Gee, a year down the road, I think we ought to get these textbooks for this program," I've never seen any kind of major problem. I mean, you might have to wait a year for something, if they decide that the English department is in greater need than you people.

In most districts, materials and equipment must be ordered from authorized distributors, even if better items can be purchased for less money elsewhere. Teachers said that by restricting purchases to designated vendors, districts limited their choices and often wasted precious dollars. Some staples of elementary-school teachers' work, such as reward stickers and felt-tipped pens were not permissible purchases in many school districts. An elementary-school special-education teacher said that her district has "a book" from which teachers must choose their materials. Seldom do such catalogues include the unconventional supplies that creative teachers might need.

When administrators consulted teachers individually or by teams and departments about their spending priorities and then proceeded to grease the procedural wheels in the central office, staff received timely and appropriate materials. One elementary-school teacher told of his surprise when a new principal with long experience in the classroom asked the staff how the school's allocation for supplies should be spent. His previous principal had typically said,

> "Here are the books. Which one would you like?" And you might get something totally different on your desk come September. We had money. Each classroom is supposed to have a certain amount of money. Well, that got spent for you. You may have asked, but you didn't go to the store.

By contrast, his new principal said, "Okay, you three teachers have seven hundred dollars. What would you like to spend it on?" The respondent and his colleagues bought thirty calculators at a retail store and the kits for weather instrument boards which he assembled over the summer. "If we had gone through a catalogue, it would have been maybe about three or four hundred dollars per kit." They "stretched the dollars" with their own effort and ingenuity.

Encouraging teachers to purchase supplies together seems to promote collegial interaction. One middle-school teacher said that once "moneys are allocated to the various schools," staff decide how they will be spent:

> This year, we received twenty-seven dollars and some odd cents for each student who will be coming from the sixth

> grade into the seventh. The teachers will meet, each level will meet, and decide what they might need. They might concentrate the purchases. For example, last year we concentrated on social studies. We bought new social studies texts, workbooks, and supplementary materials to go along with them. And maybe the year before, we bought English. So it's a cooperative venture, and we pool all the money together.

A small number of teachers received a discretionary sum of money to spend each year, either from the principal or PTA. Although the sums reported never exceeded 250 dollars, and were typically less, teachers were grateful for the chance to buy what they thought they needed when they needed it.

In schools where funds were short, where administrators disregarded teachers' priorities, or where the budgetary procedures were rigid or slow, teachers reported serious constraints on how and how well they taught. Some lacked essential materials. One middle-school teacher said that she was permitted only one pencil per child per year. A high-school English teacher in a vocational school had only thirty-five grammar and thirty-five literature textbooks for 350 students. A reading teacher in an urban middle school said that her department had received no new materials in five years. An urban high-school social studies teacher said she had found it impossible to get a new set of books for her American history classes. A suburban high-school English teacher said that the district refused to purchase lined writing-paper for student compositions: "It drives me crazy."

Beyond the basics, elementary-school teachers told of needing film for photography projects, groceries for cooking projects, felt-tipped pens for art projects, and tissues for students' runny noses. One, who said that he wished for "different things than textbooks and work sheets," imagined using science kits, "doing a unit on flight," and "teaching plant life with seeds rather than books." Middle-school teachers told of educational games and computer software that would have enhanced their teaching. High-school teachers described scientific equipment and supplies that would have expanded and modernized their curriculum.

There was considerable evidence that teachers adapt their teaching to the supplies and equipment that are available. Over time, they learn what they can expect and they exercise discretion within the constraints they encounter. One teacher, who already had five computers in her classroom, apologized for wanting what people in industry might consider basic equipment:

> If I could get five more computers, I'd be dancing on the roof. If I could get a printer, I'd by happy. Little things. It's unrealistic and I know it. Because how many teachers can say they've got five computers at their disposal any time to do anything with? I'm being unrealistic.

Respondents' accounts suggest that supplies and equipment strongly influence what they teach. An elementary-school teacher who had enough computers in her school for students to be assigned to them one-half day each week explained that her third-grade class used them to prepare a poetry anthology. A high-school physics teacher said that when he was able to purchase "thirty programmable calculators at forty dollars each" his students could "do real pendulum problems that only people at upper levels could do. I can do motion with friction. I can do orbits."

Many other teachers pointed to teaching opportunities that had been forfeited because of limited supplies. Anna Capello said that her allotment of twenty-two cents per student per week for eighteen weeks each term restricted the kinds of food preparation that were possible. An urban elementary-school teacher wanted to produce a puppet show with his fifth-grade students, "making puppets, making a stage. . . . I would love to do it and get lights and a speaker system. I would like to really do it. I will do it about halfway, and spend my money." A secondary-school Spanish teacher, who was dissatisfied with the reel-to-reel audio tapes that were available in her department, observed,

"Like all teachers, we make accommodations. That is the great flexibility of teachers. We survive."

Many respondents in this sample refused to accept the constraints of limited teaching supplies and spent their own money to equip their classrooms or exploited the opportunities of government grants and PTA fund-raisers. Again and again, teachers told of spending two hundred to five hundred dollars of their own money annually to support their teaching. Gary Stein, who taught second grade in a prosperous district, said that he routinely spent

> Three to four hundred dollars a year on school supplies, school stickers, little books for rewards. . . . I buy materials that the school might not. . . . There's a paper-supply place that has a yard sale, and I'll go there and spend seventy-five to one hundred dollars at a whack, buying a model of the digestive system or something like that—things that just couldn't be provided that I want to deal with, that I want to teach.

He offered an explanation others echoed: "You buy them because otherwise you do without them. I care too much about what I'm doing." A middle-school music teacher concurred:

> My melody bell is up here and my metronome. I bought that. I have my own tape recorder. I have my own portable record player. I have one book that teaches basic skills in music. That book cost thirty-four dollars. I have a whole program of songs to read by that cost seventy-four dollars. But I feel like that's important to me, and I can keep it and use it from year to year and move it from school to school. If I had all the materials I need to teach with, I would feel that I was almost in heaven.

Because teachers were already coping with low salaries, many who spent their own money did so with reluctance, even resentment. One who had spent six hundred dollars that year because of a change in grade levels said, "First, I think about how lousy my pay is, and then for me to go ahead and do things like that—it's like taking food out of my own family's mouth. . . . I'm spending money on doing my own job better. That negatively impacts me." Another observed,

> When Proposition 2½ came into effect, the only reason the schools didn't go down the drain—you wouldn't see firemen buying their own fire trucks or policemen buying their own guns—teachers bought their own materials. They kept it going.

Some teachers who resented having to equip their own classrooms had stopped spending their own money, while others, such as this suburban middle-school teacher, had curtailed personal spending over time: "I will do that in a limited way, but I will not subsidize the town of ———. The average resident here is far, far richer than I." An elementary-school teacher who had experienced similar misgivings—"I'm a single parent and my income is very low"—had reluctantly decided to continue buying equipment, "because it makes things better for me in the classroom." However, she had drawn the line at buying consumable materials, such as workbooks and art supplies.

Teachers were inventive and entrepreneurial in stocking their classrooms. One had bought twenty copies of the first volume of an encyclopedia at nine cents each so that she could "teach the use of the encyclopedia for one dollar and eighty cents." Others scavenged for art materials from business and industry. Some had become experts at equipping their classrooms with money from grants. A reading teacher said that she had "written two grants, and now I have the computers and printers and software, and I'm attempting to get some more." After all this enterprising effort, however, she had trouble convincing the school department to install the necessary electrical outlets for the computers.

PTAs were often the source of materials and equipment that could not be bought through the regular purchasing process. These organizations financed subscriptions to magazines and newspapers, equipped classrooms with televisions and VCRs, and purchased microwave ovens for classroom cooking. Reliance on such fund-raising raises issues of equity, however, because more prosperous schools and districts typically can muster greater financial support. One teacher, who said that her school's PTA had bought a microwave oven for the teachers' room, colored televisions for all the classrooms, and computers for every teacher, went on to observe that other PTAs in her district did not have the resources to do the same for their schools.

Many teachers relied on what they knew to be illegal photocopying of music scores, magazine articles, and short stories to supplement their teaching. Having made certain that he would not be identified in this study, one high-school teacher confided:

> The Xerox machine has created a whole educational underground. If I can't get it, I'll make it. I'll take the time and the energy to make it. Why should I hesitate to tell you? I ask for examination copies, and I take the best that they have to offer, right? Make copies of the good stuff and just reject the same old trash. I think the key here is accessibility of a duplicating service.

Another also ''engaged in certain kinds of activities that are illegal:''

> If there's a chapter in a book that I want the kids to have, and I can't have the book, I will photocopy the chapter and run it off with Thermofax masters, and the kids will have the stuff. So my kids are well supplied, but that has nothing to do with the city's budget. It has a lot to do with my willingness to spend time, usually very early in the morning.

Given such accounts, it should be no surprise that the most crucial piece of equipment in many schools is the photocopier, which is often out of order.[3]

GOING BACK TO BASICS WITH SPACE AND SUPPLIES

The need for safe, functional space and sufficient, up-to-date teaching resources would seem to be self-evident. However, because so many public schools fail to provide these, proposals to improve schooling must begin with an assessment of the physical components of work in schools. Well-designed, well-maintained, well-supplied schools express the public's commitment to schooling. Decrepit, crowded schools and inadequate supplies convey a different message—that public education is low on the list of a community's priorities. When the distribution of resources favors wealthy over poor districts or schools, the message is even more troubling—that some students and teachers are more deserving than others.

Not only does the quality of space and supplies influence morale, it also determines, both directly and indirectly, what is taught and how it is taught. Functional and flexible classrooms and schools permit teachers to shape their instructional approaches to the needs of their students instead of to the limitations of the facilities. Crowded schools afford no room for science laboratories, language laboratories, and resource rooms. Inflexible walls or fixed desks perpetuate solitary, teacher-centered instruction. Dated or unsuitable materials, books in short supply, and ordering procedures that are slow and confining discourage teachers from thinking creatively about what and how they might teach. Resourceful teachers may scavenge for supplementary materials, apply for grants, or even spend their personal funds, but not all teachers are resourceful, and some who are have begun to resent the money and time that such efforts consume.

Independent schools were widely reported to be well maintained and well supplied, and the teachers were granted considerably more discretion in ordering and purchasing resources for their classrooms. Although church-related schools were said to have far less money, teachers there did not regard problems of building maintenance and supplies as political issues. Charges of political favoritism or systematic inequities were rare in the private sector; instead there was general confidence that the schools were being managed well, given limited funds.

If schools are to be improved, it is necessary to grant teachers greater authority in designing and redesigning the spaces in which they teach. Architects cannot fully anticipate the developmental needs of kindergarten children or adolescents. They do not seem to appreciate the effects on teachers of working year after year in misshapen or windowless classrooms, in classrooms that lack the floor space for group meetings, or in those that have insufficient storage or inflexible seating.

Teachers must be given discretion also in ordering equipment and supplies, so that they, rather than a vendor's catalogue or central-office bureaucrat, determine what they teach and how they teach. Principals can involve teachers individually or as teams in spending the schools' financial allotment for materials and supplies, and they can work to ensure that teachers' priorities are honored by district officials. The district or school should routinely allot teachers several hundred dollars of discretionary funds each year to buy what they need for new projects or teaching units. If valued teachers are to commit their intellect, ingenuity, and enthusiasm to teaching, they must know that they will have the right space and the right tools to do the job.

CHAPTER FOUR

Building Bridges Between Home and School

Accountants manipulate numbers of constant value; plumbers work their trade on inert pipes; the objects of teachers' labor are children, who vary, respond, and react in their own irrepressible ways. However committed and inventive teachers may be, their success hinges on their students' interest, effort, and responsiveness.[1]

Some students are healthy, eager, well-prepared and socially mature. Too many are malnourished, fearful, lacking self-control, and deficient in basic verbal and motor skills. Schools have long expected parents to deliver their children primed for education—physically and mentally healthy, demonstrating self-control, and holding appropriate beliefs about the value of schooling. In many communities, there has been an implicit, if not explicit, division of labor, by which parents provide sound raw materials and continuing support for the schools' efforts, while teachers provide academic training.

Sociologists have documented how this division of labor often makes rivals of parents and teachers. In 1932, Willard Waller characterized parents and teachers as "natural enemies, predestined each for the discomfiture of the other," and explained that such enmity resulted from conflicts between the school and the family about what was best for children. The teacher, according to Waller, "desires the scholastic welfare of children even at the expense of other aspects of their development."[2] More recently, Sara Lawrence Lightfoot concluded that because of their divergent interests parents and teachers have fundamentally different views about how children can best be schooled.[3] Dan Lortie found teachers preferred to be "gatekeepers," regulating and restricting parental involvement in schools.[4]

Parents have often been kept at a distance by teachers who rely on their principal to buffer them from the community. Teachers, research suggests, expect parents to voice complaints in the main office before approaching their classrooms, and they prefer to restrict parents' presence to formal occasions, such as back-to-school nights, and marginal roles, such as selling raffle tickets for the PTA.

While not ideal, such a standoff may have been functional when parents and teachers filled their respective roles. However, society has changed over the past decade, and the relationship between parents and teachers has changed as well. Because of financial hardships and social problems, many parents are unable to ensure that their children enter school healthy and ready to learn. Many parents fail to encourage achievement, monitor attendance, or supervise homework because their own lives are so burdened or because they, themselves, failed in school. Teachers in urban, rural, and many suburban areas increasingly encounter students who are unprepared and parents who are unavailable. The teachers interviewed for this study frequently said that they did not want to see parents distanced from classrooms. With few exceptions, they believed parental involvement in schooling is essential for children's academic success; they hoped for parental confirmation that students were learning, and sought parental insight and support when they were not; and they urged parental involvement in school and classroom activities. It is difficult to account for the differences between these teachers' stated attitudes and those reported by other researchers. It may be that while the teachers describe themselves as welcoming and cooperative, the parents perceive the situation differently.[5] Or it may be that the particular teachers in this study, selected for their competence, felt less threatened by parents and thus responded more to parents' concerns and suggestions and desired more significant roles for parents in the schools. It may also be that continuing changes in society are making it more apparent how interdependent teachers and parents really are. Where once school observers characterized students as being caught in a tug-of-war between the teachers and parents, teachers may now see that if parents refuse to participate and let go of their end of the rope, teachers too will lose their hold on children.

Teachers in this study seemed at once distressed by the situation and determined in their efforts to develop more productive relationships with parents. Some felt overwhelmed by the responsibilities and multiple roles they perceived being piled onto them—parent, social worker, drug counselor, sex counselor, parole officer. They reported conflict about deciding whether to try to meet students' physical and psychological needs or confine their efforts to instruction. Virtually all agreed that they needed parents' presence and support if they were to educate all children.

Many have found that they cannot forge successful home/school alliances on their own. Those who worked in schools that systematically shut out parents had found their independent efforts to solicit opinions and assistance from parents ineffective. These teachers believed that schools must affirmatively engage parents in the education of their children and must mediate the growing cultural differences that exist between teachers and families. Districts must fund support personnel—social workers, translators, community organizers—to reduce the distance between homes and schools. Moreover, they said, school districts must coordinate their efforts with those of social service agencies that could assist staff in addressing the array of social and economic problems that students and their families bring to schools.

STUDENTS' READINESS TO LEARN

Teachers agreed that if students are to succeed in school, they must be physically and psychologically healthy. Teachers told again and again of impoverished students lacking adequate food, housing, or medical care. Some of these children exhibited severe psychological problems. A student of one suburban high-school teacher had committed suicide. A "really violent" urban fifth-grader had killed the class salamanders, and staff were constantly on edge with worry about what else he might do. Students of several teachers had been convicted of violent crimes. Having observed a steady increase in the personal problems of students over her twenty-year career, Anna Capello concluded:

> They seem to be poorer. They seem to be in worse health. Their day-to-day problems are just very, very serious. I feel guilty sometimes requesting a homework assignment or asking someone to pay attention when I know that they might pull me aside and say that—one of them told me that her father had been shot the night before. Another had just found out that she was pregnant. Some serious things. And you can really understand why education at that particular moment is not important.

Students who are hungry, exhausted, unwell, or unstable require special kinds of attention, but few schools are organized to respond effectively to complex personal needs.

Teachers also wished that students might begin school equipped with a modicum of self-discipline. Sitting still, waiting one's turn, and following instructions were listed as necessary social skills in large classes, and many teachers observed that economically poor students were unpracticed in such conventions of middle-class conduct. An urban middle-school teacher said,

> So many of the children come to school just for some place to come. They don't know how to act in a classroom. A lot of the children have never had anybody say "No" to them. They have an awful lot of problems that are noneducational, that tend to spill over into the school.

An urban elementary-school teacher added:

> Many parents teach their children to fight no matter where—I guess for survival. I recognize that when a kid is in his neighborhood, he might need to do that. But it doesn't work in a classroom when you're trying to teach.

The growing diversity of school populations—often three or more racial groups and ten or more language minorities—increases both the urgency and difficulty of ensuring tolerance among students and compliance with any common standard of behavior.

Notably, only a small number of teachers said that they were preoccupied with matters of student discipline.[6] One urban high-school teacher complained that her classes were routinely treated as "dumping grounds" by administrators who believed that anybody could succeed there. She estimated that she often had no more than ten minutes of truly productive teaching time during a class period because of disruptions among students. Similarly, a music teacher said that she often spends thirty of her forty-five minutes "doing discipline." Suburban teachers, too, complained of students' behavior, although disruptions seemed subtler there than in urban schools. A suburban physics teacher said that the greatest source of stress in her work was "the behavior of the students who don't seem to be interested in learning, who are rude, or who don't do any work, or who talk to each other when you're trying to do something." Although they expressed concern about chronic absence and passivity, few teachers reported significant discipline problems within their classes. More often, they were troubled by disruptions in the corridors, cafeterias, and neighborhoods that spilled into classrooms.

Teachers believe that their prospects for success are increased when students believe in the promise of formal education. For economically privileged children, the payoff of school success is readily apparent in the lives of their friends and neighbors. For children living in communities where few adults finish high school, and even those who do remain unemployed, the value of a sustained personal investment in schooling is far less obvious.[7] When a high-school teacher tried to convince a student not to drop out of school, the student argued, "My sister has a high school diploma. What is she doing? She has an ordinary job." An urban middle-school teacher described the effects of unemployment and poverty on her students' expectations: "It's been so many generations of people who didn't have an education, that they don't quite know how to motivate their kids and be a part of this educational experience." Students may see little purpose in schooling and receive double messages about the worth of regular attendance and serious work, though teachers try to persuade them that school success is important. Sometimes teachers can compensate for their students' lack of commitment to schooling, but they seldom compete successfully with influential peers who consider school a waste of time.

Some students demonstrate their disdain for education by physical absence or lack of effort.[8] An urban high-school teacher said that the greatest source of stress in her work is students who do not "seem to even care. Students are satisfied with a D-minus. 'Give me a D-minus and let me get out of here.' No one cares about striving to be excellent any more." In some suburban schools, where students competed aggressively for grades, teachers observed that many of their students respected the power of formal credentials, but had lost their interest in real learning. A suburban physics teacher described her frustration:

> They all want to go to the good colleges, and they want to get good grades, and they want to do whatever they have to do to get a good grade, but they don't really equate that with understanding material or working—just whatever little tricks they might do that would get them a good grade without working too hard. That's what they're looking for.

Finally, teachers said that successful teaching depended on students' arriving in class adequately prepared for the subject to be taught. Some children began first grade steeped in story books and "Sesame Street" while others couldn't follow simple directions or understand the difference between words such as "first" and "last." Some secondary-school students had mastered basic skills and exhibited competence in work covered in prior courses, but teachers told of other students who had fallen far behind in reading or mathematics and, as a result, were deficient in other subjects as well. A music teacher described the difficulty of teaching songs with lyrics to students who cannot read. A suburban social studies teacher who had once taught the U.S. Constitution to eighth-graders said that he could no longer assign it for homework or ask students to read it aloud in class, because they found the language too difficult. In his "continuous search" for new ways to teach the material, this teacher had devised a simulation, "The Road to Religious Liberty," which included competition among teams of students and "very, very easy readings that describe Puritan New England."

Many other respondents modified their approaches to teaching as student populations changed, but they often did so with ambivalence. A mathematics teacher in a selective urban technical school said:

> Some of the teachers live in the past where all you had to do was get up and lecture to the kids and they'd learn. But you have to improvise. You have to be an entertainer to compete with what they see on television. It's really true. You have to be a professional entertainer.

Another teacher said, "As time goes on . . . you can't teach the things you want to teach because of the type of students you have. And you start to lower your standards. And you don't want to. But if you don't you're going to flunk everybody, and I hate to do that." An urban elementary-school teacher described the challenges presented by what she called "the city reality" and said that she had made a "major adjustment" in her expectations: "I was expecting too much from these kids. I was being idealistic. I wasn't taking into account where they were coming from and what they go to every day." She went on to argue, however, "It doesn't mean that the kids cannot learn. You just have to find a way to get through all of those layers." No respondent disputed the proposition that all children can learn, but many seemed uncertain about how to adapt their teaching to the disparities among their students, particularly when there were wide differences within large classes. Most respondents viewed students' attitudes toward learning as far more important than their academic preparation, because, whatever their deficits, if students valued education and were willing to work, teachers believed that they could succeed. The challenges these teachers encountered in teaching reluctant students were like those faced by a doctor whose patients are not sure that getting well is worth the effort. Diagnostic skill and expertise in prescribing treatment fall far short of the need.

Some teachers advocated dealing with the full range of students' personal and academic problems while others chose to concentrate on those directly related to instruction. For example, Richard Sand told of a student in his suburban middle school who lived with his stepfather, having been abandoned by both his natural parents:

> This kid doesn't know which end is up. He's bright. He can't sit still. He is constantly pushing [his stepparents] to see if they like him. . . . Of course, that spills over into the classroom. This kid can't learn until we deal with that.

Other teachers believed that they should confine their attention to academic matters. One argued:

> Some factors are beyond our control. If you dwell on the fact that this one doesn't have a parent, or this one has a lack of money, you can get lost. You must focus on why we are here and what we are trying to do with them and help them see that goal for the future. Maybe it sounds harsh to you. I try not to get wrapped up in their daily lives. I feel that those things are beyond my control. I really can't change what goes on in their homes.

More teachers believed that they must simultaneously address students' personal and learning needs. No one suggested that they could ever sufficiently resolve students' personal problems, but they believed they must take such matters into account when thinking about how to teach. For many that meant less formal teaching and less academic learning than they would have hoped.

Predictably, teachers felt more confident about achieving success in economically privileged settings. A middle-school teacher who said that she works in "a yuppie town" explained that her students bring the community's values to school: "There is a very, very strong success motivator. Get ahead. Do more. Have more." However, it is important to note that teachers in low-income schools were also encouraged by incremental gains and modest achievements. One elementary-school teacher who recounted such triumphs said, "These kids are getting something that, probably, I'm the only one who's going to give it to them. That's very important to me." For many urban teachers, though, success was too uncertain and short-lived to be professionally reassuring. A middle-school teacher described the frustration of seeing "a large proportion of my students dropping out and never finishing high school." She reminded herself that

> when they were with me, I made a difference, during that time. Unfortunately—and I don't know what to do about it—I couldn't make that big a difference in their lives. They still dropped out, generally within two years of [entering] high school.

Anna Capello described sadly how her best student had planned to attend a community college to study culinary arts when she became pregnant. Capello had begged the student—"Promise me that you'll think about it, that someday you'll try and go." She acknowledged, "It's discouraging that you can't even see somebody go out in the world and make it. I experience that often." By contrast, teachers of able, highly motivated students could point to visible and lasting evidence of their success.

PARENTS AS MEDIATORS OF SCHOOL SUCCESS

Teachers routinely spoke of the crucial role parents play in students' school performance. Although a few elementary-school teachers, particularly those in private schools, regarded parents as consumers to be satisfied, and others, particularly those in urban public schools, considered parents as clients in need of services, most thought of parents as potential partners and mediators of school success. When parents encouraged their children, monitored their progress, and involved themselves actively in school life, teachers could anticipate success.

An urban elementary-school teacher said that the single most important factor enabling her to do her best teaching was "wonderful parent cooperation and support. I feel that's very necessary when you are teaching. The children and the families work together with teachers." A high-school mathematics teacher argued, if "children are not learning [it is] because adults don't care. That's the bottom line. I have good classes where parents care and those children do learn." An urban elementary-school teacher who called parental involvement "that missing piece to the puzzle" contended that reading scores would not rise until "parents are not only involved in the school, but in the school work of their children." A middle-school teacher who characterized parental involvement in his school as "nonexistent" said that with "very little feedback at all from parents, we're waging the war by ourselves." It was clear that many teachers felt the need to work closely with, and be supported by, parents. As one said, "Kids need that backup from parents. The teachers need that backup from parents."

Many teachers saw a connection between students' readiness to learn and parents' social class. When we asked teachers about parental involvement in their schools, they often described patterns of attendance at open houses or back-to-school nights, patterns that usually mirrored those of socioeconomic status. Teachers in low-income communities repeatedly told of disappointing attendance at such events. A new kindergarten teacher in an economically depressed community said that only one parent of her 20 five-year-olds attended her open house, a fact that shocked her, since "children at this stage really need to see a tie-in between Mommy and the teacher." An urban middle-school teacher who had sent repeated notices to parents encouraging them to attend an open house in her classroom said that only 10 of her 125 students were represented. A middle-school teacher in a church-related school serving a low-income community was dismayed when only one-fourth of her students' parents came to an open house where she distributed report cards, even though she had "sent a personal letter to each parent stating what it would mean to me and to their children" for them to attend.

By contrast, schools enrolling upper-middle-class students attracted large numbers of parents. An elementary-school teacher said that 18 of his 20 students were represented at parents' night and the two sets of parents who were out of town "came at a later time to see me." A teacher of English and Latin in an independent school said that parents attend such meetings "in droves. They're very much interested in their kids, very much so."

In schools serving economically diverse student populations, teachers frequently told of low attendance by parents whose children were in lower academic tracks, tracks that typically include the school's low-income students.[9] At least one teacher interpreted this as evidence of differing levels of parental concern: "Why are most of those kids in the low academic groups? Because on parents' night, when those parents come in, if I'm lucky I have three. And in the top academic groups, they're lining the walls. You can take anything you want from that, but I think that tells a lot." Most respondents argued that socioeconomic status rather than parental concern was the meaningful predictor of attendance at such events. An urban elementary-school teacher argued that parents from higher-income districts were simply more able to participate in their children's education than were lower-income parents. She cited the results of a recent survey in her own affluent community, where she served on the school board:

> Ninety-nine percent of the families had fathers and mothers at home and ninety-nine percent had fathers that worked full-time. Now, are you going to tell me that you can compare communities like that with this community, which, for the most part, has one-parent families, one parent at home? They are killing themselves working, trying to keep the family eating, clothed, and warm in the winter.

Low-income parents often have little time or energy to spare. Moreover, when students attended schools far from home as a result of desegregation programs, parents were even less able to visit teachers. One teacher, who said that his middle school drew "from the lowest of the socioeconomic scale," observed:

> Many of the parents we have are overwhelmed by the situations that they are trying to cope with. They live a distance from the school, and the neighborhoods that they live in, in many cases, are quite unsafe. They do fear going out at night.

In their effort to explain low parental involvement, teachers also mentioned that working-class and poor families were more likely to believe that the schools would be unresponsive and intimidating, and that often these expectations were well grounded. An elementary-school teacher said, "Most parents either feel alienated or feel inadequate in presenting themselves at school and participating in their children's education. Maybe they had bad experiences growing up; maybe they're immigrants who don't speak the language." Differences in language or social customs presented particular problems, as one elementary-school teacher explained:

> One of the problems in our school is that most of the parents don't speak English. I speak Spanish and have always had very good associations with my parents. . . . Most of the parents are really cooperative, and they're very concerned about their kids' education. What happens a lot of times is that they're intimidated by the system, by the teachers, by the whole thing.

Another teacher said that problems in his school resulted from a combination of lagging parental interest and low school responsiveness. The parents, 80 percent of whom were immigrants, were "not very interested in education. And they feel uncomfortable about coming to school. But nobody speaks Portuguese in the office."

Despite extensive evidence that socioeconomic status was associated with levels of parental involvement, wealth did not inevitably lead to more productive home/school relations. Independent-school teachers told of parents who rarely saw their children and who had delegated all responsibility for education to the schools. A teacher from an elite day school said, "I've had students who literally only saw their parents on Sunday afternoons. They were raised by somebody totally foreign to them, and to try to communicate with those parents is really difficult." Others spoke of the disruptions of divorce and the strains of single parenting. A Catholic-school teacher cited a

> very large number of single-parent situations, which is highly unusual in Catholic schools. We have a lot of broken homes where children are being bounced between mother for a few days and father for a few days, or weekends and weeks, and it shows. It makes a difference.

Another Catholic-school teacher said that she was puzzled by parents who spend fifteen hundred dollars in tuition but do not go to the school for routine meetings unless they are required or "bribed" to do so.

Teachers repeatedly expressed an interest in closer collaboration with parents; for only one suburban teacher, who had but four years experience, did parental inquiries signal trouble. Asked whether he had achieved satisfaction in his work, he responded, "You don't get really a lot of satisfaction. The satisfaction you get is, if you don't get any complaints from parents, then you must be doing a good job." This response, which other studies would lead us to expect as common, was not repeated in this study. However, several teachers observed that their open relationships with parents were unusual within their schools. Gary Stein said that some of his colleagues felt very much intimidated by parents and never invited them to help in their classrooms. He recalled that he had done the same thing as a beginning teacher. A suburban high-school teacher, who said that he liked talking to parents, observed that there are some teachers for whom "the prospect of talking to a parent is really anxiety producing, is really a stressful thing. I don't generally find that to be the case, really." A foreign-language teacher in an independent school described similar fears among his colleagues:

> Parents and teachers are on the same side in that they both want to do what is best for that particular child. So, therefore, if you look upon the parents as allies, then you can establish communication. Now there are some teachers who feel that parents might do something to be afraid of, and they're frightened to death of parents.

Teachers said that they did not expect their professional authority to go unquestioned, but at times parents stepped beyond appropriate bounds. A few teachers told of instances when parents harshly criticized their practice. A suburban first-grade teacher said that she reprimanded a child for "coloring all the tiles on the floor of the bathroom" and required the child to clean the tiles, only to be confronted by the child's mother, who "came in and yelled and screamed and swore at me, and said that I should never have disciplined her daughter, that it was my problem." This teacher also told of a father who was "going through a terrible custody fight" and threatened to file a lawsuit because his child was not getting enough warmth and attention at school: "I spent a good eight hours over a weekend filling out forms, talking to social workers, trying to get this mess straightened out, because he couldn't handle what had happened in his family." In each instance, this teacher believed that parents had failed to assume sufficient responsibility for their children.

A suburban high-school teacher said that "teachers want to think of themselves as professional people, people with a specific expertise and a specific training which enables them to be effective at what they do." He described disputes between some parents and teachers about the choice of textbooks: "It's not that the books contain anything objectionable. . . . The arguments are quite technical and specific, that they teach this tense first rather than that tense, that there is more emphasis on conversation than on something else." He argued that "a lot of teachers really resent the fact that, more and more, parents take these decisions into their own hands, that parents are really denying that the expertise exists on the teachers' part."

Teachers in prestigious schools often distinguished between parents who approached teachers as equals and those who approached them as subordinates, seeking to humiliate or censure them. As one independent-school teacher wryly observed, "There are parents, and then there are *parents.*" A suburban high-school teacher, who said that he had "mostly positive interactions" with parents, explained that in the "teaching mythology" of his school there is an

> oral tradition rich in stories of the individual parent who has made a teacher's life hell for an entire year by questioning every decision, by constant phone calls, letters, assailing every individual term paper or grade or college recommendation.

Richard Sand said that there are parents in his district who believe that, by virtue of having bought three-hundred-thousand-dollar homes, they can expect teachers to serve as their children's private tutors. A high-school teacher in a prestigious district told of three lawsuits filed by parents from his school challenging their children's course grades: "They were not failing grades, but grades that were between a C-plus and a B-minus or something like that." Teachers emphasized that, although such parents could preoccupy a teacher's time and energy for months at a time, they were exceptional.

Predictably, teachers working in schools that served upper-middle-class or wealthy populations were more likely to report that parents challenged their practices than were teachers in working-class or low-income communities. Where teachers held positions of superior status, few parents complained; where teachers were outranked in training or status by large numbers of professionals, they were subject to more constant oversight and frequent criticism. One suburban middle-school teacher characterized the parents in her town as "well traveled, well educated, and always willing to come in to share with the children things that they have done." But the relationship was two-way: "They telephone quite frequently if there are things that have gone on that they don't care for." Teachers in private schools reported similar challenges from parents who surpassed them in training, income, or social status. One elementary-school teacher, whose school was located in an academic community, said, "No matter what you want to bring up in class, you're guaranteed to have a parent who's an expert in the field, at least one, sometimes two or three. And that can work for or against you. . . . There's less respect for a teacher here than there would be in a public school." Janice Gagne said that she works hard to meet parents' expectations, knowing that the "last three teachers that were in this class were let go because they weren't doing what the parents wanted."

Despite the difficulties and tensions that teachers sometimes felt when they were outclassed financially or academically, many respondents said they continued to seek parents' active involvement in schools. They emphasized that the occasionally intrusive parent is less worrisome than the habitually absent one. As a suburban elementary-school teacher explained:

> These people are very well off, there's no question about it, and I attribute that to education. They're very interested in their kids' education, and they come to PTA meetings, and they come to open houses, and sometimes they come too much. But the fact is they're there. They're also there when you need them. I feel as though I have tremendous support.

A fourth-grade teacher in a public school where parents are "very, very welcome" agreed:

> Every once in a while, I get a little twinge of "Oh, no. She's at the door again!" But my immediate instinct is to make that feeling go away, because I'd rather have them feel welcome, and I don't think they overstep.

Private school teachers concurred. One said that many parents in his school "have been the first generation in their families to finally achieve a high level of social status" and, consequently, they have "frantic notions about what education ought to be all about." Despite this, he said, these "very energetic" parents were "very concerned and not meddlesome." An eighth-grade teacher in a church-related school characterized parents there as "supportive. Some teachers would say a little too intrusive, but it's much better than their not being here at all." By contrast, an urban elementary-school teacher, who said, "We don't get the parental involvement," explained that she would like to tell parents in her school: "You belong here. Your child is here. Feel freer about it."

Overall, teachers in this study were grateful for parents who were attentive to their children's experiences in school. They were annoyed by the few parents who discounted teachers' expertise and treated them like functionaries, but they were tolerant of parents who demanded more than their share of attention and influence, perceiving them as well-intentioned.

SCHOOLS AS MEDIATORS OF PARENTAL INVOLVEMENT

Teachers said that they wanted to work closely with parents, and many described their individual efforts to do so. Some called parents regularly or visited their homes. Some relied on written notes about students' accomplishments or shortcomings. Some sponsored early-morning breakfasts or afternoon coffees in order to express their interest and commitment. Sometimes teachers wanted to bridge the cultural and economic distance between them and their students' families but simply did not know how. All of the teachers' efforts to build or maintain better working relationships with parents were enhanced or limited by the school context. Some schools were more open, accommodating, and responsive to parents than others. Predictably, open schools and active parents were more likely to be found in privileged communities where parents insisted on becoming involved, but there were exceptions.

In some schools that had very permeable boundaries, parents shared responsibility for support services and exercised roles in governance. These schools often had strong and influential PTAs, or groups of parents who assisted in the office, staffed the library, sponsored social events, provided supplies, raised funds, served as classroom or office aides, or offered special academic or extracurricular programs. In one suburban school, parents had responded to the superintendent's invitation to participate in setting goals for school improvement, proposing changes that resulted in a new homework policy and a new basal reader. The kindergarten teacher who worked in this school said that she could easily engage new parents to support her instructional goals, given these norms of participation:

> They are supportive, interested in learning about their kids, interested in learning about what kindergarten is about, and they'll just go to bat for you. Most of them would just do anything on request for a teacher. . . . I've had a lot of parents in my classroom working and reading with small groups of kids and writing stories with kids.

Gary Stein, who said that parents were more active in his suburban elementary school than in other schools that he had seen, told of "an excess of volunteers. Right now I think I have four parents who will come in. They are great. They'll do anything." Parents from his class tutored students in a special reading program, prepared weekly spelling lists, transcribed stories narrated by special-education students, and ran off dittos.

Active parents were not exclusively suburban. In some instances, schools in low-income communities made resolute and systematic efforts to increase parental involvement.[10] An urban elementary-school teacher said that "wonderful parent cooperation and support" were the most important factors in promoting her best teaching. Volunteers raised money at bake sales, taught in an art appreciation program, and worked in the media center. One school with a largely Hispanic student body and a determined Hispanic principal had instituted lively open houses twice a year where report cards were distributed. As a teacher explained, "That makes a lot of them come. He gives food. It's a big event." She estimated that 40 to 50 percent of the parents attend.

In contrast to the schools where parents were vital participants in administrative and instructional activities, were others where parents participated, but only as fund-raisers, cookie bakers, or field-trip chaperones. Parental involvement in one elementary school was confined to fund-raising by "a small group of PTA parents who are really wonderful, but it's just a small group, a minority." Finally, there were a number of schools where parents participated only infrequently and peripherally. An urban middle-school teacher who called parental activity in her school "nonexistent" said, "For the most part, the parents certainly don't actively come to school."

DIFFERENCES BETWEEN PUBLIC AND PRIVATE SCHOOLS

Because private schools served families who, with few exceptions, could afford tuition, parents were likely to display the active concern for their children's education that is characteristic of upper-income communities in the public sector. As one teacher observed, the tuition was "not a drop in the bucket," and parents expected a return on their investment.

Because parents in private schools had deliberately sought enrollment for their children, they usually brought with them a respect for formal schooling and a commitment to support their chosen school's standards and practices. An alternative-school teacher explained that when parents selected a special type of school, staff could assume that they wanted what the teachers there had to offer:

> The parents choose the school for the style of education. So it's not like people think, "Hey, what's going on here? Where are the basal readers?" . . . They choose this specifically, knowing that, so you're very supported by the community. . . .

The fact that the schools could select their students mattered as well. One elementary-level teacher explained that admission decisions rested, in part, on how much the "parents [can] support this education, in their home life . . . [and] if the child has problems, how much they are committed to helping them change. If they are not, if they expect the school to do it all, then it's not going to work." Furthermore, because school membership was always conditional in the private sector, educators could better enlist parental support when a student's performance deteriorated. Many private-school teachers said their schools made a long-term commitment to students and worked hard with parents to resolve problems that might develop, but most could cite instances when students had been asked to leave. That prospect reportedly increased parents' willingness to attend meetings and cooperate with the school's efforts.

Finally, because parents were often influential in the governance of independent schools, they generally were ready to listen, and in turn, the school staff were obliged to respond. A middle-school teacher, who noted that his school's board of trustees was composed of parents, observed only partially in jest, "There are parents here all the time. Some parents are here every day. . . . They're in the way." He made it clear, however, that he valued their participation:

> It's real nice in a school to know that you have parents' support—that the parents love the school, that they've made a choice to send their children here for all of the right reasons.

Although many of the independent-school teachers said that parents were present and active in daily school life, some said they were not. Allen Rondo explained that parents in his prestigious secondary school were "very active in auxiliary ways," supporting extracurricular activities and raising funds, but they did not participate on the curriculum committee. Another teacher from an elite secondary school told of administrators carefully circumscribing parental influence:

> [Parents] are actively employed to raise money. They are given absolutely no opportunity to affect the policy or the running of the school. They can come in to [the headmistress] and make their complaints known, and they may or they may not have a lot of influence. But there is absolutely no parent organization. . . . That is considered a good thing on the part of the administration, that nobody is trying to get their fingers into the control.

She said that teachers' interactions with parents were monitored as well. There were defined procedures for dealing with complaints, and all written communications with parents were reviewed by administrators who "want to make sure that not too many contacts between parents and teachers come up that aren't somehow regularized."

Catholic schools, unlike most other private schools, maintained clear role boundaries between teachers and parents. Generally, teachers taught and parents raised money. When parents had complaints, they typically registered them with the principal rather than with the teacher. Parents had high expectations, but were less likely than their independent-school counterparts to question teachers' judgment directly and more likely to maintain a respectful distance from daily life at school.

THE SCHOOL'S ROLE IN PROMOTING PARENTAL INVOLVEMENT

It may not be possible to delineate clearly all the factors that promote or inhibit parental participation in public schools.

Unquestionably, some parents' life circumstances—wealth, work, health, family obligations—influence the extent of their involvement, and patterns of involvement mirror those of socioeconomic status. Because public-school parents do not exercise the same kind of choice that their private-school counterparts do, they may not demonstrate the same level of commitment to their children's schools. The results of this study suggest strongly that schools can do much to encourage or discourage, promote or impede, greater interaction between parents and teachers. Teachers who seek closer working relationships with parents achieve those relationships far more readily in schools where parents are often present and active in school life and where norms that endorse close home/school relationships are well established.[11]

Some schools clearly encouraged parents to volunteer in meaningful ways—performing clerical work, providing tutoring and special programs, participating in school-site councils—while other schools relegated parents to peripheral roles as fundraisers or chaperones. Where parents were present in the classrooms and corridors, they were perceived to have a better understanding of how the school worked and what teachers expected. Moreover, they influenced teachers' expectations. Their presence in the schools indirectly conferred the community's endorsement of formal education. Students could not so readily dismiss the value of schooling if parents visibly supported it, even if those parents belonged to someone else.

Some schools instituted special support services for students whose parents were most difficult to engage. Social workers, bilingual aides, and visiting teachers helped classroom teachers accomplish more than they could on their own. By coordinating social services, translating documents, letters and conversation, or providing home tutoring, these members of the school organization drew parents closer to schools. One elementary-school teacher told of a colleague serving as a "redirect person," monitoring the attendance and performance of students who had "been absent and missed work." He characterized the position as "versatile" and the person holding it as "gifted." He had begun to regard her "small space," which helped to link the school with its families, as "an extension of [his] own classroom." Such support personnel enable teachers to better bridge the distances between school and home, but they are costly and school officials who scrutinize budgets often regard them more as luxuries than necessities. In fact, many more may be needed. A teacher in a suburban district that enrolled black inner-city students as part of a metropolitan bussing program believed that the school fell short of meeting the families' needs in what seemed to many students an alien setting. He argued that the program presented

> special demands and needs for them—needs that should be met. But there are trade-offs. And I don't see solutions to these problems except money, a whole bunch of money. But the community is only willing to put up so much money.

Teachers, therefore, seem able to achieve cooperative working relationships with parents primarily under two sets of circumstances: affluent schools where parents initiate such contact or respond to teachers' invitations whether or not the school is organized to support their involvement; and less-advantaged schools where principals and teachers purposefully welcome parents, give volunteers meaningful work, and provide support services to those in need. Well-intentioned teachers whose schools systematically ignore or rebuff parents find it difficult to promote different, more trustful and responsive relationships on their own. One elementary-school teacher in an urban school argued:

> It's very hard without a real school plan, a faculty plan, to give a child, instill in a child, certain ideas or values about life, about education, about why what he's doing here is important to himself and to others, when he's getting the opposite or no similar message at home. I think it's important to make parents feel part of school. It's important to have a chance to discuss with parents and agree with parents

on what we're going to do with their child this year, and to enlist their support right from the beginning.

TOWARD MORE PRODUCTIVE HOME/SCHOOL RELATIONS

There remain perplexing unresolved questions about the appropriate boundaries between school and home, between the responsibilities of parents and the obligations of teachers. Should teachers assume child-rearing tasks that parents abdicate or cannot manage? Can teachers instill respect for education if parents and community members explicitly discount its worth? Many respondents expressed concern that the schools are not equipped for all that society expects of them and argued that communities must assume more responsibility for socializing youth and building respect for the schools. They said that the balance of home and school responsibilities had shifted in recent years in ways that were detrimental for students, families, and public education. Richard Sand reflected:

> Society has changed. American society is very different than what it was twenty years ago—ten years ago. Somebody had better wake up and realize that. What they're doing is driving schools to the point that they are making decisions that they shouldn't be making.

With very few exceptions, respondents believed that concerns about students and their education could better be addressed with than without parents. By drawing parents into the life and work of the school, they could better encourage them to endorse the value of schooling, to exercise their parental responsibilities, to encourage their children to succeed, and to oversee educational choices. Teachers endorsed efforts by their schools to promote parental participation as a way of increasing parental commitment; they preferred as workplaces schools that sought to ally with parents and that committed scarce resources to building solid bridges between home and school.

While the composition of the student population in public schools has changed dramatically over the past decade, the composition of the teaching ranks has remained much the same—predominantly white, female, and middle class. Aggressive efforts to recruit minorities to teaching will likely affect this profile only slightly.[12] Not only is the gulf "widening between the culture of public schools and poor, predominantly minority students," as researchers at the Institute for Educational Leadership observed,[13] the disparity is also increasing between the backgrounds and life situations of teachers and their students.[14] The teachers we interviewed, who came from a range of racial and ethnic backgrounds, but were committed to solidly middle-class values, felt uncertain about what role they should assume in their students' lives and how they might venture beyond conventional boundaries if they chose to do so. They expressed concern about demanding too much and about being patronizing. They said they would welcome efforts by the school and community to reduce the cultural distance and misunderstanding that existed between them and their students' families.

There were few urban schools in this study that engaged parents in meaningful ways in school life, but when they did, the results were encouraging. The work of James Comer in New Haven, Connecticut demonstrates that city schools can build productive home/school relationships and that it is up to the school to initiate the effort.[15] Principals can assume leadership in this area by working with staff to assess existing parental involvement and teacher responsiveness. They can help to devise more meaningful roles for parents and more frequent occasions for exchange. Parents can serve as visiting experts or aides. They can translate school documents into the languages of the community. They can help to organize school activities, such as multicultural fairs or sports days, designed to draw members of the community into school life. They can hold positions on school-site councils that decide matters of policy and practice.

School districts must recognize that teachers need assistance if they are to maintain productive relationships with parents. Special staff positions for social workers, tutors, translators, and community workers are vital to building and sustaining contact with families who might otherwise be beyond the school's reach. These auxiliary staff can also help teachers to recognize and move beyond their own cultural limitations. Too often such positions are eliminated by school officials who consider them frills, tangential to the schools' instructional mission. However, schools and teachers are now expected to do far more than instruct their charges, and districts must provide the support necessary for them to do so.

Teachers must be assured that they and their schools are not solely responsible for the health and well-being of their students. District officials must coordinate their efforts with those of social service agencies. Because schools are the institutions with the greatest and most continuous contact with children, they must take the initiative to collaborate with counseling centers, welfare offices, courts, shelters, and community health clinics. Allen Shedlin Jr., who heads a program in New York City that supports such collaborative programs, contends that the school "is the strategic, sensible, and appropriate institution, working together with families and the community to act as ombudsman, broker, and advocate on behalf of all children."[16] If teachers could teach in schools and communities organized to address the many noninstructional needs of students and parents, they would likely achieve greater instructional success in their classrooms.

CHAPTER FIVE

Teaching and Learning in a Bureaucratic School

During the early 1900s, educational efficiency experts touted what has come to be known as the industrial model of schooling. Schools were likened to factories, students were treated as raw materials, and teachers dealt with like laborers. Although most school reforms fade fairly quickly, this one endured. Throughout the United States, administrators applied to public schools practices of accountability drawn from business and industry. They focused on economies of scale and calculated returns on investments. They instituted departmentalized teaching in the form of "platoon schools," devising blocked schedules that rotated teachers from class to class. They constructed tests and rating scales for measuring school efficiency and instituted quantitative measures of teachers' productivity. Raymond E. Callahan concludes that school officials did not succeed in making schools more productive: they achieved economy but only the appearance of efficiency.[1] Although the effort to rationalize schooling failed to better educate children, it was not abandoned, for it reduced costs and enabled school administrators to look responsible in the eyes of the business community.

The image of the school as a factory is no longer fashionable, and today education is rarely characterized as a production process. Schools are known to be complex social organizations, and children to vary in abilities and interests. Educators voice respect for diversity and speak of being responsive to the individual and recognizing the need for flexible school structures. Features of industrial organization persist nonetheless, and today's schools continue to operate as bureaucracies even though the work that goes on inside them cannot be productively standardized. Blocked schedules, Carnegie units, age-graded classrooms, competency testing, and ability-group tracking remain the norm; open schools and classrooms, the integrated day, interdisciplinary courses, ungraded classes, and modular scheduling are the exception. The rhetoric of educational mass production is no longer heard, but its structures endure.

Bureaucratic forms in education are resilient because they keep costs down and permit schools to cope with large numbers of students in a seemingly orderly way. They do not, however, meet the needs of teachers and students who are engaged in the business of teaching and learning rather than management and accounting. If schools were structured from the inside out rather than the outside in, if they derived their form from the needs of teachers and students rather than the priorities of administrators and business, they would be smaller, more flexible, and varied organizations.

In this chapter we will explore what happens when rationalizing structures are applied to work that is not wholly rational; when schools are organized as if pedagogy could be prescribed, instruction delivered in uniform doses to clients in large groups, and the products of learning measured and summarized for public scrutiny. The public-school teachers interviewed for this study strained to make their schools work on behalf of good teaching, despite school structures that often hampered them from doing so. They committed much energy to coping with institutional constraints, energy that might have been better used in teaching their students. They learned that much of what school departments do in the name of efficiency, productivity, or fiscal responsibility is neither efficient, productive, nor fiscally responsible. They found themselves obliged to prop up ineffective practices and apologize for unrealistic expectations even while they saw their students ill-served. Ironically, the factory model of schooling prevails most strongly in those urban schools that enroll the neediest and most diverse populations—the very students who require the individualized approaches to instruction that bureaucratic schools can least deliver.

Although teachers in independent schools of the private sector also encountered some bureaucratic elements in their workplaces, the constraints were far less restrictive than in the public sector. Classes were smaller; instructional loads were lighter; teaching time was disrupted less often; clerical duties were fewer; and instructional autonomy was greater. As a result, teachers expressed more confidence in achieving success with all their students and reported more often that they could teach as they thought they should. But before examining these valued teachers' responses to the bureaucratic features of their workplaces, we should consider in more detail why schools are such poor candidates for mechanistic control.

WHY SCHOOLING IS HARD TO RATIONALIZE

Organizational analysts have observed that work can be successfully rationalized only under certain conditions. First, the work cannot be subject to uncertainty; only in a predictable and unvarying environment can work be routinized reliably.[2] Where there is little uncertainty, as in the paper industry, organizations can safely standardize practice. Where uncertainty increases, as in computer software development, organizations must be able to adapt their responses to sudden and unexpected change. Second, organizations with clear goals can more readily standardize practice than those with unclear or conflicting goals. The organizational purposes of a fire department are far less ambiguous than those of a human rights commission and, consequently, the work of fire fighters can be prescribed more precisely than that of human rights advocates. Third, the technology, or way of doing the work, must be such that it can be planned in advance and clearly specified. An organization that is to provide standardized services or products must be able to ensure conformity of process and consistency of product. McDonald's has developed such a technology for preparing fast food and has devised methods for training its predominantly unskilled, teenage work force to carry out those procedures. By contrast, the technology of writing poetry is difficult to specify and creativity cannot be programmed. Fourth, organizations that adapt well to rational structures typically use raw materials of constant quality. Assembly-line production of microchips requires consistently high-quality silicon; given suitable supplies, work can proceed in a routinized manner. By contrast, a chef's raw materials are less constant and predictable, and those who cook must adapt their techniques to the unexpected delivery of unripe avocados or sinewy beef.

When environmental uncertainty is low, goals explicit and achievable, technology narrowly specified, and raw materials consistent, an organization can specialize workers' roles and standardize their activities, whether they are manufacturing frisbees or administering inoculations. However, when uncertainty is great, goals ambiguous or contradictory, technology weak, and raw materials uneven, organizational structures must be more flexible and permit workers to experiment and adapt in doing their work. The structures must allow time for workers to coordinate their efforts and exchange information about progress and problems; they must tolerate inefficiency; and they must be responsive to the demands of an individual client rather than controlled by programmed routines of the service-delivery system.

Schools are clearly organizations of the second sort. They operate in uncertain and sometimes volatile environments. They encounter unexpected budget cuts, sudden arrivals of large immigrant groups, new mandates from state and federal governments, and constant political demands from all segments of the community. Their goals are notoriously ambiguous and conflicting; schools are expected to provide everything for everyone, to teach children both conformity and creativity, to inculcate respect for authority as well as critical thinking. Teachers are simultaneously told to attend to the needs of the individual and the group. They are expected to teach broad concepts, but their students are often tested for proficiency in discrete skills. Nor is there much consensus about the technology of teaching. For some subjects, such as typing, there are tried and true approaches. For others, such as creative writing, methods vary widely. Finally, as we saw in chapter 4, students—the raw materials of schooling—vary physically, intellectually, socially, and psychologically. As schools reach out to serve increasingly diverse student populations, they necessarily must cope with the even greater variation in ability, interest, and behavior that these students present.

A review of these features of school organizations—the environment, goals, technology, and raw materials—suggests that, if schools are to be effective, they must have adaptive structures, experiment with varied approaches, and prepare for different kinds of outcomes. Theory would lead us to predict that standardized structures and preplanned practices would enable educators to serve only some students and achieve only some goals, that rationalizing instruction overall would be ill-advised and ineffective. In some public schools education is not arranged in bureaucratic fashion or doled out in uniform doses to large groups of students. Joan Lipsitz describes several such middle schools.[3] Theodore Sizer's Coalition of Essential Schools is nurturing similar efforts across the country.[4] Most persons familiar with public education can cite other examples. But these are exceptions, created and maintained at considerable personal cost to teachers and principals who must contend with strong organizational forces in public education that suppress variation in favor of standardized treatment of students in large schools and classes with uniform, though not necessarily distinguished, outcomes.

BATCH TEACHING

Although teaching is inherently an interpersonal activity, teachers in our society rarely work with their students one at a time. Rather they encounter diverse groups of 15 to 40 students.

Although elementary-school teachers may work with the same 20 students throughout the day, secondary-school teachers are routinely assigned 125 students in five rotating classes. The teachers in this study regularly noted the constraints of large, diverse classes and demanding course loads and expressed concern about their ability to meet the needs of all their students. In general, classes were both larger and more varied in public than independent schools; teachers in Catholic schools sometimes taught more students at once than their public school counterparts, but their classes tended to be more homogeneous in student composition.

Class size. Research to date on the effects of class size has yielded inconclusive and contradictory results.[5] Lacking clear demonstration that students learn more in small classes, critics of public education often argue that class size is simply a matter of teachers' self-interest—smaller classes make work easier and protect more jobs. Given the considerable expense of reducing class size, school districts usually avoid the cost unless they encounter strong pressure in the community or at the negotiating table.

Teachers in this study expressed strong opinions about class size, opinions formed by their own experience rather than research findings. They told of large classes forcing them to lecture rather than lead discussions and reducing the time available for them to interact with individual students. They were convinced that class size made a difference in how and what students learned, and they held remarkably consistent notions about what levels of enrollment were intolerable (over 30), acceptable (25–30), preferable (15–25), and ideal (10–15).

Public-school elementary classes generally ranged from 20 to 25 students; the largest regular class represented in this study totaled 30 students.[6] Classes in reading, bilingual education, and special education were smaller, those in physical education or music sometimes larger. At the middle-school and junior-high-school level, class size varied as a result of ability grouping.[7] A mathematics teacher's smallest class included 13 students while her largest had 33. High-school classes also varied in size—7 to 35 students—as a result of both tracking practices and elective offerings in specialized or advanced subjects such as restaurant management or Latin. Class sizes in Catholic schools were similar, although a few elementary-level classes exceeded 30 students. Since some of these schools offered only one class per grade level, a particularly large class was often said to be a temporary demographic quirk. Teachers from Jewish and Quaker schools in the sample reported consistently smaller classes, reflecting their institutions' commitment to personalized instruction. Independent-school classes were often half the size of those in the public sector. With one exception, all teachers interviewed from these schools taught fewer than 20 students in a class, and most had no more than 15. Allen Rondo said that in his school the average class size was about 15: "It varies from four or five in the smaller, upper electives up to, very occasionally, a math class might have twenty." One secondary-school teacher, who said that she had never taught a class with more than 12 students, characterized class size in her school as "very manageable." The sizes of any single teacher's classes also varied in secondary independent schools, but the average size was much smaller than in public and parochial schools. One independent-school teacher's classes ranged from 5 to 14 students, another's from 7 to 18. The smallest classes of most secondary independent schools were half the size of those in public schools, while their largest were approximately two-thirds the size of comparable classes in the public sector.[8]

Public-school teachers generally considered classes with more than 25 students difficult to teach. One elementary-school teacher with 30 students called her class "enormous" and described the practical problem of arranging thirty desks for a class discussion. Another middle-school teacher of 32 students complained that her class was "huge." A middle-school teacher with classes of "about twenty-six to twenty-seven kids" called this "way too many," causing difficulties in "really getting to know them." Teachers generally doubted that policy makers understood the importance of class size. A suburban high-school

English teacher said that her assistant superintendent had decided to increase certain college preparatory classes from 25 to 27 students, thus eliminating three sections and "saving the town a lot of money." The change was made in the name of efficiency, but this teacher argued:

> What she has done is create classes that people are uncomfortable teaching, and what they've lost is far greater than anything they've gained by eliminating that half of a position. . . . Numbers make a big difference in any classroom. You know. I can do fine with a class up to twenty-five, really I can. But when it gets over the line of twenty-five, just in terms of physical layout, trying to get those extra seats in, it's a problem. I like to get to every kid at least once a period. The periods are forty-eight minutes long, and you have thirty kids. If I get to everybody, I'm not going to hear much from any one person.

A middle-school mathematics teacher in an economically poor community agreed:

> As you get up into the twenty-twos and twenty-fives and twenty-eights, effective instruction is compromised because we're dealing with kids who, ideally . . . should have individualized instruction in math. . . . They have poor math backgrounds, and they don't have a grasp of mathematical concepts or figures.

He, too, believed there was simply not enough time to go around: "In a class of thirty it's impossible. No matter what anyone tells you, in a forty-five-minute class, it's virtually impossible." Public-school teachers who taught fewer than 20 students at once said that good teaching was possible in that situation. An elementary-school teacher said that classes in her school are typically 18 to 20, which she finds "ideal." A high-school mathematics teacher whose classes averaged fewer than 20 students echoed: "It's really ideal."

Although most public-school teachers thought that classes with fewer than 20 students were ideal, independent-school teachers preferred, and generally expected, classes of no more than 15. Prior experience in private schools had led them to believe that they could and should succeed with all their students,[9] and they often argued that personalized attention was only possible when they were teaching 15 or fewer students. A history teacher in a prestigious day school, who contended that small class size is "the most crucial thing for good teaching," said that there is a "critical number" that permits, even obliges, all students to participate in class discussions. But "when classes get beyond fifteen or sixteen for me, I know that students can slip by. . . . At fourteen, they can't."

Class size, therefore, affected teachers' choice of teaching methods and expectations of success. Classes approaching 30 students were termed manageable, but only with teacher-centered instruction in which teachers took the role of experts delivering information and students became passive recipients, seldom raising questions, offering interpretations or entering into real discussion with their teachers or peers. Teachers believed that such classes met the needs of only some students some of the time. Those who taught classes of 20 to 25 students said that they had more opportunity to address individuals' interests and needs, and they suggested that reducing class size by even 2 or 3 students made a big difference in their work. Teachers whose classes were smaller than 20 in the public sector and 15 in the private sector were decidedly more optimistic that they could truly reach and teach each of their students.

Class composition. Numbers were only part of what concerned teachers when they talked about responding to students' needs in large groups, for class size interacts with class composition. A teacher of severely handicapped children may not be able to teach more than 3 students in one class, while in Advanced Placement mathematics a teacher might feel confident of success with a class of 25.

Student bodies in independent and church-related schools were more homogeneous than those in the public sector by virtue of parents' choices and school admission standards. Many such schools refused to accept students with special learning needs and there were few low-income students, given the high costs of tuition and limited scholarship funds. Therefore, although any group of children is inevitably diverse, the range of abilities, experience, and attitudes toward formal education was reported to be far narrower in the private than the public sector.

City schools were more diverse racially, ethnically, and economically than suburban schools, and even those urban classes that were homogeneous in race or economic background often included students with an array of social, health, and learning problems that required considerable individualized attention. Urban school teachers felt the greatest demands to adapt their teaching to the individual needs of students, but were the least able to do so because of large classes.

Handicapped students, present in virtually all public-school teachers' classes, presented particular demands for individualized instruction. A fourth-grade teacher in an urban school argued that her class of 20 was too big given the large numbers of such students:

> On paper, it's a regular mainstreamed classroom, but there are children here who have special needs. . . . That is the greatest source of stress in my work: time, and having children who need more help than the help I can give them.

Similarly, a science teacher in an urban middle school, who argued that class size is the single factor that most compromises his effectiveness, explained that the difficulty of teaching many students is augmented when a number of those students present unusual needs:

> I think that it makes any teacher less effective. In my case, I feel that I have a large number of special-ed children. I make tremendous adjustments for them in the classroom. In other classes, the class size might be drastically reduced because of

> the children going out to special ed, but it's a policy in the school that all children will have science, and I am the science teacher.

The interview data provided testimony of great variation among students, the raw materials of the educators' trade, and teachers were well aware that they could not apply the same set of expectations and teaching practices to all students and expect common outcomes. In fact, they found the notion laughable. Yet schools are organized as if they could and should.

Teaching load. For secondary-school teachers, the teaching loads—the total number of students and sections they taught—further influenced their ability to teach well. Secondary-school teachers from public and Catholic schools had comparable teaching loads, with 75–130 students in middle and junior high schools and 80–130 students in high schools. By contrast, teachers in secondary independent schools taught a maximum of 70–80 students.[10]

Theodore Sizer has persuasively argued the case for smaller teaching loads in public schools, contending that Horace Smith, his fictitious though typical teacher, "should not have to compromise; he should be responsible for only 80 students at a time, not 120 or 150 or 175, as is common today in many public and parochial schools."[11] A teacher's student load determines the amount of sustained attention available for any individual student. A teacher who considers the learning needs of 75 students simply thinks differently than one concerned with twice that number.

Public- and independent-school teachers also differed significantly in the number of course sections assigned to them, and thus the number of class preparations and hours of stand-up instruction. Most academic teachers in public and Catholic secondary schools taught five classes five times a week. With few exceptions, independent-school teachers taught four courses four or five times each week. Anna Capello compared her schedule as a home-economics teacher with that of her academic colleagues:

> I think I would have a hard time if I were an academic teacher, teaching the same subject every day for five periods. But my schedule is different every day. I have six classes. I see them two days a week for a total of four periods. I see them longer. They're double periods, which is sometimes difficult, but it also works well when you're preparing food. It gives me flexibility within my curriculum.

She was glad to have longer blocks of time, even though it meant that she was assigned more students.

The combined effects of five large and diverse classes meeting one after another each day exhausted many respondents. The urban high-school teacher who is responsible for 130 students in five sections each day simply cannot provide the attention to class preparation or individualized instruction that is possible for the independent-school teacher with 75 students meeting in four sections, four times each week.

Grouping and tracking. With small classes, teachers can adapt their instructional approaches to respond to individuals' abilities, learning styles, and levels of motivation. With large classes, they must either accept that they will reach only some students or devise ways to reduce the diversity. The most common response is to group, or track, students by ability. Ironically, this response often leads to a schoolwide system that is both impersonal and inflexible and reinforces the very bureaucratic practices that teachers initially sought to moderate.

Throughout this study, teachers reported grouping students by ability for instructional efficiency. Elementary teachers often regrouped students from one or more classes for reading or mathematics. For example, one urban teacher said that she exchanges students "with another second-grade teacher in our school just so we can have a top math group and a bottom math group and different reading groups, so you can get to a different group of kids."

Middle- and junior-high-school teachers also frequently organized classes into more homogeneous groups. A suburban teacher of social studies and English described the complicated arrangement in her school:

> Social studies is heterogeneous in both seventh and eighth. Science is heterogeneous in seventh, and in eighth it is semi-heterogeneous. There are a couple of top-level science classes. But in math and English, they are definitely tracked into three levels, A, B, C.

Although a few school districts prohibited tracking in the elementary or middle schools, others encouraged it. Most classes at these levels differentiated broadly among groups (advanced, regular, remedial). At an extreme, one urban English teacher, whose largest class had 32 students, reported that there were sixteen different levels in the seventh grade. The school had coped with enormous class size and its accompanying complexity by creating many discrete, homogeneous groups of students. With few exceptions, high-school teachers' academic classes were stratified either by an explicit tracking system that designated courses by level (honors, standard, or basic: Curriculum I, II) or by an elective system that differentiated courses by difficulty (Medieval History, Modern Living).

Most teachers agreed that teaching was more manageable in a homogeneous than a heterogeneous class, because one could prepare materials and approaches that were geared to a greater proportion of the students. Those who taught advanced classes might find the task demanding, but they were not confused about whose needs to meet. The goal of the class was clear and the students able and focused on their work. Many teachers of low-performing students also reported that teaching homogeneous classes was easier than trying to address such students' needs within heterogeneous groups, provided the classes were not too large. But the teachers were well aware that sometimes only the best students profit from such arrangements; that large concentrations of weak students reinforce poor study habits and low expectations among peers; and that average students often get lost in a huge, gray middle. Moreover, the teachers knew that tracking is often socially and academically stigmatizing. Several mentioned that research findings discredit tracking,[12] and some, particularly in elementary and middle schools—said they preferred to work with heterogeneous groups. However, few teachers believed that sufficient individualization was possible given the size and diversity of most public school classes, and they believed that students' needs could best be met by reducing diversity through grouping students with others of similar interests and abilities. Tracking was the accommodation they made to a school organization that requires batch processing of learners.

SPECIALIZATION OF TEACHERS

Workers on an industrial assembly line have highly specialized assignments. In manufacturing a product, whether it be a bicycle or a coat, they become experts at particular subtasks such as welding spokes, assembling brakes, cutting sleeves or making buttonholes. No single person performs the total task; no bicycle or coat bears the stamp of a craftsperson responsible for its construction. At best, an inspector tucks a slip of paper into the carton or pocket to verify that the product meets company standards. An assembly line can produce goods of uniform quality quickly and at far lower cost than items custom made by a single mechanic or tailor for particular customers.

In a school organization modeled on manufacturing, teachers would be experts in computer technology, right-brain learning, phonics, or scientific inquiry, and over the course of thirteen years, students would move from one expert worker to the next to be informed, treated, and tested until they emerged as certifiably educated graduates. Teachers would repeat routine, predetermined tasks rather than adapt their approaches to changing students. In the extreme, all students would pass through the same set of procedures, and those who failed periodic inspections would be rejected. By contrast, schools organized in response to clients would orient their approaches to individuals or small groups of students and fashion instruction to meet their particular needs. Working alone or in teams, teachers would attend to the whole child, considering physical development and social skills as well as capacity to reason abstractly or compute accurately. Predetermined teaching patterns would be replaced with individually fashioned education plans. These organizations would make it possible to diagnose and respond to the students' complex and varied needs, but only at a cost in dollars and inefficiency.

Elementary schools. Most respondents from elementary schools, both public and private, taught self-contained classes and, thus, could be considered generalists rather than specialists. Teachers who preferred this instructional format valued the opportunity to teach the whole range of subjects to a small group of students. A fifth-grade teacher said that he had been "resisting team teaching. I guess maybe I don't want to let go. I like having the kids in all the different areas." Self-contained classes provide consistent, if unspecialized, attention to student learning. With one teacher responsible for all of a student's major subjects, that student's total instructional experience is more likely to be coordinated and coherent than if several teachers were assigned parts of the total task.

Even in self-contained classes, however, selected students were taken out of class for work with specialized tutors under the auspices of programs in special education, Chapter I, or English As a Second Language. Four elementary-school teachers of self-contained classes reported that such disruptions were the greatest source of stress in their work. One explained:

> The major problem that teachers have is fragmentation in our day. We have kids going everywhere. They go out to the reading lab, and they go out to Chapter I, and they go out to the resource room. We have kids going in and out all the time, and then you don't know how to make up what they're missing.

One teacher did not question the value of such specialists' work, but reflected on the costs of a fragmented schedule:

> I have twenty-three interruptions in the course of a week in this room, and I never have my full class together, ever at one time. And parents say to me, "Well, will my child miss anything?" Well, of course they will. Of course they will.

Classroom teachers saw some irony in the fact that schools increasingly seek to serve the needs of the whole child by interrupting their core instructional time for work with outside specialists. In a few schools, specialists' services were scheduled with a regard for the integrity of core instructional time, and teachers praised those arrangements. One respondent explained that grade-level teachers in his school designate two periods each day for reading and mathematics, which could not be interrupted. Several respondents recommended that special education programs be modified to bring specialists into the classroom to support instruction there, making students' learning more consistent and classroom teaching more coherent.

Middle and junior high schools. The tension between teachers' roles as specialists and generalists increased in grades five through eight of the public schools, which are typically thought to provide a transition between client-centered instruction in the primary grades and subject-centered instruction in the high schools. Few teachers at this level taught self-contained classes; most were assigned to either subject-specific departments or interdisciplinary teams or clusters. The structure of teaching units reflected the extent to which schools and teachers oriented their programs to either the student or the subject.

In some schools teachers were organized by interdisciplinary teaching teams and assigned to work exclusively with a single group of students. Typically, such teams included teachers in English, mathematics, social studies, and science, who together took responsibility for 80–100 students. In the most successful examples, these teachers met together regularly, planning and coordinating their curricula and constructing schedules that were consistent with their students' instructional needs. Teachers could monitor students' progress closely, and if one began to fall behind in a particular subject, that teacher might ask his or her colleagues whether they saw evidence of similar problems. Study skills, personal development, and in-class behavior were of concern to all staff, and meetings with parents usually included all teachers rather than just one. Richard Sand, who collaborated with 4 colleagues in teaching 100 students, described his team's interaction:

> We meet every single day. Basically, we discuss the kids; that's why we're here. We bring up problems. We let each other know what we're doing so we don't all schedule a major test the day before Christmas, things like that. We deal with parents' problems and parents' requests. We have parents come in and talk about the kids. Sometimes we request; sometimes they request.

Teachers who favored this teaching structure valued the coordinated, holistic attention to students that it permitted, as well as the curricular insights that interdisciplinary work offered. Often classes were heterogeneous rather than homogeneous. One teacher called it "very, very healthy for students." Another said that it permitted her to respond quickly with other staff and parents when she saw a problem developing: "There's no lag time."

A departmentalized structure characterizes the organization of most junior-high schools. Teachers worked far more closely with colleagues who shared their subject specialty than with teachers from other departments who shared their students. As the day proceeded, students assembled and reassembled for their different classes with different collections of their peers. In departmentalized schools, a fixed schedule subdivided instructional time by subject, and all teachers had to work within the constraints of its uniform blocks. Many teachers liked working with colleagues who had similar academic interests, but several respondents from departmentalized schools expressed concern about the effects of specialization. One said:

> I like [departmentalization], but then there comes a point where, if teachers were working together, we could get more out of students. It seems like we're always fighting the battle alone. It's one teacher, one class, and it's either sink or swim with that class.

This teacher contended that students' experiences were too fragmented under the current departmentalized arrangement:

> They come from elementary schools where they are with the same teacher every day, all day, and then the first day of the seventh grade, they see seven different teachers, and that's the way it is for the rest of the year. I think a lot of kids don't adjust too well. . . . It's tough.

Teachers who had worked in both interdisciplinary and departmental structures generally favored the cluster structure. Richard Sand had taught in both situations and emphatically preferred the team approach, because teachers could quickly identify and deal with problems as they developed:

> It's quick. There's no lag time. Before, if a kid was having a problem, if I remembered, I would speak to another teacher at lunch time or after school or before school. It might be a week. It might be ten days. I might forget completely. We just didn't pick up on some of the problems kids were having. This is, by far, much better.

A teacher whose school had returned to a departmentalized organization regretted the change:

> We had a certain flexibility that we don't have now, the ability to double up, to have two periods without hassling all the other teachers in the school. There were lots of advantages

> like that. And being able to get together with the members of the team and talk about the kids, being able to send kids back and forth. There were a lot of advantages.

Her school had returned to a departmentalized structure in order to promote schoolwide curriculum development, but most other teachers whose schools had moved from clusters to departments said that the change had been made for financial rather than instructional reasons. As one teacher explained, "They didn't want to pay. We weren't teaching five full periods, which the other schools were." In order to work as they are intended, cluster structures require extra staff time for meeting and coordination and teachers' preparation periods must be aligned. By contrast, scheduling by departments can be done without assigning joint planning time and, therefore, is less costly both in dollars and administrative effort.

High schools. Specialization was extensive in the curriculum and schedule of both public and private high schools, where virtually all respondents' work was organized by subject specialties. A high-school English teacher was far more likely to meet and talk regularly with another member of the same department who taught an entirely different group of students than with a mathematics teacher who taught the same students. The curriculum of the large comprehensive public high school was extensive and varied, featuring elective courses in subjects as diverse as Chaucer, Chinese studies, auto repair, and Advanced Placement physics. Public high schools responded to diverse student needs by offering many courses and alternative paths to graduation. As a result, students' scholastic experiences in most public high schools were highly differentiated, some would say fragmented.[13]

Three teachers in this study taught in schools-within-schools that resembled the cluster structure of some middle and junior high schools. One alternative program for 100 students restricted their course options, but enabled them to participate in setting policies and practices for their schooling. One teacher believed the smaller class size, personal commitment, and democratic structure contributed to a community that supported student learning.

A second respondent, in cooperation with a science and mathematics teacher, taught English and social studies to a group of 68 students in a vocational high school. Students attended academic classes one week and vocational classes the next. This teacher thought that the small, tight structure was "good for the kids." He and his colleague were able to monitor students' progress and adapt the schedule to fit their teaching needs:

> I like the control that the two of us have. If we want to extend a period or shorten a period, we can do it. We can do anything we want academically. The week we have them, we're in complete control.

A third respondent instituted a cluster program in his school when officials in his suburban district moved the ninth grade to the high school and he became "very concerned" that ninth graders would get "totally lost and fail academically." Under the new arrangement, each cluster consisted of English, social studies, and science teachers working with a group of students, "monitoring them socially and academically." Teachers eventually hoped to "get together to do interdisciplinary teaching." The program was working well, though students taking accelerated courses in science and mathematics could not be accommodated in the schedule.

Except in alternative programs such as these schools-within-schools just described, public high schools provide virtually no systematic means for staff to monitor individual students' progress or to intervene when difficulties arise. Counselors with very heavy case loads—typically 250–300 students—were expected to oversee students' course selection, personal and social development, academic achievement, college applications, and career plans. No one really expected them to effectively integrate the complex and highly differentiated structure of the school on students' behalf, and yet no one else was in a position to do so.

As in public high schools, the primary reference group for most independent-school teachers was the department, where collegial interactions centered on curriculum rather than individual students. But because of the small size of these schools, teachers were often assigned to more than one department, thus promoting more exchange across disciplines within the faculty. Allen Rondo estimated that two-thirds of the teachers in his school belong to more than one department. In most independent high schools, the entire faculty met regularly to review students' progress one by one. They drew on their varied perspectives as instructors, administrators, advisors, coaches, and dormitory supervisors to identify problems and to devise strategies for intervention. An average of 378 students, compared with 1262 in public high schools, made such oversight possible and ensured that no student fell between the cracks of the departmental structure. Few public high schools are small enough to make such continuing attention possible. Moreover, faculty who may know less than 10 percent of the student body in large schools can hardly be expected to hold this schoolwide concern for individual students' progress.

Pressures to departmentalize. For a number of reasons, no high school encountered in this study was organized predominantly by clusters or interdisciplinary teams. Many teachers liked working in departments, with opportunities to teach highly specialized courses that they found both challenging and rewarding. Graduation requirements and standards for college entrance reinforce a departmentalized structure; interdisciplinary courses are misfits in traditional academic accounting systems. Standard departmental structures also survive because alternatives are costly. Faced with budgetary constraints, teachers preferred smaller traditional classes to interdisciplanary innovations. In some cases students resisted interdisciplinary structures. Able and motivated students benefited from specialized academic and vocational coursework, appreciating the opportunity to choose from 150 or more specialized courses; the less able or poorly motivated students who had more to gain from cluster structures were typically less vocal and influential.

Teachers in this study from all levels saw advantages in both specialized and unspecialized school structures. The specialists can hone subject-specific skills that generalists cannot, and the content of instruction may be richer as a result. The sixth-grade teacher who works exclusively as a writing specialist may contribute more to students' learning than he or she could if expected to teach all subjects. The Advanced Placement physics teacher arguably can offer better training to aspiring engineers than someone teaching general physics to all students.

However, highly differentiated, rationalized schools hindered teachers from integrating students' experiences from different courses or monitoring their progress effectively. Although able, self-motivated students might provide that integration for themselves, many others could not, and the price of specialization may be too often academic fragmentation and social disintegration. Ultimately, teachers' desire to see students progress may be more frustrated than facilitated by specialized structures. With lighter teaching loads and smaller schools, teachers might gain the opportunity to be both specialists and generalists, pursuing their interests and abilities in environmental science and Tolstoy while attending to their students' total schooling experience.

Constraints of nonteaching duties. Although some teachers' instructional roles were highly specialized, very few teachers in this study were permitted to specialize exclusively in teaching. If teachers' scarce and precious time were not claimed for extraneous clerical or supervisory duties, they might move more easily between the demands of subject matter and students. Any teacher's time, no matter how devoted she or he may be to students or school, is ultimately limited. Time that is spent monitoring cafeterias, supervising detention, or counting lunch money cannot be effectively spent correcting homework, meeting with parents, or tutoring students. One might expect that school officials who were concerned with efficiency and productivity would see that teachers' time is used for teaching, but often they do not, and teachers routinely function as monitors, security guards, and clerks.

Elementary-school teachers generally believed that their students needed close supervision and sustained care and they accepted supervisory tasks such as lunch duty, bus duty, and recess duty. Secondary-school teachers perceived less need to monitor students' behavior outside of class, in part because they considered their students to be sufficiently independent to fend for themselves. Many secondary-school teachers said that the greatest source of stress in their work was the shortage of time, and yet virtually all had to reserve forty-five minutes each day for noninstructional tasks. A bilingual teacher who spent third period each day in the main corridor of a large urban high school "guarding the door against intruders" considered herself lucky that it was generally quiet enough there to allow her to grade papers. However, for most teachers, supervisory time was lost time. A foreign-language teacher observed, "My main concern should be my classes and my students, not my study hall. I know I resent having to do that duty." Five of the more experienced public-high-school teachers in the sample had devised ways to substitute instructional or administrative responsibilities for supervisory duties. One who taught twenty-eight periods rather than the standard twenty-five explained, "I'll trade two or three more teaching periods for babysitting detail any day."

The problems of custodial care in public secondary schools are very real. Faculty and administrators cannot depend on positive student norms to ensure socially responsible student behavior as they might in smaller, more homogeneous schools; they cannot leave students to their own devices during free time. School facilities must be protected from disruptive or dangerous intruders. But teachers do not believe that the answer lies in seizing their already scarce professional time.

Extracurricular activities were optional for most public-school teachers, although many respondents participated. By contrast, independent-school teachers at the secondary level were usually required to coach two out of three seasons, a responsibility that some enjoyed as an integral part of their work with students and others disliked because it detracted from their "real work" of teaching. In either case, coaching claimed a great deal of after-school and weekend time. One respondent said that when she finishes teaching each day, she spends "two and one half hours out on the playing field. I spend all Wednesday afternoon at games and all day Saturday at games. It's exhausting. Perhaps if that time weren't consumed by coaching, I could spend more time thinking up new ideas." Another teacher agreed that coaching claims time that otherwise might be spent on classroom teaching: "A good soccer practice takes as long to prepare as a good chemistry class."

Throughout these interviews, teachers distinguished between nonteaching duties that required their expertise and those that did not. Richard Sand observed humorously:

> Student contact stuff we have to do. Standing in bathrooms—I don't think we have to do that. . . . They could bring a gorilla in and chain it to the wall and give it just enough rope to reach the little buggers. The student contact tasks I really don't mind for the most part.

All agreed that collecting money—whether for pictures, insurance, lunches, field trips, or candy sales—should be delegated to aides or secretaries, as should tallying daily racial counts, completing the state-required attendance register, authorizing welfare forms, and filling out truancy cards. Schools varied widely in the extent to which they subjected teachers to such tasks. Some teachers handled no money, while others had to tend several accounts. Two teachers complained about being "insurance agents" without commissions. One second-grade teacher collected lunch money daily and submitted a detailed order for hot and cold lunches, noting preferences for white or chocolate milk and ice cream or chips. She estimated that it took "a good twenty minutes" each morning to get it all right. Some schools simplified attendance procedures with computerized systems, while others required hand-tallied accounts from each classroom teacher. One elementary-school teacher said that she had few such clerical responsibilities: "We've had good leadership along the way that has seen to it that our time is put into working with children. That's probably why I'm still here." By contrast, Gary Stein said that attending to such administrative business in his second-grade classroom consumed half an hour each morning. He regretted the waste: "Time for me is very precious because the rest of the day we're going full steam."

Teachers in some schools were required to file reports listing the number of minutes they intended to devote to each subject, detailed accounts of their compliance with special education plans, and their own lesson plans for subsequent weeks. Often they suspected that no one read these documents.

Teachers spent additional time on clerical tasks such as typing handouts and tests, ordering supplies and books, and photocopying or duplicating materials for class. A few teachers objected to these chores, but most were grateful if they had access to typewriters with ribbons, photocopiers that worked, and purchase orders that would be honored. Gary Stein said that he had managed to

> barter with the principal to get a second field trip on the condition that I take on all additional responsibilities of collecting money, keeping records of money, and getting a final check that is ready to go to the bus company. The only impact on the office is that they call to arrange for the bus and they mail the check that I've given them.

Although much of teachers' routine clerical work could have been performed by others, virtually no public school in this sample had designated aides or secretaries for the purpose.

CURRICULUM AND PEDAGOGY

If schools were to operate like factories, producing educated students in large batches, teachers would be equipped with standardized curricula and trained in proven pedagogies. In fact, there has been growing optimism in some quarters that such an instructional technology is possible. Proponents of so-called effective teaching practices have sought to describe and prescribe failproof approaches to instruction. However, since 1985, researchers have raised increasing doubts about finding formulas for successful teaching.[14] More recently, those seeking to define a "knowledge base" for professional teachers have found such a definition to be "elusive" despite "a 'dramatic explosion' in research about teaching and learning over the past 20 years."[15] Despite such uncertainty, state officials and school districts throughout the country have become increasingly prescriptive about exactly what and how teachers must teach.

The teachers in this study expressed skepticism about the wisdom of any search for one best pedagogy; they believed the strength of their teaching rested in their ability to diagnose the needs of individual students and classes and to adapt their instructional approaches in response. One junior-high-school teacher said that she did not know how people could survive who rely on a single technology and do "the same thing year after year." She likened them to industrial workers who "work in an automobile plant and put the taillight bulb in every Nova that goes through." She argued that teachers must be responsive to differences among children:

> The kids are different every year. They might be the same number, and there might be some of the same problems, but they're all different. Each class that goes through has its own personality. You have to adjust; you have to adapt.

Respondents also spoke of the importance of encouraging teachers to feature the strengths of their individual teaching styles. An elementary-school teacher argued: "I don't think there is one way; I really don't. I think that for every person, it's a different way, and I think you need that." Richard Sand contended that "the worst kind of teacher is the teacher who opens the textbook and starts on page one, and at the end of the year wants to get to that last page." An urban middle-school teacher said that he and his principal agree that a good teacher "is one who does as many varied things as are necessary to meet the needs of various kids within the subject areas." A suburban English teacher was disparaging of peers who took pride in a prepackaged approach to technology:

> Their curriculum is more like a machine than anything else. They've got eighty lessons and they've got eighty days, and they click through it. It may be a pretty fancy and elaborate and detailed machine, but I think they're taking pride in something that doesn't warrant any particular pride. I'm not impressed with their curricula. I would like to see them be more motivated, more energetic, rather than trot the kids through this French Revolution for the twelfth year in a row.

Because this research was conducted in Massachusetts, where state officials do not try to regulate teaching directly, few teachers participating in this study said that they were obliged to follow a regimented, preprogrammed curriculum, and most from both the public and private sectors reported exercising a good deal of freedom in their teaching. Private-school teachers were rarely guided by more than rough outlines of course content. One elementary-school teacher, who said that he had a "tremendous amount of freedom," explained that he is constrained only by a "set of ideals and philosophy." A sixth-grade independent-school teacher explained that faculty at her school are

> given the general area, and then they decide what they want to do. I was told to teach classical Greece, and I sat down and looked at what classical Greece meant to me, what it had meant to the previous teacher, and pretty much sorted out what I wanted to do.

An English teacher from an independent high school said that she could choose her books and move at her own pace: "I can digress as I please or do other sorts of special projects as I please." A chemistry teacher in an independent school reported having much the same discretion:

> In chemistry classes, I'm pretty much free to take those classes anywhere. . . . I can go fast or slow, and I can spend three months on nuclear power or acids and bases, and nobody would ever question that.

Allen Rondo elaborated: "How many tests you give, how you want to do them, even your grading scale. . . . Do you assign homework or do you not? Do you collect it for a grade? That's up to you." Although public-school teachers spoke less confidently about their freedom to teach what and how they wanted, many in this sample did exercise as much discretion as private-school teachers. They were grateful that, unlike their counterparts in states such as Texas, they worked in a place that did not regulate their teaching practice or textbook selection.[16]

The curricula these teachers used were often local products prepared by teachers themselves. Anna Capello mentioned a home-economics "curriculum guide for the city. In fact, I wrote it." A middle-school teacher observed, "We have tremendous control over what we teach. We've designed our curriculum and change it frequently as a department." Another explained, "The prescribed curriculum is there, but it was developed by us in summer workshops a number of years ago. We set it up the way we wanted it. So it still came from us."

Teachers spoke eloquently, even passionately, about their need for autonomy in teaching. An elementary-level teacher in an independent school said, "I love making curricula for kids, for individual kids, for groups of kids, specific to learning styles." A number of respondents said that they would not continue to teach if they lost autonomy in their classrooms. An elementary-school art teacher said that if her supervisor had told her "what to teach and how to teach," she "probably wouldn't be here." A physics teacher who said, "I love the autonomy," argued similarly:

> If somebody came in here and told me to teach this way or that way, it wouldn't work—not for good teachers. . . . If you want to set a mine field . . . for failure, that's how you do it.

A middle-school teacher whose district had no centralized curriculum said that autonomy "keeps you motivated." She found that prescription "really takes away all desire to [teach]. It's irritating. I invent my own projects in the class and my own goals. It's a lot easier to work that way." A high-school English teacher argued that when "competent people who are enthusiastic about what they're doing" have "creative input so that they actually have an individual stamp, then I think that really you're going to support good teaching. It's self-motivating."

This celebration of autonomy should not be read as a demand for license. Teachers recognized the importance of a coherent program and acknowledged their responsibility to colleagues who would teach their students in subsequent years. A middle-school science teacher, who said, "I don't like to be restricted and I'm not," also argued for an articulated curriculum and said that he felt an obligation to children as they moved on to another teacher or grade:

> There are certain basic assumptions that are being made about the material that has been covered, and certain concepts that should be understood in order to deal more effectively with the following grades. So I do follow the curriculum, though I may not teach exactly like many other teachers.

A middle-school mathematics teacher said that he was free to devise units and lessons "within the guidelines of what our curriculum describes. I mean, I can't just go and teach whatever I feel like teaching." A junior-high-school teacher, who said that she had "felt very hemmed in" by a curriculum some years ago, still did not advocate abandoning all guidelines: "I don't think I should be free to wander outside the curriculum even if I don't like it. It's the only way certain expectations can be met." Several teachers mentioned the importance of consistency among schools to permit relatively smooth student transfer from building to building. Others explained the need for agreement within a school about the sequence of skills to be taught. In fact, several respondents criticized the absence of any orderly approach to curriculum in their districts. One said that he had been granted autonomy by default: "I teach the basic things, but if I didn't want to . . . I could teach anything I wanted." He would have preferred some general guidelines. Although the teachers in general prized their autonomy, they also expected to exercise that autonomy within a framework that coordinated their efforts with those of other teachers.

A few public-school districts and a number of Catholic schools had assigned curricula that defined not only the scope but also the sequence of topics to be covered and skills taught. Janice Gagne described the structure in her Catholic school:

> The textbooks follow one on the other. They do want us to go by the textbook. Whatever I find most important within the textbook, I can devote more time or attention to that. . . . You have the manuals. . . . How you [cover the course material] is up to you. But they want it covered. . . . So it does put some pressure on you, I think. There are some things that I would rather give more quality time to, rather than worrying about having to get on. There is some pressure there.

Many teachers resented such prescription, and some refused to comply. A public-elementary-school teacher said that he had "played it right by the book" one year and found that he "wasn't satisfied. I had thought maybe they had a magical formula here. I did everything that they said to do. Then I said, 'No way. . . . I can do this much better,' and I have." He reorganized the sequence of stories, introduced novels, and prepared exercises to promote higher-level thinking skills. He reclaimed his autonomy with little difficulty, but others encountered more constraints. Several teachers from one urban district chafed under mandated curricula that specified both content and outcome by grade level and subject. The amount of material to be covered was another serious concern, and some of the teachers eventually rejected the requirements. An English teacher said that her centrally prescribed curriculum was far too comprehensive, but that she had decided not to cover it all: "To me, if I can cover half of it, and they understand half of it fully, I would rather do that than go through one hundred percent and have them understand nothing." Asked whether such adjustments required approval from above, she said, "I don't ask. I just do it." By contrast, a social studies teacher felt very confined by the requirements of the district's prepackaged curriculum. She compared teaching her American history class, where the program was prescribed, to teaching in her "best" class, Afro-American history, "where you don't have all those curriculum and objectives to follow" and she could do "exciting things." In the required course,

> you're a robot and it's an assembly-line kind of thing, where you're not doing anything well. You're just on some kind of a schedule. . . . Trying to cover a whole textbook before the end of the year doesn't leave you any room to do creative kinds of things.

She argued that the prescribed program discouraged creativity among teachers: "You tend to take the safe route out. 'We're on chapter twelve today.' Boom. Boom. Boom. Boom."

Policy makers who advocate prescribed curricula for public schools do so in part because they believe that all children should be taught the same things. These teachers would undoubtedly agree that all children should learn to read and compute, that those studying Latin must master the ablative case, and that those studying chemistry must attain an understanding of valences. But there are topics and courses that are less dependent on content, where teachers aim to instill concepts more than content and develop intellectual habits rather than discrete skills.[17] A science teacher who said that he and his colleagues were "given a lot of freedom as to what we teach" explained that they had taught meteorology, in part "for our own stimulation." He explained that in earth science, the content can vary because "it's the thinking process that we're trying to develop." He, like many other teachers in this study, believed that curricular objectives could be accomplished in various ways and that a good teacher attended both to the learning needs of students and to his or her own ever-evolving interests.

SUPERVISION AND TESTING

In a mechanized production process, quality control can be obtained either by closely supervising the workers or by inspecting their products.[18] In an effort to exercise closer control over the process and product of public education, some policy makers and school officials have instituted programs to evaluate teaching practices directly by observation or indirectly with student test scores. In Massachusetts, where the data for this study were collected, state officials called for teacher evaluations every other year as well as testing of students' basic skills, relatively modest requirements compared to those of other states. Local school districts administered a variety of other tests. Private schools, which were not subject to the state requirements, administered tests of their own. Most of the teachers said that neither classroom observation nor testing resulted in significant regulation of their work, although some found the programs intrusive and counterproductive. For the most part, the programs provided the semblance, rather than the reality, of control.

Classroom observation. Formal evaluation procedures that included periodic classroom observation by administrators served as spot checks on teachers' basic competence, but did not provide school officials with continuous data about the teachers' compliance with the curriculum or prescribed teaching methods. For the teachers interviewed, observation of their work by administrators was largely symbolic. Most teachers reported that school officials monitored neither what nor how they taught, that they were left alone in their teaching. One urban elementary-school teacher said, "There's no one standing over my shoulder watching me." Gary Stein, who called evaluation "a rote process," said that his principal "really doesn't know what's going on in my classroom." Anna Capello agreed:

> I feel that I'm basically left alone. I think it would have been harder for me to stay if someone was, for lack of a better expression, breathing down my neck all the time. I really feel very independent in that no one is watching me all the time.

An urban English teacher concurred:

> No one looks over your shoulder. I could do anything I want and no one says anything. And I mean no one says anything. It's just one of those things. They just take for granted that you're in your classroom, doing what you're supposed to do.

Teachers offered several explanations for this absence of oversight. Some said that their principals and department heads trusted them as professionals. One elementary-school teacher said that her principal had announced to his staff that he had selected them to teach in his school because they were "strong." She agreed:

> We are all strong; we all do our job, and we don't need anyone to be looking over our shoulder. So we feel a certain amount of freedom in our school because we all are real professionals and do what we're supposed to do.

Similarly, another elementary-school teacher said, "I have a principal who basically respects me and what I do and says, 'I hired you to do this. Do it.' He doesn't get involved." Other teachers attributed the absence of oversight to neglect or lack of interest on the part of school administrators. One suburban elementary-school teacher said, "The fact is, there isn't anybody out there who knows what is happening. I'm not sure they care, either." An art teacher echoed, "I don't know if they care that much, to tell you the truth." These teachers, being respected as they were by administrators, may have experienced less oversight in their work than their peers, but their responses suggest no special treatment. Classroom observations were conducted to meet contractual obligations, but rarely to monitor practice.

Some administrators sought to oversee teaching indirectly by examining documents such as plan books or grade books. Anna Capello said that she had to submit weekly lesson plans but, "the person whom I submit the lesson plans to knows nothing about foods. He's the department head, a former business teacher." One middle-school English teacher said that she had to send a set of compositions to the curriculum supervisor monthly. Gary Stein was required to submit chapter tests in mathematics for review by administrators. None of these teachers complained that such techniques significantly restricted what or how they taught, but complying with administrators' requests for documentation and maintaining the pretense of accounting consumed valuable time.

Student testing. Standardized tests, a second oversight mechanism, were reported by the teachers to be increasingly prominent in their work. There was considerable evidence that test results influenced some teachers' work, but the respondents themselves seldom viewed the systemwide tests as professional tools enabling them to teach better. Because students vary and develop at different rates, it is difficult to isolate any single teacher's contribution to a student's test scores. However, some teachers believed that tests could be used by administrators to reveal individual teachers' shortcomings. One said,

> If there is a teacher who really isn't making it, the following year when the kids are tested, it really shows, and I think

> they can pretty well be identified. Maybe not for one year, but if it's a pattern over a period of years, it shows up.

Most respondents objected to administrators' using tests to single out individuals. One who acknowledged that it was "beneficial" to identify gaps in students' proficiency said that she did not think it appropriate to "blame the third-grade teacher" for students' being "low in some area." She argued that others must share the responsibility:

> She's not the only one who's been teaching math to those children in the last three years. We have first-grade teachers, second-grade teachers, and we have third-grade teachers. They test the children in the third grade.

In the case of academic programs taught exclusively by individuals, several teachers accepted standardized tests of students as appropriate measures of teaching performance. A teacher of advanced physics said that he felt "constrained" by the Advanced Placement exam, but that this was "fine. I teach to that test. That's supposed to be very bad, but it's an excellent test. I don't mind that at all." Districts seldom administered achievement tests in secondary subject areas and, therefore, teachers' practice was virtually unaffected by testing.

In the middle schools, tests often had greater influence in English and mathematics than in other subject areas. A junior-high-school social studies teacher explained that he was "dealing not so much with skills as with values and concepts, much harder things to test," and, as a result, he was safe from scrutiny:

> The pressure is on in math and English. That's what parents think is important. So they don't value us [in social studies] as much, but they don't put as much pressure on us either.

At the elementary level, where reading and mathematics are the core of the curriculum, teachers were much more attentive to standardized tests, a fact that some teachers thought perverted rather than improved classroom teaching. One said,

> The object is that children should learn, that they should start where they are and progress as far as they can during the year. The teachers should put their best effort into that process. You should try to motivate the children to make their best effort. That's what it is all about. But if it hinges on a score at the end of the year—no.

Notably, some of the same respondents who claimed that they are autonomous in their teaching also said that tests affect what and how they teach. A first-grade teacher said that she is "more aware now of getting [her] children prepared for second grade, because I know that the big push is on for competency-based testing." Although she didn't believe that she should be "teaching for tests," there was a belief in her district "that if the kids fail, then it's the teacher's fault." She said that she disciplines herself not to be driven by the tests—"I teach my curriculum, what I think is sound and what they need"—but she acknowledges that the prospect of tests influences her work: "In the back of my head, I know that's coming, and I want them to be able to go in and do it." Two elementary-school teachers reported that they had rearranged the sequence of units in their curriculum to ensure that students studied key topics before the tests were administered in the spring. Another teacher, who thought that tests could be used constructively to identify students deficient in basic skills, nevertheless criticized colleagues for overresponding to each year's results:

> The tests come back. They're low in some area. The third-grade teachers get blamed for that. What didn't you do? So they work on the math area, maybe. Then the next year the tests come out, and the math has gone up but the English is down.

Some teachers thought that their districts used tests appropriately to identify strengths and deficiencies in the program. A few who were dismayed by the lack of curricular order in their schools and districts advocated increased testing in order to pinpoint weaknesses in the curriculum. An urban elementary-school teacher said that he and his colleagues had "been unhappy, all of us, very unhappy, about the lack of testing in the city to begin with," and he called it "absurd" that students were "not tested on a regular basis so we can see where they're at when they come into a particular classroom, and where they're at when they leave. We can't follow kids' progress."

Teachers' responses to standardized testing often depended upon whether the results were used by outsiders or by teachers themselves to improve their practice. Many criticized the public's current preoccupation with test scores and the way in which some school officials inappropriately cite test scores as evidence of a faculty's success or failure. One suburban teacher said that her district publicizes high scores with pride—"Aren't we wonderful?"—although the scores can be best explained by the students' privileged backgrounds. By contrast, a teacher from a large urban district criticized administrators who were "very, very concerned" about test scores and encouraged competitive school-by-school comparisons, holding teachers solely responsible for the results. Richard Sand was angered by recent comparisons of schools' scores in local newspapers:

> We just had all the state testing at grades three, seven, and eleven. A year ago, when all this was introduced, it was: "This is to help you better understand what you're doing for the kids. It is not designed for comparisons." Yet in the last three weeks . . . all they did was compare. It is extremely depressing to pick up newspapers and read about schools being weighted by their CAT scores, their SAT scores, when at the same time, we're being told by so-called experts . . . that we have to do more hands-on work with the kids, get out of the schools more. It's the same people saying these things. "Scores have to go up. Get them out in the world." Yet, if I don't have them here and can't sit down and work with them, I can't help them with their skill problems.

A number of those interviewed recognized the need for some indicators of progress, but objected to test scores being used as the only one that counted. A junior-high-school teacher who said, "Frankly, I resent them" also acknowledged that school officials needed some way to demonstrate progress: "They need somehow to put a candle to it . . . to measure it and quantify it and qualify it. That's very difficult in education."

The context for these teachers' responses must be remembered: at the time of the interviews, state officials had only recently instituted minimum-competency tests permitting district-by-district and school-by-school comparisons, and the scores had, as yet, little influence on important decisions about funding, staffing, or promotion. These were, therefore, low-stakes tests. By contrast, teachers in other states encounter tests which are used to make important decisions. Research by H. Dickson Corbett and Bruce Wilson in Maryland and Pennsylvania indicates that such high-stakes tests move districts to become "more focused on testing than learning."[19] Administrators in these states that were devising strategies to improve test scores expressed concern that they were "compromising a standard of good professional practice."[20] Teachers were spending time preparing students for test taking even while doubting the long-term value of their efforts. The tests tended to become ends in themselves rather than means to better teaching. Richard Sand said of teachers in other states, "They ignore the individual and teach to the tests. That's what is happening. We're very fortunate. We haven't been pushed that way."

The teachers in this study said that tests provided them with general evidence about program success across grades and schools. Some diagnostic, criterion-referenced tests provided more detailed, individualized information about students' performance, which teachers could use in addressing particular students' learning problems, but, most standardized tests told teachers little, if anything, more than they already knew. Confronted with a list of summarized scores, teachers were left to guess whether these were complete and valid measures of their efforts, to wonder how changes in their practice might affect test outcomes, and to question whether adjusting their teaching to achieve higher scores was the right and responsible thing to do.

BEYOND BUREAUCRACY

Public schools have been far more bureaucratized than private schools. Indeed, one of the most striking features of independent schools is their very independence. They set their own policies and practices and are not obliged to coordinate their programs or procedures with those of other schools. They do not have to contend with "the people downtown," and they are not beholden to the state for money. Because they are embedded in no larger system prescribing or limiting what they must or can do, teachers in these schools were far less subject to the "large-batch" expectations of specialization, standardization, and oversight. Schools and classes were smaller, teachers were more often responsible for the whole child, curriculum was more flexible, and oversight was modest and indirect. As a result, teachers found that they could adapt their work to the needs of individual students and infuse their teaching with their own academic and personal strengths.

Church-related schools varied in degree of bureaucracy. Some Catholic diocesan school systems rivaled public school-district bureaucracies in formality and complexity. Individual schools and teachers were required to respond first to the larger organization's demands for conformity, efficiency, and accountability; students' needs came second. Other Catholic schools, however, were virtually autonomous and decidedly nonbureaucratic in character, featuring smaller classrooms, unregimented practices, and a focus on individuals rather than large groups.

Teachers in all schools clearly believed that highly bureaucratic schools, whether in the public or private sector, made poor use of them as professionals. Their special interests and expertise were neutralized; they were expected to comply rather than invent. They doubted their students' needs as learners were well met. Why do schools carry on with these attempts to mass-produce learning when they are seen to be futile by those most closely involved? First, only rarely do teachers, those who are most aware of the complexity of instruction, design schools. Formal authority in public education has traditionally rested with those (mostly male) administrators who manage the enterprise rather than with those (mostly female) teachers who provide the service. From the early part of this century, administrators following the industrial model of organization have advocated efficient and productive schools with the greatest possible yield for each educational dollar. Schools are, moreover, embedded in state and local political systems that demand accountability for both what is taught and what (presumably) is learned. School funding formulas, which depend on student enrollments, lead to large classes and large schools. Graduation and certification requirements drive the organization of instruction both directly and indirectly toward standardization. Although large, centralized districts occasionally experiment with alternative schools, those who staff such schools are seldom free to organize teaching and learning solely on behalf of the teachers and learners, for they must coordinate their school practices with others in the district. The cost of alternative, adaptive organizations is another factor. Many administrators who would like to encourage more flexible, client-oriented practices find that they cannot pay the price of smaller classes and instructional loads, teacher aides, schools-within-schools, or variable schedules. Tight budgets force schools to moderate their expectations and to discount individual differences.[21] Those who seek smaller, less mechanized schools often must look outside the public sector. Finally, nonbureaucratic schools—those lacking schedules, bells, formal curricula, credits, levels, large classes, and teacher-centered instruction—do not look like "real" schools. John Meyer and Brian Rowan have insightfully described the ways in which the rationalized attributes of schools convey legitimacy on an enterprise which is otherwise filled with uncertainty, even failure.[22] Schools may have muddled goals and serve students poorly, but they remain tenable institutions if they *look* like schools, and so those both inside and outside the schools rely on predictable structures, such as bell schedules, tracks, and course credits, to define education, despite much evidence that those structures interfere with the work to be done.

State officials persist in efforts to reform schools by prescribing curriculum and pedagogy; by requiring close observation and rating of teachers; and by imposing high-stakes tests that promote comparisons among classrooms, grades, schools, and districts. These policies are likely to increase the impersonal character of schooling; improve students' capacity to take tests rather than think critically; and continue to drive outstanding teachers out of teaching.

Other reforms offer more promise. Public and private high schools participating in Theodore Sizer's Coalition of Essential Schools are reducing the scope of their curricula to a "limited number of essential skills and areas of knowledge," decreasing teachers' workload to 80 students in order to personalize teaching and learning, and reorganizing the schools so that teachers are generalists first and disciplinary specialists second.[23] Other school districts are attempting to subdivide large urban high schools and create several smaller schools within the same building, where students and teachers can have more continuing contact. Although small school size may limit the breadth of the academic program, advocates contend that students benefit more from the close attention and interdisciplinary teaching that these schools permit. There are also increasing efforts to decentralize school governance throughout the United States. Dade County, Rochester, Chicago, and Boston have transferred substantial powers for setting policy to school-site councils composed of teachers, parents, and administrators, giving public schools the kind of autonomy that typifies independent schools. District offices are being reduced in size, and administrators are being directed to assist rather than control those working at the school site.[24]

These reforms promise to reduce the bureaucratic control of districts and return to the school site the design and control of teaching practice. However, many of the changes needed to personalize schooling also will require new understandings and attitudes on the part of school officials and the public. Important differences exist among both children and teachers, differences that must be valued rather than eradicated. Teaching and learning are complex processes that require large areas of discretionary action. The outcomes are inherently varied; standardization cannot be achieved except at the most superficial level. Variation is not evidence of irresponsibility, nor is standardization a virtue in itself. Much that must be changed in public education must begin with a change of mind.

Nor will the bureaucratic elements of schools be eliminated without money. Large classes and teaching loads, standardized curricula, and tight schedules persist, in part, because they are economical. If teachers are to establish more continuous and intimate relations with students, if they are to participate in both departments and interdisciplinary teams, if they are to replace multiple-choice tests with more meaningful assessments of student achievement, more personnel and more time must be found, and both cost money, which must either be newly allocated or reallocated within education. Those districts with the largest central bureaucracies have also the largest opportunity, for they can redistribute funds that currently support large administrative staffs and purchase more people and time in the schools.[25] In many districts, if less money were spent on efforts to formalize and standardize education and more were spent to permit and promote flexibility and adaptation, schools might, ironically, become more productive.

CHAPTER SIX

The Reality of Isolation and the Search for Collaboration

In the ideal world of schooling teachers would be true colleagues working together, debating about goals and purposes, coordinating lessons, observing and critiquing each other's work, sharing successes and offering solace, with the triumphs of their collective efforts far exceeding the summed accomplishments of their solitary struggles. The real world of schools is usually depicted very differently, with teachers sequestered in classrooms, encountering peers only on entering or leaving the building. Engaged in parallel piecework, they devise curricula on their own, ignoring the plans and practices of their counterparts in other classrooms or grades; when it occurs, conversation offers a diversion from teaching rather than the occasion for its deliberation—travel plans rather than lesson plans are said to dominate faculty-room talk. Although such portrayals are often exaggerated, they contain more truth than most of us would like to believe.

Those who study the collegial relations of teachers have found instances of the ideal—"places of intellectual sharing, collaborative planning, and collegial work,"[1] and they have concluded that such schools are more satisfying for teachers and more effective for students.[2] However, as Judith Warren Little observes, such schools are also "not the rule, but the rare, often fragile exception."[3]

Why are such schools so unusual? Why is continuing, constructive interaction among colleagues hard to come by and even harder to sustain? In part, the answer lies in the dual nature of schooling, which includes both the short-term task of teaching students day-to-day and the long-term task of broadly educating them. The first is usually an independent activity, requiring intense, undivided attention by individual teachers at work with their students. The second is ultimately an interdependent effort extending over many years, but teachers may not see it as such and are unlikely to deliberately coordinate their efforts beyond a year or two at a time. A lone teacher can impart phonics, fractions, the pluperfect tense, or the periodic table, but only through teachers' collective efforts will schools produce educated graduates who can read and compute; apply scientific principles; comprehend the lessons of history; value others' cultures and speak their languages; and conduct themselves responsibly as citizens. Such accomplishments are the product of a corporate venture. In a sense, teachers are like doctors and schooling like health care: surgeons may succeed heroically in removing a tumor, but have little to do with the internist, nutritionist, or psychologist whose work is also necessary for the patient's continued well-being. Health care, like education, is usually a composite of interdependent enterprises, extending over years and involving many persons who may never meet each other.

The tension is considerable between the role of the classroom teacher focusing on one group of students and the role of the faculty member considering education in the school as a whole. A teacher can be a star within the classroom while remaining oblivious to the work of a colleague next door. She or he can achieve short-term success while the school fails over the long term. It is not difficult to understand why teachers invest their limited time and energy in their own students and classes rather than committing themselves to the uncertain enterprise of schoolwide change. Moreover, many teachers are so compelled by the student-teacher dyad that the importance of working with peers pales by comparison. Allen Rondo said:

> My greatest frustration, one of them, is this feeling of always being pulled away to something. . . . Kids are more interesting than faculty and all their various gripes.

Only when teachers consider their part in the long-term task of education do the interdependence of their efforts and the need for coordinating them become apparent. However, the intense and immediate demands of daily instruction often discourage teachers from taking such a long view.

A second answer to the question of why there are so few collegial schools can be found in the organizations of schools themselves, which more often thwart than promote collegiality by withholding time, encouragement, and responsibility from those who try to work more cooperatively. The composition of teaching units, the schedule of the day, and the principal's assumptions about teachers' roles in leadership can enhance or diminish teachers' efforts to become better colleagues. Many of the bureaucratic constraints of schools discussed in chapter 5 impede teachers who would prefer to collaborate in their work.

Ironically, yet another part of the answer lies with the teachers themselves, some of whom choose to remain distant from their colleagues, either out of disregard for others, reluctance to share their best ideas, or fear that their shortcomings will be exposed. Well-established norms of privacy among teachers provide the excuse for those who prefer to remain apart. Fellow teachers are a crucial component of any teacher's workplace, and sometimes they, too, fall short of what individuals need to do good work.

Given the primacy of classroom teaching, the absence of organizational supports, and some teachers' reluctance to venture beyond their classrooms, it is not surprising that teachers remain largely isolated, their efforts uncoordinated. The valued teachers of this study were, indeed, concerned first and foremost about their relationships with students and teaching on a day-to-day basis, but they also recognized that colleagues could increase their chances of success with those students. Moreover, they knew that informal and formal interactions with fellow teachers could satisfy their needs for adult company as well as invigorate their teaching. They looked to other teachers for personal support, for instructional assistance, and for institutional coordination.

Few respondents termed their schools isolating organizations, but their collegial relationships were actually very few. Most worked closely with only one or two teachers, who taught nearby or were members of their departments or teams. They wished for workplaces that more effectively supported their efforts to become better colleagues and they believed the quality of teaching and learning in their schools would improve with collaboration. Their accounts suggest that collegial workplaces depend on teachers' openness and readiness to improve; reference groups of peers for identifying problems and taking action; ample time for observation and discussion; and administrators who both encourage teachers and accommodate their needs as they explore new collegial relationships.

HOW ISOLATED ARE TEACHERS?

The teachers in this study voiced different views about whether they were alone in their work. Only a few characterized their workplaces as isolating or teaching as solitary work; those who did were about evenly distributed between public and private schools. An English teacher said that staff in his regional high school avoid each other and "just seem to be going to work and going home." Two other teachers said that no one knew what or how they taught. One emphasized: "I am isolated. I do what I want when I want to do it, and how I want to do it." A high-school social studies teacher explained:

> Teachers are isolated people. They don't know what others are doing. Things that work for them, they keep them year after year. You don't have the time to sit down and discuss with each other from different areas. As small as this school basically is, I don't know all the people who are here.

Such accounts of isolation were not the norm in this study, but neither were descriptions of schools where teachers shared a common set of expectations and standards, observed each other's practice, or collaborated in planning curriculum or teaching. Two schools seemed nearly ideal—interdependent, interactive workplaces, where personal preferences, professional norms, and institutional arrangements converged to support continuing collaboration among a large segment of the staff. Notably, both were small, alternative schools in the private sector, serving kindergarten through eighth grade. A fifth-grade teacher in one of the schools reported developing thematic social studies units with the Spanish and music teachers and a computer specialist. She said that she and her colleagues met "all the time," and often observed each other's classes. "There is just an awareness and sensitivity on all of our parts that we should tell one another when something is going well. There is just so much cooperation." Another teacher, who cotaught a first grade class in a Quaker school, had previously worked in several public schools. She said that at the Quaker school "support for peers is very built in, which it has never been anywhere else that I've taught." Staff met for lunch once a week in support groups organized by the school psychologist. Teachers also had "buddies" from other grades whom they watched teach and talked with about pedagogy. She said that the support of other staff gave her a "feeling of empowerment. You don't feel like, 'Here I work all the time and no one respects my mind.' You don't have to feel that way."

Although these two independent schools were unusual in the collaboration they fostered, teachers from several public schools also told of frequent interaction. A suburban elementary-school teacher, who called hers "a family school," explained:

> We're just not individuals coming to work. We work together for the kids; we work together as colleagues, too. If I have an idea, I can go to people and say, "I think this might work with what you're doing." We communicate as far as

> what we do in our classrooms. I get a lot of support from the teachers here.

Similarly, an urban elementary-school teacher reported that in her school, the faculty "work as a team," a practice that they themselves had initiated:

> That's a voluntary thing that we decided among ourselves, that we could pull from each other and be able to have more grouping and do some things that could help out the children. Having a support system of other teachers who work with you is what supports good teaching.

A third elementary-school teacher described a similar set of practices, noting how her principal's systematic encouragement made it possible:

> The teaching structure is self-contained, but we have a lot of team teaching. There are two other first grades in my school, and we get together every week, share lesson plans, go over things. We have a system where we can go into each other's classrooms—any classroom in the school up to grade four—and observe other teachers. The administration gets someone to [cover the class] so we can do that any time we want.

Although these teachers described interactions that extended throughout the school, the overwhelming majority of teachers maintained close relationships with only a few colleagues, sometimes a teacher in an adjoining classroom, often members of a team or subset of a high-school department. A suburban kindergarten teacher worked closely with two other kindergarten teachers, but confessed to not having "much contact with the other teachers [in the school], I'm sorry to say." A second-grade teacher, who had described his colleagues as "basically friends," considered whether others knew what he was teaching:

> Yeah, I think so. The third-grade teacher does, and the first-grade teacher does because I work from her, and the next one, I work toward her. But if you asked the sixth-grade teacher what I do, she probably has no idea because she's on the second floor.

Another elementary-school teacher, who contended that there was not a "slacker on the staff," acknowledged that he didn't know that from firsthand experience: "We really don't know what's going on in somebody else's classroom. We just don't. So I'm assuming that everybody's doing their job."

Many middle-school teachers told of meeting regularly with three or four colleagues from their clusters or teams who shared teaching responsibilities for the same group of students. However, as Richard Sand observed, such subgroups were often isolated from other teachers in the school:

> This is one of our absolute, major problems. With the cluster, we work very closely—a lot of communication. . . . But if there's isolation, it's from the rest of the building.

High-school teachers usually described ongoing discussions with colleagues from their own departments, but could cite few exchanges with teachers from other departments who taught the same students. Where faculty interaction flourished, it was typically within small units that functioned independently of the rest of the school.

Although the extent and intensity of faculty interaction varied widely for the teachers, they agreed virtually unanimously that the threat of isolation was ever present and that the benefits of collegial interaction were many. Teachers valued the contact they had with peers, actively devised ways to promote it, and lamented its absence or curtailment. One middle-school teacher said that she "hunger[ed] after conversations with adults, talking about teaching." Gary Stein, who worked in a self-contained classroom, wished for a "team-teaching situation where you could bounce ideas off of each other." Another elementary-school teacher, who informally coordinated his lessons with other teachers in his grade, would have liked to observe their classes as well:

> I think I do better if I'm working in conjunction with other adults. . . . I don't get into anybody else's classroom. That's just the way it is. I don't sit in. . . . I will talk with the two other fourth-grade teachers, but I really haven't seen them teach.

Similarly, an urban social studies teacher yearned for a teaching situation where sustained interaction among colleagues was the norm:

> I think that we could learn from each other. We really could. Ineffective teachers could learn from those effective ones. Effective teachers could begin to grow in new ways and affect each other.

As a group, these valued teachers viewed collegial interaction as an essential component of their work. Most wished for more frequent and systematic discussion about matters of education with their peers. Only a small number of public-school teachers said that they preferred to work independently and avoided contact with peers. It is worth noting, however, that these individuals had come to prefer isolation largely because of problems in their workplaces. A secondary-school teacher of English As a Second Language said:

> I tend to isolate myself. I was at a junior high school that had a lot of problems with discipline. But I found that I could just have my own little world and control that.

Similarly, Anna Capello said that on a typical day she might never leave the home-economics area to talk with other staff. This separateness had begun to concern her:

> [Recently, I've been] trying to figure out why I have been somewhat isolating myself, and the best that I can come up

> with is that it's peaceful where I am. . . . When I go out into the halls, it's very stressful. There's craziness in the halls—yelling and screaming and kicking and pushing.

Several teachers who avoided extensive interaction with colleagues said they did so because time was short and demands many. One said that the school day was "absolutely nonstop." Others told of spending all nonteaching time with their students so that they could offer makeup work or extra help. One who called himself "a bit of a loner," found that he could "eat lunch and get work done at the same time" if he stayed in his room. He considered social conversation with colleagues no more than "letting off steam," a distraction from work rather than work itself.

These teachers were the exceptions. The large majority considered isolation a continuing concern and said that they valued productive collegial interaction and would like more consistent attention to instructional concerns in their contacts with peers.

WHAT DOES COLLEGIALITY OFFER?

"Collegiality"from the perspectives of the teachers in this study ranged from friendly staff relations to closely coordinated coteaching. The teachers looked to colleagues to meet their *personal needs* for social interaction, reassurance, and psychological support; their *instructional needs* for pedagogical advice and subject matter expertise; and their *organizational needs* for coordinating students' learning, socializing new staff, setting and upholding standards, and initiating and sustaining change. The format and activities that served each of these purposes differed; teachers who conceived of teaching as a largely independent activity still might rely on peers to meet personal and instructional needs, while teachers who recognized the interdependent character of education sought to collaborate closely with colleagues in meeting organizational needs.

Personal Needs

Social interaction can serve as an antidote to the separateness of teachers' classroom experience, and it appeared from these teachers' reports that the more sequestered they felt in their work, the more important social encounters and the company of adults became. An English teacher who worked in a very difficult school described his lunch period as "a ball . . . just a lot of fun . . . super." He argued that

> teaching's a lot more than just sitting in the classroom and teaching kids. . . . If you just do that, you're going to be burned out real quick. You just can't do that. You have to talk with people.

One middle-school teacher described an "all-for-one, one-for-all" spirit among the staff of her school, and another said, "There's just a very nice camaraderie." A third observed, "There aren't two people in this building that don't speak to one another. That is unheard of."

All schools were not so congenial; several teachers described cliques that divided staff. A fourth-grade teacher said that she had encountered more negative than positive attitudes among teachers in her school. As a result of "back-stabbing and jealousies," she found relationships with colleagues "very stressful" and had withdrawn from schoolwide activities: "That's the joy of teaching. If you don't like [the people you work with], you close your door and they're gone." Two teachers in urban schools attributed divisions to racial and ethnic differences. One said:

> The group here is not the most together group. It's very segregated. It's racially segregated. Hispanics stick with Hispanics. We have the blacks and then the white people. Very segregated.

Others whose faculties were unfriendly or fragmented withdrew from social interaction or maintained only the most superficial relationships with peers. As one said, "I go out of my way to say Merry Christmas and Happy New Year."

Virtually all of the teachers in this study had one or more colleagues in their schools on whom they could rely for encouragement and reassurance. More than a few teachers said that when they needed to talk about problems that came up with particular students, lessons, or classes, often they sought empathy as much as answers. As Richard Sand remarked, members of his cluster did a "lot of sharing—sharing a shoulder sometimes instead of just materials." An urban elementary-school teacher agreed:

> That's why I think this staff is so tight, because we share our problems. If I'm having a problem with Danny, I can go and talk to them about it. If I'm frustrated by something administrative . . . I can share it with them. Just getting it out is very important. Occasionally, you get an idea. Most of the time, you don't get solutions. Most times you just get the knowing nod, the laugh—"Yeah, I know. I've been there. Just keep plugging away."

Although these teachers were recognized within their schools as very good teachers, many met setbacks in their work and described them candidly. A middle-school teacher explained that in talking with peers, "you find out that you have a lot of similar problems. You're not the only one. You're not sitting in a vacuum here with all of your problems." Empathic colleagues provided welcome solace in work that inevitably brought disappointments.

Fellow teachers also offered recognition for good teaching in an environment of scarce rewards. Peers' praise was highly valued because, as one elementary-school teacher explained, "They're right there where I am." A middle-school teacher said that colleagues are the sole source of recognition in her school. "People actually say, 'Oh, what a great job your kids did on something.' There are a lot of compliments."

Colleagues' understanding, acceptance, and continuing support mitigated the isolation that some experienced in their work. Some researchers have discounted the importance of teachers' social interaction or discussion of problems with their peers because these exchanges do not advance the instructional agenda of the school; these teachers' accounts suggest that such talk provides the basis of trust for more organized collegial exchange.

Instructional Needs

Not only were colleagues important in meeting teachers' personal needs for adult contact and support, they were the primary source of pedagogical advice and academic expertise. Many teachers described sharing lessons and ideas, a practice that was said to occur in all schools. One elementary-school teacher explained: "If I figure out something that really works well, that I've invented, I very freely welcome anyone to come and plagiarize it." A junior-high-school English teacher shared some of her best ideas for oral book reports and opened her files to colleagues: "I have tons of work sheets on everything you can imagine, and I share those with anybody." Most teachers said that they both initiated and welcomed such exchange, although one observed that, as members of her department became more experienced, they expressed less interest in new ideas: "I don't think there's that much sharing, really. I think we're all pretty—we know exactly what we're doing and how to do it."

Despite widespread informal exchange of materials and ideas, few teachers reported observing each other's classes; many said that they knew what colleagues were doing and could have walked in and out of their classrooms if they chose. Those few who did actually observe their colleagues at work said that productive discussions ensued. One said that she would discuss ways "to improve the educational environment. 'Have you tried this?' 'Geez, these kids are going off on a tangent.' 'Well, I drew them back by doing this.' " A middle-school social studies teacher said that visits to other classrooms, common when team-teaching was popular, were now rare but still valuable:

> One of the best things was having another adult in the room occasionally who would say, "You're using that 'teacher's voice.' " . . . Just somebody to keep you on the ground, instead of getting into that pompous, teachery, preaching thing. So we do it, and I think it's terrific. It's not as much as I would like.

This teacher, like many in the sample, believed that the benefits of observing others' classes were many and wished that such visits might happen more often.

Teachers also spoke about the importance of meeting regularly with colleagues who taught the same grade or subject and, thus, had especially relevant experience. Although small schools or departments might be hospitable settings where faculty could socialize, exchange tricks of the trade, or even watch their peers teach, they were often inadequate forums for more specialized talk about instruction. Teachers in elementary schools rarely had more than two or three colleagues working at the same grade level. Large departments, such as English or social studies, included enough people with similar teaching specialties to support discussions about process writing or the use of simulations. Other departments, such as business or home economics, were usually too small to promote specialized discussions, while still others, such as foreign languages or science, were diverse assemblies of specialists in subjects insufficiently related for easy exchange, such as French and Russian or biology and chemistry. If teachers wanted to discuss curriculum with a larger cohort of grade-level teachers or subject specialists, they usually had to leave their schools, but their districts did little to organize exchanges among schools, and the need generally went unmet.

Several teachers in this sample had found groups of subject-matter colleagues from other school districts. One junior-high-school science teacher met monthly with other earth-science teachers from the area:

> All of us who joined [the group] have found it of tremendous use because we see other earth-science teachers and departments and what they're doing and what they're learning.

> They all have their specialties. It's better than taking college courses.

Another middle-school science teacher met regularly with a group of science educators teaching marine biology and environmental science: "We have a couple of conferences a year. There are presentations from other practitioners, and we're able to adapt a lot of those things into our own classrooms." A physics teacher, who had but one other subject-matter colleague in her school, was pleased when a local university organized an association of physics teachers "so that people [could] get together and exchange ideas and hear speakers."

Organizational Needs

Teachers search for new materials and methods for their classes, generally more intent on improving their own teaching than the program of a grade, department, or school. However, many teachers also recognize the interdependent character of their work and cooperate with colleagues on broader matters of curriculum and instruction.

Some of the teachers we interviewed reported meeting frequently with other staff to coordinate instruction for their students. In elementary schools, groups of grade-level teachers worked to achieve greater consistency across classes. A second-grade teacher said that she worked closely with her less experienced second-grade colleague so that all second-grade students would have the same program. Third- and fourth-grade teachers in another school coordinated their teaching to ensure continuity of student learning:

> We share a lot as far as our curriculum concerns go. We're keen on what we're doing as far as our objectives for our grade levels and how we can progress from one grade level to another. For instance, we may be aware that the third-grade studies certain grammatical rules or some kind of syntax or English skills from which we decide, "Well, should they be mastered by the end of third grade and do we need

> to continue in the fourth grade? Do we review? Do we need to supplement?'' In that sense we share a lot.

Such collegial accommodations were noteworthy; more often, instruction in the primary grades was coordinated only loosely, if at all. In higher elementary grades and middle schools, the staff of interdisciplinary teams or clusters were more likely to meet regularly to discuss the curriculum and the progress of their students. One science teacher in an urban school worked with team members from math, English, social studies, and reading, as well as specialists in art and music. While studying dinosaurs in his class, students read and wrote stories about dinosaurs in their English class, and drew or made models of dinosaurs in art classes. Because the teachers' scheduled planning periods coincided, they could "meet, discuss, and deal with situations that affect children.''

In some junior high and virtually all high schools, teachers met with their departments to plan sequences of skills and courses. This junior-high-school teacher's enthusiastic comments were typical of many:

> Our department works extremely well together. We're in constant contact with each other. Everybody knows what everybody else is doing and gets ideas from each other.

Although teachers might successfully coordinate their efforts within departments, there were no comparable schoolwide mechanisms in public high schools to coordinate teachers' efforts among departments. As we saw in chapter 5, little in such schools serves to integrate students' instructional programs. Math teachers worry about the sequence of math courses, but pay little if any attention to the relationship of their work to that of the science department.

For a few teachers in this sample, collaboration extended to coteaching classes. An urban fourth-grade teacher who shared her students and classroom with a colleague contended that the experience provides "a model for the children to see that we are working together and that they should work together and cooperate." A junior-high-school science teacher who coteaches ten sections of earth science with a colleague said:

> We really work together. All lesson plans are planned together so that we try and give all eighth graders the same education. A lot of our teaching, at least the planning part, is done together. Some days, I teach his classes, and some days, he teaches mine.

Many teachers said that coteaching and team teaching had been much more common in the 1970s, when resources were plentiful, schedules were flexible, there was greater encouragement for experimentation and less concern about measurable outcomes. Some would welcome more opportunities for team teaching, but found little encouragement in their schools these days.

Colleagues also participated in setting and upholding standards for good teaching. Given both the lack of agreement in the teaching profession about the tenets of good practice and the varied practices in public education, pedagogical standards are often determined school by school, cluster by cluster, department by department. Schools that support open and continuous exchange among staff are more likely to promote a consistent set of standards. Sometimes this is an informal process. A middle-school teacher described her hopes that fellow teachers will have regard for her work: "Certainly there are peers that I respect, fellow teachers. I would like them to think that I'm a good teacher. It's a peer pressure type of thing." Another middle-school teacher said that the sixth-grade teachers in her school had banded together to promote higher standards for teaching and discipline. They wanted a "tighter ship" and raised the issue in faculty meetings and talks with administrators. She said that in the course of these discussions, they "made a lot of enemies" among peers, and some of those peers eventually chose to transfer to other schools: "So either people left or they changed their habits.'' A middle-school art teacher believed that his team's efforts to maintain standards had improved everyone's teaching:

> I think this team is a good thing, one of the best things that's happened. The quality of work they do has improved. . . . The top people are doing better work, and the bottom people are doing better work. Everyone has been lifted up rather than down. Everyone has benefited in some way.

Colleagues were also seen to be crucial partners in efforts to institute change within a school. An isolated individual, no matter how able and determined, could not promote new programs or practices without the support of a critical mass of peers. Several of those interviewed told of joint efforts that had made a difference in their schools. One high-school social studies teacher said that he and several other peers had transferred from the junior high school to the high school and ''took them by storm.'' An elementary-school teacher recalled moving to her current school with a group of colleagues already accustomed to instituting change together:

> I think the biggest influence that we had on policy was when we arrived here as a group of sixth-grade teachers and didn't like what was going on. We were really vindicated. We were delighted with what happened. We were able to change this school around within two years. And we were given the credit for doing it.

Gary Stein observed that change was possible in his school only if a number of teachers focused on the same issue:

> If we get our act together, and we want something to happen, we can make it happen for the most part, within the confines of what a school will allow. If we choose to pick an issue, that issue has to be addressed. If there's no universal feeling towards it, then it doesn't get addressed.

According to these teachers, when that critical mass of colleagues was lacking, change was difficult to initiate and programs were hard to maintain. One high-school English teacher who wanted his peers to assume more schoolwide responsibility found that he did not have sufficient support among the staff. He speculated: "People are pretty afraid of change at the school, even though they're not very happy."

In other cases influential coalitions of teachers were decimated by layoffs and transfers. One urban elementary-school teacher said that before declining enrollment forced many teachers out of her school, it "was known for having a very avant-garde faculty that stuck together and were constantly writing letters downtown. . . . We were a very vocal, organized group, and we were known for that citywide." But with declining resources and desegregation, "people have come and people have gone," and as a result, the staff's organized influence has diminished.

Teachers also depended on their colleagues to socialize new staff, a process that appeared haphazard at best. It is a commonplace among teachers that teacher training falls far short of adequately preparing fledgling teachers for the demands of their work: teachers learn to teach by teaching. In isolation, they rely by necessity on their own wits, doing their best to approximate the practice of their own good teachers. If colleagues are available to offer a variety of pedagogical models and lead them through the uncertainties and hazards of planning lessons, showing films, and meeting with parents, new teachers are far more likely to achieve success in their work.

We found little evidence of any organized efforts to socialize new teachers, even in schools of high repute. Mentor-teacher programs were just beginning to appear in some parts of the country; where mentoring occurred in these schools, it was informal and unplanned. Without established structures to promote collegial orientation, the quality of a novice's experience depended largely on chance—who taught in the room next door, who cared enough to offer help. One veteran physics teacher reflected:

> I don't know what they do with a new teacher. That must be terrifying, with the door closed and you're on your own. There's nobody there nurturing you as you go along. It must be pretty tough.

In fact, the junior teachers in this sample had encountered a wide range of experiences as they learned to teach. Several had found little support and felt ambivalent about their teaching careers as a result. Others had been quickly embraced by one or more experienced teachers and expressed greater confidence about their future in teaching. For an elementary-school teacher who called himself "the new guy on the block," working with a team of veteran staff who were "very supportive people" made all the difference: "They're experienced. They've seen a lot. They know what's important. . . . I walk into their classrooms, and I see something amazing that never even occurred to me." But even in this supportive environment, he wished for more systematic assistance:

> But I'd like someone to tell me, "That's not really the best way to do that," or "Here's a better way to do that. Have you ever tried this?"

Teachers spoke of their obligations to new staff, often recollecting their own inadequate induction into teaching. But there was very little in the structure of teaching assignments, the allocation of time, or delegation of responsibilities that contributed to the orderly socialization of new teachers. An urban high-school teacher who said that he "love[s] rookies," explained that he actively offers assistance and advice: "I proselytize." But he does so as a lone agent rather than as one participant in a system of support. Both the need for help and the potential to provide it were present, but organized efforts to socialize new staff were lacking in virtually all of these teachers' schools.

PREREQUISITES FOR COLLEGIALITY

Teachers, therefore, valued many kinds of collegial interaction in their work. Given that interest and given preliminary evidence that schools work better where teachers cooperate and collaborate, what factors seemed to permit and promote greater interaction and interdependence among teachers? Six stood out: good teachers, supportive organizational norms, reference groups for identification and action, sufficient time, and administrators who provided encouragement and accommodation. Each deserves comment.

Good teachers. Collaboration will never occur, these respondents agreed, unless teachers cooperate in making it work. Again and again, these teachers spoke of "good" or "outstanding" teachers as those who are committed and generous, who are open to change and eager to learn, and who see beyond their own private successes and failures. One elementary-school teacher described such staff in her school:

> There are two teachers especially whom I'm thinking of who are not just good teachers, they're good people. In fact, I think they're very healthy, happy people. They've worked on themselves, and they like what they're doing. It's catching. If you have people who are bitter or angry all the time around you, unhappy with what they're doing, then that would be catching.

A foreign-language teacher working with a "very congenial group" of colleagues from different disciplines described their "sharing and cooperation":

> We always got along very well with each other from the beginning. There were a lot of complementary personalities, people with strengths in areas where they could help other people out.

The closer the collaboration, the greater the demands for interpersonal harmony. An elementary-school teacher who worked closely with two other first-grade teachers emphasized that such joint efforts "depend on the personalities. We happen to work very well together. . . . That was not always the way it was." Another elementary-school teacher, who cotaught in an open classroom said.

> In order to do that, you really have to get along with your peer teacher. You have to have the same disciplinary points there and the same likenesses and dislikes, really. . . . You really have to find someone that has the same thinking that you have. . . . It's more like a family—parents.

By contrast, a special-education teacher described how difficult work was with a coteacher whom she found disagreeable:

> He and I have hit heads a few times, and we aren't too happy about that. But we clashed on philosophy . . . and he has his master's—"I know more than you do." So we clashed on that too.

Even teachers who were fundamentally compatible needed time to develop respect, trust, and consonant practices.

Organizational norms. Schools often shield staff from criticism by parents and the public, but they rarely provide sufficient security for teachers to move confidently beyond the confines of their classrooms and engage in collegial discussion, debate, or experimentation. Teachers' feelings of vulnerability in their interactions with colleagues may derive, in part, from the very personal character of teaching and the uncertainties that pervade it.[4] As Gary Stein observed, "There is a certain kind of safety, or lack of pressure, just being there by yourself." To share curriculum, to be observed while teaching, or to coordinate the instruction of students is to open oneself to scrutiny, knowing that even the best teacher will inevitably be found wanting in some respect.[5]

In the past ten years, teachers' already fragile security has been further threatened by highly publicized comparisons of student test scores. In some of the schools studied, teachers had been laid off on the basis of administrators' assessments of their work. In the process, many schools came to be seen as perilous environments where teachers had to be cautious and self-sufficient rather than candid and open to influence. The teachers in this study offered varied accounts of the organizational environments that surrounded their classrooms. A few said that their schools were open and accepting, encouraging experimentation and exchange, but more told of mixed messages from administrators, who encouraged them to share resources and take risks but warned them that there was a price for failure. An elementary-school teacher working in a school where peers were reluctant to discuss their work explained:

> I think a lot of us feel that we don't want to tell what we do for whatever reasons—competition, fear of being fired, fear of being thought of as a braggart.

Janice Gagne spoke of a "little bit of jealousy, a certain competition that shouldn't be there." Another teacher suggested that school organizations do little to reassure staff who hold back because of self-doubt:

> I don't think teachers, on the whole, have enough self-confidence. I think they tend to feel that they're not doing a good job. So to have somebody move in and out of their classroom makes them very self-conscious. If it were done more often in a way so that teachers were encouraged to communicate . . . I think they would become very comfortable with it.

Many teachers told of administrative practices that discourage cooperation. This elementary-school teacher spoke of the fears that performance-based layoffs had generated in his school when competent teachers found themselves competing with colleagues to keep their jobs:

> I don't get into anybody else's classroom. That's just the way it is. The [reduction in force] was really a problem, you know. We were worried about it. . . . Not so much that it

> was ever said, but in between the lines, it was "Why are you sitting in my room?"

Others, like this foreign-language teacher from a prestigious district, ascribed the unspoken wariness among teachers in his school to a department head who promoted competition:

> I think some of them, whether this is real or perceived, see the department head as somebody who really wants to weigh and judge everybody and is always looking for ways to do that. . . . I think he sees anxiety and tension as a motivating factor for people. He's willing to let that feed into what people do.

Teachers did not believe that a safe environment had to be free of criticism, but they wanted to be able to offer suggestions without fear of censure and to open their practice as they chose to the scrutiny of those whom they respected. An urban elementary-school teacher emphasized the value of honest exchange and open dissent in discussions with members of his team:

> One of the most important things we share is that we all have the right to disagree with each other, and we tend to respect that. Whereas, I think a lot of people who work for the school system are intimidated just to give their opinion, and if they should give it, do not expect any kind of argument or discussion. When they find themselves confronted with a different opinion, they tend to either shrink or get very aggressive. I find that very counterproductive. It makes things happen very slowly.

Reference groups. The teachers who said that they ventured beyond the isolation of their classrooms in the pursuit of collegiality usually were members of subunits that endorsed collaborative practices. Grade-level teams, interdisciplinary clusters, and academic departments served as such reference groups for these teachers. Several small schools with staffs of 10 to 15 teachers were said to operate as effective professional units. In one unusual situation, a centrally located urban school housed eight kindergarten classes whose teachers worked together closely. More often the elementary-school teachers in this study referred to subgroups of teachers within their schools—the first-grade teachers, the fifth-grade interdisciplinary team, the third-and-fourth-grade group. The school as a whole was a meaningful unit for making decisions about discipline, lunch, dismissal, or standardized testing, but teachers turned to grade-level or subject-matter groups for curricular concerns, perhaps one reason why schoolwide improvements have been so difficult to organize and maintain.

For teachers in many junior high schools and virtually all high schools, the department was the primary reference group. In teachers' day-to-day practice, departments influenced the way instruction was carried out—the selection, supervision, and evaluation of staff; course definition and sequencing; tracking; curriculum development; textbook selection; and the assignment of teachers to courses and students to classes. From the teacher's perspective, much is at stake in decisions that are made by departments, and they made an effort to participate there. Moreover, secondary-school teachers regularly identified themselves as members of particular departments, even when they participated also in alternative house or cluster structures: "I'm in math"; "I'm in the social studies department"; "I teach English." In a few instances, departmental loyalties were strong enough to engender rivalries with other departments. A math teacher whose department had its own faculty room said that teachers worked together closely, but that departmental collegiality also spawned parochial attitudes:

> I have interaction with the math department, not with any other department. We're isolated, more or less. We wouldn't go out of our way to talk to those English teachers or those IA [industrial arts] teachers.

Although departments offered the readiest and most meaningful reference groups for secondary-school teachers, it appeared that interdisciplinary teams might provide similar satisfaction if schools had been structured differently. A Latin teacher, whose school had recently abandoned an interdisciplinary house system in favor of departments, regretted both the loss of the interdisciplinary perspective and the increased competition that departments created in his school. However, virtually all the high schools in this study were organized by departments, and teachers involved themselves in decision making in order to obtain the courses, schedules, and students they desired. Teachers who pursued interdisciplinary collaboration typically did so outside the conventional structures, often on their own time.

Sufficient time. By far the most frequent explanation teachers offered for scarce collegial interactions was inadequate time. It appeared, however, that even if more time were available, teachers might not use it for more meetings with their peers; students always need more help; professional caution and competition seep in. In any event, peer observation, curriculum development, and collaborative planning are rendered impossible by schedules that isolate teachers at work in different classrooms. Business and industry put discussion and decision making at the center of their enterprises and allocate vast resources to ensure that work is coordinated, but the educational workplace requires that teachers continuously deliver services during all but a small portion of their time, necessarily pushing collegial interactions to the margins of the workday—before and after school, while supervising recess or eating a hurried lunch. Very few teachers have more than one hour of unassigned time each day, time already insufficient for all that must be done to prepare lessons, grade papers, and confer with students. Teachers routinely said that short-term obligations to their students took precedence over long-term goals of improving their practice or their schools. Nor did the small amount of noninstructional time provided by any of the schools convey a serious institutional commitment to collegiality. Gary Stein said,

"There really isn't the opportunity that I think we need. . . . There's nothing built into the system." An elementary-school teacher contended, "They're reluctant to provide time. They don't see that as productive."

Nonetheless, teachers coped, finding moments to talk and share materials before and after school, in the halls between classes, at lunch, and during preparation periods. One said, "If there is a need, it will happen. In my situation, we ended up having a coffee club in the morning." A high-school teacher who coordinated a cluster program in a large building described the challenges of maintaining daily contact:

> We just make it a point. We try to see each other before homeroom. Even though we're scattered all over. Might see each other at lunch. Might. We make it a point, if we have a free period, if it's important, to run over to the other teacher and just say, "Did so-and-so show up for class?" or "What's going on here?" or "Don't forget the field trip coming up." So, you just have to make the time to do it. . . .

However, scarce time often led to superficial exchanges. An elementary-school teacher observed, "The interchange is very much on the surface. It is always with a bunch of papers in your hand as you're flying down the hall, knowing that you're supposed to be in the classroom."

Coteachers and those who closely coordinated their teaching made time to plan and review their work in the late afternoons or evenings. Several said that they lived near each other or shared rides and could work at home or in transit. Virtually never did schools reserve adequate time to encourage teachers' continuing collaboration or convey the organizational message that time spent with colleagues was legitimate and would likely improve teaching and schooling.

Accommodating administrators. Research on school improvement often points to the principal as the originator and perpetuator of collaborative school practices. Susan Rosenholtz studied seventy-eight elementary schools in Tennessee with continuing collegial interactions and found the principals of those schools were distinguished

> by their everyday accessibility and involvement in classroom affairs. And perhaps because they ubiquitously monitor instructional matters, they find greater opportunity to render technical assistance.[6]

Few of the valued teachers in this sample of schools looked to administrators for advice about their teaching, but they believed that principals and department heads could promote greater interaction among staff through their administrative policies and practices, since they controlled the teaching schedule and the use of meeting time.

Although school finances usually ultimately determine how much time teachers have to work together, school-site administrators are the stewards of what time there is. They schedule it, and they can protect or reclaim it. Teachers frequently complained that their nonteaching time was scheduled ineptly, leaving them free when the colleagues they needed to meet with were in class. Gary Stein, who observed, "If preps coincide, it's dumb luck," also explained that the arrangement of lunch periods in his school stymied would-be collaborators:

> I am one of two second-grade teachers who has this lunch. The third second-grade teacher is by herself. Each of the fifth-grade teachers is at a different lunch period. They cannot get together to talk. They can't say, "Are you up to this story yet? I did this and it worked great."

He regretted the lost opportunity: "We're some of our best experts, and we're not utilizing the resource." Janice Gagne said that because of her school's schedule, she regularly encountered only two teachers in the course of her day:

> It's the same two that I see all the time, because recess is at the same time in the morning. There are two different recess

> schedules, two different lunch periods. The teacher in that room and the one across the hall are the ones that I would see most often.

Given most teachers' expectations of arbitrary scheduling, they were grateful when principals and department heads coordinated preparation periods for teachers who shared students or subject specialties. An elementary-school teacher explained that, in the past, administrators had "tried to set up planning periods so that teachers at the same grade level could get together. . . . If you wanted to see somebody and share ideas and talk about concerns, you knew they'd be available." But the budget had been cut, and specialists' schedules became less flexible. "The scheduling problem of sending our special teachers to four different schools has short-circuited that." Similarly, an urban kindergarten teacher explained that time for collegial meetings had appeared fortuitously in her school when bus schedules required changing students' dismissal time from 2:15 to 1:30 for the year. She observed, "We're lucky this year . . . because we have that extra time. We are able to meet as often as we want. I don't think we'll ever see that again."

Administrators also control the time that teachers spend in faculty meetings. Most teachers said that this meeting time was administrative rather than collegial time, serving a different set of purposes than those that mattered to them, and as a result, most reported taking passive roles rather than becoming active participants. Teachers routinely complained that principals discouraged meaningful talk by staff at schoolwide meetings. An elementary-school teacher said, "They will relegate fifteen minutes at the end of a faculty meeting for a team to discuss 'What have you done in critical and creative thinking in the last month?' . . . It is not given the priority that it should be given." A few respondents told of productive meetings where staff were encouraged to wrestle with difficult issues.

Teachers often assumed responsibility for directing the discussions in team or departmental meetings. A middle-school teacher, whose interdisciplinary team met for two periods every six days, said that the time was used productively to "meet and discuss what we're going to do. Very often it's about individual children and how we're going to help them. And very often we meet with their parents." By contrast, another middle-school teacher, whose team met for one hour each week, said that administrators attended every meeting and "monopolized" the time.

Generally, the teachers' accounts suggested that the more removed meetings were from their classrooms, the less productive they became. Team, grade-level, and departmental meetings promoted the most exchange, while school-level or districtwide meetings were perceived to be progressively less relevant. The key variable may not have been distance from the classroom, however, but the extent to which teachers were at the center of such meetings, active in both the design and the discussion. When teachers took responsibility, discussion was likely to center on instruction rather than school management.

Some principals who espoused an interest in collegial exchange failed to provide the released time or the encouragement to make it happen, thus conveying the message that it really did not matter. One urban middle-school teacher said:

> At the beginning of the year, our principal said, "This year, we're going to put some emphasis on being aware of other people's teaching methods, and we'd like you to observe somebody in your discipline and somebody else in another discipline." But we haven't heard anything more about it. It just hasn't existed.

Few of the teachers interviewed regarded their principals as instructional leaders, but some respondents did praise their efforts to engage staff in collegial leadership. Richard Sand said that his principal finds substitutes for teachers who want to observe others' classes and raises money to support teachers' collaborative ventures. Teachers in his school use their meeting time as they see fit. "The principal has given us that kind of power. In other school districts . . . they're told. They're given agendas saying exactly what they have to do. He doesn't do that."

Principals who were said to be effective in promoting productive exchange among colleagues did not set the agenda at meetings or direct the interaction, but rather encouraged and enabled teachers to do so. They created coffee areas for informal discussion, arranged for skilled aides to cover classes so that teachers could observe each other, scheduled time carefully to permit collaboration, and asked teachers to design meetings and workshops. They were very influential, but not controlling.

Department heads in secondary schools appeared to be particularly well-placed to promote collegiality among staff, in part because most continued to regard instruction rather than administration as the central task of schools. Because they were obliged to prove themselves in the classroom day after day, department heads could command the respect of their peers. Because their roles combined both the formal authority of an administrator and the professional authority of a teacher, faculty respect came more readily than it might for nonteaching principals. Moreover, a department head who was engaged in teaching the same subject as his or her teachers could more readily discern their instructional concerns and ensure that departmental time would be used meaningfully. The quality of department heads varied, and the interviews included descriptions of both heroes and dullards, but the role itself seemed consistent with promoting constructive work among teachers.

ENCOURAGING GREATER COLLEGIALITY

Colleagues matter to teachers. They are a source of personal support, new ideas, and subject-matter expertise. They are essential allies in maintaining standards or promoting change. They are coworkers whose interdependent efforts combine to determine the success of schooling. The teachers in this study sought collegial interaction and regretted its absence, citing many explanations for its precarious character. Faculties were sometimes uncongenial. Some teachers did not have meaningful groups of colleagues with whom to work. Rarely was time sufficient for serious and sustained interaction. School officials seldom regarded systematic, continuing exchange among teachers as worthwhile, particularly in cases where they themselves were not prescribing its form and content. Staff were sometimes reluctant to collaborate. In schools where teachers described interaction among staff as constructive, and administrators provided the time and the encouragement for sustained discussions, observations, and collaboration, teachers were eager participants.

The teachers made it clear that continuing collegial interaction benefits both them and their students. It sustains them through difficult times. It deepens their understanding of both subject matter and pedagogy, supplies them with novel approaches, and allows them to test and compare practices. It encourages cooperative approaches to school change. It promotes high professional standards and a more coherent instructional experience for children.

The barriers to achieving collegial workplaces are both structural and attitudinal. Poorly designed schedules, inadequate time, random room assignments, or the absence of meaningful subunits within schools can discourage new collegial ventures and undo existing ones. School officials who hope to facilitate frequent and purposeful exchange among staff must ensure that preparation periods are productively aligned, classrooms are arranged to permit frequent interaction, schools are not disrupted by frequent staffing changes, and substitutes are available when teachers leave their students to observe or work with their peers. However, even when the schedule is right and time is sufficient, distrust, disrespect, and dissension can undermine collaboration. School officials must do what they can to promote cooperation rather than competition while recognizing the limits of administrative control and genuinely respecting teachers for their expertise.

Whatever support administrators provide, teachers themselves must ultimately take responsibility for collaboration.

Teachers both constitute and create the context for collegiality. Removing the structural barriers to exchange will not alone ensure that teachers eagerly and confidently cooperate and critique each others' practice. Strong norms of autonomy and privacy prevail among teachers. Creeping fears of competition, exposure of shortcomings, and discomfiting criticism often discourage open exchange, cooperation, and growth. Until teachers overcome such fears and actively take charge of their own professional relations, teaching will likely remain isolating work. The initiative is theirs, but the responsibility for creating more collegial schools cannot be theirs alone.

CHAPTER SEVEN

The Teacher in Governance: A Voice Not Heard

Teachers are the would-be professionals, seeking the influence exercised routinely by doctors and lawyers in our society. They face numerous hindrances as they pursue professional status, from difficulties of defining the tenets of good teaching practice to convincing the world that those who work with children deserve respect. Finally, however, teachers will not be recognized as professionals until they have more say in how children are educated and how schools are run.

Analysts often portray teachers as powerless and disenfranchised, the underlings of the educational enterprise. Others argue that teachers and their unions dictate far too much in the schools, that they have edged the public from its rightful place in setting policy for education and that they impede administrators from managing their schools well. Some contend that the professionalization of teachers is a misunderstood and misguided effort that will sanction poor practice, shield teachers from public scrutiny, and deprive parents of the right to intervene on their children's behalf. However, even those who fear the unwarranted exercise of professional license generally agree that good teachers deserve a say in how schools operate and that instructional priorities should prevail over administrative priorities.

The public-school teachers in this study did participate in decision making, but the majority exerted their influence intermittently and informally rather than through systematic and sustained procedures. Many had held, over the years, positions in school governance—in advisory committees, school councils, faculty senates, or teacher unions—but they generally believed that their efforts had come to little. Although a few teachers worked in settings where decision making was what one elementary teacher called "a back and forth thing, a sharing," more reported having little influence in decisions of consequence. An English teacher observed "a deep feeling of powerlessness to affect any policy" in his suburban school. An urban middle-school teacher argued, "We don't really make policy. We follow it." A suburban middle-school teacher said that, although she could "make certain kinds of choices," those choices were "so mundane as to be almost forgettable." Another suburban teacher who was asked whether she felt any sense of power as a result of her involvement on several committees, responded, "Powerful? No, I feel drained."

Although teachers from many public and church-related schools expressed discouragement, cynicism, or resignation about their scant roles in governance, many independent-school teachers reported that their voices were heard. One asserted, "We have tremendous influence"; another said that her elementary school "is run by committees." Some independent schools were said to be as repressive and authoritarian as any public or religious school, but a far higher proportion of teachers from independent than from public schools reported having a significant say in the educational policy of their schools.

Why do public-school teachers exert so little influence in governance? Is it, as some argue, because formal authority, and consequently power, remain in administrators' hands that, as one teacher said, "Policy is always presented to teachers," or as another complained, "They just don't listen to teachers . . . they think that they know it all"? Is it because the formal structures that would promote collegial governance simply don't exist in schools? Or does the responsibility lie, at least in part, with reluctant or inadequate teachers whose beliefs about being powerless are self-fulfilling? As one teacher we interviewed contended: "The faculty whine a lot."

Additionally we can ask why so many teachers in independent schools reported confidently that they do influence the policies and practices of their schools. Is it a consequence of formal governance structures, faculty norms, administrative roles, or organizational traditions? In those independent schools where collegial governance thrives, what role do parents play in policy making or teaching practice? Does strong collegial governance preclude, as some fear, active parental influence? By investigating these questions, we may better determine how public schools might promote more constructive involvement by teachers in decision making and the implications of such changes for administrators and parents.

THE DOMAINS OF DECISION MAKING

Decision making in public schools takes place in a set of loosely connected domains where different groups of participants set the agenda and control the outcomes. The decisions made in one domain may directly affect those of another, but in many cases, interaction is irregular or negligible.

The classroom. Although teachers generally exert only modest influence on decisions made outside their classrooms, they control most of the instructional policy within them. Throughout the day, they make countless decisions about curriculum, instructional technique, classroom management, and standards of discipline. Centralized curricula and mandated testing have compromised their autonomy in some schools, but most teachers continue to report that classroom policy—what to teach, how to teach, how to use time, and how to assess progress—remains largely theirs to decide. As one suburban elementary-school teacher observed, "Teachers have a lot of say in curriculum and what's happening in the classroom and how things are run."

Any discussion of school governance must take note of teachers' preeminence in this setting where the real work of education takes place. Teachers like those quoted above, who assert that they have no role in governance, usually are referring to the formal policies that regulate matters such as discipline or hiring rather than the day-to-day work of planning lessons, writing tests, or allocating their time and expertise.[1]

In most districts, teachers seem to have made an implicit treaty with school administrators, gaining instructional autonomy in exchange for keeping silent about school management. The teachers we interviewed did not describe such a pact explicitly, but they did suggest that having discretion in their teaching was essential and that, although they regretted being excluded from policy making outside the classroom, it was far more tolerable than having their day-to-day work prescribed by others. As one elementary-school teacher observed:

> I have this great faith in individuals' ability to affect their own little worlds. Somebody, way back when I started teaching, said . . . , "You are going to outlast the majority of superintendents and principals, and ultimately what you have to do every day is go into your classroom and do the best job that you can." I think that is what has kept me going, what happens in here, and I can shut out the outside.

Departments, clusters, and teams. Although individual teachers may decide how to teach from day to day, departments, clusters, or teams often determine the sequence and content of courses or the overall instructional policies for a subgroup of students. The staff of an English department may decide that the short story will be taught in the ninth grade and research skills will be taught in the tenth grade, leaving individual teachers to choose how each will be done. Staff may jointly select textbooks for the department and individuals decide how best to use them. Within a group of social studies teachers working with the same curriculum, individuals may choose to emphasize dates and facts or social processes. Similarly, teams of middle-school teachers may work together on discipline policies or teaching schedules for an overall program, while individual teachers retain the right to structure the use of time within their classrooms.

In schools that include such subunits, teachers report exerting within them the greatest influence over policies that extend beyond their separate classrooms. One suburban middle-school teacher explained that, in her English department, "We have a lot of input, true input. It isn't 'Let's pat them on the head and make them feel like they actually are saying something.' " Further, she distinguished between her department, which she said was run "very democratically," and the school, which was not. An urban middle-school teacher described her school being organized into fairly independent units, each with 4 to 7 teachers: "You are basically allowed, within reason, to run your unit. You have an awful lot of input." Another teacher from her school explained that "within our unitary structure, we teachers establish the policies that we maintain in our classroom and in our unit . . . ," while the principal is "very involved in the day-to-day management of the school," making decisions within another, larger domain.

These subunits command teachers' respect and receive their involvement because decisions at these levels are close to the classroom and concern substantive issues that matter to them, such as elective offerings, course sequence, student discipline, scheduling, and student assignment. Teachers feel confident that decisions they make with their peers will be implemented, though in other parts of the school, decisions about policy may never find their way into practice. Teachers can justify their investment of time. A mathematics teacher is more likely to commit energy to a departmental discussion of the advantages of offering prealgebra than to a schoolwide meeting about student smoking. A departmental decision has a good chance of being enacted, while the full faculty will, at best, explore alternatives and offer an advisory recommendation to the principal.

Teachers may view their responsibilities to departments,

teams, and clusters more seriously because these subunits are typically headed by colleagues who both teach and administer. Department heads are rarely distant bosses with managerial concerns, but rather peers familiar with teaching and their colleagues' concerns, sharing the burden of transforming policy into practice.

The school. Teachers' commitment to decision making is less apparent at the school level, despite the fact that important decisions are made there profoundly affecting teachers' work—scheduling, the assignment of specialists, student placement, discipline, and the provision of supplies. With few exceptions, public-school teachers in this study were pessimistic about their power to influence school policy. A middle-school teacher said:

> The biggest frustration that I hear in the school in recent years is the lack of leadership and encouragement to participate in decision making at the bigger level. . . . People want to have faculty meetings, would like to sit down and be able to discuss educational issues, not drivel. We have few opportunities to do that, where what you have to say is valued and considered beyond your department.

Another teacher reported that his colleagues have come to expect administrators to discount and disregard their views:

> We have a monthly faculty meeting with the principal, at which time, if the teachers wanted to bring something up, they certainly could. I hate to say it, but most of our major decisions are already cast. In other words, they come down as orders from high up, down to the principal. Once in a while, you fight them.

The absence of meaningful opportunities for schoolwide governance troubled a number of teachers. One from a suburban high school observed that "teachers feel particularly impotent in the area of policy making," because in her school, there was nobody to make decisions about the issues that faculty discuss among themselves. An urban elementary-school teacher reported that the failure to address schoolwide problems is a great source of stress in his work:

> Let's solve that problem. . . . What can we do about the fragmentation? We just tested kids, and in grade three they were already falling behind the national norm. We have no remedial program in grade one and two in my school. There's no plan for a remedial program. I said, "We just found out that we need a program—we need something. Why don't we have a meeting? Why aren't we doing something about this?"

Although many such problems remain unaddressed at the school level, principals often made unilateral decisions that affected teachers' work and students' learning, and sometimes those decisions had serious instructional consequences. In one vocational high school, the principal revised the schedule so that academic and vocational teachers met their students only on alternate weeks. An English teacher who believed that her students would lose momentum with such a disjointed schedule voiced her concerns to the principal, but said she "got totally shot down, not listened to at all. He didn't want to deal with it." A middle-school teacher said that when she objected to her principal's decision to create clusters of "on-level" and "off-level" groups of students, a practice that would establish de facto tracking in violation of desegregation guidelines, the principal dismissed her complaints. When he later decided to eliminate the position of a much-revered shop teacher in order to expand the foreign-language program, she objected again:

> He doesn't listen to any of us. We've had arguments with him—every single cluster, every group. I don't think there's one teacher in the building who agrees with it. But it's still going to be what he wants.

Some schools, particularly those at the elementary level, lack any forum where teachers can raise schoolwide issues. One suburban elementary-school teacher said, "If we disagree with something, there's nobody to address. I think it would be good if we had a faculty council or something. But there's none of that at all." Where faculty councils existed, teachers' input was virtually always advisory rather than binding and, in these teachers' views, remarkably ineffectual. Again and again, they said that principals controlled the outcome of school-level meetings. One high-school mathematics teacher whose principal had established an advisory council described how it fell into disuse:

> He started out pretty well with a principal's advisory council. You could go and talk with him, and people liked him. Then all of a sudden, after about a year or two, there was no more advisory council. We went to see him with a couple of suggestions, and he became very defensive. As a result, nobody goes to see him anymore.

Many such councils and senates were transitory, their membership and activity irregular from one year to the next. An urban high-school teacher wasn't certain whether an advisory council was still functioning in her school: "We do have the school-site council. It was active last year. This year, I don't know. I don't hear that much about it." An urban elementary-school teacher said that there had been a "faculty council that met once a month. It has deteriorated." When the principal gradually neglected to schedule meetings, this teacher and several colleagues

> called the office to ask if the faculty council meeting was this week or next week. The principal overheard, got on the intercom, and said, "So I guess you want a faculty council meeting?" We said, "Yeah."

The teacher voiced suspicion of the cancellation of previously scheduled meetings: "It's not like there haven't been issues. There have been plenty of issues."

Many respondents considered advisory councils to be purely symbolic. A middle-school teacher claimed that the council was "just there in name. So they can say, 'Oh yeah, we brought that up at the faculty council.' " Others criticized councils for dealing with short-term, irrelevant, or marginal issues. Teachers listed an array of issues they termed wasteful of their time that had been addressed in advisory council meetings: the use of vacant rooms, plans for Education Week, bus duty, the condition of the labs, dismissal procedures, the location of trash barrels, and the scheduling of announcements. Other meetings were preempted by teachers' immediate problems or complaints—"anything that may not be going right"—making them forums for informal grievances rather than planning and policy making. Even when advisory councils took up long-term issues, such as discipline or facilities maintenance, they were usually matters tangential to teaching and often remained unresolved. A middle-school teacher who had been on her principal's advisory committee "for quite a number of years" said that staff repeatedly asked the council to address the fact "that the school is dirty." A high-school foreign-language teacher said that her faculty council had addressed the same "topics of concern for a very long time, and it doesn't seem like many of them change . . . three lunches versus two. In-school lunches versus out-of-school lunches. Discipline. . . . Roaming the corridors."

In addition to advisory councils, full faculty meetings were typically scheduled monthly, as specified in the teachers' contracts. Some teachers said that their principals usually cancelled meetings for lack of important issues. One elementary-school teacher, interviewed late in the school year, said that her school had held only two faculty meetings so far. Teachers were pessimistic about the prospects for making policy in such meetings where many said that principals simply dispensed information—"three-quarters of the things you could read on a sheet"—or chastised staff—" 'Make sure you're here on time.' 'You're using too much paper.' " Teachers complained that discussion was seldom serious and, if it was, almost never culminated in a faculty vote. An elementary-school principal who announced that all students would be required to write a paper or story each week reportedly prohibited discussion of his decision: "A second-grade teacher said, 'Gee, I think that's a lot,' and he almost took her head off."

Anna Capello contended that, in her large urban high school, faculty meetings had become less and less meaningful over time:

> Even when we have meetings, we never get to address educational issues. . . . We end up talking about either violence or crimes or anything extraneous to education. I remember years ago, when we used to have meetings about updating the teaching skills or finding out what was going on in other parts of the country—mind-broadening, more professional matters. Now it's really depressing; it's stressful.

The mathematics teacher whose principal had ceased holding advisory council meetings also considered faculty meetings to be unproductive, largely because staff were convinced that their concerns would not be taken seriously:

> There's no faculty input. We have faculty meetings every first Monday of the month, and there's a section on the [agenda] for "faculty items." There was a time when there'd be one or two at every meeting. But we just don't bother now.

A teacher's decision not to bother is often assumed to illustrate a lack of interest; however, these teachers suggested that a commitment to participate is closely related to an opportunity to have real influence—being deprived of any genuine chance to influence policy was for them the root cause of withdrawal and cynicism. Only 7 of 75 teachers in public schools believed that they exerted ongoing influence over important schoolwide matters. A suburban elementary-school teacher told of a Japanese bilingual program proposed for her school, which would have increased class size in the early grades. The principal "didn't want to make the decision without consulting the staff, so that was a large topic at one of the staff meetings." In another case, a suburban middle-school teacher said that staff in his school were active in governance

> because the principal gets us all involved in decisions. All decisions are done in committees. People volunteer for all the committees they sit on. If there's a problem, he'll form a committee and ask teachers to sit on it and offer solutions.

The teacher whose urban middle school was organized by units also said that staff made important educational decisions: "Nothing is ever done without a consensus." Although he had found that many districtwide committees were intended only to "look good on paper," governance structures within his school actually worked:

> If I do get involved in things at school, people are expecting an end result, and you have to come across. Someone comes up with an idea, or we have to make some kind of policy decision, and it is done [with a vote].

At one large suburban high school, teachers had several structured opportunities for schoolwide influence: meetings of the full faculty, where issues of substance were discussed but votes rarely taken; a student/faculty advisory committee, where "voting takes place" about such issues as grading and scheduling, and the decisions made were binding; and an informal faculty forum organized during a labor dispute several years previously. In this third forum, teachers met before school each week to discuss school issues, and sometimes the principal, whom a social studies teacher described as a "bright, alert, articulate administrator," attended their meetings and sought their advice. Recently, when staff were dissatisfied with a proposed change in the instructional schedule, they prepared a position paper and met with the principal, who acknowledged the legitimacy of their complaints and urged them to draw up an alternative proposal; they did. By contrast, teachers' influence in the large majority of public schools included in this study appeared to be meager.

Some principals listened to staff; others discounted faculty opinion and aggressively asserted their authority. An urban middle-school teacher complained about her new principal's approach: "It's his school, you know. It's like he walked into our territory and just wanted to make it his and take it over." A suburban high-school teacher said that her principal "pretty much has his mind made up about what he wants to do. And, in spite of whatever input you might have had, it ends up coming out as he planned to begin with." A suburban elementary-school teacher explained his reluctance to initiate discussions with his principal: "I think you're hesitant because if it's taken the wrong way, you're dead." Other principals were said to be responsive to teachers and, in some cases, to seek out their opinions. Some teachers said that their principals' doors were "always open." Richard Sand, who said that he influenced policy informally by "being a pest," contended that "having a principal who listens is ninety-nine percent of the battle." Gary Stein said that his principal was "very receptive" to Stein's analysis and advice about school problems. An urban middle-school teacher praised her principal's responsiveness:

> He's very involved. He's always around. He never turns anyone away, never is too busy to deal with anything. He's always open to suggestions of any sort. . . .

Several teachers said that they could get their principal's attention because they were respected, but that all staff did not enjoy such access. One observed:

> My relationship with both the principal and other leaders in the system is a good one. There is respect for my opinion. I don't get shot down a lot. Yet I know there are some people who have terrible relationships with the principal. If they ask him anything, he'll say no. . . .

One must remember that principals who attend to teachers' concerns and solicit teachers' advice in making policy do so at their discretion rather than in response to any formal obligation. Final decisions remain theirs; sometimes those decisions are informed by teachers' views, but often they are not. A suburban elementary-school teacher believed that teachers in her school should have had greater influence than they did, that their expertise should have been granted more attention:

> Our principal is very open on the one hand. He will listen. Yet he's very stubborn in many ways. If he makes a decision, that's the decision. Maybe that's the way it should be. He is the administrator. But I think that when you're dealing with kids and you're in the classroom all day, that you know what's going to work and what's not going to work. I think it needs to be discussed. Very often it isn't.

Overall, at the school level, teachers' roles in governance are largely informal and dependent on the principal's personal style of management. Meetings that may be scheduled do not necessarily occur or lead to policy decisions. Many teachers see such meetings as ceremonial assemblies consuming time and energy and serving only to dramatize their powerlessness in school governance. Few teachers have any guaranteed role in making decisions about schoolwide issues, and many seek to exert informal influence. In some cases, principals and teachers alike avoid important educational choices, and policy becomes simply the sum of sudden, unplanned decisions.

The district. At the district level, teachers participate in two policy-making forums—districtwide committees and collective bargaining. In the first, teachers exercise weak influence over a broad range of matters, while in the second, their influence is strong, but the scope of issues that they address is typically narrow.

Teachers in this study reported having very little to do with policies that emerged from the central office or school board, despite the fact that school officials at that level make important decisions about curriculum, testing, budgeting, hiring, the school calendar, purchasing, staff assignment, categorical programs, and building maintenance. Teachers were generally unfamiliar with the work of this bureaucracy, even in relatively small districts.

They felt ignored by school officials outside their schools and expressed contempt for top-down managerial styles.

A suburban middle-school teacher contended that teachers in her school "would feel a whole lot better about being here . . . if we had a lot more to say about what is done systemwide." She observed:

> It just seems as though things are done by edict. Very often they are things that we are the experts on and they're not. Not that I expect them to allow us to make the decisions without them, but consulting us would be really nice.

A number of teachers, who said that they could exert influence in their schools, felt powerless outside those schools. A suburban teacher explained:

> A lot of times around here, you're asked, and it feels like it goes right . . . into the trash can. Not in this particular building. In this building you are polled and respected. In the system you are not.

Several teachers told of occasions when the central office notified staff that their schools would be reorganized. Teachers in one urban high school were told that their school would become a magnet school, and they were asked to suggest "novel programs" to attract students. Another teacher said that school officials were likely to change her junior high school to a middle school: "But that kind of issue doesn't seem to be discussed with the faculty. It is somebody on high who says, 'Okay, from now on this is a middle school.' " A third respondent said that, in September, the central office announced that her school was to become a magnet school. Teachers spent the year making detailed plans for the transition; in the spring, central-office administrators decided that "we're not going to be a magnet school. . . . They're just having one magnet school in the city."

Other teachers resented instructional policies that originated in the central office. A suburban high-school teacher told of a district-level proposal to triple the physical education requirement in his school, a change that would dramatically affect course enrollments in other departments, but that had never been discussed with staff. A middle-school teacher described how central administrators' enthusiasm for cooperative learning techniques led quickly to a decision that all teachers should use them in their classrooms:

> [They] were taking the approach: "Well, this is a great idea. We're going to provide in-service training, and the teachers are going to do this from now on. . . ." Somebody gets an idea, and the school committee approves the idea, and then we are told, "This is what you are going to do."

Such apparently unilateral decisions had convinced many teachers that central office administrators worked in a world apart, one untroubled by teachers' concerns, uninformed by their expertise. Teachers seemed to attribute to these administrators a distant but binding authority, like that which airline passengers often ascribe to the faceless air controllers who govern their flight schedules in unpredictable but powerful ways.

Many districts offer teachers the chance to serve on districtwide committees concerned with matters such as staff development, student services, or curriculum articulation. Virtually all such committees are advisory, charged with studying issues and submitting recommendations, but given no authority over decisions. Teachers often complained that their efforts on these committees and task forces were futile; they told of written reports that were never read and recommendations ignored by school officials who had had different plans in mind from the outset.

A few teachers said that the advice they offered at the district level did influence decisions, most often on textbook selection. One teacher felt encouraged when, having met with a group of colleagues to consider the causes of persisting low achievement among black students in a predominantly white school district, the superintendent translated their recommendations into action. With very few exceptions, however, teachers believed that even if the district offices solicited their opinions, ultimately those opinions would carry little weight.

Many teachers had worked on committees that studied such topics as staff development, middle schools, or teacher evaluation. Only rarely was the group given a specific charge, and participants often found their efforts unconnected to decisions or policies that followed. Some, like this suburban middle-school teacher, found the teachers' majority position overruled by the administrators who ultimately issued the committee's report:

> I served on a committee, and when the report came out, it was the exact opposite of everything we had decided on, so that I really am very skeptical about that way of running the school system.

Most of those who criticized the work of districtwide advisory committees gave examples of findings or recommendations that had taken months to arrive at and then were simply ignored by school officials. Richard Sand emphasized that he had had his fill of such ventures:

> Two years, two full years of afternoons, nights, a couple of weekends. A year later, the report couldn't be found anywhere. I had the only copy in the district. They had been thrown out.

Although many teachers told similar tales of wasted effort, at least one reported that teachers on committees in his district "actually have a say in policy." He served on a joint committee of teachers and administrators charged with evaluating staff proposals for spending educational improvement funds. This committee, atypical in that it had a specific charge as well as recommending authority, met but once a year, and by this teacher's account, the central office routinely honored its recommendations:

> We go through this report, which is pretty thick, item by item, discussing whether we would give [the proposals] a number one, two, three, or four priority status. It seems to me that anything that is given a number one priority really does go through the following year.

Such purposeful meetings and assurance of influence were unparalleled in the experiences of other respondents.

In contrast to the uncertain course of advisory committee work, collective bargaining provided teachers with leverage legitimated by law and leading to enforceable outcomes; not just an advisory process that precedes policy making, collective bargaining is policy making.

Opinions varied among those interviewed about the appropriate role of unions in public education. Some respondents believed them constructive agents of change, while others felt ambivalent about belonging to organizations that focused too much on workers' rights. Richard Sand said, "I'm a union officer, but I don't like unions." Another teacher explained, "I think we're getting paid like factory workers because we're always trying to equate ourselves with factory workers. . . . It's distracting for us as professionals to be spending all our time haggling over sick days and money. . . ."

Teachers agreed, however, that their influence as contract negotiators could be far more powerful than it ever would be as members of advisory committees. An urban middle-school teacher said, "You do have a lot of voice, and this goes back to the teachers' contract. Collective bargaining came in probably about twelve years ago, and teachers really began having a say in their working conditions." Respondents told of contract provisions that protected them from arbitrary dismissal, prohibited administrators from overloading classes, and regulated transfers within the district. Administrative violations of the contract could be redressed through grievance and arbitration procedures that might require the school district to change its practices or make financial amends to the aggrieved party. Unlike the advisory committee reports, the collective bargaining agreement was not likely to be ignored or misplaced.

Although collective bargaining is a binding process, the range of issues it typically addresses is narrow—class size, teaching load, working hours, grievance procedures—and virtually never includes instructional matters such as curriculum, pedagogy, or testing. An urban high-school teacher told of his union's negotiating an agreement which included a salary raise and an increase in teaching load to five periods each day, accompanied by a reduction in class size—important changes, but ones that would affect instruction only indirectly. Several factors interact to limit the scope of the large majority of teacher contracts, including state laws that expressly restrict negotiation to wages, hours, and working conditions; the difficulty of enforcing contract provisions about matters that are not easily verified; and teachers' desire to preserve their instructional autonomy.[2] Although some districts are experimenting with ways to expand the scope of bargaining,[3] their efforts are unusual.

The fact that most teacher contracts address but a narrow range of working conditions leads some teachers to argue that academic interests are not adequately or fairly represented by their unions. These teachers wished for the collective bargaining process to be used to ensure greater professional influence in the schools, but others preferred to limit union negotiations to the most basic features of their jobs.

Legislatures, courts, and state departments of education. In legislatures, courts, and state departments of education, far-reaching policies are made on behalf of schools and students without the participation of the teachers who must implement them, and teachers are increasingly troubled by the unintended consequences of the array of procedural regulations, administrative rulings, and judicial remedies affecting public education. Several teachers described pull-out programs that disrupt classroom instruction and student learning. Two teachers in a large urban district told of desegregation orders putting parents at great distance, both physically and psychologically, from their children's schools and teachers. No teacher reported any personal involvement in the state legislature's debate about schooling reform, and yet new laws would certainly affect their classrooms. Increasingly, governmental regulation of school practices, whatever the merits of that regulation, contributes significantly to teachers' sense of disenfranchisement.

Taken together, these teacher interviews suggest that school policy is not the product of any rational process systematically integrating the priorities of participants from all levels of interest or involvement; rather, it is a loosely coordinated assemblage of preferences and practices, which are variously set in the classroom, the department, the cluster, the principal's office, at the bargaining table, the central offices, the school-board room, the state department of education, the legislature, and the courts. Policies made by individual classroom teachers vary widely and may bear little resemblance to central-office directives. Policies established by the school board, with far-reaching consequences for individual schools or programs, may be little informed by teachers' expertise. Policies set at the negotiating table may enable teachers to hold school officials accountable for their action, but fail to address many matters of pressing concern to teachers. Respondents believed that traditional patterns of dominance and subordination persisting in educational policy making create a decidedly Us-versus-Them situation. The problem is, at least in part, a structural one, for even when school administrators are responsive and accommodating, it is because they choose to be, not because they are required to be. Even in collective bargaining, the only forum where teachers can command the attention of school officials, the obligation to bargain in good faith requires only consideration, not concession.

Informal channels. Because the domains of decision making are so loosely coupled,[4] much educational policy is ultimately the result of personal influence and political bartering by an ever-changing array of parties. A high-school social studies teacher, who said that he was given "a certain amount of power in designing [his] program," also argued:

> Ultimately it has to pass through your superiors—the superintendent and ultimately the school committee. Often . . . by the time it passes through the various steps, it's unrecognizable. So the opportunity is there to participate in the policy-making of the school, but what happens to whatever you decide on by the time it gets amended and refined and tailored to satisfy everybody who has to approve it makes you think that you didn't have very much influence on policy making.

Recognizing the limits of their influence in this system, many respondents suggested that they could better effect change by voicing their concerns informally to a key individual—the principal, a school-board member, or a central-office administrator—than by participating formally in advisory bodies or bargaining sessions. One urban middle-school teacher said that she often stayed away from committee meetings because "it was just a lot of people airing problems and not getting anything accomplished." However, she was not without influence: "I feel so comfortable now, being in this school so long, I feel that if I have any complaint I can just go and air it. . . ." A suburban high-school teacher who was similarly disenchanted with formal meetings agreed: "In the long run, I really think that an informal recommendation coming from a teacher carries as much weight as a formal response." He also recognized the inequity of such influence: "To effect policy as one of two hundred teachers in the building, to do it alone, isn't right. It gives you more status than you deserve." Notably, another teacher in the same school said that she did not try to influence policy informally, although

> other teachers do, . . . [who] feel more comfortable doing that kind of thing. They will go to the principal or to the superintendent or even to a school committee member and say, "Look, I don't think this is a good idea. I think we should do something about that."

She did not disapprove of such actions, but was uncomfortable taking them herself.

For teachers in large districts, informal influence was usually exercised at the school site, where teachers urged their principals to hear their concerns and consider their recommendations. Those in small districts could more easily find their way to central administrators who held power. One elementary-school teacher said:

> [This district] is small enough that I'm on a first-name basis with the superintendent. I know all his assistants and so forth. A school system of that size is nice, because if you really have a problem you can go right to the top and say, "This is my problem. What are we going to do about it?" And I think that is good.

The exercise of informal influence at all levels depended on the presence of responsive administrators and good personal relationships. A suburban elementary-school teacher explained that she influenced policy

> through relationships—not necessarily through formal organizations. If I have anything to say, usually it is listened to by [the principal]. I will get some action or consideration. I think she respects me, and I respect her. It's on that basis.

This emphasis on personal relationships suggests that it is commonly the well-positioned individual rather than the expert professional who successfully influences the decisions of the powers that be.

PUBLIC-SCHOOL-TEACHERS' ATTITUDES TOWARD GOVERNANCE

Some respondents argued that the opportunities for formal influence are available, if teachers would only take advantage of them. We found evidence that, although teachers doubted the capacity of administrators to make good decisions, they themselves were sometimes unwilling to participate in alternative forums or exert what power they did have. In explanation, respondents noted their preoccupation with students and classrooms, excessive demands on their time, norms of equity that discouraged individual teachers from stepping forth and taking the lead, and skepticism about the prospects for success. Notably, these constraints parallel those that teachers offered in chapter 6 to explain the dearth of collaboration among staff.

Some teachers objected to being distracted from teaching by the demands of policy making. They believed that teaching well required their undiverted attention, and they wished that administrators would simply anticipate their needs and respect their views. Precisely because administrators have historically controlled policy, some teachers regarded peers who moved into that realm as turncoats seeking undue status or political advantage. Anna Capello said that in her school, "People are careful about doing too much. . . . Even at general meetings, people are afraid to say things, because you might be labeled a Goody Two-Shoes." A high-school teacher who had expressed confidence about teachers' power to influence policy said that there had been "some fairly disagreeable needling that I've experienced, that other people have experienced, who have been willing to work with the superintendent and the principal on this plan."

Other teachers doubted that their efforts would lead to anything important. One teacher, who continued to try to influence policy, said that she understood the reluctance of others:

> Sometimes we go through the motions of making it look like it's democratic, but it really isn't. In some cases, people have gotten so discouraged, they'll go to meetings where they do have voice, and not want to get involved, not want to offer anything. Their attitude is, "We've done it before. We've tried it. We've failed. We give up."

Teachers in large districts where decision making was often fragmented and highly politicized, expressed even more cynicism. When we asked Anna Capello if she participated in formal policy making, she said, "That's where I've given up. About three years ago, I just stopped having anything to do with that. Maybe I felt that there was no sense to it, that it wouldn't do any good. . . . I lost something. I just did. . . . Politically, there are things that go on that make you not want to participate." She told of a school-board decision to merge her school with another, a yearlong effort by teachers to prepare for the change, and the school board's subsequent decision to scrap the plan. "That's been pulled out now. That's no longer going to happen."

Two suburban high-school teachers, who were confident that teachers could affect policy in their schools, rejected their peers' skepticism. One said that his principal had instituted a committee that would be

> a pipeline for input. You've got input that people have complained that they don't have. And yet, very, very few people were interested in it. . . . [They think that] the principal's going to do what he wants to do.

A teacher from another district voiced similar criticism of teachers:

> I think there's a perception on the part of people that the input doesn't count, that the decision is made beforehand. You can hear people very often say at faculty meetings, "What are we doing here? They know what they're going to do already." I think that that's not the case. I think that's simply not true.

Both of these teachers were from small districts where one might expect teachers to have more direct influence on policy. For them the possible payoff, though never certain, was worth the effort. For others, particularly those in large urban schools, the unlikely prospect of making a difference simply was not compelling; the disincentives for participating in the formal policy-making process outweighed incentives.

We found considerable evidence that teachers are peripheral to the formal policy-making process in public education. While some teachers described themselves or colleagues as active, confident, and influential, far more were skeptical and discouraged about the prospects for effecting change beyond their immediate teaching situations. Some teachers were satisfied to teach as they wished within their classrooms, and have a say within their teams or departments, but leave district policy to central officials. Many of these valued teachers were considerably more ambivalent about their circumscribed, subsidiary roles. They sought more respect for their opinions and a more decisive role in setting policy. Having been discouraged by token assignments and politically motivated decisions, they had withdrawn from formal committee work and resorted to their own informal politicking. However, many would have preferred to participate in a more orderly process that consumed less time, sapped less energy, and offered more certain outcomes. Teachers' reluctance to participate in policy making must be seen in its context of past failures and disappointments.

EXPERIENCES IN THE PRIVATE SECTOR

Some respondents from church-related schools said that they expected and exercised even less influence in school policy than their colleagues in public schools. Janice Gagne said that her Catholic elementary school lacked any forum for teachers' participating in policy making. Nor did she have much informal influence, apparently because the hierarchical school structure prescribed practice at the top. An elementary-level teacher in a Catholic diocesan school said that she was not involved in setting policy because that was done by the principal "who attends many meetings, principals' meetings and staff meetings, in the parish and the archdiocese." Similarly, an elementary-level teacher in a Jewish day school said there were no faculty committees, that "all policy and all decisions of that sort are made by the head rabbi." In such cases, teachers were expected to comply with their superiors' expectations rather than presume to take charge of their schools. Collective bargaining at church-related schools, when it occurred, generally addressed only a very narrow range of issues.

At other church-related schools, self-determination rather than obedience was the prevailing norm, and teachers exercised far more influence than at most public schools. In one Quaker school, the faculty screened applicants for teaching positions, teachers reviewed student admissions, and staff participated in an array of influential committees, including the school's governing board. These teachers did not struggle for influence or vie for power with authoritarian administrators, but shared authority and were expected to do their part in governing the school. A middle-grade teacher in this school explained that because Quakers value consensus, "unless everyone agrees, it doesn't happen." Such an arrangement obviously requires staff with a common set of values, who are committed to making the process work; it depends on a strong organizational culture, and it takes time. But teachers in this school reportedly regarded the time as well spent, for the decisions they made became school policy, both on paper and in practice. As a first-grade teacher observed, "There is a lot of input on everything, which means a lot of work. It also means a lot of feeling that you have some power."

In a Waldorf School, run in accordance with the spiritual and pedagogical principles of Rudolf Steiner, the faculty assumed collective responsibility for the school and its teaching. Instead of a principal, members of the staff served as faculty chairperson for prescribed terms. An array of faculty committees, to which teachers were elected by colleagues, administered the school. One teacher explained that the system of governance was intended to "involve all human beings and their strengths and weaknesses," but that it was "not meant to be a democratic system where everyone votes on everything. It's meant to be a republic where there are individuals and committees who are given authority in their realms." Parents were active in the school's governance, although teachers retained the authority to hire and, if necessary, fire staff. When asked what features of the school supported his best work, this teacher extolled the system of collegial governance:

> Teachers are involved in the running of the school. This is not hierarchical in any sense. Those who work in administration do so as colleagues, each of them as a teacher in addition to these administrative responsibilities.

Like the teacher in the Quaker school, this teacher emphasized the practical demands of shared governance:

> It means more meetings and more struggles. But it also means that this does not become a we-they struggle. There is no they. If I'm dissatisfied with something, I can't say, "They did it." I have to say, "We did it."

For these teachers, the opportunity to govern carried with it the responsibility to govern.

The small alternative school cited in chapter 6 for its extensive collaboration among staff was nonhierarchically governed, though there was an administrative head. The teacher we interviewed explained that new staff are sometimes unprepared for this egalitarian relationship and expect that eventually the head will make the decisions. When she does not, teachers do their part and, reportedly, "come to value it." All faculty are members of the school's corporation, and their representatives serve on its board of directors. Committees meet regularly and set virtually all policies for the school—"Most everything is done by consensus." Although pay is considerably lower than in neighboring public schools, teachers said they remained at this school because they "have a voice—knowing that you can really effect change if you want to."

These three schools stand out because of the teachers' far-reaching roles in governance, comparable in many ways to the collegial administration of hospitals and law firms, with which schools often are compared unfavorably. The schools were atypical, even within the sample of private schools, for featuring both the structures and the norms that encourage teachers to set policy and oversee standards of practice in their own institutions. For the majority of teachers in these schools, such opportunities were said to contribute substantially to their satisfaction as professionals.

A number of the independent schools with more conventional governance provided staff with opportunities to both shape and implement school policy. A junior-high-school teacher in a private boarding school said that faculty there establish curricula with their departments and set schoolwide policy through full faculty meetings: "It's all a matter of discussion," with the final policy being "written up by a committee of faculty members . . . and administrators." Although faculty are very influential,

> the final, final decision always lies with our headmaster, who utilizes that now and then, sometimes to speed up the process so that it's ready on time, and other times because a decision needs to be made and he's heard enough opinions.

The headmaster's "final, final" decisions might not satisfy all staff, but teachers could expect that those decisions would be consistent with the positions taken by a significant number of their peers. Although the headmaster did have formal authority to set policy that contradicted prevailing faculty views, strong collegial norms made it difficult to do so.

In a college-preparatory high school, teachers

> set policy at faculty meetings. We'll vote on issues, and we have a pretty strong say in what's going to be taught and how things are taught and, . . . if a [student] is in academic difficulty, who's going to stay on and who's going to be dismissed.

Here, too, "there were a few things that the headmaster does on his own," and in some cases, he aroused teachers' ire by acting contrary to strong faculty sentiment. For example, "No one wanted to have lacrosse at the school, and he bowed to parental pressure and put it in on his own, despite the fact that the faculty was . . . eighty percent against it." This teacher concluded that, although "certain things are done maybe a little bit behind the scenes, in general, I would say that we have a pretty strong voice."

An art teacher characterized governance of her private, alternative high school as "very democratic"; faculty served on the board of trustees and voted about curricular, attendance, and disciplinary policies. Through an assortment of committees, faculty kept a close watch on school practices. "If we need to make substantial changes that require some extended study, a committee is put together and we investigate it. They're just constantly trying to improve things." This teacher argued that any headmaster who tried to assert hierarchical control of school policy would violate strong expectations of collegial governance: "I don't think any headmaster would try and change it or make a substantial policy change in a different way."

A biology teacher in an independent high school contended that private schools have a fundamental respect for faculty opinion. He recalled how little his expertise had been valued at a prestigious public high school where "for years, I'd been banging on tables" about the appropriate sequence of science courses. He was surprised, when he raised a similar concern at his current school, to find both serious consideration and ready acceptance of his proposal: "After an hour, everybody said, 'That sounds reasonable. Let's do it.' "

Although teachers in his school had long exercised curricular influence through their departments, their experience with schoolwide collegial governance was relatively recent. According to this teacher, the prior headmaster had been authoritarian and "absolutely called the shots himself. The faculty was here to teach and shut up. Just let him take care of everything else." With the appointment of a new head, the school shifted toward "more collegial responsibility for schoolwide affairs." However, in this teacher's view,

> engaging the faculty is not an easy thing to do. They want representation without taxation. They want to be able to make pronouncements about policy . . . [but] they don't particularly want to put in the enormous amount of time it requires to reach those kinds of decisions.

The transition to a new pattern of faculty governance required an attendant change in faculty expectations and norms.

The enthusiastic descriptions of faculty influence in these nonpublic schools suggest that teachers can play decisive roles in policy making, that faculty meetings can be used as democratic forums for exploring proposals and making decisions, that teachers and administrators can share authority and responsibility for the school, and that greater collegial governance can ultimately promote greater professional influence and greater satisfaction among staff.

Although our research uncovered many instances of faculty influence in private schools, it also revealed that independent status does not inevitably lead to collegial governance. Many private schools have committee structures, but only some provide for true faculty governance, others offering little more than democratic trappings for otherwise hierarchical organizations. Some faculty bodies render binding decisions while others are only loosely advisory. Some headmasters are committed to faculty governance, but others only give it lip service; a few repudiate it altogether.

Allen Rondo said that teachers in his elite preparatory school have no meetings to discuss schoolwide policy.

> So it's more informal. The headmaster's door is always open. . . . There's no formal structure to suggest a change, except a curriculum committee. But as far as other things, it's pretty much . . . if you have a concern, say it to somebody and let's talk about it.

Because administrators in his school were responsive to teachers' views, staff were generally satisfied with these informal practices. In another prestigious high school, which was similarly structured, teachers were said to be battling for greater control. A history teacher said that faculty had historically been subordinate to administrators: "In fact, it has been, up until now, a totalitarian rule that is sometimes benevolent and sometimes not so benevolent." Although she was an active participant on the admissions committee and was influential in curricular decisions, "to say that I have had a hand in policy, I think, would be a complete distortion." She said that at her school "it was a tedious effort to get things that . . . many institutions would take for granted, like finding out how much you're going to be paid before you walk in the door in September." At the time of the interview, the school was preparing to replace the retiring head, and teachers were demanding representation on the search committee. This respondent perceived the school to be at a turning point: "I think the faculty understands that if they don't win this one, the chances of things changing really, in terms of input from the faculty, are very slim. And I think the faculty is determined."

These teachers' experiences offer several lessons about the prospects for collegial governance in public schools. Several organizational features common in nonpublic schools seem to foster faculty involvement in policy making. Because most of these schools function as independent units, the school site is the place where change can best be initiated and implemented. With the exception of some church-related schools embedded in larger organizational structures, private schools were truly independent; in deciding to alter practices, staff did not have to consider the implications of change for any larger system. The size of the faculty, which seldom numbered more than 30 even at the secondary level, encouraged frequent interaction among all members. Because those who served as assistant headmasters or academic deans also were teachers, instructional values were well represented in school decisions. The limited number of administrative positions in nonpublic schools meant that teachers served on governing committees that dealt with admissions or community relations not only because they considered these matters important, but also because the organization depended on their efforts to keep the school running. Each of these schools had a unique and familiar history, and teachers shared a set of expectations about "how things are done here." In the public schools, where teachers and principals can be transferred from one building to another without warning, such continuity of practice is often lacking. Without strong traditions of collegial governance, schools seem to fall back into conventional, hierarchical modes of operating, if only to be sure that the organization functions from one day to the next.

Independent-school teachers expected to be consulted about policy and to have their views taken seriously. It is not clear where their attitudes originated—whether independent schools attract teachers intent on self-determination or the schools themselves foster such attitudes; both factors may be at work. We found evidence that, although independent-school teachers' expectations for involvement were greater than those of their public-school counterparts, those expectations were heightened and sustained by individual schools' histories of faculty participation. Teachers from schools that had only recently shifted away from authoritarian governance evidenced much the same skepticism and reluctance as public-school teachers.

Although norms and expectations that support collegial governance seemed essential to sustain faculty involvement, they appeared insufficient to withstand the force of administrators who chose to retain control of policy and practice. No independent school teacher mentioned that he or she would prefer to work in a unionized setting, but some would have welcomed common gains of collective bargaining—a standardized pay scale, grievance procedures, and advance notification of teaching assignments. Respondents in schools where teachers could exert collective influence through committee work, faculty meetings, and representation on boards of directors rarely mentioned such concerns. Teachers who lacked formal influence and worked under authoritarian heads reported feeling ineffectual and vulnerable and withdrawing to their classrooms.

EFFORTS TO INCREASE TEACHERS' ROLES IN GOVERNANCE

The issue of faculty governance in public schools has received considerable attention in recent years. The Carnegie Forum on

Education and the Economy[5] and the Holmes Group[6] have made strong cases for increasing teachers' roles in determining how their schools work. Local teacher unions have allied with school officials in a number of school districts to bargain collectively about restructuring governance and decision making.[7] With the encouragement of business, numerous state legislatures and school boards have taken steps to decentralize control of the public schools.[8] Data gathered in our interviews cast light on several of these initiatives.

School-site management. Proposals to decentralize school districts, to grant greater autonomy to individual schools, and thus, to the teachers in those schools, have considerable appeal for we have grown suspicious of large organizations and the impersonal bureaucracies they spawn. As we saw in chapter 5, highly centralized school organization favors conformity and compliance over variation and independence, and reinforces the preeminence of an administrative hierarchy that excludes parents and teachers from important decisions.

School-site management is currently advanced by many reformers as a means to return decision making to the site of instruction. Chicago schools are now governed directly by school-site councils composed of parents, teachers, community members, and principals. These councils have the power to evaluate and rehire principals, approve school improvement plans, determine staffing needs, allocate funds, and build the school budget.[9] Under a new teachers' contract in Boston, school-site councils will set instructional priorities, prepare budgets, disburse funds, hire new staff, and approve teacher transfers; council decisions, unlike those in Chicago, will require the principal's approval.[10]

These changes are recent and radical. Only time will show if they will be fully implemented, if the powers that have been delegated to teachers and parents will, in fact, be theirs, and if they will actively exercise them. In themselves, the proposals are consistent with the kinds of changes that the teachers in this study proposed.

The experiences of independent-school teachers suggest that if teachers are to influence school governance, they must do so in a context that is meaningful and within an organization that is manageable. Although one might hope that public-school teachers would become active and influential districtwide, it seems more likely that they will invest energy at the school site. Our evidence supports the belief that if school officials will truly delegate authority over the important matters of staffing, budget, and curriculum to those in the schools, teachers will become more active policy makers.

It is important to note that in private schools where teachers were influential and decisive, parents also were visible and active, serving as equals on committees and closely watching the schools at work. Augmenting collegial governance for teachers does not inevitably result in distancing parents from schools. School-site management may well provide greater power for both groups, and the best schools are likely to be those where the perspectives of both teaching and parenting are well represented and respected.

Joint teacher/administrator committees. Encouraging results are emerging from experiments with district-level committees in which administrators and teachers jointly assume responsibility for ongoing policy making and administration in such areas as staff assignment, evaluation procedures, and curriculum. In Cincinnati, teachers and school officials participate on joint committees to administer a peer evaluation plan, oversee the assignment of surplus teachers to understaffed schools, and direct an experimental program in school improvement.[11] In such arrangements, teachers hold equal powers with administrators rather than serving as their advisors; they address real problems, not contrived ones. The data of this study suggest that strengthening the formal powers of teachers and specifying their relationships to administrators would indeed encourage greater participation by teachers in districtwide governance. Public-school teachers repeatedly complained that their work on advisory committees was inconsequential, and many had withdrawn to their schools and classrooms as a result. The vitality of faculty committees in some independent schools suggests that public-school teachers like those interviewed for this study would increase or renew their efforts if they felt confident about the result.

The provision of authority to both teachers and administrators is important. The Carnegie Forum on Education and the Economy has suggested that executive committees of lead teachers might run schools, hiring principals, setting policy, and monitoring practice.[12] The evidence in this study suggests that such a model of collegial governance is possible, but also that teacher-run schools are unlikely either to gain widespread support among teachers or to serve the interests of most public schools. The image of the subservient principal carrying out the mandate of a decisive professional staff seems seriously misdrawn. Principals have repeatedly been shown to be central to school success,[13] and our respondents agreed that principals truly matter. Although individuals might fail to meet the demands of the principal's role, the role itself is vital, not vestigial. As teachers continue to focus their attention on the classroom, principals must remain attentive to the organization's larger purposes, holding as they do a schoolwide perspective that no single teacher can be expected to have.

The interviews with independent-school teachers suggest that the policy-making activities of teachers and principals can and should overlap more than they typically do in public schools, and that there need be no pact exchanging teachers' classroom autonomy for principals' school-level authority. Nor is there strong evidence to suggest that teachers either wish to, or should, assume responsibility for the entire enterprise. The only teacher-run school in the sample, a Waldorf School grounded in a set of explicitly shared values, staffed by a group of like-minded individuals, and serving a relatively homogeneous group of students, is no easy model to replicate in larger, more diverse and complex schools. Overall, however, the evidence from independent schools suggests that there is much to be gained when faculty and administrators deal jointly with policy making.

Differentiated staffing. Differentiated-staffing plans by which teachers' roles and responsibilities vary, some holding greater authority than others, have been proposed as an antidote to repetitious and unvaried teaching and as a better use of staff resources. Beginning teachers might spend most of their time in the classroom while master teachers would combine teaching with other responsibilities, such as teacher training, curriculum development, or departmental administration. Such plans hold promise for extending expert teachers' influence in decision making beyond the boundaries of the classroom, thus augmenting their roles in school governance. Differentiated roles, such as mentor teacher or department head, span instructional and administrative responsibilities. Many independent schools, which have fairly simple administrative structures, already feature differentiated roles for staff. In this study, we found classroom teachers simultaneously serving as department heads, academic deans, and assistant headmasters. Their presence and prominence in the schools tended to blur the distinctions between teachers and administrators, thus keeping instructional concerns and values more at the center of school policy.

Many proposals for differentiated staffing would delegate more of teachers' custodial and clerical responsibilities to aides, thus making it possible for the teachers to commit more time to governance. Teachers who are now expected to monitor study halls, supervise the cafeteria, or cover the classes of absent colleagues, might be called upon to review the discipline code, prepare a teachers' handbook, or design a master schedule. Teachers in independent schools are routinely expected to serve on committees that make admissions decisions, prepare curriculum, or review the quality of student services. They assume these responsibilities both because there are not enough administrators to do the jobs and because the tasks are thought to require teachers' expertise. Reconfiguring the use of public-school teachers' noninstructional time might make it possible for them to exert similar influence.

GETTING FROM HERE TO THERE

For the teachers in this study, students and classrooms were what mattered most, but they were not all that mattered. These valued teachers understood that they worked within a loose network of policies and practices that either supported or subverted their best efforts. Decisions by others to change a textbook, require hall passes, redraw attendance boundaries, or institute transitional classes affected their teaching. Many of those interviewed would have preferred enlightened administrators to make good decisions about such matters, but they had become increasingly doubtful that this would occur. Most would have welcomed opportunities for greater influence, but were skeptical that teachers' opinions could ever be decisive given the politics of their large, complex schools. Some independent schools provided examples of collegial governance, where instructional values prevailed and teachers had a major say in how the institution was run. Current proposals for school-site management, increased formal authority, and differentiated staffing offer promise to those who would make the governance of public schools more like that of these private schools. Such plans return decision making to the school site where teachers teach and students learn, where the costs and benefits of alternative choices can be calculated and practices fashioned to meet local need. These plans ensure that teachers share formal authority with administrators and exert decisive rather than merely advisory influence. They would permit more productive and efficient use of teachers' scarce professional time.

However, these teachers made it clear that such opportunities are necessary, but not sufficient, conditions for achieving collegial governance of public schools. If teachers are to exert more professional influence in public education, they must commit energy and time to that effort. Independent-school teachers were frank about the costs of attending to matters of schooling beyond their classrooms, but they were also candid in describing the rewards of such work when it went well. Many of the public-school teachers are ready to commit the time and reap the benefits. In the past they have participated extensively, often patiently, on principals' advisory committees, districtwide curriculum committees, and community task forces. They have already taken the lead in their teams, departments, or unions and sought to influence school officials both formally and informally. One or another, working alone, had initiated changes in a district's report card, instituted a study of bilingual education, promoted lengthening the hours for kindergarten, rewritten a school's discipline code, and undertaken a plan to better integrate specialists' work in the school day.

Several teachers in the study argued that they cannot wait for others to remake their work and hand them the authority they need, particularly when those others have their own administrative interests and positions to protect. In response to an early discussion of this study's findings, one teacher agreed that he and his colleagues wish that their needs and views would be understood by responsive administrators: "I, too, would like to go into my classroom and engage kids in fine talk about stories and ideas" while "a group of powerful men and women somewhere down the hall make sure I could continue to do that in peace. . . . But I don't think that it's likely that teachers are ever going to be so lucky." Later, inspired by the discussion of self-governance in *A Nation Prepared,*[14] he assumed the presidency of his union and initiated several reform efforts. He argued that teachers cannot leave decisions of professional practice to principals, superintendents, or school boards:

> It's awful, but it's true, I think. Those other folks just don't know enough about the job. It's also true that they often don't care enough about the job. And since it's the most important job there is, those people who know and care about it ought to be the watchful custodians of the conditions under which it is done.

With support, such teachers may begin to demonstrate that administratively governed schools are not inevitable after all.

CHAPTER EIGHT

Forging Stronger Cultural Bonds

When a soccer team enters a tournament, a software company embarks on developing a new product, or an orchestra prepares for an historic concert, the participants are drawn together by a clear and common goal. Individuals who might otherwise pursue personal interests commit themselves to the organization and adopt its principles and purposes, often giving more than ordinary effort and devising ways to reduce discord, minimize differences, and work cooperatively. They interpret their contributions and rewards in light of the organization and its accomplishments. The team, company, or orchestra benefits because members work in concert rather than at cross-purposes, and individuals benefit from finding greater meaning and success in their work and enjoying the privilege of belonging to a coherent community.[1]

The ideal world of organizational community always sounds easier to achieve than it is. Despite a joint purpose, individuals inevitably veer off on their own personal courses, and external pressures or internal adversity make it difficult for the group to remain unified. The goalie on the soccer team has a bad game. Threats by a competitor provoke complaints and blame among the software developers. A peevish conductor generates uncertainty and dissatisfaction among the musicians. Entropy ensues. When common purposes blur, when individuals act more selfishly than selflessly, or when short-term losses threaten people's confidence in the collective wisdom of the group, the organization may change, replacing the values, purposes, and traditions that served to unite, reassure, and motivate its members with rules, penalties, and the exercise of formal authority.

Two kinds of bonds—cultural and rational—bring organizational order and purpose to otherwise disorderly enterprises.[2] Cultural bonds include the shared purposes, values, traditions, and history that promote harmonious behavior and a sense of community. They are internal links that draw participants together through shared meaning. They promote commitment rather than compliance. By contrast, rational bonds include the rules, roles, functions, penalties, and formal authority that specify and regulate the behavior of individuals in organizations. They presume reluctance and dissent rather than commitment and accord. They unify participants externally by defining their responsibilities, roles, and relationships, by telling them what they can, cannot, and must do.

Cultural bonds are more efficient than rational bonds, being independent of external monitoring and control. They generate rather than consume energy. However, they are not always easy to promote and sustain, particularly in organizations with diffuse purposes, shifting memberships, or many discrete and specialized tasks. Public schools present particular challenges to unification through cultural bonds. The purposes of schools are multiple and sometimes contradictory. Success is difficult to define or measure. Teachers and students come and go.

The underlying core transaction of schooling, however, is what occurs between an individual teacher and a child. Who these teachers and students are as individuals—whether they are confident, inquisitive, authoritarian, or fearful—shapes any single relationship, and schooling is ultimately the sum of these myriad interactions among teachers and children who are assembled and reassembled in various combinations over days and years.

When we view schools from the inside looking out, we can see that the personal character of teaching is more likely to fragment the organization than unify it. What provides direction and coherence to this assembly of discrete efforts and interactions? All schools rely on some combination of rational and cultural bonds. Even the most rule-driven school is imbued with beliefs about the importance of education, and the most value-driven schools rely on some formalized practices; they differ importantly in the extent to which they rely on rational or cultural bonds to ensure coherence, and these differences affect both teachers' conceptions of their work and their satisfaction with it.

Those schools that primarily are bound by rational structures are likely to be more confining than inspiring and to narrow teachers' notions about what is possible and what their own contributions to the school might be. By contrast, schools bound by symbol and culture are likely to promote a shared sense of responsibility among staff and to encourage teachers to find in the school organization ways to meet both their own needs and the needs of the school community.

THE PROMINENCE OF SYMBOLIC BONDS

Private-school teachers in this study described cultural bonds as prominent in their work. Compared to their public-school counterparts, they expressed clearer notions of their schools' goals and purposes; they identified the values that they shared with others in their schools, they explained how these understandings were grounded in their schools' histories and were reinforced and expressed in their traditions. As Allen Rondo said, "Faculty here have a very clear sense of what this school is hoping to accomplish."

By contrast, public-school teachers seldom mentioned the presence of cultural bonds in their schools, schools which were notable for their mixed purposes, hazy histories, artificial traditions, and neutral stance toward values. Gary Stein said, "I've never felt a strong community sense within the school; I've never felt a strong thing that would pull us all together."

The prominence of cultural bonds in private schools and their virtual absence in most public schools can be explained by differences in their organizations. Because private schools are typically independent, small, stable, and homogeneous, those who work in them can better agree on goals, champion hardy values, celebrate their successes, find direction in their history, and rekindle purpose with traditions. Public schools, by comparison, are large and heterogeneous and embedded in public bureaucracies. They are subject to frequent and wholesale changes in membership and are responsible to diverse interests. As a result, public-school teachers and administrators are often tentative about proclaiming their purposes and cautious about espousing their values. They rarely have a reassuring history on which to rely or meaningful traditions to celebrate.[3]

The public-school teachers in this study suggested that, in some schools, there are small groups of teachers sharing standards or expectations who choose to work together. Overall, however, the symbolic glue is weak, and most public-school activity is ostensibly coordinated by rational bonds—the curriculum, the discipline code, the schedule, the chain of command, attendance and dismissal procedures. Teachers are told what to do and when and how to do it, and they, in turn, convey the rules and penalties to their students. Sometimes these bonds hold; often they do not. When they fail, teachers may withdraw and withhold, carefully reckoning what they give against what they get. Students testing the limits of rules and regulations lose sight of their obligations to fellow students and staff.

Public-school teachers were often perplexed when we asked whether a set of values, purposes, history, and traditions unified their schools. Those who had responded fluently and articulately to other questions stumbled over this one. Whether they taught in urban or suburban settings or worked with students at the elementary or secondary level, public-school teachers had to strain to identify symbolic bonds in their schools. One said that in her school there was "nothing unusual—maybe that's what holds it together." Another reflected, "I'm really hard pressed to come up with common goals and values." A third observed, "I don't know. It probably does have some unifying culture and I'm just not aware of it." A fourth echoed, "I don't know that I can label any one thing." A fifth who asserted, "I've never been in any school that did," attributed this to the "nature of teaching. . . . You have to be an individualist. . . . Everybody kind of brings their own agenda with them."

When public-school teachers did suggest that some set of shared purposes or values brought order to their combined efforts, they attributed it to the presence of particular colleagues rather than any larger meaning conveyed by the school organization. Such teachers cared about their students and about each other. Gary Stein said,

> I think the only theme you could even pull out as a unifying thing is caring for kids. I think that everyone who works here does care for the kids, at least at a reasonable level, some more than others.

Another teacher explained, "I think that what holds us together is that we know what's right; we know what needs to be done; and we're not there for ourselves. We're there for the kids." Richard Sand voiced similar views: "I think there's a sense that we have to work for these kids. That's why we're here. We have to work with them. We know what's right."

Others spoke of personal bonds of friendship. One described "our camaraderie, our feeling of friendship and sharing," while another said that she had "very close friends here" whose values coincided with her own.

Thus, when public-school teachers found an answer to this question, they most often spoke of the aggregate efforts of good people doing their best to do good work. But it was also clear that groups of good people happening to be in the same school was largely fortuitous. Moreover, the bonds that did exist among them were often loose and temporary. As one teacher explained,

> Everybody supports each other. We all have something in common. I'm not sure what we have in common, because once we leave, we go our separate ways. . . . I think we're all just thrown together and then come out being like each other in a way.

Unlike their public-school counterparts, the private-school teachers answered this question handily, describing an array of goals, values, historical events, and traditions that provided a meaningful context for their work. In private schools, unifying bonds were more enduring and less dependent on accidental circumstances. An elementary-school teacher observed, "I'm sure everybody thinks their school is special, but I particularly feel something very strong here. And it's part of the community of the school." A teacher in an alternative high school described how her school fueled personal commitment: "It's the kind of place that once you start, you just don't want to quit. It's like a family in a way."

Not all private-school teachers commended their schools for the strength of their cultures. One junior-high-school teacher said:

> Probably the worst thing that compromises my teaching is when things aren't clear, when there's no apparent philosophy guiding decisions. That is the bane of this school.

He was distressed by the school's reluctance to confront moral issues, a

> kind of lackadaisical attitude toward taking moral stands. . . . We don't ever say to a kid, "No, you can't do that. That's wrong," in the same way that we don't celebrate what's right.

Similarly, an elementary-level teacher in an elite independent school observed that, although values and traditions had been prominent in the last two schools where she had worked, her current school had not "pull[ed] together a basic philosophy. . . . Our school does not really have it."

Nor did private school teachers always approve of the values and purposes that guided their schools. One described a "kind of obsession with winning" that left students "not able to tolerate losing very well." Moreover, she said that the "dearth" of minority students in her school "exacerbate[d] the feeling on the part of the students that they are a select few, that there is an elite core of people entitled to the perks of that sort of education." In these teachers' views, private schools did not always make the most of the symbolic bonds available to them, nor were their schools' values and purposes always constructive. However, private-school teachers widely believed that their schools could achieve direction and unity. Closer analysis of these cultural bonds suggests how powerful they can be.

Private Schools' Goals

With very few exceptions, teachers in private schools could identify their schools' central goals. Most independent schools were committed first to achieving academic excellence. A high-school teacher in a very selective independent school observed that the students had "enormous talents. . . . We take that talent and transfer it into an academic setting." A junior-high-school teacher in an urban Seventh-Day Adventist school said that she and her colleagues have "striven for academic excellence." Sometimes, the students were very able; other times they were not. A Catholic high-school teacher observed, "A lot of low achievers really excel in this school." Many such schools concentrated on preparing students for admission to selective secondary schools or colleges; one high-school teacher said, "A big concern of ours is to get kids prepared for college."

Often achieving academic excellence was coupled with developing positive values among students. A kindergarten teacher in a selective independent school said, "We are committed to honor and excellence." Allen Rondo, whose students routinely gain admission to elite colleges, explained, "Our first line is, 'We care most of all about the kind of person a boy is.' "

For teachers in independent schools that featured experiential learning and were guided by the tenets of Progressive Education, goals of personal development and the acquisition of skills for lifelong learning took precedence over more conventional notions of subject mastery and college admission. One teacher in an alternative secondary school explained,

> To educate students to the best of their ability, to respect the individual. These are really old saws that we have in every school. But we really do it. We really try. It's a belief in the youngster, a belief in the best of the youngster.

Other private schools, particularly those that were church-related, joined spiritual and academic goals. An elementary-level teacher in a Waldorf school explained, "We deal with the whole child—the spiritual, physical, and intellectual parts of the child, seeking to reunite these." An elementary-level teacher in an urban Catholic school said, "Basically, we are here to teach the whole child, to teach the child academically, to teach the child spiritually. That is probably the bottom line." For some of those interviewed, religious purposes took precedence. Two Catholic-school teachers offered ready answers when asked about their goals. One said, "To train them in the way of Christ." Another echoed, "To teach as Jesus taught."

These goals, whether they were academic excellence, independent learning, personal or spiritual development, enabled parents to know what they were choosing in a school and helped teachers understand what mattered most in an organization where many demands competed for attention.

Private Schools' Values

Those schools advocating academic excellence and character development often set forth clear expectations about students' personal conduct within that context. A secondary-school teacher, who characterized her faculty as a "very dynamic, goal-oriented, no-nonsense group of people," said that they would not tolerate deviant behavior. She explained, "There's a strict code of discipline pertaining to drugs and alcohol and cheating. . . . There is a very strong notion of what is expected, of how students are supposed to behave, and where the limits are."

Allen Rondo's faculty relied on principles in its effort to develop character among students. The headmaster was said to be reluctant to reduce those principles to "hard and fast rules," but he spoke frequently and fervently about their importance in all facets of students' lives at the school. Rondo said that if he were to meet a student in the hall and ask, "What do we expect first?" that boy would very likely respond, "Consideration and honesty."

Several teachers made it clear that their concerted effort to reinforce such social values was necessary because of their school's emphasis on academic achievement. A middle-school teacher said that his faculty had deliberately introduced moral education in response to the pressures of ambition and exacting standards. Although the students were "incredibly bright," they were also "incredibly competitive" and "sometimes very vicious to each other." The program in moral education was a school-wide endeavor that teachers and administrators had created over several years: "It's implemented into all that we do—teaching, coaching. We spend a lot of time on it."

In alternative schools, values centered on respect for individuals' needs and contributions. One teacher said that hers is a "school that's really committed to looking at the way children learn and designing the education around that, rather than trying to fit children into one specific learning style." She explained that this individualized attention was apparent not only with reference to "the cognitive aspect of the kids' development," but also their emotional, social, and physical development. Another school, avowedly student-centered in its pedagogy, was described as "a humanistic, humanitarian school." A teacher from a third school spoke about the importance of developing close friendships with students so that faculty became "a real important connection and part of their lives."

Shared values also guided the work of teachers in church-related schools. For example, in a Quaker school where all staff decisions were made by consensus, students were taught to be patient, attentive, and respectful of others' opinions. As a result, one teacher said, "Everyone feels heard." Students were expected to include others in their activities and, even on the playground, were not permitted to exclude children from their games. Quakers' beliefs in pacifism were routinely reinforced, with students forbidden to play guns at recess and expected to "settle conflicts in a peaceful way."

Some Catholic schools also deliberately promulgated values of honesty, obedience, and service. Students were frequently involved in social-service projects, sometimes on school time. One teacher arranged with a nursing home for students to visit after school each week and help elderly patients. The teacher explained that this effort gave her "the opportunity to bring the values [she] taught—peace and justice—into the community."

Private Schools' Histories

Private-school teachers often said that their schools' goals and values were historically grounded, and therefore stable and more resistant to shifting values in the society. For example, Allen Rondo's school had always enrolled a diverse student body. The founder had been a champion of "abused people" and "in the struggle between colonists and Indians, he more or less took the side of the Indians." Today, the staff "can go back and say that it was a school where diversity was encouraged and recognized. . . . I think that's a special edge, to have that great history, that great tradition."

Similarly, a teacher from an independent girls' school said that she and her colleagues offered an education that is "a lot more radical than what one would have expected. It is certainly feminist, by and large." These radical, feminist values, muted though they might be by the social prominence of the current students' families, had their roots in history—"coming out of the Progressivism of female education. . . ." Today the school is proud that it always was committed to serious education for women: "It was seen as a real place of academic preparation and not a finishing school. From the very beginning, it was not a finishing school."

Although only a few schools can draw on such long histories, many achieve constancy over time by serving a particular congregation or community. A teacher in a Catholic elementary school observed: "It's got real roots in the community, a spirit in the parish. . . . People want to pass on what they had, hoping that their children will get some of the values that they knew." Similarly, a teacher in a Catholic secondary school said that his was a "family school" where "everybody's sister and brother comes" and parents expect that their children will be taught traditional values.

Private Schools' Rituals and Traditions

Often private schools sustained or revived their histories with rituals and traditions. Several sponsored founder's days, when they recalled and celebrated their origins. Others held regular convocations of the school community to rekindle common commitment to the schools' goals and values. A Quaker school had "meaningful worship" once each week in addition to all-school meetings, which promoted "a real feeling of community, of everybody being together." A Jewish school held a religious service every morning, and a number of Catholic schools sponsored weekly mass. The community of an independent school gathered three times each week for programs, announcements, and celebration.

Private schools sponsored many annual events—fairs, academic competitions, athletic events, musicals, and awards ceremonies—that promoted community and reinforced values. For example, on the day following one teacher's interview, her school was to celebrate Prize Day, when students would be recognized for their athletic achievements. She said that the activities, which began with two bagpipe players marching down a hill to an assembled school community, were "very structured, very nice, and very much a tradition." Private-school teachers explained that such rituals and traditions, whether frivolous or solemn, drew students and teachers together and directly or indirectly promoted commitment to the central purposes and values of their schools.

Public Schools' Goals

Where private-school teachers could easily list their schools' goals—academic excellence, character development, individualized learning, spiritual growth—public-school teachers seemed at a loss. They often spoke enthusiastically about their personal goals for students, but they had little to say about corporate goals.[4]

In suburban middle-class districts, school goals seemed to be understood to be the aggregate expectations of the local community. Teachers were expected to successfully move students on to college and a standard of living that was at least as good as their parents'. A middle-school teacher said that the prominent goals in her school were "very middle America—every child should go to college—great expectations." Similarly, teachers said that schools in working-class or lower-class communities were devoted to improving or maintaining the lot of their students. In order to satisfy the community expectation that students achieve more productive work lives and more secure economic futures, the content of schooling sometimes became less important than its completion. One teacher in a working-class high school expressed his frustration with the discrepancy between his goals and those of school officials:

> The problem is this. My goal is education. The school's goal is diplomacy. What can we do to get her graduated? Not even to see that she graduates—to get her graduated. . . . That sort of thing is anathema to me, not so much because it compromises my values, but because I see it killing a small society immediately and a larger society eventually.

For many, the schools became instruments by which to achieve economic or social success rather than organizations to be valued in their own right.

In searching to identify their schools' goals, some public-school teachers referred to the written philosophies that staff had prepared for teams of external evaluators. Although they recalled having spent many hours debating and refining these statements of purpose, no teachers suggested that faculty actually were guided by them. One teacher from an urban high school said that she had believed in the effort at the time that the philosophy was written, but that the words themselves were not enough: "We did try to state certain things. But I think that the reality of this is that there isn't a school philosophy." Similarly, a teacher in a competitive public high school found the school's statement of goals general and uninspiring: "It includes twenty different items. But it's things like 'To provide the student with the best possible background in a variety of subjects. To give every student the ability to read and write at a certain level.'" She said that she could not find guidance for her work in such a statement: "You do the philosophy once every ten years when you're going to be evaluated, and then you put it into the file drawer." Although her school achieved considerable academic success, she expressed concern about its lack of purpose and direction: "We are a ship without a rudder. No one is really sure where we're going, and if we're going somewhere, why we are going there."

The one theme that seemed to unify public-school staffs was caring for children, but as several teachers noted, this concern did not translate easily into specific goals. The notion was that if all staff could share this attitude, then the school would achieve its purposes, but many teachers could not explain what the school as a whole sought to achieve, beyond narrow instructional outcomes.

A number of teachers doubted that their colleagues truly held the goals that they espoused. One urban elementary-school teacher said, "Everyone would profess that they would have the same goals. I'm not sure that I would buy that that is really happening." Similarly an urban secondary-school teacher observed, "They'll talk about it: 'Get the best out of your kids.' But that's really not true. They talk. They talk. They talk. But no one's really doing it."

One elementary-school teacher was optimistic and confident that "people share the same philosophies. . . . It's there, but people aren't aware of it." His personal goal was to serve every child: "I truly believe in my heart that a school should be able to take any child no matter what their home problems are . . . and provide them with a totally safe, separate, and encouraging place." He hoped that, over time, he might bring others to realize that they, too, shared this purpose.

Public Schools' Values

Where private schools openly advocated personal values of honesty, respect for others, diligence, and inquiry, public schools were largely value-neutral.[5] Teachers said that the schools often simply transmitted the varied values of their local, frequently diverse communities. A high-school teacher said that "what we need in ——— High School is 'Masterpiece Theater.' What we have is 'Let's Make a Deal.'" He was distressed that his school refused to address matters of principle, for he saw a close relationship between instructional success and an ethical society:

> When I read of people dumping battery acid in farm fields, I think, "These are the same people who are passed along without having to learn to read." I really believe that. Without having to learn to think.

He recounted an incident in which a politician had "argued the case of a parent whose child was horribly deficient academically" and advocated for her promotion. After the teacher had "provided copious data," explaining why the student had not passed his course, the politician responded: "What the hell difference does it make anyway?" When teachers challenged prevailing local values, they did so as individuals. Because of their political context, schools were careful not to provoke their only constituency.

Since most public schools did not promulgate or uphold explicit values, teachers were left on their own to address moral and ethical concerns. Such efforts were uncertain and sometimes hazardous in institutions that provided little direction or support. One middle-school teacher explained, "There's so much divergence here. There are moralists . . . [and there are those] who couldn't care about morality at all."

Public-School History

The history of most public schools is confined to the construction date chiseled above the door and a trophy case standing in the front hall. Because they are public, these schools can rarely point to being founded with any purpose beyond housing burgeoning student populations.[6] The teachers interviewed knew little about their schools' pasts; only one, who taught in the country's second oldest high school and had participated in a research project to rediscover its special past, spoke about the unifying influence that this history might have for what was otherwise a very disunified faculty.

Not only did schools maintain only tenuous notions of their distant pasts, many also had little sense of recent history. Schools had been closed in response to budget cuts and demographic changes. Demands for staff shifted and court-ordered desegregation required massive reassignments. Faculties in large districts were moved from school to school like temporary help while junior faculty in smaller districts moved from town to town in search of secure employment.

Public schools' ties with their pasts are also disrupted when demographic changes alter the composition of students and staff. One high-school teacher said that he and many of his colleagues had once been students in the same school: "Many, many, many of the teachers were born, brought up, and went to school in ———." However, as residence patterns changed, that continuity changed as well. New teachers were not local residents, and staff could no longer rely on the past to provide direction for the present or hope for the future.[7]

Public Schools' Rituals and Traditions

Most public schools sponsor annual events, but very few celebrate traditions. In order for traditions to have meaning they must be tied to a past, but few public-school communities keep in touch with their past. Schools sponsored assemblies, field trips, and athletic competitions, but teachers said that these were generally disconnected from any explicit goals or values. Many events were explicitly nonacademic, designed as much to provide an escape from learning as to support it.

Teachers searched their memories for events that warranted the label "tradition." One middle-school teacher offered a typically equivocal response:

> Each department has traditions. As for the whole school having a tradition, nothing jumps out at me. But each department has annual events, if you want to call them that, that pull the school together.

When asked whether her school had traditions, another teacher said,

> Not many, not any that I can think of. As a matter of fact, every once in a while, the principal will say something like, "This is a tradition," and usually will get a response of laughter.

Although many teachers said that they enjoyed some of the annual events in their schools, those occasions were not taken very seriously. One said,

> Every year we have this and that. You will have the Turkey Trot and the Christmas assembly program. There's a lot of that because there are a lot of people who have been work-

ing together, working in the community over the years. Each school is its own little world. So they do this and they do that.

Public schools have long relied on the calendar to provide occasions for such events—Christmas, George Washington's Birthday, Valentine's Day. However, several teachers said that increased secular pressures and changes in student populations had moderated the schools' recognition of these holidays, particularly those with religious origins. For example, one teacher said that the traditional Christmas concert had become the Holiday Concert in an effort to explicitly separate church and state. Although faculty acknowledged the legitimacy of this change, "nobody knew exactly what to do."

A recently devised celebration sponsored by several urban schools had begun to attain the status of tradition and was linked to the value of respect for cultural diversity. Several teachers said that their schools sponsored multicultural fairs in recognition of the national and ethnic origins of their students. A middle-school teacher said that the three days before Thanksgiving were used to "celebrate ethnic diversity" and to "develop a sense of cohesiveness." Students wore ethnic clothing, taught and learned ethnic dances, and enjoyed the music and art of various cultures. Whereas some school traditions had been abandoned because they lost meaning for diverse student populations, multicultural events gained meaning and relevance by virtue of that very diversity. However, such events that celebrated individual differences were still too new to rank as traditions.

THE SOURCES OF DIFFERENCE

Why are cultural bonds so prominent in private schools and so lacking in public schools? Why do most private-school teachers respond almost without hesitation when asked to name the central goals of their schools while public school teachers seem perplexed? Why do private-school staff usually articulate their schools' values with confidence while public-school teachers lament the demise of moral and ethical standards in their schools? Why are history and tradition salient in private schools and negligible in public schools?

Private schools are small, voluntary, selective, independent, stable, and relatively homogeneous. By comparison, public schools are generally large organizations embedded in even larger school districts. With the exception of examination high schools or specialized magnet schools, public schools cannot select or reject students. Seldom can parents choose the school most apt to meet their child's needs. Student bodies are likely to be as heterogeneous as the communities that they serve. Moreover, because public school membership changes rapidly, cultural memory is short. No single feature is decisive, but together they create a setting that discourages strong symbolic bonds.

Size

Public-school teachers rarely discussed the effects of school size on the culture of their schools, seeming to accept the inevitability of many classrooms, many teachers, and many students. The average enrollment of public elementary schools in this study was 432; four exceeded 800 students. Middle schools averaged 644 students; again four exceeded 800. Public high schools averaged 1262 students; eight had more than 1500 students. By contrast, independent schools averaged 173 students at the elementary level, 297 students in junior high and middle schools, and 378 students at the high-school level. Church-related schools averaged 319 at the elementary level, 265 in middle schools, and 659 in high schools. Enrollments in church-related elementary schools approached those of public schools, but otherwise the average private school was less than half the size of a public school at the same level.

Private-school teachers believed that small size affected the relationships among teachers and students. One said that her preparatory high school

> likes to have the feeling of unity and a small, close-knit community. It is a small school. There are only three hundred students and fifty faculty members. It prides itself on that smallness and, therefore, its closeness. And you can get very close to the students. The faculty is very approachable. We're very available.

Allen Rondo's independent school had 44 students in the senior class, and, as a result, "We know them well." Janice Gagne said that in her Catholic elementary school of 244 students, "The principal knows every child. Every teacher knows every child," and as a result, "You're responsible for everything you see." Anonymity, often said to be a problem in larger, public schools, was not even a possibility in these small private schools.

Two private-school teachers described how their schools had been affected by growth. One who taught in a Catholic high school observed that family-like traditions nurtured there during the early 1970s were hard to maintain during the 1980s when school size climbed to 950 students. Similarly, a teacher explained that her Jewish day school, which includes both elementary- and junior-high-school grades, had grown and split into two buildings, making it difficult to conserve the school's values: "It's no longer a family. We used to speak of the ——— family, but we have four sections of one grade, multiplied by eight. It's no longer a small family."

When large schools also have large student/teacher ratios, as most public schools do, the problems of anonymity and impersonal relationships increase exponentially. It is much less likely that teachers will have a shared understanding about their school's goals when faculty size exceeds 100 and teachers rarely encounter their colleagues. Furthermore, faculty will not assume the same level of personal responsibility for students in large schools where sheer numbers make knowing every student an impossibility.[8]

Independence

It must be remembered that most private schools operate as autonomous units, while public schools are embedded in educational bureaucracies. A private school, like one in our sample, can focus on a program of moral education without concern for other schools' programs or priorities. Decisions can be made on site by faculty, administrators, and trustees with virtual certainty that they will not be reversed by some distant administrative hierarchy. By contrast, those who work in public schools are always at the mercy of central-office administrators who may prefer standardization and discourage efforts by individual schools to foster unique identities. Moreover, schools that experience a great deal of student transience—in some places, as much as 60 percent annually—are obliged to offer programs that are relatively interchangeable with those of other schools.

Choice and Selectivity

In addition to being small and independent, private schools are both voluntary and selective. Parents choose to enroll their students and schools choose to accept them. As a result, student bodies are similar in background and expectation. By contrast, most students in public schools attend by default rather than choice, and the schools must not only accept all comers but actively work to retain them as members.[9]

Each child in a private school represents a parent or guardian who believes that that child will be better educated there; parents often choose schools explicitly for the values that they represent. Janice Gagne said that parents choose her Catholic school because they seek "a special set of values, traditional values." A teacher in a Jewish school explained that parents enrolled their children because the school was known to inculcate strong interpersonal values:

> They are under the impression that there's not much going on in the teaching of values in the public school. . . . Parents sometimes are not terribly observant with regard to Judaism, and so that certainly wouldn't be the reason to draw them here, but they do know that we pay a great deal of attention

> to values, and by that I mean not just right and wrong, but how you treat the other person, what flies and what doesn't, what's proper, good behavior. And it's everything from meeting your obligations to not teasing your fellow student.

The support and commitment that are expressed by a parent's choice to enroll a student in a private school are further enhanced when that school is selective and membership is seen as a privilege. One teacher in a very selective independent school explained that "the kids who are here are generally happy here and proud to be here. It's tough to get in and . . . we don't have a whole lot of discipline problems." Although independent schools generally were more selective than church-related schools, all private schools could ultimately reject an applicant or expel a student and, consequently, could exert a stronger influence on students' behavior and a firmer hold on their loyalty. As a result of the choice and selection that preceded enrollment, private schools were considerably more homogeneous than public schools, and therefore more inclined to espouse consonant goals and values. The large majority of students in highly selective schools were wealthy, white, and academically able. Some private schools, particularly those that were church-related, purposefully sought to create student communities that were more racially and ethnically diverse. However, because they were self-supporting, these schools could only waive tuition for some students, and minority students usually came from the middle class.

By contrast, several Catholic schools in cities served populations that more closely resembled those of urban public schools. One teacher, who said that her school is "striving to be a Christian community," observed that

> those values are being assailed on all sides, and the children here are from broken homes, beating-up homes and drunken homes. . . . It's not an elitist school. It's kind of a solid, substantial parochial school.

A middle-school teacher in a Seventh-Day Adventist school also described a student population that was considerably more diverse than that of most other private schools. But even it was selective, with more than one-fourth of its graduates moving on to a competitive public high school that required examinations for admission. One high-school teacher explained that the educational goals in her urban Catholic school had changed as the student population had changed. "If you're admitting a different type of student, then, of course the educational goals have to undergo a look-at." Once firmly committed to college preparation, the school now tries to serve students who do not intend to go to college as well as those who do.

Public-school teachers were well aware of the challenges that diverse student populations presented. Many saw heterogeneity as one of their school's strengths, but recognized the difficulties of promoting clear goals and consistent values for so many different students. Although individual neighborhoods might be fairly homogeneous, a school in a desegregated district might draw students from many different neighborhoods. One teacher believed such reassignments promoted competition and hostility among different groups of students, while another argued that they generated apathy: "The students are bussed from all over, and there's no neighborhood feeling, and nobody stays after school for anything." When the school board threatened to close one teacher's high school, there was sentimental talk about "the [school] family. But I don't personally feel it. Amongst the faculty, I feel a lot of disillusionment and low morale. . . . I feel that most of the students are not really involved."

Other communities that had been only moderately heterogeneous confronted new challenges with the arrival of new immigrant populations. A middle-school teacher said that forty years before, his school had been multi-ethnic, but solidly middle class:

> . . . Jewish, Polish, some Italian, hard working, blue collar; nice community. That was forty or fifty years ago. Now the city is fifty percent Hispanic, forty percent white, and ten

> percent Cambodian and Vietnamese. . . . There is not this idea of a close-knit community. There are all sorts of pressures, internal and external on [the city].

In its effort to respond to so many different families and students, the school, he argued, had lost its focus.

These public school teachers did not yearn for the homogeneous student bodies they believed populated private schools. In fact, a number emphasized that they prized the diversity that distinguished their schools. One suburban elementary-school teacher who said that her school had "all races, all religions," called this a "delightful mix." Another proudly called his school a "League of Nations." However, teachers also recognized the difficulty of sustaining common support for any body of core values when their colleagues' goals and their students' and families' experiences varied so widely.

States and local school districts are increasingly enacting policies of choice that would enable parents to select public schools for their children. Minnesota, Iowa, and Arkansas have passed laws giving parents considerable latitude in selecting both districts and schools. Local school districts such as Milwaukee, Boston, and Cambridge, Massachusetts, have instituted controlled-choice plans that offer choice within the guidelines of a desegregation plan. It is not yet clear either how many parents will choose to educate their children outside their local communities, or whether school-choice plans will increase or diminish the gap between poor and wealthy students' performance in education. It does seem possible, however, that they will permit school communities to forge clearer understandings about their purposes.

Stability and Continuity

Although private school faculty did not enjoy the guarantee of tenure, few experienced rapid turnover.[10] Once novice teachers had been reappointed two or three times, they could consider their jobs to be secure. Since the majority of private-school teachers had made the choice to work at a particular school, they, too, could be expected to perpetuate the culture of that school.

By contrast, many public schools—particularly those in urban areas—were marked by instability, uncertainty, and transiency. These schools were built in response to growing student populations and are closed when populations decline. Because any particular public school is but a component of a larger system, there is no guarantee of constancy. Students and teachers may be reassigned; buildings may be closed; schools may cease to exist or merge with others, losing their names and the threads of their pasts. A number of teachers in urban, small city, and suburban school districts described the effects of this instability.

Anna Capello said that with declining enrollments, "the fate of our school has been kind of dangling the last couple of years. As a consequence, morale is low." Two urban elementary-school teachers described the demoralizing effects of staff layoffs. One, who taught in a magnet school, said that the teachers had once been unified, but with "layoffs back a few years ago, we lost it all." Another said layoffs had decimated her school's staff: "Up until desegregation, we were a totally stable faculty. . . . The school was a totally different school for half of its years, than it is now." Staffing formulas and layoff and transfer provisions based on seniority operated without regard for the value or constancy of school community. This teacher argued that a school could not be expected to maintain clear and consistent goals without a stable and continuous staff: "Faculties grow together when they've been together for a long time." A teacher in a school that housed a number of recently transferred staff concurred:

> A lot of them transferred here without wanting to be transferred. A lot of them were kind of dragged here. They come, leaving their old schools behind them, and their friends behind them. It hasn't really clicked yet.

Although many teachers noted that instability and disruption make it difficult for schools to promote sustained commitment, understandings, and expectations, several teachers observed that stability, in itself, offers no certainty of excellence. In some cases, it promotes complacency, as large groups of senior, tenured staff reassure themselves that there are no better answers than the ones they already have.

THE IMPLICATIONS FOR LEADERSHIP

What do these differences between rule-bound and culture-bound schools imply for the work of school administrators? Do those who work in schools with strong cultures approach their work differently? The teachers we interviewed suggest that they do. It would be simplistic to say that heads of private schools can be leaders while principals of public schools must be managers, but it did seem that public-school administrators were more encumbered by procedures and responsibilities to the larger district and less supported by school cultures than were their counterparts in private schools.

Independent-school heads are often thought to be of heroic proportions, but, in these interviews with private-school teachers, we found only two examples of strong, symbolic leaders who closely tended values, nurtured traditions, inspired staff and students, and personally embodied the high standards that the school espoused. Allen Rondo said that the clear sense of purpose in his school "starts with the headmaster." He described how this headmaster publicly addressed values:

> We're a nondenominational school, so he doesn't speak religion, he speaks principles. He will give a speech before midyear exams, and again at the end, talking about the temptations to cheat. No grade, no test is worth sacrificing a reputation. We can get the whole school together sitting in those chairs at one time, and he makes use of that to reinforce these types of things, I think, quite effectively.

Another independent-school teacher observed that such revered, symbolic leaders were no longer common, even in independent schools:

> Up at Deerfield, it was Cappy Boyden, and at Exeter, it was Saltonstall. At Groton, it was Peabody, and these men were giants, in the sense that they had a vision of what they wanted their school to be, and they set about to instill that vision in others. Now the headmasters in the schools have a different character.

Private-school principals and heads could seldom wield the unchallenged authority that had permitted heroic leadership in the past, but they could still rely on strong school cultures to unify their school communities and carry on a shared sense of purpose. This same teacher said that his current headmaster

> is a person who has his vision, and his vision exudes a kind of a fairness and a balance. . . . He is also concerned about the issue of minorities and the introduction of an increased representation of minorities in the school. . . . The fact that he, himself, was concerned about those issues—I don't like to use the word "force"—but he guides the school in those directions. . . . He's a guide for us to follow.

The middle school that developed a schoolwide program in moral development did so in response to "the beliefs of the headmaster who spent a long time thinking about it. . . ." In schools such as these, administrators need not depend on close oversight or formal policies to direct teachers' work. Rather, a skillful leader might reinforce others' commitment to the school and its culture by making pronouncements about what the school stands for and reminding staff of the meaning their work has for the larger school community.[11] Teachers expected private-school administrators to take advantage of this opportunity and sometimes criticized them when they did not. One high-school teacher observed, "The headmaster doesn't have a lot of direction, in my estimation. To me, he doesn't have a lot of sense of what the school should be.''

When public-school teachers described administrators, it was usually with reference to their formal authority and the rational structures that surrounded them rather than their roles as leaders. Often teachers spoke with admiration. A junior-high-school teacher praised her principal for his managerial strengths: ''In fourteen years, this is the only principal whom I've worked for that I think runs the building better than I could run it.'' A middle-school teacher described her principal's clear expectations and skill in dealing with the school bureaucracy:

> She doesn't waste words. She'll let you know right up front what's expected of you, what she expects you to do within your job limitations. If you have any problems, contact her. She'll get you through to the union if you can't settle it here. She'll go to the supervisor. If not, she'll go right over them to the superintendent or the school committee.

A suburban elementary-school teacher described her principal as ''very much the head of this school, the head of people's thinking,'' but acknowledged that the principal's efforts to inspire staff and students were decidedly authoritarian and sometimes failed:

> She expects a lot from us. She very often will have something inspiring written on the daily bulletin. Every morning over the intercom she will read the children stories, and she often has something inspiring to say. Frankly, not everyone is impressed by this, as you can imagine. . . . It's very, very rigid sometimes, and sometimes you feel that it's a little military.

An urban middle-school teacher who was dissatisfied with her principal's approach to leadership complained that he only ''tells us what we have to do.'' She, like a number of other teachers in our sample, accepted directives from administrators, but relied on fellow teachers and department heads for what inspiration or sense of purpose they found.

Several public-school teachers said that their principals "set the tone" for the school by establishing clear standards for student discipline and high expectations for staff. Although the phrase, "set the tone," might imply a symbolic approach to leadership, the teachers clearly meant something different. Administrators who successfully "set the tone" were said to be visible and demanding, personally enforcing the school's standards. One urban middle-school teacher explained how her principal made good teaching possible:

> The tone he sets in the building has so much to do with how difficult or how easy your job is. [He sets that tone] just by being there, by saying, "Here's the line, cross over the line, and that's it. We will deal with you." . . . The principal is setting the tone by making sure everybody is doing what they are supposed to be doing, including the children. He's very visible; he's constantly in the halls. He's probably worn out about six pairs of shoes already this year.

Several public-school principals were said to be virtually omnipresent in their schools, reminding others of their own responsibilities. An elementary-school teacher in an urban school also praised her principal's direct and pervasive influence, but observed that the school does not function well without him:

> You can tell when he's not here. If he's ever out, you smell it in the air. You feel it. . . . It's scary because it shows that he has assumed all the responsibility for the place. When he is not around, people goof off a lot. A lot goes on.

Some teachers praised principals for facilitating their teaching by making the school bureaucracy work on their behalf and by assuring them discretion in their classrooms. Other teachers lauded principals who chose not to exercise their formal authority in ways that might restrict teachers' initiative. One middle-school teacher said that as long as "things are reasonable," her principal "seldom pulls rank to say, 'This is how you're going to do it.' " Another middle-school teacher said that her principal exerted leadership indirectly: "He's not very dynamic, but just by letting us function, I think he exhibits some leadership." Principals were praised not for providing inspiration, but for ensuring that staff were not encumbered by the rules and constraints that might have been imposed.

Often public-school administrators are characterized as narrow-minded bureaucrats, intent on managing their buildings rather than leading their school communities. The teachers suggested that such can be the case, but that it may result more from the features of public schools that limit the development of cultural bonds and discourage symbolic leadership than it does from the character of the individuals who fill the positions. Large schools dependent on a public bureaucracy cannot be intimate settings where school leaders inspire others with visions of what a school might become. Diverse student bodies and staffs generate disparate goals and purposes, and the school that seeks to serve them all may eventually assume a neutral stance toward values. Hazy histories and manufactured traditions do little to sustain schools that regularly endure uncertainty about staff transfers and layoffs or threats of closure by a vote of a distant school board.

Edgar Schein has argued that "*the only thing of real importance that leaders do is to create and manage culture,*" (Schein's italics).[12] Public-school principals who work to create and manage school culture suffer severe constraints. Some public-school leaders search for statements of purpose and value to unify their schools, but given demographic changes and the demands that society has placed on public schooling those are difficult to compose. Slogans such as "All Kids Can Learn," "Differences Matter," and "Diversity Is Strength" point to both the opportunities and the difficulties of sustaining commitment and strengthening school communities.

Many people look to principals to resolve the problems of the public schools, hoping that these school leaders will provide unity, direction, and commitment for students and staff alike.

But such expectations may be unrealistic given the weak support for cultural bonds in school organizations themselves.

IMPLICATIONS FOR TEACHING AND LEARNING

An intriguing puzzle for school watchers is why private schools continue to attract well-educated, highly motivated staff when pay is low and job security uncertain. Explanations include prestige, the quality of students, and the more comfortable settings of many private schools, but the findings of this study suggest that a large factor is the sense of identity, belonging, and ownership that teachers experience in a school that has focused purposes, explicit values, rich histories, and compelling traditions. Most public-school teachers must sustain their commitment to their profession on their own, with little support from their school organizations, even while the rule-bound school organization assaults productive relationships among students and staff by requiring order, compliance, and accountability.

Anthony S. Bryk and Mary Erina Driscoll, who studied data on 357 schools, found that schools with communal organizations provided "substantial psychic rewards" for the adults who worked there. Teachers reported greater satisfaction and higher morale and had lower rates of absenteeism. Students, too, did better in such settings, having lower drop-out rates, fewer problems with classroom disorder, greater interest in schooling, and greater gains in mathematics achievement from sophomore to senior year.[13]

Public-school teachers in this study routinely described themselves as struggling with a mechanized system that had been designed to coordinate and control their work. They praised school administrators who buffered them from the constraints of the system and enabled them to enlarge their roles as teachers, but made clear that freedom from external constraints was not the same as participating in an organization that gave meaning and direction to their work. There may well be a significant number of public-school teachers who require direction by rules and formal procedures to do good work. However, for these respondents, whose work has been judged to be "very good," such external controls were often problematic and interfered with their best efforts. These valued teachers preferred work settings that were unified by cultural rather than rational bonds, that treated them as central to the future of their schools rather than as replaceable parts to be sent from the central office.

Our interviews suggest that public schools would be well advised to promote stronger symbolic bonds and support more symbolic leadership. Even under the best of circumstances, it will be difficult to serve the diverse student populations of the public schools. That the task is difficult does not mean that it is not worth doing. But when the organization and management of public schools add to the task by insisting on large schools, by centralizing management, by frequently transferring staff, and by arbitrarily terminating programs, one wonders whether anyone really expects teachers to succeed in their work. This does not mean, as some argue, that the public schools would be fundamentally improved by privatization, for there is no guarantee that all students would be well served under such a system. But, if public schools are to succeed in meeting the needs of their students and communities, they must be given the best possible opportunity to do so. The experiences of private schools suggest changes in public education that deserve attention and support.[14]

First, as many have argued, schools must be smaller. Staff cannot become sufficiently well acquainted with each other, let alone their many students, in organizations too large for regular deliberation about the schools' purposes.

Second, schools must have the greatest amount of independence possible, given the minimal, but necessary, constraints of formal district structures. Decentralized decision making and school-site management deserve support not only because they enlarge participation in school governance, but because they support the possibility of building and sustaining unique school cultures.

Third, school officials must become sensitive to the need of individual schools for stability and continuity. Teachers and students are more likely to invest meaning in their schools when they believe that those schools will endure. Where school life is not grounded in rich history, it can at least have the prospect of a secure future. Too often, teachers live from year to year, uncertain whether their jobs will be available the following September. With the support of union leaders, some large urban districts have begun to restrict individual teachers' transfer rights in the interests of minimizing disruption to school faculties; these efforts deserve support. If staff cannot believe in a future, they cannot be expected to contribute to it.

Fourth, schools should be encouraged to develop a clear set of purposes and affirm an accompanying set of core values that distinguish them. Magnet schools have provided the opportunity for school staffs to develop unique identities, often with impressive results.[15] However, some districts' experiences with magnet schools have demonstrated that internal bonds do not automatically develop once a school has been labeled different and special. The Aeronautics High School does not generate a set of meaningful purposes and unifying values by virtue of new hardware and a flashy name. Teachers must be encouraged to jointly develop such organizational identities over time in response to students' needs, and they must be granted administrative patience and financial support to do so.

The mission of the public schools must not be undermined in the process of developing symbolic bonds. Public schools will lose their one clear purpose—to educate all—if they mimic private education and focus their energies on designing and supporting exclusive school communities.[16] *All* students, not only the able and well behaved who have enterprising parents, must find a meaningful place in school. However, the inclusive principles of public education need not preclude creating small, locally governed schools and programs with individual purposes and values, where teachers want to teach and students want to learn.

CHAPTER NINE

Investing in Teachers' Growth

Schools are in the business of promoting students' learning and growth. With an array of academic and vocational programs, tests, grades, and diplomas, they set goals and define routes by which to reach them. Progressive steps to mastery are identified with the completion of units and courses, the achievements marked by awards and formal ceremonies.

Ironically, public schools are not in the business of promoting teachers' learning and growth. For teachers, learning and growth are personal rather than institutional responsibilities, occurring largely at the margins of their work. Although most school districts sponsor in-service training for their staff, the teachers in this study generally considered the programs superficial and irrelevant. Evaluation and supervision practices, which consume enormous amounts of administrative time and energy and which advocates believe improve instruction, were said by the teachers to have virtually no effect on their classroom practices. Those who chose to train prospective or novice teachers as part of their own professional development did so independently, without compensation or institutional support from the school. Career development, like learning, was a personal matter. Teachers who sought to fashion a career our of their teaching experience had to set their own goals and celebrate their own progress, for there were virtually no milestones set out by the school along the way. One veteran suburban high-school teacher explained that teachers' learning, growth, and career development are personal rather than organizational concerns: "We have grown all by ourselves in management skills, in curriculum skills, by hit, miss, trial and error—hard work."

These teachers sought to learn and grow in a variety of ways. They wanted to keep abreast of developments in their fields; an English teacher wanted to learn about deconstructionism; a music teacher longed to study electronic music. Others wanted to know more about how students learn and develop—right-brain and left-brain learning, stages of moral development. Teachers sought out new pedagogies—process writing, computer-based instruction, cooperative learning. They hoped to grow through opportunities for increased influence and responsibility. One veteran teacher explained, "I think that the key to my wanting to stay here for a while is that glimmer of hope that I can grow as an individual and a professional."

Given these teachers' interest in learning and growth, why are schools not better organized to promote it? Why do the structured opportunities that do exist—in-service training, supervision and evaluation, increased compensation for advanced course work—miss the mark by so much? The teachers offered several explanations. First, administrators rather than teachers shape the opportunities for learning and growth that do exist in most schools. Since those administrators are usually removed from teaching and must typically offer programs that apply to all staff, in-service training tends to be generic in character and, thus, disconnected from teachers' real concerns. Second, policies that regulate supervision and evaluation are formulated to ensure procedural correctness rather than personal or professional development. Evaluators often lack teaching expertise in the actual subjects that they supervise, and therefore, can assess competence only broadly and offer only general rather than subject-specific advice. Evaluation is designed to ensure minimal standards rather than to promote continuous improvement. Third, financial constraints force teachers' learning and growth to the perimeter of their workday. Given scarce funds, school officials often narrowly define efficiency and productivity, scheduling teachers' time for teaching rather than learning.

It is revealing to compare teachers' scarce opportunities to remain current in their fields with those of other professionals. For doctors, lawyers, psychologists, and business people, continuing training and independent study are central features of their work. They routinely attend conferences, meet with consultants, and jointly review their professional problems and progress. Nor are they expected to do so on their own time or at their own expense, for such learning is financed indirectly by their patients, clients, and customers who value their skilled services. While other professionals combine practice with training, schedule time for reading, attend workshops in their specialties, and benefit from the supervision of experts, teachers teach on, hoping that the next school vacation will bring enough time to read Auden's poetry or to find out more about perestroika.

Teachers themselves bear some responsibility for their schools' failure to address their learning needs. They express little sense of entitlement about their right to grow on the job or their employer's obligation to provide continuing training. They seldom contend that they, rather than administrators, should design in-service training, and they remain largely passive participants in the endeavor. Moreover, strong norms of equity among teachers discourage even valued teachers from contributing their expertise and acquired wisdom in training their peers.

Good teaching depends on good learning. If teaching were simply a rote act that could be carried out by faithfully complying with the prescriptions of textbooks and handbooks, there might be little need for intellectual renewal. But good teaching is a creative process, demanding the constant injection of new information, new perspectives, and new psychic energy. Over time, teachers who lack opportunities for learning and growth become intellectually depleted, their classes intellectually barren. They eventually find that they have given out far more than they have taken in; as they lose their reservoir of provocative insights, puzzles, facts, and stories, their work becomes increasingly routine and pedestrian. Teachers were recommended for this study because they continued to be good teachers, valued for their commitment and contribution to the schools. One of the notable features of this group was the extent to which they were self-sufficient learners, relying little on the school organization to meet their needs for intellectual growth and development. They carried on alone. However, their accounts reveal the many ways in which schools neglect teachers' learning and undermine their professional development. They suggest how much more teachers might contribute to schools if learning were considered part of their job.

REFLECTING ON PERSONAL PRACTICE

As a group, these teachers looked to their own experience for new understandings about how to teach. Although they might not have been familiar with Donald Schön's terminology, they functioned as "reflective practitioners,"[1] relying largely on their own judgments about how well they were doing and how they might do better. They experimented with new materials and methods and then adapted their practices in response. They perfected favorite lessons and generated new ones. They studied their students for evidence of why they succeeded or failed. These teachers learned through teaching. As one respondent explained, "Experience is the greatest teacher," and another observed, "Every year I teach, I feel like I've learned something."

Often this self-reliance was a response to institutional neglect. Gary Stein, who planned to leave teaching for administration, complained that his school district disregarded teachers' learning needs:

> I'm learning my best stuff from just being in the classroom, just living through it and figuring out how I'm going to do it differently when I leave here, and hoping I can accomplish what I want.

Although it is clear that these teachers profited from independently improving their practice, it also seems likely that isolation limited their growth. For the reasons discussed at length in chapter 6, teachers rarely observed their colleagues or jointly examined their teaching. One urban elementary-school teacher acknowledged,

> It's true that you can get stagnant. I do the same lessons each year. They might be a little bit different, but they are to a different group of children. I would love to see somebody else teach. I would love to be able to go to a different system and see what's done and walk around. . . . I'm tired of seeing the same things. I would love to have the opportunity to go and observe and pick up something new.

However, regular class visits and sustained review of practice are very rare, and most teachers are limited by the boundaries of their own insight.

INSTITUTIONALIZED LEARNING OPPORTUNITIES

Virtually all public-school districts offer three structured learning opportunities that might be expected to supplement teachers' reflection on practice—in-service training, course work tied to raises, and formal supervision and evaluation. As the following discussion demonstrates, however, these valued teachers do not believe that any of these promotes their learning and growth.

In-service Training

In-service training typically occurs intermittently on early-release days throughout the school year. Although one school district set aside two hours twice a week for elementary-level teachers' staff development, most designated no more than two hours each month. Respondents observed that such infrequent injections of training could scarcely be considered worthwhile.

An elementary-school teacher explained that in her district "workshop days" occur "once a month, but not in February. So, it's less than six times a year—an hour and a half." Gary Stein made a similar calculation: "We have probably nine scheduled workshops during the year where the children are dismissed at twelve o'clock. Then we have from twelve-thirty until three." Even these opportunities occurred only "on paper" because four of these sessions were preempted for parent conferences and the fifth, in June, for "clean-up day." Because of the need to supervise the children, in-service training was invariably scheduled at the end of the school day, when teachers are least able to think clearly and contribute freely. Richard Sand complained:

> They try to run some afternoon in-service. Forget it! You can't even see straight at that point. I can go home and chop a cord of wood, but don't ask me to sit down and work on curriculum at that time of day. My mind is just completely mush.

For the large majority of teachers in this study, in-service training occurred fewer than eight times each year, lasted less than two hours each session, and was scheduled at the end of the teaching day.

In the array of sessions presented by their districts, teachers rarely discerned any systematic plan for professional development. More often they described a haphazard sequence of speeches and workshops addressing unrelated topics. Criticizing the lack of logic in such programs, a suburban English teacher said, "They get taken up by . . . whatever." Teachers' assessments of in-service training ranged from condemnation to modest praise. One elementary-school teacher explained that at the previous week's staff development session, teachers were instructed in the use of a teacher's manual. Reading scores in the district had been low.

> So one way they thought of handling the situation was to bring out a person from the book company to explain a new series. All she did was to go through the teacher's manual. It was really an insult.

Most respondents who did not dismiss in-service training out of hand offered but faint praise. An elementary-school teacher concluded, "They aren't that bad."

In the few instances where in-service sessions focused closely and systematically on pedagogy, teachers voiced appreciation. In each case, consultants had presented a series of workshops over several months. A veteran physics teacher who had volunteered to attend twelve sessions on skilled teaching praised the program:

> That was very valuable. It gave you a way of seeing whether you were in a rut. It introduced a few new ideas of things that you might try, looking at it all from a slightly different perspective, pulling back and getting an overview. That was good. I don't think it makes a teacher of you, but people who are decent teachers pick up on all of that.

An urban social studies teacher had volunteered to participate in a series of sessions on cognitive learning styles and looked forward to training colleagues in the material the next year. An urban English teacher praised his district for offering an eight-part series on computers, taught by instructors from a local university: "I think it's been great."

Remarkably few sessions addressed teachers' concerns about their teaching. Many dealt with what respondents regarded as administrative matters—testing procedures, special education referrals, approaches to discipline, preparation for ten-year evaluations. Those sessions that were concerned with students typically focused on their social rather than their intellectual needs. An urban chemistry teacher noted, "We've had in-service training in drugs, in suicide. The sessions are pretty much about the students rather than teaching." A suburban physics teacher observed, "There's very little that applies to science teaching." A middle-school history teacher who had recently attended a session on critical thinking found nothing that she could take from the workshop to apply in her classroom:

> You do know that there is such an animal as critical thinking. And you do know that this guy was very, very quick in putting paper up on a poster board. But, beyond that, what can you do with it?

She argued that in-service training fails to address teachers' subject matter concerns because the sessions must be acceptable to a wide variety of staff:

> They're operating at a very, very general level, and so they have to bring in the presenters who are going to hit on the least common denominator. Usually what happens is very, very unsatisfying. . . . It has to be general. The more general it is, the more useless it really is.

Teachers argued that in-service training failed to meet their needs not only because it was intermittent, poorly organized, and superficial or tangential, but also because it was organized by administrators and tolerated passively by teachers. In the language of teachers and administrators, the word "in-service" has become a transitive verb with teachers as its object. Teachers are "in-serviced" in suicide prevention, race relations, and critical thinking. Administrators decide what should be taught and require of teachers only their compliant attendance. Teachers described many districtwide workshops where they were no more than reluctant spectators. One teacher who was to attend a session later in the week couldn't recall the scheduled topic if her "life depended on it. . . . All I know is that I have to be in the auditorium at one o'clock. I'm debating whether to bring my knitting, just to make a statement." A suburban middle-school teacher criticized administrators in her district for

> thinking that they have to have a speaker. On occasion, we've had some wonderful people, but very often it's incredibly horrendous, boring, and stupid. We'd love to be able to just be with the departments and get some work done. But they don't consider that to be valuable. You've got to justify it somehow. Early release has to mean something unusual.

A number of teachers admitted that they passively attend the few required sessions and rarely convey their assessments to administrators or suggest alternative approaches. When we asked one suburban high-school teacher if he or his colleagues ever refused to participate, he was puzzled:

> I don't know. It's a funny question. I'm trying to imagine how we would go about it. We're such a docile group that we'd probably hold the discussion because we were told to. But it wouldn't mean anything to anybody. "Okay, can we go now? Give me the time. I want to get out of here."

Sometimes administrators not only arranged the sessions, but presented them as well. One urban elementary-school teacher said that the substance of most in-service sessions at her school was "committee reports. Our principal will stand up there and read superintendent circulars. . . . It's called in-service." A middle-school teacher complained that administrators in her district scheduled in-service meetings so tightly that they did not allow time for discussion of classroom practice, what she called "the nitty gritty goings-on."

By contrast, in a small number of schools, teachers were active in planning and conducting in-service sessions. A suburban elementary-school teacher described an "incredibly successful" professional day:

> The superintendent had a group of teachers who got together, and planned it, and pulled it off. They brought in some absolutely incredible speakers. It was a full day of activity. It was planned from A to Z. It was something we were all very, very proud of.

A suburban elementary-school teacher whose district scheduled a remarkable four hours of released time weekly, described a successful series of workshops on writing. All of the district's second-grade teachers met

> to work and to try out some new materials and literature. There is a meeting where you are presented with the materials. You go back to your classroom, try it, and go back to another meeting to discuss what you liked, what you didn't like, how you could improve them. We would pool activities and ideas from all of us and then it would finally get put into a unit of study that we could use later.

Although many teachers criticized the structure and content of in-service training, few were active in seeking to reform it. It is unclear whether they were reluctant to confront administrators, skeptical that their suggestions would be heard, unwilling to commit the necessary time and effort, or wary that stepping forth as leaders would transgress norms of equity among staff. Several teachers mentioned that they had recommended changes that were ignored by administrators. In another district, where teachers were being encouraged to participate in planning in-service training, a department head observed that few teachers had responded:

> They just instituted an in-service and curriculum day committee, inviting any teachers to join with other people to decide what they would really like to focus that time on. What is interesting is that many people do not come forward to volunteer. But that is an extra meeting. On the one hand, they would really like some more input, but on the other hand, the time commitment for doing that and helping it grow is a different story.

In general, teachers who find that existing in-service training fails to meet their needs would prefer to use the time to work with colleagues or pursue more relevant training on their own rather than organize alternative sessions for others.

Conferences and Workshops

Many of those interviewed explained that, while they found formal in-service training of little use, workshops that they attended outside of school were often very valuable since they could select topics that addressed their areas of interest and choose instructional approaches that gave them hands-on experience. Several attested to such workshops' restorative powers. A high-school teacher called them "rejuvenating activities." An elementary-school teacher explained, "Whenever you have any experience like that, you're just so much better, ready to teach."

Districts offered meager support for teachers' independent learning activities. One bilingual teacher wished that her supervisors "could at least order some professional journals and have them in our hands. Of if they could tell us about some conferences coming up. But they don't." A middle-school teacher said that her English department supervisor distributed a list of workshops, but only permitted one or two teachers to attend, thus putting teachers in competition with peers for the right to improve their practice. By contrast, several teachers told of principals who offered abundant information about workshops as well as continuously encouraging their pursuit of learning opportunities. Teachers were grateful for that support. As one said, "That's his strength because he'll seek you out and encourage you in different opportunities."

Few districts permitted teachers more than two or three days each year to attend conferences and workshops, and sometimes even days that were contractually guaranteed were withheld or granted reluctantly. A teacher who had been encouraged by his principal to take three days to attend a workshop was refused permission by the superintendent because the district had already spent too much on substitutes. This teacher acknowledged the financial constraint, but also queried, "In the meantime, do you want someone who's better skilled?" Another teacher, who reported that she had recently attended an exciting reading conference, said that teachers were not permitted enough time for such endeavors: "We're not allowed to go out of this room as much as we'd like. . . . You can't measure what you learn at these workshops. We're given the opportunity once or twice a year. That really isn't enough." A history teacher in a suburban school described the diminishing support for out-of-school learning in her district:

> I'm going to the social studies conference in March. This will be the first time I'll have to pay for it myself. And I will not be given a professional day. I will be permitted to go, but I'll have to take either a sick-leave day or a personal day. In other words, I lose something by going. But I'll go nevertheless.

By contrast, teachers in several affluent districts said that they had sufficient time to attend training outside school. One explained, "We have professional days where we can ask to go to some workshop or conference. They're very good about trying to get us there." Another reported that he would soon attend a daylong session on tide pools and that he had just returned from another on process writing; he anticipated that each of these would enrich his teaching.

Sabbatical leaves, which once offered paid leave for sustained learning, were eliminated by most districts during the financial hard times of the 1980s. For Gary Stein, this had strongly influenced his recent decision to leave teaching:

> That would have been something they could have dangled in front of my face, that I could have at least had some benefits in staying. But from a financial point of view, if I can't even get some time off . . . to make myself a better teacher, then that's fine.

Even those public-school districts that provided time and encouragement for teachers to pursue professional training, rarely paid their tuition. There was very little money to support course work or workshops. An urban teacher explained, "You have to be able to pay for your own tuition to take courses outside. . . . If you can't manage to pay for it yourself, there is nothing." A suburban physics teacher said that although he once attended conferences, he no longer does: "If somebody else paid, I'd go." An urban elementary-school teacher had not yet pursued an advanced degree because of tuition costs: "I know too many people who are getting their master's and doctorates for free because they're not teachers. I'm waiting for someone to offer me some money."

One teacher said that she had seen information about two conferences that interested her, but each had cost ninety-five dollars. She reflected:

> Now the days are gone when the school system can even make the effort to send everybody to conferences that wants to go. So it seems like every time you want to better yourself, you're paying out of your own pocket, whereas in business, they pay for everything. . . . We're supposed to be so education-minded, and yet, we don't have enough incentive to really broaden ourselves.

Course Work and Salary Scales

Milbrey Wallin McLaughlin and Sylvia Mei-ling Yee distinguish between school organizations that are "investment-centered" and those that are "payoff-centered," contending that the former promote professional development while the latter stifle it.[2] Investment-centered organizations fund workers' training, ideas, study leaves, and research proposals, while payoff-centered organizations compensate workers for degrees earned, discoveries made, or books written. According to the teachers of this study, public schools are decidedly payoff-centered.

Although districts are seldom organized to invest in teachers' training, they are obliged to pay salary raises for those who obtain training on their own. Salary scales in all public-school teachers' contracts include raises for completed graduate work. Such scales encourage many teachers to complete master's degrees, but many of our respondents believed that this advanced study did little to improve their teaching. Teachers often chose courses for their financial rather than their academic payoff. One respondent explained that courses costing 165 dollars at a state college are far more popular among staff than more expensive courses at a more demanding private institution.

A number of teachers found conventional academic course work irrelevant. Richard Sand said that he "stayed away from education courses," choosing instead those "that can be used in the classroom." While preparing an instructional unit on fire safety, he had attended classes taught by fire department personnel. Other teachers expressed interest in course work that was not directly related to their fields of specialty, but that would enrich their teaching. One explained that the salary scale had not provided her with the intended incentives:

> I didn't get my master's until about three years ago because I took all my courses any place I felt like it, anywhere, time, or shape. So I ended up with ninety-seven credits beyond my master's degree. . . . If you go out and get your master's, and then you get your thirty credits, they will pay five hundred dollars per course beyond that. I have yet to see a penny because I've never taken courses that have qualified. It has to be something that directly relates to your field. I took art education, but I don't teach art.

Teachers' perceived needs for income and learning often fail to coincide. As a result, school districts commit considerable funds, both directly through in-service training and indirectly through salary scales rewarding advanced course work, for sessions that teachers routinely regard as mediocre or irrelevant. The two notable exceptions were externally funded programs for academic study. In one, a high-school mathematics teacher received a federal subsidy to attend a summer institute in curriculum development sponsored by a local college:

> They are subsidizing the tuition. They supply the textbooks and they pay us a stipend. So what they are saying is: "We realize that you have to supplement your income with summer work and know that you couldn't come and pay for this. We would rather see you going to school, because it will help us."

Another respondent told of a program that paid science teachers to work in a state university research center during the summer. Such opportunities for paid learning and increased involvement with both specialists and other teachers promoted learning and renewed teachers' commitment to their work.

Learning in Private Schools

Formal opportunities for learning in public schools differ markedly from those reported by teachers in independent schools, where learning was also expected to be an individual matter, dependent on individual initiative, but supported with encouragement and school funds. These schools were, in McLaughlin and Yee's terms, investment-centered. In-service training was far less common in the private than in the public sector, although two teachers did report schoolwide workshops on communication and writing. More common were opportunities for independent learning, often in subject-matter specialties.

Independent-school teachers repeatedly told of attending conferences and workshops at their schools' expense. A high-school teacher said that he and his colleagues are encouraged to attend professional meetings—"There's money available within the department for such a thing. You can get excused very easily to attend anything you feel it is appropriate to attend." Some schools could not afford to subsidize teachers' attendance at conferences, but respondents said that they felt encouraged to attend nonetheless. One elementary teacher explained:

> If I want to go to a conference . . . they really try very hard to send us, and I get a feeling that that's a reward. I've never been turned down and that's a nice feeling.

For most independent-school teachers, summer was understood to be a time for learning and personal restoration, and their schools frequently subsidized both. An elementary-school teacher said that she had attended weeklong workshops during each of the previous three summers. A high-school teacher said that her school had supported her summer study and travel for three years by supplementing a National Endowment for the Humanities study grant for one year, paying her to prepare a course during the second, and covering her travel costs to study in France during a third. At the time of the interview, she was planning another summer in France where she would work as an investigative reporter. The school was to pay 750 dollars toward that trip—"They can't pay the whole way, but they encourage us to the hilt." She said that these opportunities revitalized her: "It's a time for self-renewal. It's important so that I have the drive to start again in September."

Virtually all independent schools paid for part or all of teachers' graduate study. Several said that their schools covered three-fourths of their tuition. Allen Rondo said that his school had paid the full costs of his master's degree. One middle-school teacher described his school's generous support:

> The school is willing to pay for your graduate work, your summer course studies, and your night courses during the year. For anything under five hundred dollars they definitely pay the whole deal. For anything over five hundred dollars, they definitely pay for eighty percent and sometimes up to one hundred percent. So they want you to develop professionally. You get more points on your salary scale for having received your master's or having received advanced graduate degrees. So there's a lot in there that encourages it.

Most independent-school teachers could also look forward to sabbatical leaves for sustained work or travel. One respondent said that two to three teachers in his school are on leave each year.

Unlike public-school teachers, those from independent schools expressed confidence that their schools were committed to their continued professional growth. By providing ample time for leaves and grants for study and travel, their institutions demonstrated that they valued teachers' independent pursuit of learning. Almost as important as their schools' financial support was the clear message that teachers deserved to learn and grow, and that individuals rather than institutions should decide how best to do that. As Allen Rondo said, "You make your request. You're very much encouraged." Several teachers we interviewed deliberately traded the chance to earn higher salaries in the public sector for the chance to work in an organization that valued adult learning. A high-school teacher explained:

> Most of your independent-school faculty are a self-selected group . . . making this conscious choice: "I am going to go to a place that values what I do, where I can grow, and where I can practice the craft of teaching . . . and I'm willing to be paid less money." . . . That tends to produce a group of people who are very highly devoted professionals.

Teachers in Catholic schools experienced far less support for their learning. Although their schools occasionally paid for workshops and conferences, they seldom offered study leaves and rarely supported graduate tuition. Teachers said they were encouraged to learn new methods and materials, but they described no institutional commitments to ensure that they could do so.

SUPERVISION AND EVALUATION

Within the past decade, public-school districts throughout the country have devoted much money and administrative time to improving the practice of teacher supervision and evaluation. Many states and school districts have adopted policies that formalize a process that was once haphazard or nonexistent. Researchers have documented local evaluation practices judged to be exemplary in promoting high standards and continuous improvement.[3] Consultants thrive on preparing administrators to observe and assess classroom teaching. This fervid activity, fueled, in part, by the research on effective schools, assumes that principals should be instructional leaders, equipped to supervise and improve teaching practice. Also, the past decade of financial constraints and staff cutbacks has eliminated the slack that once allowed schools to hide incompetent teachers and has made it apparent that classroom teaching must be improved. Finally, a number of states have mandated systematic evaluation of teachers' work as part of overall reform programs. Together, these forces have brought unprecedented funding and attention to teacher evaluation.

In practice, the assessment and the improvement of teaching tend to be at odds, the first requiring administrators to make tough, summary judgments and the second calling for them to give teachers sustained support. The prospect of assessment promotes caution among teachers, while improvement depends on their taking risks. The teachers interviewed for this study roundly criticized formal supervision and evaluation practices, observing that they are effective for dismissal but not for improvement, that administrators are rarely prepared to offer genuinely useful advice, and that the procedures invariably take precedence over the content of supervision, virtually never providing an opportunity for learning. Despite the considerable expense of administrative training and time that many local districts now invest in teacher supervision and evaluation, the effects are said to be felt by only a few marginal teachers. Others, particularly the very good teachers included in this study, regard the practice as an institutional obligation to be endured rather than an opportunity to be seized.

When we asked teachers to describe supervision and evaluation practices, they virtually always responded with procedural accounts, describing the frequency, length, format, and criteria used in their districts. Most elementary-school respondents said that they were evaluated by principals who observed and assessed their teaching using standardized forms. A suburban respondent explained:

> Every third year we are evaluated. The principal will come anywhere from three to five formal visits. We have a pre-evaluation meeting where we plan and tell what we are going to do. Then she will come in and observe, take notes. Then we will have a post-evaluation meeting, where we discuss what happened.

A second suburban elementary-school teacher also focused on the process of the experience:

> There's an evaluation instrument. There's one for tenured teachers, and one for nontenured teachers. There are about fifteen different characteristics that we are rated on as being "unacceptable," "acceptable," and "excellent." Then there are some questions where they have to describe our teaching and comment on it, and so forth. And that's it. He has to sign it, and he has to observe our teaching four times in order to do this, and he has to have a conference with us before about it, and a conference after. Those are the rules. It doesn't always work out that way, but those are the rules.

Several teachers described practices requiring them to set goals by which they subsequently would be judged, but most told of standardized criteria. A few received written evaluations that contained only narrative comments, while most received checklists and ratings that labeled their teaching as "excellent," "satisfactory," or "unsatisfactory." Although the criteria used by districts were similar and included such items as "command of subject matter," "classroom management," "responsiveness to individuals," some were vague and left teachers puzzled. One urban middle-school teacher considered many of the "qualities and requirements" by which he was assessed "quite questionable. The one that we haven't been able to figure out at this point is 'demeanor'—'maintains a professional demeanor.' We've never had a definition of it."

These valued teachers widely believed that supervision and evaluation in their schools were intended largely for other, far less competent staff. Gary Stein observed, "Unless there is a yellow flag or a red flag to [attract] the principal's attention, [he] will leave us pretty much to our own devices." One urban high-school teacher, who dismissed the process as "a joke," went on to amend his judgment: "I shouldn't say that, because they did get rid of a science teacher [who] was pretty bad and they put him down in central administration." A suburban middle-school teacher said that, three years before, the district had "let three teachers go, basically for incompetence, because we have an evaluation system. So the pressure now on the evaluators is incredible, to do the process correctly, to assess a teacher's merits and strengths. It's extremely difficult."

During periods of declining enrollment, three school districts had instituted merit-based layoffs, which generated anxiety among staff. A high-school English teacher described the lingering fears in her school:

> Everybody's afraid of [evaluation] because it's what's going to be used to decide whether or not you keep your job. So people become defensive—"What do you mean I didn't look at Johnny and looked at Jane?" People get very neurotic about it because of the fact—and this is one of the things I think is wrong with teaching—that it's the only criterion to be used in deciding whether you're going to leave or stay.

In two instances, evaluation ratings were also used to grant or withhold salary increases and therefore took on extra meaning. A suburban social studies teacher described evaluation as "an economic instrument, more than a pedagogic instrument." He concluded:

> It does nothing, in my experience. No one I know (and I know quite a few teachers) feels that it does anything to influence their ability as a teacher who supplies content, selects methodology, engages kids, evaluates them, and writes something on a report card. Yet it can have economic implications because a bad, poor, negative evaluation could result in the teacher's being denied a step increase.

Most respondents concluded that although supervision and evaluation practices were billed as opportunities for improvement, they failed to serve their advertised purpose. A suburban English teacher said that the process, repeated every two years by state law, is "very elaborate, very specific, and marginally useful." Gary Stein called it a "rote process. It's going on so that we can say we're doing something." An urban high-school teacher summarized the judgments of many:

> It's an absolutely worthless process, in my opinion, and I've said so publicly. . . . Evaluation allegedly is a tool to improve the quality of teaching. That's the avowed aim and goal of the evaluation process. In fact, I've never seen it either function that way or even be used that way. I have seen it used as an obligation: you have to be observed three times during the school year; that's the regulation. I've seen it used to put pressure on certain individuals, to change certain practices. I have seen it used as a method of stroking people.

Those few who valued the process itself generally participated in a system that required them to set their own goals for improvement. One suburban physics teacher said that the formal obligation to set goals gave her "just that little bit of push to take the time to do something new or different that I might not do otherwise." She suggested that she might use the opportunity to devise three new lab experiments but noted, "I can't say that anybody's supporting you; you're doing it yourself." Another teacher said that supervisors had uneven expectations for the goal-setting process:

> The goals come from the individuals, but some department chair people are very, very strict about how teachers set up goals. You'll see a teacher who has ten objectives, and they can be the picky things, like xeroxing. Other department chair people say, "Go ahead. Do what you want. Write them up, and we'll look at them." Then you might only have two or three.

Another teacher explained that because evaluations are used to make summary assessments, staff are unlikely to risk setting goals that might reveal their weaknesses: "So what I will do is take an area of strength and say, 'Well, I'm going to accomplish this, this, and this in my area of strength,' which looks good on paper."

Only 5 of the 75 public-school teachers interviewed praised supervision and evaluation and, in each instance, they attributed its value to particularly able supervisors. One middle-school teacher said that she finds her evaluation "helpful because I have confidence in the professional opinion of my department chairperson." Richard Sand, who contended, "any evaluation system is only as effective as the evaluator and what's done with it," said that his principal

> will give you any support he can. . . . The document is just a piece of paper with certain questions and responses. You can read into them whatever you want. What helps is the fact that he is constantly coming up with suggestions. . . . The procedure is him. It's not the document.

A third respondent characterized his new principal, who had recently been promoted from the classroom, as "a wonderful teacher. . . . She's an expert in language arts and reading. . . . She's very much down to earth and she'll make suggestions if I need it. If she has suggestions, they are probably warranted. She knows what she's talking about."

The overwhelming majority of teachers doubted that their superiors could adequately supervise their work, even after rigorous training in observation and assessment techniques. This situation seemed largely a result of supervisors' distance from classroom teaching. An urban elementary-school teacher explained:

> I personally don't think the principal, whom I have a lot of admiration for in my school, could come into my classroom and do as good a job as I could teaching kids. I just don't think so. And I think it's pretty hard for him to come into the room, sit down, watch me teach, and decide whether I'm doing a good job or not. I think that's difficult for him because I have more experience in the classroom than he ever had. The last time he taught in the classroom full-time, all day, was probably fifteen or twenty years ago.

Another respondent said that her supervisors lacked "self-confidence. . . . They tend to stand back and wait for something that they see as a glaring problem before they step in."

Other supervisors were said to be inexperienced in the particular subjects or grade levels teachers taught. One teacher explained that if she needed help with mathematics, she would request it from the district supervisor of mathematics rather than from the principal who evaluated her. A music teacher complained that she is assessed by an administrator without training or experience in music. An elementary-school teacher who was evaluated by her principal contended: "If I were evaluated by a person whom I knew and admired in my field, who had criticisms, good and bad, I think I could improve. . . . If I had my choice of who would evaluate me, it would be a person in my subject area."

Administrators unfamiliar with the academic territory or uncomfortable advancing their judgments tended to be cursory in their observations and to make superficial comments and infrequent or fleeting visits. A suburban elementary-school teacher said that he had never been "formally evaluated. And I've been here five or six years. I'm sure that they fill out an evaluation form and send it up to the central office." Another said that, although he had been in his school for five years, "my principal has never really seen me teach a lesson. . . . My principal has been up a few times. He stays for a couple minutes. He may come up when we're having recess." An urban junior-high-school teacher said that although she has several formal supervisors, none observes her teaching: "All these people fill out that evaluation form, but nobody is ever in the classroom to watch me teach." An urban English teacher with twenty years of experience reported that she had been evaluated that year for the first time by a new principal: "Prior to this man, my principal never set foot in my room. Never. Yet she would write up a report on me and ask me to sign it. She never left her office to come to the classroom."

Reports of such administrative neglect were in the minority, but by no means exceptional. Many teachers explained that their principals believed that they were doing satisfactory work and therefore shouldn't be bothered. An urban middle-school teacher said:

> I don't see how a person can evaluate you when they've never really observed you teaching a class. See, he assumes that I'm a good teacher, because my class is always quiet. I very rarely bother the office. He doesn't get any complaints from parents about me. So in his mind, he thinks "Oh, she must be doing a good job."

Some teachers were pleased to be left alone, but others were wary of uninformed judgments made about their practice. The elementary-school teacher whose principal had never observed him teaching had only four years of experience and expressed concern about the "myth" that had been created about him.

> One day I'm afraid this myth is going to catch up with me. They're going to find out that I'm not like those things. I don't want to incur the wrath or resentment of people because I haven't lived up to the stories that have been told or the image that has been projected.

For the majority of the teachers, classroom observations occurred regularly, in procedurally correct ways. However, often they said that the administrative effort was perfunctory or that the process took precedence over the content. Several described excessive, impersonal note taking. Others complained of evaluators' feeling obliged to find areas for improvement and picking inconsequential problems. One teacher said that he had been praised for being well organized, but criticized for the format of headings on students' papers. In a few districts, reports that central administrators had established quotas of high ratings undermined teachers' confidence in the process. Several teachers said that the procedural obligations detracted from their learning experience:

> The amount of time spent writing all of this down is tremendous. It's written down; it's typed; it's discussed. And with every teacher in the school, they're spending all of those periods, sitting down talking about an evaluation. You need to have it if you're going to fire someone, if you're going to have merit pay, if you're going to promote people. You need

> those written lines. I understand the need for it, but I don't like it.

Respondents further criticized evaluation practices for being infrequent and ritualistic. A department head said, "It's a very artificial situation, unless it is happening a lot—you know, people in there ten to fifteen times over the course of a year. Then, maybe it's worthwhile. But twice? It's meaningless." One high-school teacher said that he had urged his supervisor to avoid making artificial and formal observations:

> Whenever my administrator has asked, "Can I come in and see you some time?" I've said, "What about now? I'm ready now. I have a class prepared now. My class will begin where the last one left off and will end up with a promise for the next class."

Other teachers, particularly those who were most critical of their supervisors, believed that many teachers conspire to keep the process meaningless by performing their best lessons when they are observed. A middle-school teacher quipped, "It's not even a snapshot. It's more like a staged production."

In general, the valued teachers we interviewed received unqualified praise from their evaluators, which both flattered them and increased their cynicism. For many, laudatory evaluations were welcome rewards in a workplace with scarce recognition. Others said that they would prefer candid and thoughtful appraisals of their work to blanket commendations. One elementary-school teacher explained:

> I would like him to be honest in his evaluation of what I'm doing. I don't want everything glossed over. "She's an excellent teacher." I hate that. I want him to be able to come in and observe and say, "I like what you did here. Here are your strengths." I'd like to be able to trust his opinion of what I do, that this is an area to work on. I would rather have constructive criticism.

A second expressed a similar concern about the futility of the process:

> I am happy with my principal and, obviously, she likes my teaching and . . . she's always given me an excellent rating and has never had complaints. But, unless there are complaints, and, therefore, constructive criticism, then the evaluation is not useful to you.

Again and again, teachers said that they did not believe that current evaluation practices encouraged them to learn or grow. This elementary-school teacher's remarks were typical:

> Anybody, in any role, feels that you should always be getting better. I think I miss that. I generally get an evaluation and it's "Check, check, check—no problem. I don't need to come back to see you"—which is all right, you know. In a way, it's nice, but in a way, I'm left thinking, "I know I could do a lot better. I know there are things out there that I should be doing."

For these very good teachers, schools offered no systematic way to productively review and improve their practice. The process of supervision and evaluation, supposedly meant for all teachers, actually addressed the problems of only the weakest. Evaluators were seldom sufficiently skilled or experienced to offer constructive criticism in subject areas and frequently limited themselves to giving categorical praise. They concentrated on the procedural demands of the process that were subject to legal review in any dismissal case. These consumed enormous amounts of administrative time while diverting administrators' attention from the substance of most teachers' practice.

The experiences of private school teachers again provide an informative contrast. Few of the private schools in this study employed formal evaluation practices resembling those of public schools. Because teachers are rehired on an annual basis and administrative discretion is unconstrained by union contracts or tenure laws, the supervision and evaluation practices that do exist are directed more toward improvement than documenting decisions to rehire or fire. When formal supervision occurred, as it did in approximately half of the private schools studied, the process tended to be more participative, intense, and peer-directed than in the public sector.

Like their counterparts in public schools, the teachers reported infrequent observation. Many teachers in Catholic schools, particularly at the elementary level, said that their principals walked through classrooms often, but seldom conducted any formal assessment. Janice Gagne's experience with a principal who "comes in once a year to sit in the back of the classroom" was unusual. By contrast, administrators in independent schools were said to treat classes as teachers' inviolate private territory. Job decisions in the private sector were reported to be based more on reputation than observed practice, with students' reports and parental satisfaction figuring prominently in administrators' decisions to offer or withhold subsequent contracts or pay increases. One teacher said that her school head seemed to judge her practice by "osmosis." Allen Rondo said that administrators make no regular observations of classroom teaching in his school, but "keep their eyes and ears open" for problems. Two teachers criticized the fact that important employment decisions were based more on hearsay than fact.

Several teachers in independent schools described supervision programs that involved a substantial component of peer review and were intended exclusively for improvement. A high-school teacher who was head of peer evaluations in his school explained that when a teacher was slated for review, a committee would be formed, including the teacher's department head and two colleagues of his or her choosing. After the teacher had completed a written self-assessment and the group had met to review the teacher's goals and concerns, each committee member observed one of that teacher's classes for an entire week. In addition, students completed written evaluations of the teacher's work. Finally, the committee reconvened to review the materials, report on their observations, and discuss opportunities for improvement. Because the process took approximately ten days to complete, only four teachers were reviewed annually and any individual might expect a review only once in eight or ten years. Two teachers praised this process, explaining that they preferred these infrequent, intensive reviews to frequent, but superficial observations. Several respondents from other schools described similar supervisory processes, all of which included peer review and extended classroom observations. Although one school had abandoned its peer review process because of the time required, a teacher there said that staff would like to return to collegial supervision if time permitted.

Virtually all teachers from both the public and private sectors agreed that, if they are to learn and grow in their work, supervision for improved performance should be separated from evaluation decisions that determine salary or job status. When teachers feel threatened, they conceal their fears and their weaknesses, treating classroom observations as occasions for parading their strengths and teaching surefire lessons rather than venturing forth in new ways. Moreover, respondents concurred that their profit from the process of supervision depended on supervisors being both expert in subject matter and proficient in pedagogy; although virtually all administrators can distinguish competent from incompetent teachers, reportedly few could offer useful advice to able teachers. Finally, if observation is to be meaningful, classroom visitations must be extended to permit consideration of a sequence of lessons rather than the display of onetime stellar performances.

TRAINING OTHERS

Many teachers commented that they learn from training others—student teachers, beginning teachers, and peers. Assisting others in the craft of teaching can be an attractive and rewarding experience—unless the surrounding circumstances make it inconvenient or burdensome.

Most of the valued teachers interviewed had supervised student teachers at some time in their careers; they recounted the ways that they learned from the experience. Able novices introduced them to new ideas and subject-matter content. An elementary-school teacher said, "I've had some extremely talented people that I learned an awful lot from. They've given me ideas that have lasted, that I use every year now. They'd come in with ideas and plans. Some people are so good. . . ." Another teacher said that student teachers "bring something into the classroom. They bring their youth and ideas." A third agreed: "It keeps you up on it. They come in and there's always something that you learn that's current." Some teachers found that having a student teacher provided an inducement for them to reflect on their own craft. One explained that the experience offers "a very good way that I can evaluate myself. I can sort of look at myself." She said that she had learned from student teachers by "watching them and having them watch me. . . . To explain why you're doing something, and how you're doing it, and get some feedback from them on that. It's a very good process. It's invigorating."

Despite many respondents' beliefs that supervising student teachers prompted professional development, circumstances often discouraged them from assuming these responsibilities. During the recent years of declining enrollment, teaching aspirants were few, and teachers reported they were rarely assigned able student teachers. Although one teacher said that she had "never had a dud," many reported that the quality of teaching candidates had plummeted. An elementary-school teacher said, "Sometimes I don't feel that they're turning out teachers like they used to." Another preferred not to take on a student teacher because "sometimes you get a blob who just makes it worse for you, because you're having to control his group plus your group." A foreign-language teacher described a student teacher so ill prepared in her subject that she required daily tutoring: "I worked with that student teacher every single day, to reteach material, so that she could go back into the classroom to teach it the next day." A high-school mathematics teacher said that he had sworn off student teachers ten years before when "one apprentice" whom he described as "the most awful person," would "come unprepared, couldn't control kids. It was horrendous." However, recently, as more jobs have become available and more college students aspire to teaching, the quality of applicants in his district has improved.

> All of a sudden this year, we have five new apprentices at our school. They're great, really great, nice young kids. Yesterday, the supervisor said, "Would you take an apprentice?" I said, "Well, last year I would have said absolutely not, but let me think about it."

Respondents also objected to poorly structured relationships between their schools and sponsoring colleges and to disorderly processes of assignment and supervision. Colleges differ in their standards for students, expectations of cooperating teachers, and procedures for maintaining communications. Teachers said that their schools frequently accepted student teachers from several institutions at the same time, without establishing productive working relationships with any of them. The foreign-language teacher who had tutored her charge through student teaching said that the university supervisor "did not show up until the Thursday before the Friday when she left." One elementary-school teacher had coped by becoming "very selective" and working only with students from one particular college where candidates were likely to be committed to teaching and where she had an established relationship with the program supervisor.

With few exceptions, cooperating teachers are not paid for their efforts although the college supervisors are. This lack of compensation figured prominently in two teachers' decisions not to train student teachers. As one explained:

> I have very strong feelings about the system. I know that [student teachers] learn to teach by getting in the classroom and teaching, and that if they can work with a good cooperating teacher, they can learn a lot. But it just sticks in my craw that the cooperating teacher doesn't get any remuner-

> ation for what is the most important component of training a student teacher. I refuse to take another one until I get paid for it. I think that is the most unprofessional thing we do. If someone else is being paid for it, which they are, there is money being spent. If they were becoming teachers gratis, then I'd say, "Sure. I owe it to the profession, and I will assist in that." But the money is being spent and we're getting none of it.

Most respondents earned college course vouchers for their efforts with student teachers, but often these were but token rewards, since teachers either did not want or could not arrange to take the courses that were available.

Some teachers avoided supervising student teachers because of the considerable time it required, time that was always in short supply. Outsiders may think that a student teacher relieves a cooperating teacher of classroom duties and thus makes work easier, but the initial investment by the teacher in observation and assistance is immense. An elementary-school respondent, who had decided that he would not supervise a student teacher because, "I don't have the time. I really don't have the time," described that investment: "It seems nice at the end when they're leaving and they're conducting your class, but an awful lot goes into getting to that point." Another concurred:

> People have to understand that a student teacher is sometimes worse than five students, in that you spend so much time talking to them. It's a tremendous investment of teacher time.

For a few teachers, the issue was less that student teachers demanded extra time than that they displaced them in the classroom. A middle-school teacher said,

> I love student teachers, because they're young, energetic, fresh, unbiased. But the issue is time again. I don't mind doing it, but my classes lose when I'm not with them. That is not saying that I'm anything special. What it says very basi-

> cally is that I know what I'm doing; I know where I'm going. It's difficult to put that on paper and have somebody come in and work with the class the same way that I work, and cover the same areas, the same material in the same ways. I'm very jealous about that. I don't like to give it up.

Therefore, although the majority of public-school respondents believed that supervising student teachers potentially offered opportunities for learning and professional development, only a few believed that the advantages sufficiently outweighed the disadvantages.

Respondents expressed far more ambivalence about training peers. Except in their roles as department heads at the secondary level, they generally had only intermittent opportunities to offer systematic assistance to colleagues. Many of them believed that they had something to offer and could benefit from the expertise of others, but virtually no formal mechanisms existed to make that exchange happen, and strong egalitarian norms discouraged any but the most unassuming assistance.

When asked if she would like to expand her informal role as a mentor in the building, an elementary-school teacher said,

> I would want to if it were a formal arrangement. I feel like I'm on thin ice because it's not a formal arrangement. I cannot justify my going in and telling another teacher how to set things up. I can only suggest. And it's a very thin line you're walking on. It's very possible to have a teacher who has fifteen years of experience, but because of the situation in the building, finds it difficult to adjust, and I'd be asked to go in and offer assistance. It could be construed by that teacher that I was pretending that I was in administration.

Many respondents raised similar concerns. One distinguished between formal supervision and informal assistance: "I don't presume to tell, but if somebody's talking about something, I will interject a good idea. 'Gee I have something that I think you'll like. Let me bring it to you and see what you think.' " Allen Rondo said that he would enjoy the chance to train others, but that he would "rather do it in conversation than by decree. . . . It seems to sound as if you are casting yourself as a great teacher. And that's not it at all. It's really sharing observations." This prohibition against being too confident and forward about one's expertise seemed to be intensified by the presence of seasoned staff who might well have benefited from others' wisdom but seldom asked for help. Notably, several teachers had taken it upon themselves to train their colleagues in computer skills, about which senior teachers were not embarrassed to admit ignorance.

One elementary-school teacher suggested that if teachers are to assume differentiated roles and responsibility for peer supervision, they should be assigned away from their regular schools:

> The problem is that people resent it. It doesn't work well with your peers. My own personal opinion is that almost the best way to do that is to do an exchange with the schools rather than the people you work with in the same building.

One suburban high-school teacher said that she and a colleague had begun to consult with staff in other school districts about process writing and about critical-thinking skills. They had provided a session for teachers in their own school, but found it "the hardest workshop we ever did. . . . It was tough and we didn't get any feedback. We're involving a few more people in the next one so that we aren't perceived as the go-getters and the know-it-alls."

Similar organizational deterrents operated in most Catholic schools, where teachers expressed great reluctance to presume to train others and where the schools themselves did nothing to formally endorse such activity. By contrast, independent schools as well as the Quaker and Waldorf schools in our sample included a variety of roles that legitimized teachers' training, mentoring, and supervising colleagues. One independent-high-school teacher said that she was "the leader of the geography crew." Several elementary-school teachers were head teachers with responsibility for training assistant or apprentice teachers.

Two teachers in one school held endowed chairs, which, as one teacher explained, "Confers upon them a prestige, and puts them in a class that is clearly different from the others." Often senior teachers in independent schools were explicitly designated as mentors for beginning teachers. One explained,

> One of the responsibilities that I have as an older teacher, a more experienced teacher, is to assist an incoming teacher who may be experienced or a complete novice, and to work with them through the year, to be their friend, to answer questions, and to try to anticipate areas where they might need help.

In the Waldorf school, individual teachers were designated as sponsors for less experienced colleagues; in the Quaker school, such sponsors were called "buddies." Unlike public schools, where teachers were cautious about claiming to know too much, independent schools often had both formal and informal systems for identifying skilled teachers and promoting the socialization and supervision of new staff.

CAREER ADVANCEMENT

For teachers, learning and growth is a personal matter. McLaughlin and Yee argue that teachers chart their own careers subjectively rather than institutionally;[4] they advance horizontally, reaching out to new ideas and responsibilities, rather than vertically ascending a pyramid of achievement. Whether teachers have resorted to defining their own personal progress because opportunities for vertical advancement are so scarce or because they simply are uninterested in acquiring greater authority, influence, and recognition remains unclear. Among the teachers in this study, there were both those who would welcome some formal, institutional recognition of their advancement, as well as those who discounted the importance of promotions and increased authority, choosing instead to increase the depth and breadth of their own practice in classrooms.

Without question, opportunities are few for promotion in public teaching. The positions of department head or team leader were the only ones that teachers understood to be potential steps within a teaching career. To become a principal or curriculum supervisor was to leave teaching and join the administrative ranks that many teachers disparaged. A high-school teacher said that when a teacher "leaves the classroom, it is a way to get into public view and to step up. The advancement ladders are not in the academics." Another explained that "in industry, if the individual is creative and puts in a little bit of extra effort, he has the opportunity to advance and become a vice president. There is not that opportunity in teaching." Several respondents observed that good teachers often failed to be promoted to administrative positions, either because they were women or members of minority groups or because they did not have sufficient political connections. An elementary-school teacher who said that there were no women administrators in her district was particularly critical of the promotion process there:

> Last year they had an opportunity to change that, but the best candidate for the job never even got past the first cut. That's what outraged everybody, because it was purely political pull. And it left a bad taste in everybody's mouth. The women teachers hold the educational system together. They're willing to work hard, and if they want anything done and done well, they ask us. But the men get the promotions.

Not all men were successful in their pursuit of promotions to administration. One who had been "frustrated" because he had not been granted an administrative job, acknowledged that he did not know if, in the end, he would have liked the work. He had pursued the opportunity because it seemed to offer the only chance for visible advancement:

> You've got to realize that in education, administration was seen as your reward for good teaching. That's been a traditional concept. So, when you don't achieve that level, there's a certain feeling—"Well, I've failed as a teacher. I'm not a very good teacher because I'm not a housemaster or an assistant housemaster, building principal, director or whatever. That must mean that there's something wrong with my teaching."

Over time, he had come to realize "that's not necessarily true. You can still be a very fine teacher without being an administrator, without being rewarded as an administrator. As education changes, somehow that has to be addressed."

Mobility and advancement, which in other professions are linked to greater authority and visibility, higher wages, and increased status, mean something different in schools. For most teachers, mobility and advancement involve much more modest changes—switching grade levels or teams, chairing committees, becoming a union leader, or developing a new course. For those teachers who chart their careers personally by setting their own challenges for teaching and learning, such limited institutional opportunities are sufficient. They hope that they can continue to grow on the job, a prospect that, unfortunately, they may not realize. But for others who seek both formal verification of their success and who would assume more responsibility or exert wider influence, such changes are insufficient.

IMPROVING THE OPPORTUNITIES FOR LEARNING AND GROWTH IN PUBLIC SCHOOLS

We can draw on these teachers' accounts for recommendations to ensure that public schools attend to the developmental needs of teachers as well as students. Some of the changes that would increase teachers' capacity to do their work well require that school districts allocate new funds, but most simply call for new policies and practices that would reallocate funds or redistribute responsibility.

One productive place to begin is to put teachers in charge of their own learning. These teachers' accounts suggest that if they, rather than administrators, were to design and carry out in-service training, it would be much more decentralized and more responsive to concerns of individuals. It would rely far more on the expertise of in-house staff than visiting experts, and it would replace passive endurance with active participation. Subject matter and how to teach it would be far more central than is currently the case in most schools.

Second, schools and districts should explore shifting from being payoff-centered to becoming investment-centered. Currently, huge sums of money are tied up in standardized salary scales that reward teachers for accumulating credits and degrees.[5] Some of those funds might be productively redirected to support teachers who embark on new learning, whether it be by attending conferences, taking courses, conducting research or developing curriculum. Several teachers in this study had recently received state grants for program development and they welcomed the chance to explore topics of interest. Independent-school teachers were clearly motivated by their schools' commitment to fund summer study, workshop attendance, and graduate tuition, and some were even willing to accept lower wages in exchange for working in an organization that promoted their continued development. Public-school officials in conjunction with teacher union leaders might do well to designate new salary money to subsidize similar opportunities for their staff. Not only would teachers feel greater support and encouragement from their schools, their learning would likely be more productive.

Serious efforts should also be made to redesign student teaching so that exemplary teachers find it a process worth investing in. A few professional development schools have better integrated teacher training with teaching. In one at the Devotion School in Brookline, Massachusetts, interns from a local college work full-time throughout the year with groups of experienced teachers in the third and fourth grades. Team teaching is common, and the novice teachers are well integrated with the regular staff. The presence of the student teachers permits the regular teachers to participate in other activities—curriculum development, research, teacher training—for the equivalent of one day each week.[6] The small number of such experimental projects is likely to expand dramatically with the publication of a final report from the Holmes' Group's project, *Tomorrow's Schools,* a yearlong effort to redesign the relationships between schools and universities, with guidelines for establishing professional development schools.

When teacher preparation is carefully planned to provide beginning teachers access to exemplary practice, when it enriches rather than compromises the quality of classroom teaching and learning, when it provides more opportunities for teachers to participate in projects that will extend their own knowledge and understanding, it will receive the support from veteran teachers that it deserves.

Public schools would also do well to reassess their supervision and evaluation practices. We found virtually no evidence that good teachers profit from the process as it currently stands, with its emphasis on procedural correctness and minimal standards. Two changes seem appropriate. The first would disengage supervision from evaluation, so that those who would use the opportunity to explore new approaches could do so unencumbered by the caution that formal evaluation engenders. Teachers judged to be in need of remedial work could participate in a separate process. Second, teachers should be granted and should assume greater responsibility for supervising their peers. Teachers cannot continue to fault administrators for being ineffectual without agreeing to serve as the experts in their stead. Currently, experienced teachers in Toledo and Cincinnati serve as consulting teachers, supervising and assessing the work of all beginning teachers and others judged to be in need of remediation.[7] Roles that differentiate the teaching staff and permit some to assume responsibility for supervising others will also provide teachers with alternative ways to build their careers.

Finally, these teachers' accounts suggest the wisdom of experimenting with career ladder programs that would permit vertical advancement. Only a few teachers in our sample explicitly regretted the absence of opportunities for advancement, but we spoke only to those who had chosen to stay in the classroom. It seems likely that others who were attracted by opportunities to advance outside the classroom left to become school administrators or to work in other fields. Had opportunities existed, such former teachers might well have been designated master teachers and their expertise tapped to enrich the learning and growth of their colleagues. Currently, public-school teachers can become department heads or team leaders, but independent-school teachers' accounts reveal additional possibilities for elaborating the teacher's role to combine teaching and supervisory responsibilities. Given the chance, teachers not only accept but welcome the variety and opportunities that such roles offer.

Such changes as these would unquestionably require reorganizing the institutional structures and roles of schools and redistributing salaries, rewards, and responsibilities. It remains unclear whether public schools are wastelands of adult learning accidentally or deliberately. One can argue that the current dearth of opportunities for learning and growth is intentional, designed to keep teachers in their place. However, one might also contend that teachers have not sufficiently insisted on increasing opportunities for learning and growth, that they have been silent co-conspirators in most districts' failure to tend to their professional needs. If the current efforts to augment teacher professionalism lead teachers to collectively assume responsibility for their own learning and professional growth, school structures and funds may well fall in line to support their initiatives.

CHAPTER TEN

Putting a Premium on Good Teaching

What makes a person decide to teach? What makes teachers work hard? What encourages their best efforts? Questions about the incentives and rewards of teaching have been at the center of debates about schooling reform since 1984. Reformers argue that the right mix of motivators will attract talented and committed recruits to the profession and ensure the revival of public education. Dispute persists, however, about what motivates teachers and what balance of intrinsic and extrinsic rewards is required.[1]

Workplaces in our society offer a variety of incentives and rewards, ranging from financial security to self-fulfillment. People choose jobs and professions partially for the rewards that various lines of work offer, and their behavior on the job can be influenced by incentives. The incentive system of any workplace is effective to the extent that it engages workers' commitment to achieve the organization's goals: to work, it must offer the rewards that matter most to them.[2]

The attractiveness, and therefore the efficacy, of incentives differs across lines of work and among individuals, but that variation is far from random. Car repair offers the challenge of diagnosing mechanical problems and the pleasure of repairing broken machines. Catering promises the chance for culinary and artistic expression as well as the opportunity to serve and please others. Arbitrage offers entrepreneurial ventures, heady competition, prospects of power, control, and quick wealth. Law attracts individuals who enjoy solving puzzles and problems, who desire professional status, who enjoy the vigors of competition, who value opportunities for financial gain, and who seek to help people or improve society. Different kinds of work offer different mixes of rewards. Extrinsic rewards, such as pay raises or promotions, provide external benefits, while intrinsic rewards, such as intellectual triumph or personal satisfaction, provide psychic payoffs. Work carrying little intrinsic reward must offer extrinsic incentives, while work offering psychic payoffs can rely less on external incentives to promote workers' effort and commitment.[3]

As we saw in chapter 2, teachers enter teaching primarily for the intrinsic rewards that the work promises—the prospect of educating children, the challenge of pedagogy, and the personal satisfaction that good teaching yields. Evidence from this study and others[4] indicates that, at its best, teaching is inherently rewarding and self-sustaining and that extrinsic rewards are far less significant than in other lines of work such as manufacturing, real estate, or even medicine.

However, teachers' well-documented response to psychic rewards has led some of the public, its policy makers, and even teachers, to discount the importance of extrinsic rewards such as pay, promotion, and recognition and to assume that teachers will happily and unendingly be sustained by the content of their work. Others who would remake the teaching profession have concluded that the best teachers are (or ought to be) more entrepreneurial and more responsive to the opportunity for extrinsic rewards. Consistent with this line of analysis, they have introduced incentive pay and competitive recognition to promote harder work and better teaching.[5]

The teachers in this study suggest that both approaches fall short. Salaries and recognition are very important to teachers, and these respondents report that the deprivation of both has demoralized them and discouraged others like them from entering teaching. However, teachers seek more than opportunities for competitive bonuses or public accolades; they seek more than what one teacher called "the stand-up-and-give-you-a-ribbon sort of recognition" gained at the expense of peers. They seek salaries and recognition that make teaching financially possible and rewarding (though not necessarily lucrative), that signal status and respect for the profession, and that ensure ready access to the psychic rewards that matter to them most. Extrinsic rewards are more a means than an end in teaching, but they are certainly not irrelevant. Anna Capello recalled the observations of a psychologist she knew, who said, "You need reinforcement from superiors or people you're working with. You need money, or you need satisfaction at the end of the day, a feeling that you've accomplished something." She observed, "Sometimes all three of those are lacking in teaching."

RECOGNITION

It is no news that teaching is short on recognition. Many respondents noted that they must look to themselves for motivation and reassurance about the merits of their work. An urban elementary-school teacher said that she is rewarded by "seeing kids' progress and the connection I make with them, realizing and seeing how influential I can be with them." This, she concluded, was "highly rewarding. It's the only feedback that I really get. It's the one I really value most." A middle-school teacher, who said that external rewards were lacking in her school, explained that "recognition is very individual, within people, inside themselves." A third teacher said that, being a professional person, "you don't really have to be recognized, because you know yourself if you're a good teacher."

Reliance on self-assessment is not without problems. Working with students who progress slowly or erratically can fail to provide any of the signals—high student test scores, insightful writing, enthusiasm for learning—that teachers look to for evidence of their success. Because there is always more work for teachers to do, they can find it difficult to stop and accept the praise that they are due. An elementary-school teacher who argued that "self-satisfaction is one of the best kinds of recognition for good teaching," also acknowledged that "if you're a good teacher, you're never satisfied." Very good teachers who rely on themselves for praise may be disappointed in the recognition that comes their way. Virtually all teachers in both public and private schools said that they rely primarily on psychic rewards in their work, but most went on to explain that they look to others—students, parents, principals, and peers—to verify their successes.

Teachers take a long view of their work and its effects, sustained from day to day by a good class discussion or a single student's mastery of fractions. A middle-school teacher explained, "I know I'm good. I know by what the kids tell me, by what they produce for me, and by what they don't produce for other teachers." However, over time, teachers look for evidence of enduring influence. They want to know not only that their students fare well on this week's test or in subsequent grades, but that they have made a difference in their students' lives. Considering possible sources of recognition for good work, a middle-school teacher said that "the ultimate" is "that very, very rare note from a kid. . . . They're the ones who really know what you're doing or what you're not doing. They're the authorities." Several teachers mentioned receiving reassuring cards or notes from students at the close of the school year. One teacher said that she prizes an essay that a former first-grade student had written about her teaching eight years after leaving her classroom. She admitted: "If I get really down, I read it."

Students' "coming back," months or years after leaving their classrooms, provided teachers with their most valued source of encouragement and recognition. An elementary-school teacher talked of "years later, children coming back, and they still remember you." The day before we interviewed one teacher, a parent had arrived to pick up her child in a nearby classroom, stopped to say hello and to tell her daughter proudly, "This was my fourth-grade teacher." An urban middle-school teacher explained, "It gives you pleasure to see someone do well, in whatever it is they're doing." He acknowledged, though, "It hasn't happened very often, frankly. I've had a couple of kids come back. One is an electrical engineer. Another kid bought up half of [the town] with an oil company. He's doing well. You occasionally get them."

A middle-school teacher who said that she liked "knowing in a very small way that I have influenced a great number of people," told of encountering a student while on vacation:

> I walked into a store and I heard "Mrs. H——" I looked up and it was a student I had taught twelve years ago. I couldn't believe it. "You were one of the best teachers that I ever had, and I will never forget you. You made such an impression on me. I want you to know, you're one of the best." . . . And things like that make the whole thing worth it.

Several other students who attend college visit her "every now and then and say how much they learned. They still have their seventh-grade grammar notebooks. It makes you feel like you've done something."

Reassurance and thanks came more readily to teachers of college-bound students in both public and private schools than to teachers of less academically inclined students. Teachers who successfully prepare their classes for competitive examinations and schools often said that students returned to express their appreciation and to garner their own measure of praise for their accomplishments. For urban teachers, particularly those of non-academic subjects, such testimonies of success are rare, and teachers must rely on their own estimates of their worth for reassurance.

Many teachers, particularly those of younger children, look to parents for statements about their success with students. A first-grade teacher said that her most important source of recognition is from "parents who say that their children are happy in school. I love to hear the parents say, 'This is great. My son can't wait to go to school. My daughter can't wait to go to school.' That makes my day."

Several teachers said that, because of their success with older children, parents request that younger siblings be placed in their classes. An elementary-school teacher with nineteen years experience in the same district said that her "best recognition" is "parents who line up their families because they like what you did with their brothers and sisters. They say, 'Wait until you get so-and-so in five years.' It's a little mystique that builds. That's rewarding." Similarly, a veteran elementary-school teacher said when "parents come in and you have one child, and then they want you to have their other child . . . it says something. They want their kids to have the same school teacher. I enjoy all those things. It makes me feel good. I'm not sure it's better than money, but. . . ."

Parents' written notes of thanks were potent sources of praise for these teachers. An elementary-school teacher confessed that "some of them are almost embarrassing. But they are really signs of sheer appreciation for the little extra things you do with their youngsters." A middle-school teacher, who contended that "teachers need stroking that they're not getting," said that "there is nothing more wonderful than getting a letter. Maybe if parents knew what that did for teachers, they'd do it more." With parents' decreasing involvement in schooling, few teachers anticipated that families would provide them with the recognition they might like.

Administrators were a source of recognition for teachers in this study, although some were said to be far more successful than others in offering meaningful praise. One middle-school teacher said her principal "has made me feel very good about myself as a teacher. We don't have a whole lot of ways of recognizing good teaching." An elementary-school teacher said that his principal "gives you a lot of recognition . . . sometimes just pats you on the back, just telling you that you're doing a heck of a job." Usually principals who provide praise that teachers value do so in the course of work rather than on formal, public occasions. In thanking one of her staff for gathering some information that she had requested, a principal told a teacher whom we interviewed that she had praised her to another administrator: "I spoke to the other principal today and told her: 'This is just the kind of person she is, and you can't have her, ever.' " The teacher said that she was gratified by the recognition: "The fact that she said that to me made me feel really good, and that kind of thing makes me want to do other things. If I didn't have the praise and good feedback, I might not be as enthusiastic as I am about doing other things, trying new things."

One teacher, who was unusually pleased with the recognition available for staff in her school, credited the principal for her generous and explicit praise:

> She comes around and she compliments, she openly compliments people at staff meetings on what she saw in the classroom or in the hall. Last year there was a Teacher of the Year award that somehow got to the school because there were more teachers nominated here than anywhere else. So, instead of giving it to one or two people, she gave it to the entire staff. That was really great. . . .

Teachers were wary of indiscriminate praise that failed to address their real strengths and achievements, and they described the importance of valid recognition. An urban elementary-school teacher explained why he valued his principal's praise: "He doesn't say that I do everything well, but he says, 'You do this well,' and I like that." Another said of her principal: "He's encouraging. If he sees a good job, he tells you that he likes what he sees." In illustrating how his principal rewarded teachers for specific contributions, an elementary-school teacher described her seeking him out to thank him for setting up a stereo system at an appreciation luncheon for classroom aides:

> It was no big deal, but she went out of her way to find out whose idea it was. I was out on recess duty, and she came out to thank me. That impressed me. She really makes an

> effort, and it makes a big difference. It really does. . . . As far as recognition goes, that's where it ends.

Several principals were said to send teachers notes of appreciation for individual efforts. Two found the gesture more perfunctory than genuine, but others believed that their principals truly valued their contributions to the school. Richard Sand gave his principal unusually high praise:

> It's the only recognition we're going to get. It's personal recognition. Kind words. Not just kind words as in "I hope you have a nice day" that you hear at the supermarket. It's kind words as in "You did a hell of a job. That was really great. Thanks a lot. I really appreciate it." You come home and you find a thank-you card, and a gift certificate to a local restaurant, and a note that says, "Take your family out to dinner." I know damn well that came out of his own pocket. I know it didn't come out of school funds.

For three teachers, recognition came in the form of their principals' support—financial, administrative, and moral—for new programs that they wanted to try. An elementary-school teacher explained, "If you're a good teacher, then he's going to give you all the rope you need—not to hang yourself, but to hold on to so you don't fall off." Several teachers said that they felt recognized for good teaching when their principals appointed them to influential committees or asked them to present in-service workshops. A music teacher said that her department head asked her to "audition voices for the all-city chorus" and to judge singing contests.

> He will recommend me highly. As a matter of fact, my principal just told me in a joking way, "I'm tired of your boss telling me what a good teacher you are." He laughed. I told him, "I like hearing that." That's the truth, and I want him to keep on saying it.

Finally, several teachers said that their principals recognized good work by asking for their advice or formally involving them in policy making. As one elementary-school respondent explained, "They do listen to me. I feel that it is because they respect me and respect my opinions. They ask for my opinions."

Teachers also look to their peers for recognition and reassurance. They feel encouraged by teachers within their schools who ask their advice or use their ideas. An elementary-school teacher said that she is heartened when "other teachers come and say, 'I'm coming to you because I know you know how to do this.' " Another described similar responses from colleagues:

> There are a lot of compliments. The fifth-grade teachers are a wonderful group . . . a very supportive group. They'll come down and say, "I hear you have a great mural in your room." They'll come in or they'll bring the children in to see it. Or they'll ask you questions—in a way, if people ask questions, it's a compliment to you.

Teachers were buoyed by the compliments of colleagues who taught their students in subsequent grades and commended them for preparing those students well. A middle-school social studies teacher said that he has been "told by the high-school teachers that my kids get far in high school, that they are the ones who do the most questioning; they are the ones who debate. That's nice to know. It's nice to know that I'm doing something."

Comments from peers, administrators, parents, and students cumulate over time and constitute a teacher's reputation within the school or community. Teachers repeatedly described how the recognition that accompanies such a reputation is one of the greatest rewards that they experience in their work.

Much has been made of the strength of teachers' egalitarian norms and teachers' discomfort with being singled out and publicly acclaimed for their achievements. These respondents did not eschew praise, although they dismissed the value of onetime prizes that momentarily illuminated them and elevated them above others. Several teachers had been selected as Teachers of the Year in their schools or districts, but they did not put much stock in these honors; one called them "phony baloney." Rather, they were encouraged in their work by gaining reputations for being excellent teachers, reputations that grew gradually and without fanfare over time. An elementary-school teacher said that for her,

> recognition would be another teacher realizing that you're a good teacher. And the kids would hear that you're a good teacher, through the grapevine, through their brothers and sisters that you've had in previous years. And the parents would also hear and know that you're a good teacher.

A middle-school teacher said that, although there is no formal recognition for good teaching in her school, "You get to know who the better teachers are. They make themselves available, and usually the department heads look to those people. The meetings are held in their rooms. They're the ones who pass out the information. They're the ones who get asked to do special things." Several teachers noted the implicit nature of such recognition: "It's kind of understood, kind of known who is thought of as a good teacher. . . . You just get a feeling. People know." It is, as a middle-teacher explained, "Just a sense of confidence that people have in you—which, to me, is a reward." Respondents believed that they deserved recognition for their work, but they were more than willing to share that recognition with others who had also earned it.

Although teachers valued the unheralded praise and reputations they earned over time, for most, this was the only form of recognition available in their work, and for some, even that was lacking. Repeatedly, teachers said that there were no sources of recognition for good work beyond their own confidence that they were making their best effort. Asked if there was recognition for good teaching in her school, an urban elementary-school teacher was unequivocal: "Absolutely not. No. Nobody even pats your head and says, 'Hey, that was a good job.' " Another concurred dejectedly: "We never know [if we're doing a good job]. We never know." A high-school teacher echoed: "Nothing. Not a thing. Nothing. Excellent teachers do what they do because they love teaching." Anna Capello said,

> There's barely any recognition in the whole school. So I think that everyone's clamoring for it. . . . All the satisfaction that I get—and people tell me that this is very different from business—is totally personal satisfaction. In our particular school, there's not time for any kind of stroking. You get somewhat abused by the students, and we all have the same title.

Richard Sand had resigned himself to the lack of administrative praise and offered this rationale: "It's like anything else. If your street is well plowed during snowstorms, do you call the director of public works and say thank you?"

Several respondents said that being selected to participate in this study was the first sign of recognition they had received from their administrators. Anna Capello remarked, "I was surprised when I was recommended for this, [study] because I didn't know that he was all that aware of what I was doing."

Many respondents said that school officials simply expected teachers to do their best without feeling obliged to praise them in response. An elementary-school teacher's response was typical of many:

> Not too many people even say, "Good job." They just expect it. So I don't think there's that much incentive. I don't think administrators realize how much time and effort teachers put into their job and what it takes out of them. They just, you know, expect it.

Some observed that, although school officials were often slow to offer praise and grant recognition, they were quick to blame. An elementary-school teacher said "if you're not doing a good job, you're going to know it. If you are doing a good job, nobody is going to say a thing." Another echoed, "I don't even get a little pat sometimes. But I know right away when I've done something wrong." A high-school teacher, who reported that administrators will "wait for you to do something bad, and then they'll give it to you," said that this response was common city-wide:

> In this city, not too many people appreciate anything. Any time you do something good around here, they want to find something wrong with it. It's a very negative city.

Very few teachers said that there was sufficient recognition, either in formal commendation or informal reputation, for the work that they do. Several teachers, particularly those who worked in urban schools where students presented difficult learning problems or parents kept their distance from the schools, made a plea for more recognition to sustain them in their work. A suburban middle-school teacher said, "Teachers need stroking that they're not getting. There is very little stroking. We hear about what we do wrong, but we don't really hear much about what we do right." An urban high-school teacher agreed: "We need recognition, if no more than a thank you or a pat on the back."

Teachers in private schools generally reported having more access to recognition in their work than their public-school counterparts. Students were, on the average, more motivated and successful, and teachers could readily point to evidence of their accomplishments. A high-school teacher said that she had achieved both personal satisfaction and public acclaim:

> I guess I'm proud of the fact that I have made an impression on students about what learning is about, what the search for truth is about. I think I've inspired some students who hated history to love history. I think I'm proudest of the fact that students like me as a human being and respect me as a teacher. I've been chosen to make the speech at the senior assembly. I've had the yearbook dedicated to me. I'm a good teacher and I'm proud of my classroom work.

Parents of private-school students were reportedly more generous and open with praise and gratitude. One elementary-level teacher in an independent school said, "I get a lot of juice and feedback from parents, and how happy they are, and how happy their kids are. So there's a lot of appreciation from parents." A teacher in a Catholic elementary school said, "Parents are very, very grateful." A teacher who had worked in public and private schools said that both children and parents were more explicitly appreciative of his efforts in the private school: "The response of the kids tends to be more open than it does in the public school. The response of their families is really a very nice thing."

Some private-school respondents said that their principals and colleagues made special efforts to acknowledge good work. Janice Gagne said, "I'll find a note on my desk from the principal from time to time. A pat on the back, or whatever. It makes you feel good." A Catholic high-school teacher said, "I think there's a basic attempt to affirm everyone in the school." An elementary-level teacher in a Quaker school who previously had worked in public schools said that recognition "does come from other people on the faculty. People are very aware of telling others that what they're doing is very nice." Her principal, like several other private-school heads, "writes each person an individual contract, which is about why that person is very dear to the school." In several private schools, staff turnover was high due to low wages, and respondents there reported that school officials made extra efforts to recognize teachers' work in order to avert such turnover. One elementary-level teacher in a Jewish day school said, "I almost feel now they would do most anything to keep me." A middle-school teacher in a Catholic school said candidly that her principal "values [her] something fierce."

Private schools seemed to offer teachers somewhat more certainty of success and consequent recognition because they were selective and stable institutions. However, some teachers from independent and church-related schools expressed as much dissatisfaction about the scarce opportunities for recognition as their counterparts in the public sector. Conditions were better, but not sufficient. An elementary-level teacher in an independent school said,

> It's hard to know whether you're recognized. I know by now through hearsay that I'm an appreciated teacher. I have never once gotten it from the headmaster, but I have gotten it via a board of trustees member who happens to be a parent I've known for a long time. It would be nice if he would come and say something.

Similarly, a high-school teacher in an independent school said, "It's rare that people come up to you and say, 'Gee, Sandy, I think you're doing a great job.' Not that I need a gold star next to my name, but every now and then, I think it would be nice if I heard that I was doing okay."

Private- and public-school teachers, therefore, voiced similar concerns about the lack of recognition for their efforts and successes. Not only did they value most highly the responses of current and former students and their parents, but for many those were the only sources of recognition available. Teachers who received the genuine praise of peers and administrators said that it encouraged them to sustain or extend their efforts. One middle-school teacher in a Jewish day school explained, "The more respect and appreciation I get, the more I knock myself out to try to do an even better job." Teachers repeatedly said that they do not work hard in anticipation of such recognition; rather, the recognition that comes their way is a testimony to their success and encourages them to persist and to expand their efforts.

SALARIES

Many of the teachers we interviewed made clear that personal and public recognition, however reassuring, are not enough. A veteran middle-school teacher reviewed the rewards he had received and observed that they could not substitute for financial compensation:

> Well, I've gotten a lot of recognition. A yearbook was dedicated to me. One year I was voted Teacher of the Year. People say nice things about me. My principal wrote a nice letter to put in my files, saying that I'm a bona fide good teacher. But none of that is negotiable, unfortunately, and it doesn't get me a lot. I got a Horace Mann [professional development grant from the state], so that gets me a little bit more. And every summer that I have put in for a curriculum project, I have received that. There have been extras sent my way. . . . But in terms of saying, "Hey, you're a good teacher. We really need the likes of you because you do things that are good for our kids"—and that's what we're here for—"so here is the 48,500 dollars you deserve. You are asking for fifty thousand dollars, and we've been paying you a paltry less than forty thousand dollars. Here's what you deserve." That has not come about. I do not think I'll see it in my career.

Given the scarce opportunities for promotion and the paucity of public awards in teaching, salaries provide teachers with the primary, if not the sole, extrinsic incentive in their work. However, for most respondents, pay—both the level and the structure—serves more as a disincentive than incentive for continuing in teaching and maintaining a strong and constant effort. Whereas doctors can expect to earn a substantial salary in virtually any setting, lawyers can expect their earnings to increase steadily over time, and business people can anticipate that initiative and extra effort will pay off, those who enter teaching must anticipate comparatively low wages, a short salary schedule that offers few increases after mid-career, and no chance to earn more for making a better effort or achieving better results. Consequently, many prospective teachers never enter teaching, while some who do leave after several years. Of those who remain, a number hold second jobs that distract them from their teaching, and many of the best resent being confined to a pay scale that compensates them no better than the worst among them. For many of the teachers, the disincentive of low, fixed salaries interfered with their enjoyment of the intrinsic rewards of teaching.

Teachers expressed far greater concern about their low level of pay than about the lack of differentiation between successful and less successful teachers. One public elementary-school teacher, who anticipated leaving teaching because of the low pay, argued that "basically we're all underpaid. It's not a matter of the better teachers making more money. I think as a group we're all underpaid." She advocated raising all salaries across the board: "I see a lot of very, very hard workers, who are very dedicated and who are good teachers." A middle-school teacher expressed the same view:

> All of us should be paid more. All of us are in the trenches every day. We really are, and none of us is compensated adequately. Even the poorest teacher is underpaid. We have very few in this school who are poor. I would say we have an awful lot of superior teachers in this system. Not just in this building, but in the whole school system.

Teachers condemned their low salaries both because they earned less than other workers and because it was difficult to make ends meet for their families. Many of those interviewed cited examples of others who are less educated, less skilled, and who contribute less to society than they, yet earn more. After four years with a telephone company, the daughter of a middle-school teacher earns ten thousand dollars a year more than her mother does after fourteen years of teaching. A high-school social studies teacher said that her husband "hires people fresh out of school for six thousand dollars more than I make after twenty-one years of teaching." An English teacher in a vocational high school said that one of her former students, who had not yet met the vocational requirement of five years in the trade, "was hired at twenty-five thousand dollars. I make twenty. I've been here ten years and I have a bachelor's degree." A middle-school teacher complained that subway employees "working in the cellar doing labor jobs make thirty-four thousand dollars a year,'' while teachers in his district begin at eighteen thousand dollars.

Many respondents interpreted these pay inequities as evidence of society's low regard for education. A middle-school teacher said that he believes his work is "every bit as valuable, or more valuable'' than that of two friends, a lawyer and the owner of a linoleum business. He argued that although people

> talk about education, they really don't want to spend money on it. . . . They go to buy linoleum and they don't mind paying top dollar for it, and this guy makes a good living on the fact that they buy linoleum. They're probably more interested in having nice linoleum than having well-educated people.

No teachers had expected high wages when they entered teaching. As one said, "I'm certainly not in it for the money.'' Janice Gagne echoed, "You know you're not going to get rich if you're going to be a teacher'' A third agreed: "Anyone who gets into it for the money will always be disappointed.'' But most had anticipated that their salaries would support them and their families in a solidly middle-class life-style; their current pay levels challenge that expectation.

Some teachers in this study questioned whether they could afford to teach at all. Gary Stein, who complained, "The money is terrible,'' said that he was applying to be a principal largely because he needed more money. While younger teachers such as he worried about their own careers, veteran teachers expressed concern over the future of education. An elementary-school teacher said that she wished something "would draw these young people in more, more than just the satisfaction of being in the classroom and dealing with children. That is a natural attraction for many young people, but they don't think they can afford it.'' For many current and prospective teachers, the intrinsic rewards of teaching cannot compensate for low pay, even if they live in what one teacher called "humble circumstances.''

Current salaries were said to provide adequate support for single individuals living modestly. An elementary-school teacher who admitted, "Personally, I am very happy with the salary that I am making," explained that she is single and "at the top of the pay scale, master's plus thirty [credits] and maximum experience. . . . If I were supporting a family myself, I would have a hard time with just my salary." A middle-school teacher who admitted, "I could always use more," said, "I'm content with the amount of money that I get, because it's only me." A high-school physics teacher voiced similar views:

> I'm single, and I don't have children, and for me the pay has been all right. I don't take expensive vacations. I don't go out to eat a lot—hardly at all, actually. I just don't have a very expensive life-style. For me, it's been adequate.

Those teachers who supported other family members were far less sanguine. Several said that the greatest stress of teaching was the difficulty that they experienced paying their bills. One said that the pressure increases at Christmas when there is not enough money to buy family gifts, "and your wife is saying, 'Hey, we need more money.' Even to the point where she sometimes suggests, 'Do you ever think of doing something else?' " A veteran teacher recalled that many times he had considered leaving teaching "because after I got married, the income was less than adequate." A teacher with five years of experience anticipated coming strains:

> The truth is, when you grow up, money seems to be, unfortunately, the real reward. It's enough for me at this point in my life to see a smile on kids' faces. . . . But I just bought a house in the fall, and I know that money is becoming more and more important every day. It's very scary. I'd like to have a child some day soon. I don't know if I can afford it.

A high-school teacher with two young children said that a job offering more money could lure him out of teaching "because

I have two little kids now of my own, and it makes all the difference." He wondered how he would educate his children:

> It sounds whiny, but I get furious because I teach in a community that wants me to prepare their kids for Harvard and Dartmouth and Brown. But my kids, unless they're superb scholars, are not going to go there unless I change jobs. The money won't be there.

This teacher only anticipated the problem Richard Sand actually faced—the infuriating plight of being unable to provide his own academically talented daughter with the education that she deserved. A veteran high-school teacher who had begun teaching after years of working as a pharmacist explained that

> even though I always liked to teach, I never did go into it because there was no money in it. . . . My children were all grown and through college before I went into teaching. So I could afford the luxury of teaching. But I often wonder how they're going to attract dedicated teachers without paying them more money.

Virtually all teachers who had family responsibilities supplemented their salaries with a spouse's income or a second job. For them, teaching was necessarily subsidized work. An urban kindergarten teacher explained, "I'm lucky that my husband is an attorney. We're comfortable, and it's not really an issue for me." Another elementary-school teacher said, "I certainly could use more money, but I have a second income. My husband is the primary breadwinner, let's face it." Several respondents' spouses were also teachers, and the combined salaries were adequate to support their families. Gary Stein, whose wife was a teacher, noted that "two teachers make what one of my next door neighbors makes. . . . I could not pay my bills on one teacher's salary—my mortgage, food, bills would exceed what I take home." A veteran physics teacher whose wife also taught was satisfied with the pay:

> If she weren't a teacher, the situation might be different. Between us, we make well over sixty thousand dollars. So as a family income, it's very nice. We have ten weeks off in the summer and the same vacations during the year. So, as a personal solution, it's marvelous. Now, if only one of us were working and the salary, therefore, was cut in half, I might really see that half of that is not a lot of money.

For some teachers—even some whose spouses already worked—the solution was moonlighting. One played music at country clubs on the weekends. Another tutored fifteen students each week in mathematics. Anna Capello taught in a chefs' school at night. One middle-school teacher ran a painting business, while another owned an investment company. Yet another middle-school teacher reported that she works "in an orthopedic practice, in the accounts receivable department. I've worked in real estate. I've worked in a bank." She works evenings, summers, and some weekends.

Although only approximately 10 percent of these public-school teachers held second jobs during the academic year, they said that more of their colleagues did. Four said that all male teachers in their buildings supplemented their teaching salaries with additional work. Their stories suggest that the proportion of teachers working second jobs is far higher than our sample indicates, and one could legitimately wonder whether the demands on such teachers' time compromise their work and make them less than "very good" teachers. One respondent explained that she cannot "do a lot of the stuff outside the classroom" because of her second job. The teacher who ran the painting company described how he managed his schedule:

> I use my prep periods to do the school work, so I don't have to take anything home. If I have another job, I leave school at three o'clock, and I work until eight or nine at night. Then I go home. So I don't have time to take work home. . . . Last summer, work took us right up until November. We were leaving school as soon as the bell rang. I'd be in here, chang-

> ing my clothes—putting my paint clothes on—and brrr-ing, out the door.

An elementary-school teacher observed that "loads of men have second jobs that become businesses, that then become their first priority." In these respondents' views, second jobs frequently interfered with teachers' ability to teach well and yet, ironically, such jobs were necessary for many teachers to remain in teaching.

A few teachers enjoyed their second jobs because they provided release from the stresses of teaching or stimulation for new learning. However, most who worked did so because they had to, and they would have far preferred salaries that permitted them to concentrate fully on their teaching. An elementary-school teacher who said that he was "behind the eight ball, as the head of a family whose wife doesn't work," contended that "if you had some money and some financial security, you wouldn't have to take a second or third job."

We cannot know how many potential teachers calculated the price of teaching and decided that they could not afford it. Nor can we judge how much better public education might be if adequate, even attractive, salaries served as incentives to teaching. However, these teachers' accounts suggest that pay influences who teaches and how they teach.

Teachers had no illusions about the prospects for achieving pay equity with other professionals or being appropriately compensated for their responsibility or effort. As one elementary-school teacher said, "I don't think you could ever pay us enough. We work with the most precious commodity in our nation, and we probably should be paid the highest of anyone." Another elaborated, "For what we're asked to do, expected to do, it's nowhere near enough. For the commitment and dedication they want—and is very often there, but not always recognized—it's nowhere near enough." They acknowledged that they had chosen to teach because the low pay was outweighed by other rewards that they sought. An elementary-school teacher expressed the views of many: "I'm not real happy about the money, but on the other hand, I couldn't be happy, no matter how much money I was getting, if I weren't doing something like this."

A number of respondents felt demoralized and angered by what their low pay implied—society's low opinion of their work. Several said that they didn't think the public understood the demands of their jobs. An elementary-school teacher was tired of patronizing remarks from people who say, "Aren't teachers wonderful?" but "aren't willing to put their money where their mouth is."

A few argued that low public regard led to low pay, while others, like this elementary-school teacher, contended that the causal relationship moved in the opposite direction, with low pay leading to low status: "I think that in this society, we are valued by what we make, unfortunately. And, in comparison to others, we should make more money." A suburban high-school teacher agreed:

> I don't mean to sound mercenary about it, but I suppose that, in this society, we do attach worth to the almighty dollar. If a lawyer holds an important, prestigious position, it's probably so because a lawyer and a doctor make more money than do teachers.

For those who shared this teacher's view, the answer to the problem of increasing the status of teachers lay in substantial salary raises. An urban elementary-school teacher argued:

> America, unfortunately, is a country that measures and judges everything by the amount of money someone makes. Now, if you don't make an awful lot of money, you're not respected as much as the person who does. Teachers do not make a lot of money, and respect for them has gone right down to the basement level. . . . If you put teachers' salaries where they should be, in the professional category, all of a sudden, because of where we live, I guarantee you, teachers would be up there with the doctors and the lawyers.

However, this teacher, like several others, emphasized that higher pay would not inevitably lead to better education, because the problems of schooling are so complex. Raising salaries to sixty thousand dollars "may attract more people, and it may attract better people, and it may raise the standards somewhat, but it's not going to improve the overall educational system."

Respondents from independent and church-related schools echoed many of the concerns of their public-school counterparts with regard to pay. Most of those teaching in independent schools earned several thousand dollars a year less than those in public schools, although recently a few had achieved competitive wage levels. With few exceptions, salaries in church-related schools were considerably lower—some by as much as ten thousand dollars—than in public schools, a factor that appeared to be responsible for rapid turnover among teachers.

A few teachers in Catholic schools had taken their positions after being laid off by the public schools, but most had chosen their schools for nonfinancial reasons—the quality of students or staff, the academic or moral standards of the school, or a personal commitment to the purpose of the institution. At Janice Gagne's school, teachers began at nine thousand dollars a year. After six years, she was earning 10,500 dollars and had been offered twice that much by a public-school district. She decided to stay where she was because her school supported good teaching and her own children were enrolled there. Private-school teachers often taught where they did in spite of the lower salaries. Independent schools sometimes made this choice possible by supplementing teachers' salaries with room and board, and for single teachers, such an arrangement could be ideal. However, many could not afford to teach once they had families, unless theirs was a second income. A veteran independent-school teacher explained that "the atmosphere of the place holds people. . . . It is a great place to be. However, that doesn't pay the electric bill." An elementary-school teacher in an independent school said, "When [the men] get married and have children, they leave." A high-school teacher in a prestigious independent school had continued to teach, but resented her low salary:

> I really hate not making more money. It didn't bother me when I didn't need it. It seemed we could live very easily, back in the old days, without money. It didn't seem all that crucial. But as you get older and . . . you have kids and it becomes more complicated, the lack of money begins to grate.

Only 2 of 20 independent-school teachers in our sample reported holding second jobs during the school year, although several took on additional summer work. Afternoon coaching assignments and dorm responsibilities seemed to preclude moonlighting. Teachers in church-related schools held many of the same jobs as public-school teachers. One, who taught in a Catholic school, relied primarily on her husband's salary, but also worked nights at a bank. The demands of her second job, which sometimes kept her at work until 11:30 P.M., made her tired and impatient with her students:

> I'll come into school and I'll be very tired, and I try to be as patient as I can. But sometimes things just bug me. Then I get upset at myself. I say, "Look at how good these kids are. How can you be impatient with them?" I get very hard on myself, and then I sit down and say to myself, "Don't be hard on yourself. If they paid you what you were worth, you wouldn't have to have a part-time job. You wouldn't be tired, and you wouldn't be taking it out on anyone." I try hard not to. I try to be patient.

Thus, for a variety of reasons low teaching salaries in both public and private schools troubled teachers. Extra jobs, taken on to pay bills, often diverted them from the teaching they loved, while for many, salary, status, and self-respect were entwined with demoralizing effect. For single teachers, or for those who could supplement their pay with a spouse's income, salaries were sometimes a neutral factor, but in no instance did they serve as incentives for respondents to remain in teaching, to work harder, or to focus their efforts on particular goals. The motivation for good teaching came from other sources, primarily from their students and the work itself. However, teachers did believe that low wages discouraged able candidates. As Janice Gagne said, "Something does have to be done if they want quality people. Something is going to have to be done."

Respondents were careful to distinguish between the problems of low pay and standardized pay. Virtually all those interviewed from both the public and private schools believed that teaching is undervalued and teachers are underpaid, but they differed in their assessments of salary schedules that determine individuals' pay on the basis of length of service in the district or amount of postgraduate education.

Most public-school teachers believed the standardized salary schedule to be the best solution to the complicated problem of determining fair rates of pay in a large and complex organization, but many spoke of problems and inequities with such pay scales. Some expressed dissatisfaction over teachers' being paid without regard to the quality of their teaching. Like one middle-school teacher, they noted the problem of a pay scale that fails to distinguish between "the better teacher, the average teacher, and the weak teacher." Others disapproved of pay scales equating experience with excellence by paying more to teachers with longer tenure. An elementary-school teacher said, "I don't think we're going in the right direction with 'the longer you stay, the more money you make.' " More than one of those interviewed complained about making less than another senior teacher who had "retired on the job." However, this was a minority view, and most teachers agreed that salaries in education should increase with years of experience.

Respondents also disagreed about the distribution of compensation within the salary scale. Some junior teachers argued for higher beginning wages to attract and retain talented teachers. Teachers with more seniority contended that the pay scales should be weighted to benefit the veterans who had committed their careers to public education. The disputes centered not on the right of either group to earn more, but on how a fixed pot of resources should be divided.

Finally, some respondents, like this middle-school teacher, criticized differential awards to teachers with advanced degrees, contending that additional course work bore no relationship to good teaching:

> I'm bothered by the fact that our salary increments are based on the number of credits we get. I think that almost all of those credits are totally meaningless. . . . The courses that I've taken say absolutely nothing about me as a teacher, or improving as a teacher. . . . I think that having a doctorate is fine, but to say that having a doctorate makes you a better teacher is really ridiculous.

Others, like this elementary-school teacher, argued that the financial incentives for further academic training were insufficient to warrant the expense of tuition:

> Unfortunately, people have decided that it's not worth their while, financially, to go on and get a higher degree or to take the courses. The way it's set up now, it would take many years to get back the money that you would spend on a master's degree.

Although no teachers believed the standardized scale favoring longevity and advanced study an ideal means for distributing income, most considered it acceptable, and few could offer specific alternatives. Their speculation centered on proposals to reward better teaching with better pay, and many teachers spoke at length about the prospects and pitfalls of merit pay.

Some teachers said they approved of compensating teachers on the basis of merit. They seemed more concerned over a few incompetent staff members receiving the same pay as others than about themselves not having incentives for entrepreneurial competition. A middle-school teacher who favored merit pay said that she had seen "cases where people simply aren't earning their paychecks." Another advocate explained, "I see a lot of bad teaching." Anna Capello said that once teachers are awarded tenure, "you could be working your tail off and the person next door is getting by doing absolutely nothing." Virtually all respondents—even those who supported performance-based pay—were quick to note its problems.[6]

They were wary of the evaluation system that would be used to competitively assess teachers' work. Several worried about teachers' being evaluated by different administrators with different standards. An elementary-school teacher said that in his district of 4000 students, 25 different administrators would conduct evaluations:

> If they're all doing it the same way, wonderful. But they're not. Some people come in, take a quick look, and say, "Everything's fine. Good job." And others will come in and sit there by the hour and take notes. It's got to be done in an equitable and fair way, and that's what's wrong with evaluation. If one person could do it all, maybe it would be done uniformly.

Many, like this middle-school teacher, criticized administrators for being poor judges of practice: "Many of these administrators are these politician and business types, and I don't think they are qualified to judge. . . . It's a very subjective judgment." Another respondent concluded cynically, "A lot of principals could care less."

Respondents also challenged the criteria that might be used to award merit pay. One middle-school teacher argued that a merit system should "assess the quality of services delivered to children," rather than the extent to which teachers satisfied administrators, but he could not suggest how that might be done. Teachers of academically slow or disabled students often doubted that gains in student test scores could fairly measure their efforts and efficacy. An urban high-school teacher objected to fixed criteria because "certain students need certain kinds of teachers. They might not do well with my kind of teaching. Everybody has a strength to give in certain areas." A department head in a suburban district agreed and said that she would "like to recognize people's different styles. Some people do things differently. Not everyone's going to be adept at handling small groups."

Several teachers challenged the notion of rewarding those who work harder. One asked: "What does 'working harder' mean? I know there are an awful lot who tend to make a lot of noise, but who don't necessarily work that hard." An industrial-arts teacher presented another view: "How do you judge who is working harder? I think that I do a real good job, but I can't say that I really work hard at it. To me it might just come naturally. I enjoy what I'm doing, so to me it's not hard work." A bilingual-education teacher observed that teachers "who just put in time after school are not necessarily good teachers." A mathematics teacher concurred: "If they're going to tell me that I have to take two clubs and get into all these extracurricular things to be a good teacher, I say, 'absolutely not.' " Many respondents would have agreed with this teacher who admitted that she was stumped about how fair assessments might be made:

> I can just think of people who shouldn't get [merit pay awards]. I don't know. The trouble is the subjectivity of good teaching in many ways. So many things are not measurable. It has to be based on some guidelines of creativity and enthusiasm, or willingness to take risks, willingness to try new things—something that could be documented and would show the characteristics of a good teacher who hasn't fallen asleep behind the desk.

These teachers were skeptical that merit awards could ever be distributed with an even hand, and they warned of patronage and prejudice. An elementary-school teacher predicted that principals would decide on the basis of "personality. Are you getting along or aren't you getting along?" Another concluded, "If your principal likes you, you're in." A third claimed that she could predict who would receive merit pay:

> People who always say "Yes." People who inform the principal of everything going on. People who inform an administrator about what other people say about him or her. These people are often honored.

One respondent was so concerned about the power of politics in her town that she suggested an "independent agency from out of town should award merit pay. . . . This town is terribly political. . . . If you don't fit, politically, you could be in a lot of trouble. It has always been that way."

Nor were the teachers convinced that merit pay would improve public education. Many were fearful that it might make matters worse. An elementary-school teacher argued that, although recipients would appreciate the financial boost, "it would certainly cause resentment among those who were not considered better teachers. You might end up losing teachers who really are good teachers." She reasoned further that merit pay would not improve teachers' performance:

> I don't think that paying better teachers would make teachers who aren't good teachers better teachers. They are either good teachers because they are doing their job and they like it or they're bad teachers because that's the way they are. I don't think that paying some of them extra money is going to change the way that others teach.

Others said that the pay bonuses under consideration by most school districts were too small to serve as financial incentives. A veteran physics teacher said, "I think that the numbers I hear bandied about aren't worth it. . . . Give me a gold watch instead." Richard Sand recognized that funds for merit pay would always be limited:

> There is only a pool of money . . . a certain amount of money. It can be cut up any way you want. But there is a limited amount. If every single teacher in your school district is exceptional, they're only going to get a small piece of the pie.

Teachers also expressed concern over unintended effects of promoting competition among staff: several worried that higher pay might discourage cooperation. Gary Stein, who said that he is eager to exchange ideas and materials with colleagues, explained his concern: "I fear that people would then start looking at dollar signs and might take a narrower look—'If [the principal] sees me doing this, but not everybody else, maybe he'll think I'm better.' " Two teachers spoke of "hard feelings" that merit pay could engender. One elementary-school teacher who supported merit pay acknowledged that it "would create incredible competition." Richard Sand, who said that he and his middle-school colleagues are "constantly sharing," dramatically portrayed the competition that he envisioned merit pay would generate:

> We would become a group of hoarders, jealously guarding things, keeping our doors locked, not leaving things around the teachers' room for people to see, taking my mail and keeping it in a filing cabinet with the good things that came in—conferences et cetera. The day that happens, public education is dead, deader than a doornail. If we can't share, then we're nothing. Merit pay will not work.

Other respondents felt less certain about the advantages and disadvantages of merit pay, but even among the small number of proponents, none expressed confidence that merit pay could succeed without major changes in school organization and practice.

Teachers from several districts had experienced the effects of merit-based layoffs or merit pay, and their stories confirmed respondents' fears. One district had awarded "super-maximum" pay to selected teachers of high merit; once selected, recipients enjoyed the increased salary benefits until retirement. A high-school teacher recalled that "the evaluation process wasn't fair or good." An elementary-school teacher said that he had succeeded in receiving super-max pay, "although only five to eight percent of the teachers who were eligible for it applied." He characterized the process as "incredibly stringent, very, very difficult"; and in the end it proved to be faulty, because "one of the teachers in [the district] who was fired for being incompetent had gone through that process and passed it. So who is the one to judge? Who is the one to identify the super teacher?"

Several teachers in another district commented on a recently instituted merit-pay plan that enabled teachers with five years of experience to receive bonuses of two hundred to one thousand dollars on the recommendation of their principal. One teacher who had just become eligible to apply said that "a lot of people are unhappy with it. They feel that they're good teachers, and they don't get any merit raises. And the people who have gotten to the top of the scale, they kind of play against each other." A more senior teacher who had received merit pay said that she found it difficult to explain why she received a bonus while other "good, creative, and deserving" teachers did not. Low absentee rates were a key criterion in this plan, and another teacher complained that she had been denied the award because she had been absent more than five times: "Merit criteria do not relate to teaching skills." Another elementary-school teacher said that merit pay had become "the subject of a lot of discussion. A lot of people don't feel that it's good for morale." She and her colleagues were uncertain about the criteria, because the process had been "kind of secretive. I have no idea how many people have gotten money and how many people haven't. That's not discussed."

Private-school teachers offered little more encouragement about the prospects for effective merit pay programs. All church-related schools and many independent schools in our sample had instituted standardized salary scales that closely resembled those in the public sector. Merit did not figure in either Janice Gagne's or Allen Rondo's wages. In some schools, salary scales had been established after teachers had uncovered evidence of favoritism and discrimination in merit-pay programs. Schools that paid teachers differentially based their awards more on extra effort in coaching and committee work than on any formal assessment of classroom performance; the details of all such systems were kept confidential. Some respondents, such as this elementary-school teacher, endorsed competitive compensation: "If someone is going to dig in and really do a good job, pay them for the job that they're doing. But it is a subjective decision—no doubt about it." However, another called the process "voodoo" and said that it is "a recognition of how much you coach, how many extracurricular things you do. You don't get paid specifically for them, but, obviously, when you're reviewed, and your salary is discussed, if you've been one of the good soldiers in the trenches, it should reflect in your pay." The headmaster in his school was said to combine objective information about coaching and extracurricular activities with feedback from students and parents about the teachers' skill in the classroom. One teacher supported such a system because it "encourages veteran teachers to get involved in more things," but others criticized it for focusing too much on nonclassroom efforts. Notably, two crucial features of merit pay in independent schools—relying on a single evaluator and maintaining secrecy—could not be duplicated by most public schools.

Although these valued teachers generally acknowledged the possible advantages of merit pay, virtually all conceded that it would be impossible to implement fairly and, as one teacher said, "could do more harm than good." Most respondents would have agreed with this elementary-school teacher's assessment: "It sounds so good, and yet it seems to have so many pitfalls."

The teachers generally saw more promise in proposals for career ladders which included several stages of professional advancement. As one elementary-school teacher saw it, those with the same title should be paid equally, while those with more or different responsibilities should be paid differently. A middle-school teacher who was serving informally as head of her English department believed that the positions of department head provided a good model on which to build systems of differentiated staffing. Another middle-school teacher suggested eliminating tenure and creating a "three- or four-tier teaching system" where teachers start with three to five years as apprentice teachers and eventually advance to the status of master teacher where "you're getting the bucks." One teacher who recommended a career ladder believed that teachers, rather than administrators, should assume primary responsibility for evaluating their peers and establishing the standards for advancement. Although these advocates of differentiated staffing and career ladders were interviewed before proposals for such plans gained national prominence, and they had not thought through their ideas in detail, they suggested policies that were more systematic and stable than most merit-pay programs of the past. They did not contend that professional career ladders would serve as focused incentives for better effort or performance, but that such plans would provide long-term incentives for able and committed teachers to remain in a profession that currently offers almost no formal advancement.

PROVIDING SUFFICIENT REWARDS FOR GOOD TEACHING

The matter of motivation in school work is complicated, both because incentives and rewards are so scarce and because the ones that matter most to good teachers are so elusive. The primary attraction of teaching and the incentive for good work continues to be the prospect of achieving success with children. Teachers look to students, parents, administrators, and peers for reassurance and recognition that they are doing a good job and getting results. However, schools are not well organized to deliver such assurances and rewards. Students seldom express their appreciation, if at all, until months or years after they have left a teacher's classroom. Parents often keep their distance from teachers, withholding both praise and criticism. Administrators are frequently removed from classrooms and fail to express genuine praise or gratitude for teachers' efforts. Meanwhile, teachers typically work in isolation that discourages peers from knowing how well they teach. As a result, most good teachers savor praise when it is available and persist on their own, despite great uncertainty, when it is not.

The present low salaries make it difficult or even impossible for many teachers to teach. Standardized salary scales that compensate teachers of equal longevity equally offer no reward for extra effort or success; pay scales that compare poorly with other professions convey society's low regard for the work. Teachers believe that their work is worthwhile, and they would be encouraged to know that others do too. While salaries in themselves would probably never provide sufficient incentive for teaching, at their current levels, they serve as disincentives rather than incentives for a sustained commitment to teaching.

Devising an effective set of incentives and rewards for teachers is a challenge because teaching itself is such a complicated task. The answer does not seem to lie in public awards that celebrate the accomplishments of a few exemplary individuals or in merit-pay plans that reward teachers competitively for their efforts and achievements. Teachers' pay must be made competitive with that of other professionals if teaching is to attract and retain good workers and enable them to devote themselves to their work. Career ladders that provide higher pay to teachers who assume more responsibilities deserve careful consideration. But equally as important, our research suggests that schools should be organized to promote ready access to intrinsic rewards, the informal and formal expression of recognition for good work among students, parents, administrators, and teachers. Although it may seem a far too simple response to a very complex issue, the ultimate reward that teachers seek appears in fact to be quite simple: the opportunity to teach well and to know that it matters.

CHAPTER ELEVEN

Keeping Good Teachers Teaching

Teachers, it appears, are like other workers. In choosing an occupation and deciding whether to stick with it, they respond to a wide range of features, assessing whether the workplace provides sufficient support for the work they set out to do. We cannot know how many people who might have become outstanding teachers never entered the field because of its low pay, low status, or poor working conditions. We do know that many of those who chose to teach eventually left the classroom because of dissatisfaction with the workplace. Many of those who left were among the most talented. If schools are to attract and retain strong teachers, they must become places where those teachers can do their work well.

The interviews with the valued teachers of this study show clearly that they attend to the *physical* components of their work, surveying school sites to determine whether they were safe, functional, comfortable, and well-maintained. Teachers assess the materials and supplies available for appropriateness and sufficiency. They respond to the *organizational* structures of schools, noting the number of students and classes assigned to them, the demands and flexibility of the schedule, the extent to which their work is monitored and the amount of discretion they are expected, or allowed, to exercise in their teaching. They consider their schools from *sociological* perspectives, noting the attitudes that their students bring to school and the relationships that their schools maintain with the families they serve. Their roles as teachers, both within the school and within the society, and the quality of their associations with colleagues contribute to their sense of belonging, efficacy, and status. *Economic* factors, such as job security and pay, determine for many teachers whether they can concentrate on their teaching or even afford to teach at all. Access to the incentives and rewards that matter most to them—appreciation from students and parents, reputations as outstanding teachers—are important determinants of their satisfaction. Teachers also view their workplaces *politically,* considering whether they can influence important decisions about school policy, such as how money is spent, which new teachers are hired, or which textbooks are bought. Teachers contemplate whether they are supported in their work by the *cultural* features of their schools—constructive norms, rich histories, and compelling traditions that engage students, peers, administrators, and parents in shared sets of values and purposes. Finally, teachers appraise the *psychological* characteristics of their work in schools, considering whether the meaning of teaching is enhanced or diminished by their workplace, whether the personal and professional stresses of teaching are tolerable, and whether their jobs provide sufficient opportunity for their own learning and growth.

The features of the workplace that mattered most to these teachers proved to be the ones that enabled or inhibited them in the classroom. If school buildings were dysfunctional or decrepit, if materials and equipment were out-of-date or out of order, instruction suffered. If they were assigned heavy workloads, whether in number of students per class, numbers of classes per week, or numbers of course preparations per term, they became exhausted and discouraged about the possibility of doing a good job. If districts prescribed, packed, and paced curricula, teachers became defiant or demoralized. If schools tested some results—such as computation and decoding—while disregarding others—such as social growth or creative expression—teachers were less likely to respond to the emerging interests of the class or adapt instruction to meet the individual needs of students. If the schedule had little flexibility, or students' days were splintered by pull-out programs and specialists' classes, teachers could not sustain a coherent approach to instruction. If students were unwell, unfed, or preoccupied with personal problems, teachers could make little progress teaching subject matter. If parents were removed from their children's schooling and the school did nothing to reduce their physical, social, and psychological distance, teachers' chances of success were seriously compromised. If teachers had no time to meet with their colleagues or observe others' classes, they were deprived of professional support and expertise that would have improved their work in the classroom and the school. If they had no say in how their schools were run, managerial rather than instructional priorities prevailed. If the school was marked by instability or lacked shared values, traditions, understandings of purpose, and responsibility, teachers were hindered in their efforts to make a significant difference in students' lives. If teachers' personal learning and professional development were confined to intermittent in-service sessions, teachers were more likely to be resentful than restored. If low pay required them to take second jobs, thus leaving little time for classroom preparation and independent learning, their teaching suffered, and they became less likely to achieve the intrinsic rewards that had originally attracted them to teaching.

These valued teachers, who had stayed with teaching through difficult periods of layoffs and transfer, budget cuts, and transformations of neighborhoods and student populations, had chosen to continue teaching. They had chosen to cope while many of their most able colleagues had decided that the personal and professional price of work in schools was too high. Even so, a significant number of the public-school respondents—9 of 75—reported that they now plan to leave teaching.

Of those who stay, many do so with enthusiasm and confidence, but others only with resignation and discouragement. For most, schools have not been the workplaces that they had hoped or needed. We saw in these interviews that some teachers had, over time, narrowed the scope of their attention and responsibility in response to the conditions of their work. When the school did not provide high standards for student behavior or high expectations for staff, some of these very good teachers withdrew to their classrooms and focused exclusively on their students, recognizing that their independent influence as individuals might be less than it could have been in a better organized, more interdependent school. Some teachers who had once spent extra time developing curricula or deliberating with their colleagues on districtwide committees had abandoned those efforts when their work was ignored by school officials or the hours of unpaid time became burdensome. Although Anna Capello continued to work intently with her students in home economics, she admitted that she had retreated from participating in schoolwide governance and found herself making less effort to meet with colleagues outside her teaching area. She spoke of feeling less optimism and enthusiasm about her work and finding no incentive for working any harder. Although she recognized that she was not responsible for all the difficulties that she encountered in teaching, she observed, "There's a lot of guilt involved. When you haven't accomplished what you set out to do, you can come up with a number of very good reasons, but it doesn't make you feel any better. . . ."

In addition to influencing teachers' satisfaction and schoolwide effort, the workplace affected the quality of teaching that was possible. No matter how talented and committed, teachers could not do their best work in settings that distracted them or undermined their efforts. Anyone has but a limited amount of time for work, time that can be used more or less productively. These teachers believed that their time was best spent on work with children, uninterrupted by clerical or supervisory duties; on meetings with colleagues centered on instructional rather than administrative matters; on classroom preparation unhindered by scarce or inadequate supplies; on parent conferences undisturbed by strained home/school relationships. When there was insufficient time for teachers to do their best work or when their time was poorly protected from disruption and abuse, the quality of teaching was inevitably compromised.

Schools can encourage or discourage collegiality among teachers. Those that promote competition among staff with merit pay or performance-based layoffs are unlikely to obtain the benefits of close collaboration. Those that schedule specialists' time efficiently but fail to provide meeting time for teachers to confer regularly, increase the isolation of staff. Those that discourage classroom observations and elevate norms of privacy and self-sufficiency will miss many advantages of their teachers' varied talents. The contributions of teachers in such schools are necessarily limited and the experiences of students inevitably disjointed. In a variety of ways, the school as a workplace determines the character and quality of schooling, promoting satisfaction, commitment, and continuing improvement of practice or causing discouragement, withdrawal, and an ever-worsening instructional climate.

VARIATION AMONG SCHOOLS

Overall, the public schools we studied proved to be deficient workplaces, although we found individual schools that supported teachers well in their work. Some schools boasted sound, functional facilities; plentiful supplies; and up-to-date equipment. Some schools enjoyed strong support from parents, and others took deliberate steps to promote constructive relationships between home and school. Some teachers shared responsibility with small teams of colleagues for distinct groups of students, exercising discretion over curriculum, discipline, and scheduling. In some schools, administrators arranged teaching schedules so that staff who needed to collaborate could do so. Teachers from several schools were influential in school governance, both formally and informally, having a say in who was hired, how money was spent, and what texts would be used. In some schools, norms were strong and positive, and students and staff shared a commitment to each other. Professional development was a serious endeavor in a few schools, where staff were encouraged to design and participate in in-service training, and sessions centered on teachers' instructional concerns. In some schools teachers felt that they were recognized by parents, peers, and superiors for their work. Some staff could supplement their modest salaries with paid work in research, writing, or curriculum development that would enrich them academically as well as monetarily. Although we found no teacher whose school succeeded in all of these areas, evidence was ample that success is possible.

Our sample provided comparisons among public and private schools that proved to be informative. To be sure, private schools have limitations of their own—low pay, limited capacity to serve the full array of student needs, excessive demands on teachers' time and privacy; however they are also relatively unencumbered by bureaucratic requirements, more responsive to parents, more reliant on teachers' assuming broad institutional responsibilities, and attentive to developing special identities.

Those private-school teachers who could afford the lower salaries that their schools typically paid, usually were more satisfied with their workplaces than were public-school teachers. In general, private schools were organized to make good teaching not only possible, but more likely. Facilities were typically well-maintained and well-equipped. Teachers could ask students to purchase books and could themselves buy additional materials as needed. Students were generally well-motivated and parents were both supportive of the schools they had chosen and cooperative in case of difficulties. Classes and teaching loads were small, schedules flexible, autonomy extensive, and nonteaching assignments centered on students rather than paperwork or building security. Teachers often held positions on governing boards and hiring or admission committees; some assumed both teaching and administrative responsibilities. They enjoyed the support of strong cultures that helped people feel part of their school communities and the values, history, and traditions those communities stood for. Private schools encouraged staff to pursue their own professional growth and often financed courses, workshops, and summer study. They provided teachers with ready access to praise from parents and thanks from students, even though salaries often failed to compensate them sufficiently for their efforts.

Although a higher proportion of private-school teachers than public-school teachers expressed satisfaction with their workplaces, there was no guarantee that private schools were good places in which to work. Some private schools were said to be rigid, punitive, isolating, competitive, and unrewarding environments. However, several features common in nonpublic schools seemed to increase the likelihood that teachers would find them satisfying workplaces that supported productive work.

First, with the exception of diocesan Catholic schools, they were usually autonomous and free of constraints from larger, sponsoring organizations. Decisions about policy and practice rested at the school site rather than in a bureaucratic office downtown, and teachers felt that they had access to those who determined policies and practices. Second, students, staff, and administrators attended their schools by choice rather than arbitrary assignment. All members of the school community had a stake in making things go well, for there was no easy transfer out. Third, private schools were smaller in size than public schools at comparable grade levels, and teachers were more likely to know all students and colleagues with whom they worked. Fourth, private schools tended to have small administrative structures, and as a result, teachers were obliged to participate in policy making and often held roles that combined teaching and administrative responsibilities. Fifth, private schools were typically well-established institutions that offered stability, certainty, and good reason for staff to invest in their futures.

The freedom of private schools to select their students and dismiss those who fail to meet their standards might be thought alone to account for teachers' greater satisfaction with these workplaces. In fact, having able and eager students did contribute to private-school teachers' satisfaction and sense of success, but seemed less prominent in these teachers' accounts than other features of their work—small classes, autonomy, voice in governance, and strong cultures. It mattered a great deal that students wanted to be in their schools; it mattered far less whether those students were among the most able.

Teachers' experience in urban and suburban schools also exhibited notable patterns of difference. One might conclude, again incorrectly, that suburban schools are more satisfying workplaces simply because their students are healthier, abler, and more highly motivated, but here too other important features supported teachers in their teaching. Suburban districts were smaller than urban districts, and more suburban-school teachers expressed the belief that they could influence policy. Because suburban districts had fewer schools than urban districts, teachers were less likely to be moved without warning from one school to the next or to encounter hosts of new colleagues each September. Suburban districts typically had small central offices, and school sites enjoyed greater autonomy than in cities, often exerting greater control over their budgets, program, and staffing. Because the reputations of such communities rested with the success of their public schools, they spent more on facilities, supplies, and support services.

Suburban schools were not inevitably good workplaces or good schools. Some were unsatisfying and unsuccessful, demanding conformity among staff, generating unsettling competition, and discouraging teachers' professional growth. As with private schools, suburban schools were more likely to provide the conditions for good work, but there was no certainty that they would do so.

DESIGNING SCHOOLS AS WORKPLACES

Comparison across and within sectors of schooling reveal the characteristics that schools require to support good teachers in their work. Clearly, there is no single model, for the capacity to adapt and evolve is an essential feature of good workplaces, but we found remarkable similarity in the teachers' accounts of features that they would recommend for their schools.

Good schools would be located in functional, well maintained, and clean facilities with classrooms large and flexible enough to accommodate creative teaching. The buildings would draw people together rather than seclude them in separate corridors and cubicles, and teachers would have comfortable work spaces equipped with computers, photocopiers, and telephones. No teacher would be expected to spend precious time cleaning floors, painting classrooms, or protecting students from broken glass. There would be current textbooks, plentiful materials, and sufficiently modern equipment to prepare students for subsequent study or employment in the contemporary world. No teacher would have to make do with but one set of texts for four classes, and no one would cope with faint, lavender-hued dittos or lack access to language labs, computers, VCRs, or Bunsen burners. Teachers would have three to five hundred dollars in discretionary funds each year to support their teaching with whatever they deemed necessary, whether it be stickers, felt-tipped pens, lumber, film, or video cassettes.

In such schools, students would have the support of families and community agencies to ensure that they are adequately nourished, clothed, and housed. If families fail to inculcate strong beliefs in their children about the value of formal education, schools would devise ways to engage parents in school life, to convince the community of the value of schooling, and to facilitate frequent interaction between home and school. These schools would put learning at the center of their efforts and devise organizational structures that enhance rather than diminish opportunities for learning. Classes of no more than 20 students and teaching loads of no more than 80 students would enable teachers to respond personally to the varied needs of their students. Tracking would be reduced or eliminated as more support staff supplemented teachers' work within these smaller classes. Small schools or schools-within-schools would enable all staff and students to know each other and teachers to maintain contact with their colleagues who teach the same students. Teachers could be both generalists concerned with the total education of their students and specialists demonstrating expertise in particular subject areas. Their nonteaching time would be reserved for class preparation, staff meetings, or conferences, rather than supervisory or custodial duties in the corridors or cafeterias.

No fixed curriculum would be handed down from on high, and staff would develop their own program in keeping with broad district guidelines. Within that curriculum, teachers would be encouraged to prepare units and lessons of interest to them and their students. Tests would be designed primarily for diagnostic use, and where they were used to assess the schools' success in imparting either skills or subject matter, administrators would interpret scores realistically, without diverting teachers' attention from other instructional purposes.

Teachers would collaborate in these schools, relying on each other for support and encouragement, new teaching strategies, subject matter expertise, insights into their own classroom practice, the development of shared professional standards, the socialization of new staff, and alliance in initiating change. Schedules, teaching responsibilities, and room assignments would encourage both interaction and interdependence among staff, who themselves would endorse new norms to discourage isolation and competition among staff and encourage continuing classroom observations and purposeful discussions about practice.

From the classroom to the central office, teachers would exercise decisive rather than simply advisory roles in setting policies and practices. Teams, clusters, departments, school-site councils, full faculty meetings, and joint decision-making committees at the district level would provide formal mechanisms for influence. Teachers and administrators would share responsibility for determining policy and practice, and thus their decisions would be informed by the wisdom of both instructional and administrative experience.

These schools would have distinctive purposes and core

values that enable staff, parents, and students to know what it means to be members of their schools' communities. Goals and values would form the nucleus of the school's culture from which traditions could gradually develop. There would be strong emphasis on belonging; everyone would find a place. High standards for personal behavior and academic effort would be widely endorsed by students, parents, teachers, and administrators.

Teachers would be active learners rather than simply dispensers of learning, and their schools would encourage them to study, explore, and write in order to enrich both their teaching and their lives. Just as there would be no prescribed curriculum, there would be no dictated program of staff development. Teachers would not be "in-serviced" by others, but would shape their own programs for personal and group advancement. These schools would be investment-centered rather than payoff-centered, funding workshops, courses, travel, research and sabbatical leaves rather than simply granting pay increases retroactively for accumulated credits. There would be opportunities in these schools for teachers to combine teaching with other responsibilities in administration, research, teacher training, and curriculum development. Teachers particularly skilled in the classroom could oversee the work of less-experienced staff, receiving compensation for their acknowledged expertise and greater responsibility.

Finally, teachers would be well paid in these schools, earning salaries comparable to those of professionals in other public institutions—lawyers in state government, physicians in public hospitals, engineers in city halls. That pay would allow them to concentrate exclusively on their teaching and, thus, more likely reap the intrinsic rewards of student progress, parental appreciation, and collegial respect that are the centerpiece of the teaching profession.

New Policies and Practices

As we have seen, the school is a complex workplace, and improving it will require attention by many people in many places. There must be changes in policies and practices as well as roles and attitudes if schools are to become the model workplaces these teachers envision, and if public education is to attract and retain the kind of teachers who provide good education for young people.

Five general recommendations for policy and practice emerge from the teachers' accounts, changes that would permit the creation of the workplaces they seek. First, *policymakers must secure sufficient funds to ensure that public schools are well-financed.* It is illusory to imagine that public education can be at once cheap and effective. If teachers are poorly paid, many who enter classrooms during the next decade will be those who cannot find jobs elsewhere. Large numbers of women are no longer willing to subsidize education with underpaid careers. If schools are not repaired and maintained to permit safe, comfortable work, good teachers will take their skills elsewhere, seeking employers who recognize the effects of physical surroundings on work. If funds are not available for new books and equipment, if there is no budget for clerical assistance, if classes and teaching loads are large, students will suffer and teachers will continue to leave teaching. This society will never obtain an educated citizenry without paying for it. If politicians think that the public will not approve the taxes needed to improve public education, then they must persuade that public that its future depends on its schools.

Thoroughly reforming schools will be costly. But schools fail not only because money is scarce, but also because it is mismanaged. Buildings deteriorate because repairs are not carried out systematically or because some principals are more successful than others in exerting political pressure at the central office. District administrators purchase equipment and materials without determining whether teachers can use them. They purchase unreasonably expensive supplies or accept low bids from contractors who do shoddy work. Central offices maintain costly records or impose unnecessary procedures that do little to support instruction. They hire outside experts to provide staff development that teachers consider irrelevant. Many costs can be reduced without compromising the quality of instruction and school services, and they should be.

Second, *public schooling should be decentralized and deregulated so that the school site, rather than the district, becomes the primary unit of organization and so that teachers, principals, and parents can institute practices that address the needs of the school community.* School-site management is consistent with the findings of this study, suggesting that schools should be individually shaped and governed by the people with the most immediate stake in how they work. The one feature that most distinguished independent schools in this study was that they were, in fact, independent, and therefore capable of setting their own priorities for the use of time, money, and personnel. Much of what public-school teachers found to be most troubling in their work resulted from their subordination to a larger bureaucracy which assigned staff, created and eliminated programs, prescribed curriculum, tested outcomes, and decided when and whether to repair their broken windows. Teachers, principals, and parents of these schools felt little sense of control, and their futures as school communities were never certain. Buildings could be closed, programs relocated, and staff reassigned without recourse.

New efforts to decentralize school governance and institute school-site councils are underway in Chicago, Boston, Rochester, and Dade County. Under Illinois legislation, central-office administrative costs in Chicago will be cut by 20 percent and the savings passed on to school sites where local school councils composed of parents, teachers, principals, and community members will choose their school's principal, control the budget, and develop a school improvement plan.[1] Similarly, under the provisions of a Boston collective-bargaining agreement signed in June 1989, school-site councils in that city will

> manage all matters that relate to the operation of the school, including priority and objective setting, design of the instructional program, budgeting and fundraising, purchasing and

> disbursement of funds, space utilization, hiring of new staff and in-transfer of staff from other schools in the system, selection and guidance of mentor teachers, parent-teacher relations, and functions, solicitation, and use of outside professionals and social service resources, and so on.[2]

These efforts to decentralize school management would be of less note if they were not occurring in school districts that have historically been among the most centralized in the country. The changes will enable teachers to have a serious voice in decisions about curriculum, budget, staffing, and program, and they could provide staff with unprecedented influence in the policies and practices of their schools. Our interviews suggest that moving such decisions close to the classroom will augment teachers' participation in policy making and increase the likelihood that their priorities receive serious attention.

Teacher unions, too, must make a serious effort to decentralize. Collective-bargaining agreements that regulate school-site practices in order to protect teachers' rights must permit for variation and adaptation as school-site councils shape local practices. Seniority rights that have enabled teachers to bump their colleagues from school to school must be amended to ensure stability and discretion for those at the school site. Staff positions that have been protected by the contract must be made subject to division or even subcontracting as school-site councils reassess their needs and reallocate their funds. Teachers must be granted the authority to assume responsibilities beyond the classroom, even when that means evaluating their peers.

Third, *policy makers should abandon industrial models of schooling that prize standardization or promote narrow measures of productivity; they must redirect their attention to improving teaching and learning for inquiry and higher-order thinking.* Good teachers have no interest in moving large batches of students through prefabricated curricula to a uniform outcome. They entered teaching to generate enthusiasm, to foster individual development, to encourage exploration, and to provoke doubt as well as certainty. They become disheartened when they are confronted with textbooks that discourage inquiry, schedules that defy variation, large classes that preclude individual attention, and tests that recognize only one correct answer.

Many of the policies enacted by states during the 1980s conveyed the message that teachers' work could and should be controlled. Legislatures prescribed curricula, tested outcomes, and sought to monitor compliance in the classroom. It has become apparent not only that teaching is difficult to regulate, but also that many talented teachers refuse to be the objects of such academic engineering.[3] If public education is to retain its best teachers—those who are creative and skilled, who think for themselves and devise alternative approaches to old problems—then districts should not presume to specify how teachers should do their work or assess their progress narrowly. If we expect children to learn to think, create, and develop their strengths, they must have teachers who are free to do so as well.

Fourth, *public schools must engage parents more meaningfully in the education of their children and coordinate public services on behalf of children and their families.* Currently, teachers in many urban schools find themselves overwhelmed by students who are poor, homeless, hungry, physically ill, and psychologically troubled. With each succeeding year, those children who arrive at school are less optimistic about formal education and less prepared to commit themselves to serious work. The schools themselves are responsible for some of this discouragement, for often they have failed to provide good education. However, without parents' actively participating in their children's education—reading with them at home, meeting with their teachers, monitoring homework, and conveying a belief that school is worth the effort—teachers' chances of success will be slim.

Teachers suggested several ways by which schools might improve home/school relations. Parents might become instructional aides or members of school councils—becoming visible participants in school life and symbolizing for students the community's commitment to education. Schools might sponsor programs in adult literacy or child rearing, or offer academic courses in continuing education. Translators, social workers, community organizers, and home tutors could assist teachers in bridging distances between home and school, mediating cultural differences between parents and teachers.

Enabling parents to choose the programs or schools that they believe will best serve their children's needs might encourage them to increase their commitment to their children's education. The accounts of private-school teachers suggest that parents who make such choices are more likely to inform themselves about the school's program and expectations. Several states, including Minnesota, Iowa, and Arkansas, have increased parents' rights to select their children's schools, and it seems likely that students will benefit and teaching will become more rewarding. However, experience with magnet schools suggests that choice plans may simply introduce a new tracking system into school districts, relegating students who are at risk to substandard schools.[4] In order for choice plans to serve students well, all schools must offer good programs so that those children whose parents do not choose on their behalf will not be further penalized.

If schools are to function as the primary social agency of the community, they must have help in supporting economically poor or troubled families. Agencies that provide health, welfare, public housing, legal, and foster-care services must coordinate their efforts either through the schools or in close association with the schools so that students arrive in classrooms with a good chance of learning.

Fifth, *schools should rely more on the professional expertise of teachers by granting them greater influence in what they teach and how their schools are run. In turn, teachers and their leaders should take steps to increase their responsibility for managing their schools and assessing the performance of their peers.* Although schools have long been under the control of administrators, local districts are increasingly granting teachers more formal responsibility for setting school policies. Unions have negotiated contracts that call for teachers' participation in setting budgets, evaluating peers, assigning staff, and hiring principals. Where once teachers' influence was almost exclusively advisory, in a few cases, it is now decisive. These initiatives are consistent with influential proposals by the Holmes Group[5] and the Carnegie Forum on Education and the Economy[6] for restructuring teachers' work. They are also consistent with the accounts of the teachers in this study who resented their lack of formal influence and would have welcomed opportunities to decide how their schools should be organized.

Adequately funding and decentralizing schooling, abandoning models of mass production, involving parents and developing systems of community support, and increasing the professional influence of teachers would enhance the quality of the school as a workplace and make it possible for good teachers to do good work. We would be mistaken, however, to imagine that the many difficulties that teachers identified in this study can be eliminated simply by a vote of the legislature or signatures on a collective bargaining agreement. There is no certainty that changes in practice follow changes in policy. Deciding that a school district should embark on school-site management is only the first step in a long process that requires many other changes to achieve decentralization—reorienting hierarchical relationships between central offices and schools, developing new decision-making skills among teachers and parents who are unpracticed in school governance, preparing principals and teachers for new kinds of leadership at the school site.

New policies provide opportunities, not outcomes. They create the climate in which teachers, parents, and administrators can improve schooling, but they cannot ensure that change will follow. There is the danger that well-intentioned school reformers, whether they be legislators, union leaders, or local school officials, will try to install new programs as if they were modular components to be mixed and matched without considering how the entire system must change in response to the innovations. The proposals for change made here are comprehensive and interrelated. Teachers cannot be expected to invest more time in school governance unless they earn salaries that enable them to do so. Schooling cannot be decentralized unless school officials relinquish expectations of standardized outcomes. Schools cannot develop productive home/school relationships unless the school itself enjoys sufficient stability and autonomy to give them an arena in which to operate. Neither the school as a workplace, nor the school itself, can be reformed by patchwork.

New Attitudes and Roles

The public-school teachers interviewed for this study offered remarkably consistent descriptions of the roles of teachers, principals, and central-office administrators in their schools. Teachers, they said, had discretion in their classrooms and pursued their work largely in isolation from their peers, with little involvement in schoolwide or districtwide decision making. Principals, who rarely ventured into classrooms, were responsible for managing their schools, facilitating instruction, and carrying out the bidding of central-office administrators. Superintendents, assistant superintendents, and curriculum supervisors from the district office were said to make policy, require compliance, and demand paperwork. From the teachers' perspectives, there was a fissure between the classroom and the school office and a chasm between the school and the central office.

Exceptions exist—teachers who continue to participate on districtwide committees, who champion changes in policy and practice, who organize collegial endeavors; principals respected for their teaching skills who promoted leadership within their faculties and shared their formal authority with staff and parents; superintendents who visited schools often, who encouraged autonomy within broad guidelines and saw to it that their offices served the schools rather than being served by them. These were the exceptions. Many of the colleagues and superiors of these valued teachers had resigned themselves to working in segmented systems where few people dared to step out of role.

For serious school reform to occur, educators' roles must change. Central-office administrators must come to understand that they exist to aid and sustain the schools rather than the reverse. Not only must they disburse the resources and functions that have accumulated over time in central offices, they must also find ways to expand school-site autonomy and to ensure school-site stability. For administrators who find meaning in controlling others' work, this will be troubling; however, those who want to establish more meaningful relationships with teachers and students will find decentralization liberating.

Principals of public-school systems have long exemplified middle managers caught between the demands of their supervisors and their subordinates, obliged to enact practices that they cannot control. Some have stood with their backs to their schools, oriented toward the central office, following directives, documenting procedures, and competing for resources. More have been intermediaries, seeking to satisfy both the central office and their faculties, interpreting the needs of each to the other, garnering supplies and services, and meeting bureaucratic deadlines. A few have stood facing their schools, disregarding demands of the central office, initiating change on their own, tending to the concerns of their teachers, students, and parents. Whatever stance they assumed, however, the fact that schools were embedded in larger bureaucratic organizations has always left the principals caught in the middle.

At the beginning of this study, I anticipated that principals would be far more prominent in teachers' accounts than they proved to be. When teachers thought their principals unusually effective, they praised them enthusiastically; when they considered them incompetent, they disparaged them. In these respondents' eyes, the effective principals were those who made good teaching possible, who minimized bureaucratic demands, ensured order among students, consulted staff about purchases and practices, respected teachers' autonomy, and rewarded good effort with a genuine "Thank you"—those who cared most about what happened in the classroom and designed all their actions to support it. The worst principals were said to be politically preoccupied, administratively driven, and instructionally inept. They were condescending and authoritarian or withdrawn and ineffectual. They pretended to know more about teaching than the staff, yet never demonstrated their expertise. Between these extremes—where most principals fell—school-site administrators were important only sometimes. They expedited or impeded instruction, often succeeding in one area, such as minimizing interference from the central office, while failing in another, such as providing useful supervision. Principals might be influential in making sure that schools functioned smoothly, but rarely were they said to be leaders.

With decentralized governance, increased influence by teachers, and greater parental involvement, the roles of principals will necessarily change. They will become accountable to school communities; blaming downtown will no longer suffice. They will have to share their authority with parents and teachers, opening matters of policy and practice to scrutiny and influence by new groups of actors. They will no longer be able to rely on their position to ensure compliance, but must earn respect from staff and parents for their competence as teachers, facilitators, and leaders. They, like their central-office counterparts, must come to regard teaching and learning, rather than management and control, as the center of schooling.

Parents, too, will find different roles in this reformed system of schooling. Not only must they oversee their children's education, but they must invest personal time and energy in making their schools work better. They will share responsibility for major decisions about budget, staffing, and program, and in doing so, will have to reconcile their personal concerns for individual children with the larger educational needs of the student body.

Finally, teachers' roles must change, for if they do not, the school as a workplace will continue to fall far short of their expectations and students' needs. Not only must teachers venture beyond their classrooms, fashioning new working relationships with their peers, and participating in decisions about their schools, but, as a group, they must become accountable for teaching standards and professional performance. The corollary to accepting greater professional authority is exercising greater professional responsibility. Over time, many of the experienced teachers of this study have withdrawn from formal roles in governance to tend solely to their own classroom needs. Few challenged norms of noninterference that allowed staff to work behind closed doors, doors which sometimes concealed unprofessional practice. Few dared to violate norms of equity that dissuaded individual teachers from assuming leadership, displaying excellence, or presuming to advise their peers. The experiences of teachers in this study who did transgress such norms suggest that it will be difficult for individuals to remake their roles as teachers, for there is much resistance among their ranks. Small groups of teachers may better collaborate to take the risks and responsibilities inherent in achieving greater professionalism. Teachers' reported successes in teams, clusters, or departments indicate that these subunits of the school can provide the critical mass of energy and support necessary to remake conventional roles and norms.

Inevitably, we must return to the question that runs throughout this study: Should schools be redesigned with only very good teachers in mind? The answer must certainly be no. However, schools must surely be redesigned with, *at least,* these very good teachers in mind. As they gradually change their roles and assume more responsibility for their schools and their profession, teachers will inevitably confront the differences that exist among them, differences that have been politely discounted or downplayed for a long time. There are inherent differences between new and experienced teachers, between skilled and merely competent teachers, between teachers who choose to exert leadership and those who are pleased to be led, between teachers who want to concentrate exclusively on instruction and those who seek educational experiences beyond their classrooms. These differences can be acknowledged and dealt with as schools institute mentoring programs, peer-evaluation plans, school-site councils, differentiated staffing, and career ladders. Without such programs, teachers will continue to be treated as an undifferentiated group, and policies will continue to be devised for the average or least able among them. However, once schools become workplaces where very good teachers can thrive, the distinctions among staff can be put to use. Outstanding teachers can be encouraged to exploit their strengths, working collaboratively with new staff, deliberating about school policy, writing curriculum, and conducting research on school practice. Teachers needing assistance can receive it from mentors, peer evaluators, and team or department members. To redesign the school as a workplace so that very good teachers can succeed is also to ensure that the needs of other teachers are addressed.

The reform of schooling and the school as a workplace are inseparable. If public education is to improve and responsibly serve an increasingly complex and diverse student population, it must be staffed by talented and committed teachers. The public cannot expect that those teachers will step forward in sufficient numbers to serve selflessly in schools that discourage their best efforts. If the quality of teaching is to be improved, then the school as a workplace must also be improved. Ultimately, good teachers must be able and encouraged to teach.

APPENDIX

METHODOLOGY

The sample of 115 teachers is an intentionally diverse one, including 75 public school teachers, 20 independent school teachers, and 20 church-related school teachers. They vary in gender, years of experience, grade level, subject of assignment, and demography of schools and districts of origin. Although the study centers on public schools and is finally designed to illuminate practices there, teachers from other sectors were included to provide comparisons. Because the workplaces of independent and church-related school teachers differ from public schools in important ways—selective student populations, independent funding, less elaborate administrative structures, less formalized labor/management relations—it seemed promising from the start to explore those differences and the implications for the public school as a workplace.

To begin, I selected an economically and demographically diverse group of school districts in eastern Massachusetts and wrote to 95 principals describing the study and asking them to recommend 3 teachers whom they considered to be "very good" teachers. My letter explained: "These should be teachers whose work is respected by their colleagues and whose contributions to the school would be missed if they were to leave."

As the responses arrived from 64 principals noting teachers' subject specialties and estimating their years of teaching experience, I built a sequential sample by selecting 1 individual from each list, always seeking to maintain as much diversity as possible in subject or grade level, gender, and years of experience. I wrote to those selected teachers, asking if they would be interviewed. If a teacher chose not to participate, I chose another from the same principal's list, again seeking to maintain diversity and balance in the total sample. Additionally, I selected a second teacher from 13 schools in order to ensure sufficient representation from particular demographic or subject areas. In all, I asked 108 teachers who had been recommended by principals to participate in the study; 76 agreed. Three of these eventually withdrew for personal reasons. Two additional teachers whom I had selected for pilot interviews on the basis of their exemplary reputations were included in the final sample of 75.

Although I asked principals to recommend "very good" teachers, I was not seeking only to interview those who were extraordinary. Rather, I wanted teachers whose work was valued by their colleagues and principals. I assumed that the standards of good teaching would vary from school to school and that, in any school, a number of very good teachers could have been recommended. In fact, several principals noted that the choice of only 3 had been a difficult one. Given the large number and geographical dispersion of the schools in this sample, I was unable to independently verify those principals' judgments.

There remains, of course, the possibility that administrators were poor judges of teacher quality or undiscerning observers of collegial respect. It is conceivable that principals intent on protecting their reputations might recommend mediocre, but loyal, teachers. However, since participation in this study was completely voluntary, I assumed that any principal who felt concerned about participating would simply decide not to. I further sought to reduce the possibility of a principal's selecting his/her single ally by soliciting 3 names and informing the principals that only 1 would likely be chosen. As with most qualitative studies, decisions about validity must rest with the discerning reader who is familiar with teachers, principals, and schools; weighs the data; and judges the subsequent analysis. The interviews provide considerable evidence that these teachers were committed to teaching, were respected by their peers, and had made special contributions to their schools. Among them were local and state Teachers of the Year, recipients of federal and state grants, department heads, team leaders, and union officers.

Of the 27 public-school districts represented in this sample, 5 are urban, 12 are suburban, 5 are located in small cities, and 5 are rural or regional. They range in enrollment from 687 to 58,977, the median being 3171. The 62 schools vary in size and character as well.

PUBLIC SCHOOL SIZE

	Elementary	Middle/Junior	High
Largest	886	1110	2019
Smallest	159	304	310
Mean	432	644	1262
Median	392	678	1154

Twenty-one schools are located in communities of "average" wealth (5–30 percent of school-aged children below the poverty line); 20 are in "poor" communities (more than 25 percent below the poverty line); and 21 are in "rich" communities (less than 5 percent below the poverty line).[1]

In soliciting the participation of teachers from independent and church-related schools, I again sought to identify a diverse selection, including both day and boarding schools that varied in selectivity and reputation. I sent 28 letters to heads and principals of independent schools, 19 of whom responded with teacher recommendations. Of the 29 principals of church-related schools whom I contacted, 15 recommended teachers. Both independent and church-related schools were smaller, on average, than those of the public sector.

PRIVATE SCHOOL SIZE

Independent	Elementary	Middle/Junior	High
Largest	225	351	573
Smallest	125	152	263
Mean	150	240	354
Median	171	216	308

PRIVATE SCHOOL SIZE (continued)

Church-Related	Elementary	Middle/Junior	High
Largest	472	365	953
Smallest	201	201	342
Mean	297	285	586
Median	240	273	402

In both independent and church-related schools, the middle-school or junior-high-school grades were subunits of schools including kindergarten through grade eight or, in one instance, grade nine. Therefore, the school size figures reported for this level are larger than the number of students actually included in these grades.

The majority of church-related schools are Catholic (11 of 16), but the sample also includes Quaker (1), Seventh-Day Adventist (1), and Jewish (3) schools. Where possible, I chose church-related schools located in the same communities as the public schools that I had selected, assuming that they might draw from similar student populations. In some instances this was the case; in others it was not.

Of the 270 teachers initially recommended by principals, 174 were women (64%) and 96 were men (36%). Gender distribution by sectors was as follows:

GENDER OF INITIAL SAMPLE

	Women	Men
Public	65%	35%
Independent	55%	45%
Church-related	17%	83%

The final sample of 115 teachers includes 73 women (63%) and 42 men (37%), with slightly more men than women teaching in public high schools and independent schools, and decidedly more women than men teaching at church-related secondary schools and at the elementary levels of all sectors:[2]

GENDER OF RESPONDENTS

	Public		Independent		Church-related	
	Female	**Male**	**Female**	**Male**	**Female**	**Male**
Elementary	19	6	4	1	9	0
	76%	24%	80%	20%	100%	0%
Middle/	17	9	1	4	5	1
Junior High	60%	40%	20%	80%	83%	17%
High	12	13	4	5	4	1
	44%	56%	50%	50%	80%	20%
Total	58	28	9	10	18	2
	60%	40%	50%	50%	90%	10%

These teachers were well educated, with 50 of the 75 public-school teachers holding master's degrees and two more holding doctorates. Of the 20 independent-school teachers, 11 held master's degrees and two held doctorates. Six of the 20 teachers in church-related schools held master's degrees and one of these held a law degree as well. However, few of the teachers, even among the independent-school sample, are graduates of elite colleges. The large majority had studied in state-sponsored institutions or small colleges of modest, but solid reputations.

Despite efforts to include a range of veteran and novice teachers in this sample, the group as a whole has considerable teaching experience. In part, this reflects the fact that developing the personal craft of teaching is a gradual process and valued teachers are likely to have at least 3 or 4 years of experience. However, the fact that the average teaching experience of those in this sample is close to 17 years probably results more from staff layoffs during the 1970s than from principals' preference for veteran teachers. In recommending respondents, they were choosing from senior, seasoned staffs.[3]

YEARS OF EXPERIENCE

	Public			Independent			Church-related		
	Elem	**Mid/Jr**	**Sr**	**Elem**	**Mid/Jr**	**Sr**	**Elem**	**Mid/Jr**	**Sr**
Mean	16.8	17.8	17.7	13.2	6.6	16.5	11.3	16.3	13.2
Median	16	18	17	10	5	18	11	17	13
Least	2	2	10	7	3	4	4	5	10
Most	37	34	35	25	11	32	25	27	17

As a group, these teachers had not only accumulated many years of experience, but the majority had done so in the districts where they were initially hired. Forty-three of the 75 public-school teachers had taught at their current schools for over half of their careers, and the mean number of years that all teachers in the sample had been in their current schools is very high:

MEAN NUMBER OF YEARS IN CURRENT SCHOOL

	Public	**Independent**	**Church-related**
Elementary	9.24	6.7	5.8
Middle	11.8	3.6	11.0
High	11.0	10.5	8.4

The low mobility of respondents from all sectors suggests either that they are content with their positions or that they fail to move because of personal inertia, institutional constraints, or financial necessity.

All schools are located in eastern Massachusetts, an area that encompasses a wide range of districts and economic conditions. Declining enrollment in the region forced substantial teacher layoffs beginning about 1980 and continuing in the secondary schools at the time of the interviews. In addition, all public-school districts were contending with financial constraints imposed by Proposition 2½, Massachusetts' tax limitation law. They were implementing a modest package of school reforms passed by the state legislature, which included a statewide testing program, increased requirements for teacher evaluation, and special research and study grants for exemplary teachers. Throughout the text, I have noted where such special circumstances appeared to influence teachers' responses.

Along with several research assistants, I conducted semi-structured interviews with these teachers from March 1986 through June 1987. Respondents were asked to discuss many aspects of their workplaces including the setting; supplies and equipment; teaching assignments; relationships with principals, colleagues, parents, and students; evaluation practices; roles in governance; pay and incentives; intrinsic rewards; and opportunities for learning, advancement, and professional growth. Questions ranged from those designed to gather facts—"Are you involved in any formal policy making?" "What administrative tasks or obligations do you have?" "Who evaluates your teaching?"—to those that probed teachers' judgments about their workplaces—"Who provides leadership in this school?" "What about this school or district makes it possible for you to do your best teaching?" "Are you satisfied with the extent of freedom or autonomy that you have in your teaching?" (Sample protocols are included below.) At a minimum, 29 issues were covered in each interview. Respondents typically became engaged in the interview and added more of their own. The interviews, all of which were tape recorded, lasted between 45 minutes and 2½ hours.

Once the interviews had been transcribed, I indexed them using the software program, "Ethnograph," a filing system designed for organizing large sets of qualitative data. The 92 topical codes that I used to index the interviews were drawn from a review of the workplace literature in other employment sectors and a preliminary analysis of these interview data. Because "Ethnograph" permits a researcher to assign multiple codes to any unit of data, I could systematically review printouts of all teachers' comments about a single topic, consider the range and distribution of those responses, and test emerging hunches and conclusions against the data.

This qualitative approach offered an appropriate method for examining complex workplace issues and generating possibilities for further research. The study has both the benefits and defects of data gathered intensively from a relatively small, purposefully chosen sample, inevitably sacrificing breadth for depth, telling a great deal about a few people, but not permitting statistical generalizations to larger populations. However, the rich and complex data that emerged from these intensive interviews can provide valuable insights for teachers, administrators, parents, policy makers and school watchers who seek to improve their schools.

SAMPLE INTERVIEW GUIDE

1. Briefly review your academic background, including the schools that you attended and the degrees that you earned.
2. Describe your current assignment (grade, subject). What type of teaching structure do you work in (self-contained, open classroom, team, cluster, department)?
3. How long have you been teaching? How many years have you been in this district? At this school? At this grade level?
4. Why did you enter teaching? Are you still in teaching for the same reasons? Have your goals for teaching been fulfilled?
5. Do you intend to continue teaching? If so, why? What could lure you away from teaching? If not, are there changes that would encourage you to stay?
6. Is this a good building to work in? Is it safe? clean? Is the neighborhood safe? Do these things affect your work?
7. Do you have sufficient materials for your work? Do you have discretionary money that you may use to buy materials? Do you buy materials with your own money for your teaching?
8. What administrative tasks or obligations do you have (lesson plans, attendance, money collection, individualized education plans)? Do you find these reasonable or burdensome? Are you requested or required to participate in extracurricular activities?
9. What is it about this school or district that makes it possible for

you to do your best teaching? What compromises your best teaching?

10. Who provides leadership in this school? Who sets the standards for good teaching?
11. Are you satisfied with the extent of freedom or autonomy that you have in your teaching?
12. Do you have a say in what grade or subject you will teach?
13. Do you design your own curriculum? Could you? Are you expected to? Is there a prescribed curriculum that you must follow in your subject area?
14. Does the school or district administer standardized tests? How are the results used?
15. Do you select your own textbooks? Do you have input into their selection?
16. Who decides how much time you allot to each subject area? Who decides what type of teaching structure you use?
    Are you free to arrange the classroom as you see fit?
    Are you free to take risks in your teaching? Are you encouraged to do so?
17. Who supervises or evaluates your teaching? Could you describe how that works? Is it effective? helpful? How might it be improved?
18. Do you supervise, assist, or train other teachers? Is that something that you like (or would like) to do?
19. Are you involved in any policy making (union, curriculum committee, principal's advisory council, districtwide committee)? Do you influence policy informally? If so, how?
20. Do parents play an active role in your school? How does that affect your work?
21. What are your views on teachers' salary levels and salary structure?
22. Is there recognition for good teaching in your school?
23. Are you a specialist in any area of your work?
24. Of what are you most proud in your work?
25. What is the greatest source of stress?
26. There has been talk recently about how teachers' work is repetitive, and that there aren't enough opportunities for personal and professional growth. Is that an issue for you? Are there parts of your job that give you more responsibility or offer more variety than other teachers have? Are these important to you?

27. Teachers sometimes say that they are isolated from other adults in their work. How much contact do you have with other adults during the day? Where does it take place and what is its purpose? Are there others in your school who teach your subject/grade level? Do you have opportunities to share ideas and materials with them or with others who teach your subject/grade level in the district?
28. How would you describe this faculty's norms and expectations about what a teacher should or should not do (hours, supervision, extra work, grading)? Do you share those norms?
29. Some organizations are said to have strong cultures, to be unified by a set of values, goals, or traditions. Is that true in your school?

NOTES

INTRODUCTION

1. Larry W. Barber and Mary C. McClellan, "Looking at America's Dropouts: Who Are They?" *Phi Delta Kappan,* 69 no. 4 (December 1987):264–67, 264; Designs for Change, *The Bottom Line: Chicago's Failing Schools and How to Change Them* (Chicago: Designs for Change, 1985).
2. National Assessment of Education Progress, *The Nation's Report Card* (Princeton, NJ: National Assessment of Education Progress, 1988).
3. John F. Jennings, "The Sputnik of the Eighties," *Phi Delta Kappan,* 69 no. 2 (October 1987); David T. Kearns, "An Education Recovery Plan for America," *Phi Delta Kappan,* 69 no. 8 (April 1988):566; Massachusetts Institute of Technology Commission on Industrial Productivity, *Made in America* (Cambridge: Massachusetts Institute of Technology, 1989).
4. V. S. Vance and P. C. Schlechty, "The Distribution of Academic Ability in the Teaching Force: Policy Implications," *Phi Delta Kappan* 64 (1982):22–27; P. C. Schlechty and V. S. Vance, "Do Academically Able Teachers Leave Education? The North Carolina Case," *Phi Delta Kappan* 63 (1981):106–12; W. Timothy Weaver, "Solving the Problem of Teacher Quality, *Phi Delta Kappan* 66 (1984):108–15; Richard J. Murnane, Judith D. Singer, and John B. Willett, "The Influences of Salaries and 'Opportunity Costs' on Teachers' Career Choices: Evidence from North Carolina," *Harvard Educational Review* 59(1989):325–46.
5. Louis Harris and Associates, *Former Teachers in America* (New York: Metropolitan Life Insurance Company, 1985), 17–18.
6. Linda Darling-Hammond, *Beyond the Commission Reports: The Coming Crisis in Teaching,* R-3177-RC (Santa Monica, CA: RAND

Corporation, July 1984); David W. Grissmer and Sheila Naturaz Kirby, *Teacher Attrition: The Uphill Climb to Staff the Nation's Schools,* R-3512-CSTP (Santa Monica, CA: RAND Corporation, August 1987).

7. Lynn Olson and Blake Rodman, "Growing Need, Fewer Teachers: Everybody Is Out There Bidding," *Education Week* 5 no. 39 (June 1986):1.
8. Joseph Berger, "Allure of Teaching Reviving: Education School Roles Surge," *New York Times,* 6 May 1988, 1.
9. National Commission on Excellence in Education, *A Nation at Risk: The Imperative for Educational Reform* (Washington D.C.: U.S. Government Printing Office, 1983).
10. Linda M. McNeil, "Contradictions of Control, Part 3: Contradictions of Reform," *Phi Delta Kappan* 69 no. 7 (1988):483.
11. Robert Rothman, "Teachers Vs. Curriculum in Philadelphia?" *Education Week* 7 no. 26 (23 March 1988):1.
12. Susan Moore Johnson, "Merit Pay for Teachers: A Poor Prescription for Reform," *Harvard Educational Review* 52 no. 2 (May 1984).
13. Rothman, "Teachers Vs. Curriculum," 21.
14. Linda M. McNeil, "Exit, Voice, and Community: Magnet Teachers' Responses to Standardization," *Educational Policy* 1 no. 1 (Winter 1987):111.
15. Carnegie Forum on Education and the Economy, *A Nation Prepared: Teachers for the 21st Century* (New York: Carnegie Forum on Education and the Economy, 1986). Holmes Group, *Tomorrow's Teachers* (East Lansing, MI: Holmes Group, 1986).
16. Theodore R. Sizer, *Horace's Compromise: The Dilemma of the American High School* (Boston: Houghton Mifflin, 1984), 184.
17. See, for example, Holmes Group, *Tomorrow's Teachers;* and Carnegie Forum, *A Nation Prepared.*
18. McNeil, "Exit, Voice, and Community," 102–104.
19. My prior research demonstrates that principals think of teachers as making particular rather than generic contributions to the school. See Susan Moore Johnson, "Performance-Based Layoffs in the Public Schools: Implementation and Outcomes," *Harvard Educational Review* 50 no. 2 (May 1980):214–33.

CHAPTER 1

1. Thomas Good, "Research on Classroom Teaching," in *Handbook of Teaching and Policy,* ed. Lee S. Shulman and Gary Sykes (New York: Longman, 1983), 42.

2. This lack of agreement is well illustrated by the ongoing debate about whether reading should be taught primarily with phonics in basal readers or whole-word recognition in regular books. See Jeanne Chall, *Learning to Read: The Great Debate,* rev. ed. (New York: McGraw-Hill, 1983).
3. Dan C. Lortie, *Schoolteacher: A Sociological Study* (Chicago: University of Chicago Press, 1975), 133.
4. David B. Tyack and M. Stroher, "Jobs and Gender: A History of the Structuring of Educational Employment by Sex," in *Educational Policy and Management: Sex Differentials,* ed. Patricia A. Schmuck, W. W. Charters, and Richard O. Carlson (New York: Academic Press, 1981); Nancy Hoffman, *Woman's "True" Profession: Voices from the History of Teaching* (Old Westbury, NY: The Feminist Press, 1981).
5. Lortie, *Schoolteacher,* 13–17.
6. David B. Tyack, *The One Best System: A History of American Urban Education* (Cambridge: Harvard University Press, 1974), 28.
7. Raymond E. Callahan, *Education and the Cult of Efficiency* (Chicago: University of Chicago Press, 1962).
8. Callahan, *Education,* 95–125.
9. Callahan, *Education,* 97.
10. Joan Lipsitz, *Successful Schools for Young Adolescents* (New Brunswick, NJ: Transaction Books, 1984), 99.
11. Gertrude McPherson, *Small Town Teacher* (Cambridge: Harvard University Press, 1972), 51, 54, 55, 164.
12. Robert Kahn, "The Meaning of Work: Interpretation and Proposals for Measurement," in *The Human Meaning of Social Change,* ed. Angus Campbell and Philip E. Converse (New York: Russell Sage, 1972), 159–203; John P. Robinson, "Some Approaches to Examining Quality of Employment Indicators for Disaggregated Segments of the Work Force," in *Measuring Work Quality for Social Reporting,* ed. Albert D. Biderman and Thomas F. Drury (New York: Wiley, 1976).
13. Robinson, "Some Approaches," 47–48.
14. Neal Herrick and Michael Macoby identified four "principles of humanization of work":

    1. Security (health, safety, income, future employment)
    2. Equity (commensurate compensation, fair evaluations, profit sharing)
    3. Individuation (craftsmanship, autonomy, learning)
    4. Democracy (participatory management, worker control)

    Neal Q. Herrick and Michael Macoby, "Humanizing Work: A Priority

Goal of the 1970s," in *The Quality of Working Life,* vol. 1, *Problems, Prospects, and the State of the Art,* ed. Louis E. Davis and Albert B. Cherns (New York: The Free Press, 1975), 64–66.

15. Richard E. Walton suggests that although the following criteria were "the result of this author's personal observations, experiences, values, and assumptions about human nature," such lists might be derived more systematically by some combination of empirical methods—surveys, observations, and depth interviews. "Criteria for Quality of Working Life," in *The Quality of Working Life,* Vol. 1, ed. Davis and Cherns, 100–101.
16. Rosabeth Moss Kanter and Barry A. Stein, eds., *Life in Organizations: Workplaces As People Experience Them* (New York: Basic Books, 1979); Studs Terkel, *Working* (New York: Avon, 1972); Robert Schrank, *Ten Thousand Working Days* (Cambridge: MIT Press, 1978); Lloyd Zimpel, ed., *Man Against Work* (Grand Rapids, MI: Eerdmans, 1974); William Serrin, "The Assembly Line," *Atlantic Monthly,* October 1971, 62–73; Barbara Garson, *All the Livelong Day* (Garden City, NJ: Doubleday, 1975); Carolyn See, "A Veterinarian," *Atlantic Monthly,* October 1971, 95–102; James P. Spradley and Brenda J. Mann, *The Cocktail Waitress: Woman's Work in a Man's World* (New York: Wiley, 1975).
17. "Steve Dubi," in Terkel, *Working,* 720.
18. See, for example, Jay Galbraith, *Designing Complex Organizations* (Reading, MA: Addison-Wesley, 1973); Paul R. Lawrence and Jay W. Lorsch, *Organization and Environment: Managing Differentiation and Integration* (Boston: Harvard Business School Press, 1986); Henry Mintzberg, *Structure in Fives: Designing Effective Organizations* (Englewood Cliffs, NJ: Prentice-Hall, 1983).
19. "Terry Mason," in Terkel, *Working,* 76–77.
20. "Grace Clements," in Terkel, *Working,* 385.
21. "Brett Hauser," in Terkel, *Working,* 371–374.
22. "Ping-Pong," in Garson, *All the Livelong Day,* 1.
23. "Hobart Foote," in Terkel, *Working,* 234.
24. Alan Harrington, "A Day at the Crystal Palace," in *Life in Organizations,* ed. Kanter and Stein, 108–109.
25. Rush Loving, Jr., "W. T. Grant's Last Days," in *Life in Organizations,* ed. Kanter and Stein, 402.
26. "Mike Lefevre," in Terkel, *Working,* 2.
27. "George Allen," in Terkel, *Working,* 508.
28. Spradley and Mann, *The Cocktail Waitress*, 15–28.
29. "Terry Mason," in Terkel, *Working,* 73.
30. "Philip Da Vinci," in Terkel, *Working,* 695.
31. "Kitty Scanlon," in Terkel, *Working,* 642.

32. Serrin, "The Assembly Line," 63.
33. Patrick Fenton, "Confessions of a Working Stiff," in Zimpel, *Man Against Work,* 19.
34. Zwerdling, Daniel. "At IGP, It's Not Business As Usual," in *Life in Organizations,* ed. Kanter and Stein, 351.
35. Terrence E. Deal and Allen A. Kennedy, *Corporate Cultures: The Rites and Rituals of Corporate Life* (Reading, MA: Addison-Wesley, 1982).
36. Thomas J. Peters and Robert H. Waterman, Jr., *In Search of Excellence: Lessons from America's Best-Run Companies* (New York: Warner, 1982); Deal and Kennedy, *Corporate Cultures.*
37. "Hobart Foote," in Terkel, *Working,* 236.
38. Robert Coles, "On the Meaning of Work," *Atlantic Monthly,* October 1971, 104.
39. "Mike Lefevre," in Terkel, *Working,* 1.
40. "Hub Dillard," in Terkel, *Working,* 51.
41. "Nora Watson," in Terkel, *Working,* 675.
42. Rosabeth Moss Kanter has studied workplaces that encourage workers to take risks and innovate and that invest in people and promising ideas; she concludes that highly segmented organizations that restrict workers to narrow assignments frequently foreclose personal growth and development. See Rosabeth Moss Kanter, *The Change Masters: Innovation for Productivity in the American Corporation* (New York: Simon & Schuster, 1983).
43. Fenton, "Confessions of a Working Stiff," 19.
44. "Jim Grayson," in Terkel, *Working,* 232.
45. "Hub Dillard," in Terkel, *Working,* 51.
46. "The Lordstown Auto Workers," in *Life in Organizations,* ed. Kanter and Stein, 206–25.
47. F. H. M. Blackler and C. A. Brown, "Job Redesign and Social Change: Case Studies at Volvo," in *Changes in Working Life,* ed. K. D. Duncan, M. M. Gruneberg, and D. Wallis (New York: Wiley, 1980), 311–27; Pehr G. Gyllenhammer, *People at Work* (Reading MA: Addison-Wesley, 1977); Steve Lohr, "Making Cars the Volvo Way," *New York Times,* 23 June 1987, D1, D5.
48. Kanter and Stein, eds., *Life in Organizations,* 183.
49. Kanter and Stein, eds., *Life in Organizations,* 183.
50. Albert B. Cherns and Louis E. Davis, "Assessment of the State of the Art," in *The Quality of Working Life,* Vol. 1, ed. Davis and Cherns, 46; for a similar argument see Stanley Seashore, "Defining and Measuring the Quality of Working Life," in *The Quality of Working Life,* Vol. 1, ed. Davis and Cherns, 111.
51. R. M. Steers, *Organizational Effectiveness: A Behavioral View*

(Pacific Palisades, CA: Goodyear, 1977); Charles Perrow, "Three Types of Effectiveness Studies," and W. Richard Scott, "Effectiveness of Organizational Effectiveness Studies," in *New Perspectives on Organizational Effectiveness,* ed. Paul S. Goodman, M. Pennings Johannes and Associates (San Francisco: Jossey-Bass, 1977).

52. George Madaus, "The Influence of Testing on the Curriculum," *Critical Issues in Curriculum: 87th Yearbook of the NSSE, Part I* (Chicago: University of Chicago Press, 1988).
53. Davis and Cherns, eds., *Quality of Working Life,* vols. 1 and 2; Duncan, Gruneberg, and Wallis, *Changes in Working Life.*
54. National Commission on Excellence in Education, *A Nation at Risk: The Imperative for Educational Reform* (Washington D.C.: U.S. Government Printing Office, 1983).
55. Callahan, *Education,* 19–41.
56. Carnegie Forum on Education and the Economy, *A Nation Prepared: Teachers for the 21st Century* (New York: Carnegie Forum on Education and the Economy, 1986). Holmes Group, *Tomorrow's Teachers* (East Lansing, MI: Holmes Group, 1986).
57. Philip W. Jackson, "Facing Our Ignorance," *Teachers College Record* 88 no. 3 (Spring 1987); Kevin Ryan, "The Wrong Report at the Right Time," *Teachers College Record* 88 no. 3 (Spring 1987).
58. John I. Goodlad, *A Place Called School: Prospects for the Future* (New York: McGraw-Hill, 1984).
59. Goodlad, *A Place Called School,* 177.
60. Goodlad, *A Place Called School,* 178.
61. See, for example, what history tells us about the prospects of merit pay. Susan Moore Johnson, "Merit Pay for Teachers: A Poor Prescription for Reform," *Harvard Educational Review* 54 no. 2 (May 1984).
62. Dale Mann, "Authority and School Improvement: An Essay on 'Little King' Leadership," *Teachers College Record* 88 no. 1 (Fall 1986):41–52; Myron Lieberman, *Beyond Public Education* (New York: Praeger, 1986).
63. Lynn Olson and Blake Rodman, "Is There a Teacher Shortage? It's Anyone's Guess," *Education Week* 6 no. 39 (24 June 1987):1, 14.

CHAPTER 2

1. Dan C. Lortie, *Schoolteacher: A Sociological Study* (Chicago: University of Chicago Press, 1975), 25–54.

2. John I. Goodlad, *A Place Called School: Prospects for the Future* (New York: McGraw-Hill, 1984), 171.
3. Goodlad, *A Place Called School,* 171.
4. Dan Lortie first labeled the school schedule an "ancillary reward" of teaching in that it is available to all as a condition of employment (*Schoolteacher*, 101). Notably, though, it is valued differently by individual teachers.
5. Michael Lipsky, *Street-Level Bureaucracy* (New York: Russell Sage, 1980).

CHAPTER 3

1. A recent report by the Institute for Educational Leadership documents the poor physical conditions in urban schools and the problems caused by deferred maintenance. Thomas B. Corcoran, Lisa J. Walker, and J. Lynne White, *Working in Urban Schools* (Washington, D.C.: Institute for Educational Leadership, 1988), 11–20.
2. These reports are further substantiated by a study sponsored by the Education Writers Association: Anne Lewis, *Wolves at the Schoolhouse Door: An Investigation of the Condition of Public School Buildings* (Washington, D.C.: Education Writers Association, 1989).
3. Among the 280 urban teachers interviewed by researchers from the Institute for Educational Leadership, the highest percentage (28 percent) said that photocopiers were the most needed equipment in their schools. Corcoran, Walker, and White, *Working in Urban Schools,* 29.

CHAPTER 4

1. Several researchers have described teachers' dependence on their students for achieving a sense of professional efficacy. See Robert W. Connell, *Teachers' Work* (Sydney, NSW: George Allen and Unwin, 1985); Patricia T. Ashton and Rodman B. Webb, *Making a Difference: Teachers' Sense of Efficacy and Student Achievement* (New York: Longman, 1986); Mary Haywood Metz, *Teachers' Ultimate Dependence on Their Students: Implications for Teachers' Responses to Student Bodies of Differing Social Class*

(Madison, WI: National Center on Effective Secondary Schools, 1988).

2. Willard Waller, *The Sociology of Teaching* (1932; reprint, New York: Wiley, 1976), 68.
3. Sara Lawrence Lightfoot, *Worlds Apart: Relationships Between Families and Schools* (New York: Basic Books, 1978).
4. Dan C. Lortie, *Schoolteacher: A Sociological Study* (Chicago: University of Chicago Press, 1975), 190.
5. Elizabeth B. Kean explores this issue from her perspective as both a parent and a teacher in "Left Behind," *Teacher Magazine* 1 no. 1 (1989):8–9.
6. By contrast, researchers at the Institute for Educational Leadership found "serious problems with students in most of the 31 [urban] schools that they studied" (p. 46); teachers' dominant concern about students was discipline (p. 38).Thomas B. Corcoran, Lisa J. Walker, J. Lynne White, *Working in Urban Schools* (Washington, D.C.: Institute for Educational Leadership, 1988).
7. For a description of how minority students lack confidence in formal education because of seeing others unable to obtain a job, even when they hold diplomas see John Ogbu, "Variability in Minority School Performance: A Problem in Search of an Explanation," *Anthropology and Education Quarterly* 18 no. 4 (1987):312–34.
8. Recently, researchers have described the informal bargains by which students refrain from disruptive behavior in exchange for teachers lowering academic expectations. See Linda M. McNeil, *Contradictions of Control: School Structure and School Knowledge* (New York: Routledge and Kegan Paul, 1986); Arthur G. Powell, Eleanor Farrar, and David K. Cohen, *The Shopping Mall High School: Winners and Losers in the Educational Marketplace* (Boston: Houghton Mifflin, 1985); Philip A. Cusick, *The Egalitarian Ideal and the American High School: Studies of Three Schools* (New York: Longman, 1983); and Michael Sedlak, Christopher W. Wheeler, Diana C. Pullin, and Philip A. Cusick, *Selling Students Short: Classroom Bargains and Academic Reform in the American High School* (New York: Teachers College Press, 1986).
9. Jeannie Oakes, *Keeping Track: How Schools Structure Inequality* (New Haven: Yale University Press, 1985), 65–7.
10. Robert Connell and his associates have richly described the complicated relationships between homes and schools in working-class and professional communities in Australia: Robert W. Connell, D. J. Ashenden, S. Kessler, and G. W. Dowsett, *Making the Difference: Schools, Families, and Social Division* (Sydney, NSW: George Allen and Unwin, 1982).

11. For a description of such schools, see James P. Comer, "Home-School Relationships As They Affect the Academic Success of Children," *Education and Urban Society* 16 (1984):323–37.
12. Patricia Albjerg Graham, "Black Teachers: A Drastically Scarce Resource," *Phi Delta Kappan* 68 no. 8 (April 1987):598–605. Louis Harris reports that black and Hispanic teachers currently account for about 11 percent of the teaching force. Forty-one percent of them report that they will leave teaching within five years. Louis Harris and Associates, *1988 Survey of the American Teacher* (New York: Metropolitan Life Insurance Company, 1988).
13. Corcoran, Walker, and White, *Working in Urban Schools,* 42.
14. For an exploration of the tensions that middle-class teachers experience in working-class or lower-class communities, see Annette Hemmings, *"Real" Teaching: How Teachers Negotiate National, Community, and Student Pressures When They Define Their Work* (Madison, WI: National Center on Effective Secondary Schools, 1988).
15. James P. Comer, "Education for Community," in *Common Decency,* ed. Alvin Schorr (New Haven: Yale University Press, 1986):186–209.
16. Deborah L. Cohen, "Joining Forces," *Education Week* 8 no. 25 (15 March 1989):8. For a description of programs that successfully coordinate such social services, see Lisbeth Schorr, *Within Our Reach: Breaking the Cycle of Disadvantage* (New York: Anchor Press/Doubleday, 1988).

CHAPTER 5

1. Raymond E. Callahan, *Education and the Cult of Efficiency* (Chicago: University of Chicago Press, 1962), 178.
2. In their research, Burns and Stalker found "mechanistic" organizational structures in industries that were stable and established, "organic" structures in industries that were more dynamic. Tom Burns and G. M. Stalker, *The Management of Innovation* (London: Tavistock, 1961). Subsequently, Lawrence and Lorsch found that organizational structures were more flexible in the plastics industry than in the packaged-foods or box-container industries; they concluded that these differences in structure reflected differences in environmental uncertainty. Paul R. Lawrence and Jay W. Lorsch, *Organization and Environment: Managing Differentiation and Integration* (Boston: Graduate School of Business Administration, Harvard University, 1967).

3. Joan Lipsitz, *Successful Schools for Young Adolescents* (New Brunswick, NJ: Transaction Books, 1984).
4. Holly M. Houston, "Restructuring Secondary Schools," in *Building a Professional Culture in Schools,* ed. Ann Lieberman (New York: Teachers College Press, 1988), 109–28.
5. U.S. Department of Education, *Class Size and Public Policy: Politics and Panaceas* (Washington, D.C.: U.S. Government Printing Office, 1986).
6. Nationally, the median class size at the elementary level is 24. Class size in Massachusetts is well below that of other states, such as California. U.S. Department of Education, *Class Size and Public Policy,* 28.
7. Nationally, the median class size at the secondary level is 22. U.S. Department of Education, *Class Size and Public Policy,* 14.
8. For comparisons of class size in the public and private schools of New Jersey, see Pearl R. Kane, *The Teachers College New Jersey Survey: A Comparative Study of Public and Independent School Teachers* (New York: Teachers College, Columbia University, 1986).
9. See also Arthur G. Powell, "The Conditions of Teachers' Work in Independent Schools: Some Preliminary Observations," in *The Secondary School Workplace,* ed. Milbrey Wallin McLaughlin and Joan Talbert (New York: Teachers College Press, 1990).
10. In her survey of teachers' workloads in public and private schools in New Jersey, Pearl Kane found that the average load for public school teachers in academic disciplines was 103. The average load in independent day schools was 69, while in boarding schools it was 50. Kane, *The Teachers College New Jersey Survey.*
11. Theodore R. Sizer, *Horace's Compromise: The Dilemma of the American High School.* (Boston: Houghton Mifflin, 1984), 197.
12. Helen Featherstone, "Organizing Classes by Ability," *Harvard Education Letter* 3 no. 4 (July 1987):1–2. Also see Jeannie Oakes, *Keeping Track: How Schools Structure Inequality* (New Haven: Yale University Press, 1985).
13. See Arthur G. Powell, Eleanor Farrar, and David K. Cohen, *The Shopping Mall High School: Winners and Losers in the Educational Marketplace* (Boston: Houghton Mifflin, 1985).
14. Barbara Neufeld, "Evaluating the Effective Teaching Research," *Harvard Education Letter* 1 no. 5 (November 1985):5.
15. Lynn Olson, "Teaching's 'Knowledge Base' Seen Still Elusive," *Education Week* 7 no. 23 (2 March 1988):7.
16. For a description of such prescriptive curricula, see Linda McNeil, "Exit, Voice, and Community: Magnet Teachers' Responses to Standardization," *Educational Policy* 1 no. 1 (Winter 1987):93–113.

17. Grant Wiggins makes this useful distinction in "10 'Radical' Suggestions for School Reform," *Education Week* 7 no. 24 (9 March 1988):28.
18. Charles Kerchner and Douglas Mitchell have argued that work which we call "labor" can be rationalized and monitored directly, while "professional" work is adaptive and can be assessed only indirectly. Douglas E. Mitchell and Charles T. Kerchner, "Labor Relations and Teacher Policy," in *Handbook of Teaching and Policy,* ed. Lee S. Shulman and Gary Sykes (New York: Longman, 1983), 214–38.
19. H. Dickson Corbett and Bruce L. Wilson, "Raising the Stakes on Statewide Mandatory Testing Programs," in *The Politics of Reforming School Administration,* ed. Jane Hannaway and Robert Crowson (New York: The Falmer Press, 1989), 30.
20. Corbett and Wilson, "Raising the Stakes," 33.
21. Theodore Sizer's Coalition of Essential Schools is working to provide alternative structures with no more than modest increases in costs, "an ultimate per pupil cost not to exceed those at traditional schools by more than 10 percent." Houston, "Restructuring Secondary Schools," 127.
22. John W. Meyer and Brian Rowan, "The Structure of Educational Organizations," in *Environments and Organizations: Theoretical and Empirical Perspectives,* ed. M. Meyer and Associates (San Francisco: Jossey-Bass, 1978); the concept of the "real" American High School is developed by Mary Haywood Metz, *"The American High School": A Universal Drama Amid Disparate Experience* (Madison, WI: National Center on Effective Secondary Schools, 1988).
23. Houston, "Restructuring Secondary Schools," 126–27.
24. Lynn Olson, "In San Diego, Managers Forging 'Service' Role," *Education Week* 8 no. 24 (8 March 1989):1.
25. Under a new school reform act, Chicago schools are projected to save $40 million by reducing the size of the central office, savings which will be passed on to the schools. Designs for Change, *The Chicago School Reform Act: Highlights of Senate Bill 1840* (Chicago: Designs for Change, 1989).

CHAPTER 6

1. Susan J. Rosenholtz, "Effective Schools: Interpreting the Evidence," *American Journal of Education* 93 no. 3 (May 1985):365.
2. Judith Warren Little, "Norms of Collegiality and Experimentation:

Workplace Conditions of School Success," *American Educational Research Journal* 19 no. 3 (1982):325–40.

3. Judith Warren Little, "Teachers as Colleagues," in *Educators' Handbook: A Research Perspective,* ed. Virginia Richardson-Koehler (New York: Longman, 1987), 493.
4. Dan C. Lortie, *Schoolteacher: A Sociological Study* (Chicago: University of Chicago Press, 1975), 134–61.
5. For an insightful examination of the opportunities and difficulties that teachers encounter as they participate in peer observations, see John McGee Ritchie, "Experiments in Promoting Teacher Collegiality: A Qualitative Study of Three Schools" (Doctoral diss., Harvard University, 1989).
6. Susan J. Rosenholtz, *Teachers' Workplace: The Social Organization of Schools* (New York: Longman, 1989), 55–64.

CHAPTER 7

1. Called the discretion of the street-level bureaucrat in Michael Lipsky, *Street-Level Bureaucracy* (New York: Russell Sage, 1980).
2. Susan Moore Johnson, *Teacher Unions in Schools* (Philadelphia: Temple University Press, 1984).
3. Julia E. Koppich and Charles T. Kerchner, *The Trust Agreement Project: Broadening the Vision of School Labor-Management Relations: A First-Year Progress Report* (Berkeley, CA: Policy Analysis for California Education, September 1988).
4. Karl E. Weick, "Educational Organizations As Loosely Coupled Systems," *Administrative Science Quarterly* 21 (1976):1–19.
5. Carnegie Forum on Education and the Economy, *A Nation Prepared: Teachers for the 21st Century* (New York: Carnegie Forum on Education and the Economy, 1986).
6. Holmes Group, *Tomorrow's Teachers* (East Lansing, MI: Holmes Group, 1986).
7. Jerome Rosow and Robert Zager, *Allies in Educational Reform: How Teachers, Unions, and Administrators Can Join Forces for Better Schools* (San Francisco: Jossey-Bass, 1989).
8. For a description of the radical reorganization of the Chicago public schools, see Designs for Change, *The Chicago School Reform Act: Highlights of Senate Bill 1840* (Chicago: Designs for Change, 1989).
9. Designs for Change, *The Chicago Reform Act.*
10. Boston Public Schools, "Agreement Between the Boston School

Committee and the Boston Teachers Union" (Boston: Boston Public Schools, 1989).

11. Susan Moore Johnson, "Pursuing Professional Reform in Cincinnati," *Phi Delta Kappan,* 69 no. 10 (June 1988):746–51.
12. Carnegie Forum, *A Nation Prepared,* 61.
13. Michael Cohen, "Improving School Effectiveness: Lessons From Research," in *Educators' Handbook: A Research Perspective,* ed. Virginia Richardson-Koehler (New York: Longman, 1987), 483.
14. Carnegie Forum, *A Nation Prepared.*

CHAPTER 8

1. The following discussion of organizational culture assumes a broad definition of the concept, such as that set forth by Edgar Schein:

> A pattern of basic assumptions—invented, discovered, or developed by a given group as it learns to cope with its problems of external adaptation and internal integration—that has worked well enough to be considered valid and, therefore, to be taught to new members as the correct way to perceive, think, and feel in relation to those problems.

Edgar H. Schein, *Organizational Culture and Leadership: A Dynamic View* (San Francisco: Jossey-Bass, 1985), 9. Others have productively explored ideas of organizational culture both theoretically and empirically. See, for example, Erving Goffman, *Interaction Ritual* (Hawthorne, NY: Aldine, 1967); Terrence E. Deal and Allen A. Kennedy, *Corporate Cultures: The Rites and Rituals of Corporate Life* (Reading, MA: Addison-Wesley, 1982); Richard T. Pascale and Anthony G. Athos, *The Art of Japanese Management* (New York: Simon and Schuster, 1981); J. Van Maanen, "The Self, the Situation, and the Rules of Interpersonal Relations," in *Essays in Interpersonal Dynamics,* ed. W. Bennis et al. (Homewood, IL: Dorsey Press, 1979). There are, as well, thoughtful studies of organizational culture in schools including, Sara Lawrence Lightfoot, *The Good High School: Portraits of Character and Culture* (New York: Basic Books, 1983); Anthony S. Bryk, Peter Holland, Valerie Lee, and Reuben Carriedo, *Effective Catholic Schools: An Exploration* (Washington, D.C.: National Center for Research in Total Catholic Education, 1984); Anthony S. Bryk and Mary Erina Driscoll, *The High School As Community: Contextual Influences, and*

Consequences for Students and Teachers (Madison, WI: National Center on Effective Secondary Schools, 1988); Mary Haywood Metz, *Different by Design: The Context and Character of Three Magnet Schools* (New York: Routledge and Kegan Paul, 1986); Peter W. Cookson, Jr. and Caroline Hodges Persell, *Preparing for Power: America's Elite Boarding Schools* (New York: Basic Books, 1985); Nancy Lesko, *Symbolizing Society: Stories, Rites, and Structure in a Catholic High School* (New York: The Falmer Press, 1988).

2. This distinction between rational and cultural bonds is similar to that set forth by Ferdinand Tonnies and later elaborated by Max Weber between *Gesellschaft,* an association of people which is based primarily on the members' rational pursuit of their own self-interest, and *Gemeinschaft,* an association of people which is based primarily on personal loyalties, shared purposes, and common sentiments. Ferdinand Tonnies, *Gemeinschaft und Gesellschaft* (Leipzig: Fues's Verlag, 1887); Max Weber, *The Theory of Social and Economic Organization,* ed. Talcott Parsons (New York: The Free Press, 1947). However, it seems that there is an important difference between the two kinds of bonds described by teachers in this study and the two kinds of social organizations described by Tonnies. Teachers from public and private schools do not seem to differ fundamentally in purpose when they enter teaching; both are compelled by an interest in children, subject matter, and pedagogy. However, once in teaching, schools as organizations seem to shape the experiences of one group to resemble *Gesellschaft* and the other to resemble *Gemeinschaft.*
3. Sara Lawrence Lightfoot's qualitative study of four public and two private high schools led her to conclude:

   > Institutional control is a great deal easier for schools with abundant resources, non-public funding, and historical stability. It is not only that private schools tend to be more protected from societal trends, divergent community demands, and broader bureaucratic imperatives; they are also more likely to have the advantage of the material and psychological resources of certainty.

   Sara Lawrence Lightfoot, *The Good High School: Portraits of Character and Culture* (New York: Basic Books, 1983), 319.
4. In his study of three secondary schools, Philip A. Cusick also found an absence of stated goals: "No principal of those schools ever talked about the school philosophy or beliefs or adherence to some common goals; the schools were always presented as an aggregate of discrete and disparate activities and events." Philip A.

Cusick, *The Egalitarian Ideal and the American High School: Studies of Three Schools* (New York: Longman, 1983), 95.

5. Robin Lovin states that "the problem of pluralism in American society is mirrored in the problems of American education. An old consensus, which established nondenominational and nondogmatic Protestantism as the country's dominant value system, has broken down under the weight of real social diversity, in which many persons no longer aspire to the values of Protestant civility." Robin Lovin, "The School and the Articulation of Values," *American Journal of Education,* 96 no. 2 (February 1988):143; Anthony S. Bryk argues that the "idea of a value-free public education is an oxymoron—it neither reflects a commitment to the public good, nor does it comprehend the distinction between an education of persons and technical training." Anthony S. Bryk, "Musings on the Moral Life of Schools," *American Journal of Education* 96 no. 2 (February 1988):258.
6. Sometimes, as James S. Coleman and Thomas Hoffer explain, a local community that built such a school constituted a "functional community in which social norms and sanctions, including those that cross generations, arise out of the social structure itself, and both reinforce and perpetuate that structure." James S. Coleman and Thomas Hoffer, *Public and Private High Schools: The Impact of Communities* (New York: Basic Books, 1987), 7.
7. James S. Coleman and Thomas Hoffer contend: "Thus the public school with a geographically defined student body has become increasingly heterogeneous in values, increasingly contentious, increasingly unmanageable by principal and staff." Coleman and Hoffer, *Public and Private High Schools,* 17.
8. In their study of 357 schools, Anthony S. Bryk and Mary Erina Driscoll found that school size was strongly related to the presence of communal organizations. Small schools were more likely than large schools to be organizations with shared values, common activities, and distinct patterns of social organization. Bryk and Driscoll, *The High School as Community,* 19.
9. Philip A. Cusick concludes that it is contemporary public high schools' commitment to the egalitarian ethic—their commitment to provide each student with an opportunity for social, political, and economic equality—that has generated diverse, fragmented curricula in today's schools. Cusick, *The Egalitarian Ideal,* 106–7.
10. Edgar Schein emphasizes that culture is "a *learned product of group experience* and is, therefore, to be found only where there is a definable group with a significant history" (Schein's italics). Schein, *Organizational Culture,* 7. In their study of private boarding schools,

Peter W. Cookson, Jr. and Caroline Hodges Persell found that "teachers are, in the words of more than one head, the 'heart and soul' of any school. Students come and go, but the faculty goes on. Senior faculty in particular are the embodiment of what the school has been, is, and will be." Cookson and Persell, *Preparing for Power,* 85.

11. Peter W. Cookson, Jr. and Caroline Hodges Persell contend, "As the symbol of authority in the total institution, the head must insure that the school forms a true collective, not merely a collection of individuals." They argue further, "Creation of a collective identity, however, requires more than outward discipline. Individuals must also be submerged in a belief system that guides their behavior and instills them with the proper values." Cookson and Persell, *Preparing for Power,* 120, 138.
12. Schein, *Organizational Culture,* 2.
13. Bryk and Driscoll, *The High School as Community,* 21–8.
14. For an exploration of some of these possible changes, see Nel Noddings, "An Ethics of Caring and Its Implications for Instructional Arrangements," *American Journal of Education* 96 no. 2 (February 1988):215–30.
15. Metz, *Different by Design.*
16. For a consideration of the potential divisiveness of selective or magnet schools, see Philip A. Cusick and Christopher W. Wheeler, "Educational Morality and Organizational Reform," *American Journal of Education* 96 no. 2 (February 1988):231–55. For an examination of choice programs in Chicago, New York, Philadelphia, and Boston, which concludes that they have increased the isolation of students at risk, see Donald R. Moore and Suzanne Davenport, *The New Improved Sorting Machine* (Madison, WI: National Center on Effective Secondary Schools, December 1988).

CHAPTER 9

1. Donald A. Schön, *The Reflective Practitioner: How Professionals Think in Action* (New York: Basic Books, 1983).
2. Milbrey Wallin McLaughlin and Sylvia Mei-ling Yee, "School As a Place to Have a Career," in *Building a Professional Culture in Schools,* ed. Ann Lieberman (New York: Teachers College Press, 1988), 37.
3. Arthur E. Wise, Linda Darling-Hammond, Milbrey W. McLaughlin,

and Harriet T. Bernstein, *Case Studies for Teacher Evaluation: A Study of Effective Practices* (Santa Monica, CA: RAND Corporation, 1984; Milbrey Wallin McLaughlin and R. Scott Pfeifer, *Teacher Evaluation: Improvement, Accountability, and Effective Learning.* (New York: Teachers College Press, 1988).
4. McLaughlin and Yee, "School as a Place to Have a Career."
5. Donald R. Moore and Arthur A. Hyde, *Making Sense of Staff Development: An Analysis of School District Programs and Their Costs in Three Urban School Districts* (Chicago: Designs for Change, 1981).
6. Barbara Neufeld and Sarah Haavind, *Professional Development Schools in Massachusetts: Beginning the Process* (Cambridge, MA: Education Matters, 1988), 9–11.
7. Wise et al., *Case Studies;* Susan Moore Johnson, "Pursuing Professional Reform in Cincinnati," *Phi Delta Kappan* 69 no. 10 (June 1988):748.

CHAPTER 10

1. Susan Moore Johnson, "Incentives for Teachers: What Motivates, What Matters," *Educational Administration Quarterly* 22 no. 3 (Summer 1986):54–79.
2. Expectancy theory, upon which incentive plans are based, was first set forth by V. Vroom, *Work and Motivation* (New York: Wiley, 1964). It has been elaborated by Edward E. Lawler III, *Pay and Organization Development* (Reading, MA: Addison-Wesley, 1983).
3. Bacharach et al. concluded that extrinsic rewards such as money will improve the performance of "uninteresting or otherwise unattractive" tasks, but that intrinsic motivation is sufficient for problem-solving tasks. Samuel B. Bacharach, David B. Lipsky, and Joseph B. Shedd, *Paying for Better Teaching: Merit Pay and Its Alternatives* (Ithaca, N.Y.: Organizational Analysis and Practice, 1984), 13.
4. See, for example, Dan C. Lortie, *Schoolteacher: A Sociological Study* (Chicago: University of Chicago Press, 1975).
5. U.S. Department of Education, *The Nation Responds: Recent Efforts to Improve Education* (Washington, D.C.: U.S. Government Printing Office, 1984).
6. These teachers' concerns were consistent with those documented by researchers who have studied merit pay. See, for example, Bacharach, Lipsky, and Shedd, *Paying for Better Teaching;* Terry A. Astuto and David Clark, *Merit Pay for Teachers, An Analysis of State*

Policy Options, Education Policy Series no. 1 (Bloomington, IN: Indiana University School of Education, 1985); Richard J. Murnane and David K. Cohen, "Merit Pay and the Evaluation Problem: Why Some Merit Pay Plans Fail and a Few Survive," *Harvard Educational Review* 56 no. 1 (1986); Susan Moore Johnson, "Merit Pay for Teachers: A Poor Prescription for Reform," *Harvard Educational Review* 54 no. 2 (May 1984); H. P. Hatry and J. M. Greiner, *Issues in Teacher Incentive Plans* (Washington, D.C.: The Urban Institute, 1984).

CHAPTER 11

1. Designs for Change, *The Chicago School Reform Act: Highlights of Senate Bill 1840* (Chicago: Designs for Change, 1989).
2. Boston Public Schools, "Agreement Between the Boston School Committee and the Boston Teachers Union" (Boston: Boston Public Schools, 1989).
3. For a persuasive discussion of the folly of "list logic," whereby public schools seek to achieve eertain instructional outcomes by complying with standards and practices derived and imposed by those outside the schools, see Roland Barth, "On Sheep and Goats and School Reform," *Phi Delta Kappan* 68 no. 4 (December 1986):293–96.
4. Donald R. Moore and Suzanne Davenport, *The New Improved Sorting Machine* (Madison, WI: National Center on Effective Secondary Schools, December 1988).
5. Holmes Group, *Tomorrow's Teachers* (East Lansing, MI: Holmes Group, 1986).
6. Carnegie Forum on Education and the Economy, *A Nation Prepared: Teachers for the 21st Century* (New York: Carnegie Forum on Education and the Economy, 1986).

APPENDIX

1. *Curriculum Information Center's School Directory, 1986–1987: Massachusetts* (Shelton, CT: Market Retrieval, 1987).
2. Of the 1062 public school teachers interviewed by Louis Harris in 1986, 68 percent of the respondents were women and 32 percent

were men. Louis Harris and Associates, *The American Teacher, 1986: Restructuring the Teaching Profession* (New York: Metropolitan Life Insurance Company, 1987), 73.

3. Fifteen was the median number of years of experience of the 1062 public-school teachers interviewed by Louis Harris in 1986. Harris, *The American Teacher,* 85.

BIBLIOGRAPHY

Argyris, Chris. *Personality and Organization.* New York: Harper, 1957.

Ashton, Patricia T., and Webb, Rodman B. *Making a Difference: Teachers' Sense of Efficacy and Student Achievement.* New York: Longman, 1986.

Astuto, Terry A., and Clark, David. *Merit Pay for Teachers, An Analysis of State Policy Options.* Educational Policy Series no. 1. Bloomington, IN: Indiana University School of Education, 1985.

Barber, Larry W., and McClellan, Mary C. "Looking at America's Dropouts: Who Are They?" *Phi Delta Kappan* 69 no. 4 (December 1987):264–67.

Bacharach, Samuel B.; Conley, Sharon C.; and Shedd, Joseph B. "Beyond Career Ladders: Structuring Teacher Career Development Systems." *Teachers College Record* 87 no. 4 (Summer 1986):563–74.

Bacharach, Samuel B.; Lipsky, David B.; and Shedd, Joseph B. *Paying for Better Teaching: Merit Pay and its Alternatives.* Ithaca, NY: Organizational Analysis and Practice, 1984.

Bacharach, Samuel B., and Shedd, Joseph B. "Power and Empowerment: The Constraining Myths and Emerging Structures of Teacher Unionism in an Age of Reform." In *The Politics of Reforming School Administration,* edited by Jane Hannaway and Robert Crowson, 139–60. New York: The Falmer Press, 1989.

Barth, Roland. "On Sheep and Goats and School Reform." *Phi Delta Kappan* 68 no. 4 (December 1986):293–96.

———. "School: A Community of Leaders." In *Building a Professional Culture in Schools,* edited by Ann Lieberman, 129–47. New York: Teachers College Press, 1988.

Baugh, W. H., and Stone, J. A. *Mobility of Wage Equilibration in the Educator Labor Market.* Eugene, OR: Center for Educational Policy and Management, 1982.

BIBLIOGRAPHY

Berger, Joseph. "Allure of Teaching Reviving: Education School Roles Surge." *New York Times,* 6 May 1988, 1.

Biderman, Albert D., and Drury, Thomas F. *Measuring Work Quality for Social Reporting.* New York: Wiley, 1976.

Bidwell, Charles. "The School As a Formal Organization." In *Handbook of Organizations,* edited by James G. March, 927–1022. Chicago: Rand McNally, 1965.

Bird, Thomas, and Little, Judith Warren. *School Organization of the Teaching Occupation.* San Francisco: Far West Laboratory, 1985.

Blackler, F. H. M., and Brown, C. A. "Job Redesign and Social Change: Case Studies at Volvo." In *Changes in Working Life,* edited by K. D. Duncan, M. M. Gruneberg, and D. Wallis, 311–27. New York: Wiley, 1980.

Boston Public Schools. "Agreement Between the Boston School Committee and the Boston Teachers Union." Boston: Boston Public Schools, 1989.

Bryk, Anthony S. "Musings on the Moral Life of Schools." *American Journal of Education* 96 no. 2 (February 1988):256–90.

Bryk, Anthony S., and Driscoll, Mary Erina. *The High School As Community: Contextual Influences, and Consequences for Students and Teachers.* Madison, WI: National Center on Effective Secondary Schools, 1988.

Byrk, Anthony S.; Holland, Peter; Lee, Valerie; and Carriedo, Reuben. *Effective Catholic Schools: An Exploration,* Washington, D.C.: National Center for Research in Total Catholic Education, 1984.

Burns, Tom, and Stalker, G. M. *The Management of Innovation.* London: Tavistock, 1961.

Callahan, Raymond E. *Education and the Cult of Efficiency.* Chicago: University of Chicago Press, 1962.

Carnegie Forum on Education and the Economy. *A Nation Prepared: Teachers for the 21st Century.* New York: Carnegie Forum on Education and the Economy, 1986.

Chall, Jeanne. *Learning to Read: The Great Debate.* rev. ed. New York: McGraw-Hill, 1983.

Cherns, Albert B., and Davis, Louis E. "Assessment of the State of the Art." In *The Quality of Working Life.* Vol. 1, edited by Louis E. Davis and Albert B. Cherns, 12–54. New York: The Free Press, 1975.

Cohen, David K. "Knowledge of Teaching: *Plus Que Ça Change. . . .*" In *Contributing to Educational Change,* edited by Philip W. Jackson, 27–84. Berkeley, CA: McCutchan, 1988.

Cohen, Deborah L. "Joining Forces." *Education Week* 8 no. 25 (15 March 1989):8.

Cohen, Michael. "Improving School Effectiveness: Lessons from

Research." In *Educators' Handbook: A Research Perspective,* edited by Virginia Richardson-Koehler. 474–90. New York: Longman, 1987.

Coleman, James S., and Hoffer, Thomas. *Public and Private High Schools: The Impact of Communities.* New York: Basic Books, 1987.

Coles, Robert. "On the Meaning of Work." *Atlantic Monthly,* October 1971, 104.

Comer, James P. *School Power.* New York: The Free Press, 1981.

———. "Education for Community." In *Common Decency,* edited by Alvin Schorr. 186–209. New Haven: Yale University Press, 1986.

———. "Home-School Relationships As They Affect the Academic Success of Children." *Education and Urban Society* 16 (1984):323–37.

Connell, Robert W. *Teachers' Work.* Sydney, NSW: George Allen and Unwin, 1985.

Connell, Robert W.; Ashenden, D. J.; Kessler, S.; and Dowsett, G. W. *Making the Difference: Schools, Families, and Social Division.* Sydney, NSW: George Allen and Unwin, 1982.

Cookson, Peter W., Jr., and Persell, Caroline Hodges. *Preparing for Power: America's Elite Boarding Schools.* New York: Basic Books, 1985.

Corbett, H. Dickson, and Wilson, Bruce L. "Raising the Stakes on Statewide Mandatory Testing Programs." In *The Politics of Reforming School Administration,* edited by Jane Hannaway and Robert Crowson, 27–39. New York: The Falmer Press, 1989.

Corcoran, Thomas B.; Walker, Lisa J.; and White, J. Lynne. *Working in Urban Schools.* Washington, D.C.: Institute for Educational Leadership, 1988.

Cusick, Philip A. *The Egalitarian Ideal and the American High School: Studies of Three Schools.* New York: Longman, 1983.

Cusick, Philip A., and Wheeler, Christopher W. "Educational Morality and Organizational Reform." *American Journal of Education* 96 no. 2 (February 1988):231–55.

Darling-Hammond, Linda. *Beyond the Commission Reports: The Coming Crisis in Teaching.* R-3177-RC. Santa Monica, CA: RAND Corporation, July 1984.

Deal, Terrence E., and Kennedy, Allen A. *Corporate Cultures: The Rites and Rituals of Corporate Life.* Reading, MA: Addison-Wesley, 1982.

Designs for Change. *The Bottom Line: Chicago's Failing Schools and How to Change Them.* Chicago: Designs for Change, 1985.

———. *The Chicago School Reform Act: Highlights of Senate Bill 1840.* Chicago: Designs for Change, 1989.

Duncan, K. D.; Gruneberg, M. M.; and Wallis, D. *Changes in Working Life.* New York: Wiley, 1980.

BIBLIOGRAPHY

Edmonds, Ronald. "Effective Schools for the Urban Poor." *Educational Leadership* 37 (October 1979):15–24.

Featherstone, Helen. "Organizing Classes by Ability." *Harvard Education Letter* 3 no. 4 (July 1987):1–2.

Fenton, Patrick. "Confessions of a Working Stiff." In *Man Against Work,* edited by Lloyd Zimpel, 19–26. Grand Rapids, MI: Eerdmans, 1974.

Freedman, Sara; Jackson, Jane; and Boles, Katherine C. "Teaching: An Imperilled Profession." In *Handbook of Teaching and Policy,* edited by Lee S. Shulman and Gary Sykes, 261–99. New York: Longman, 1983.

Friedson, Eliot. *Profession of Medicine: A Study of the Sociology of Applied Knowledge.* New York: Dodd, Mead, 1971.

———. *Professional Powers.* Chicago: University of Chicago Press, 1986.

Galbraith, Jay. *Designing Complex Organizations.* Reading, MA: Addison-Wesley, 1973.

Garson, Barbara. *All the Livelong Day.* Garden City, NJ: Doubleday, 1975.

Goffman, Erving. *Interaction Ritual.* Hawthorne, NY: Aldine, 1967.

Good, Thomas. "Research on Classroom Teaching." In *Handbook of Teaching and Policy,* edited by Lee S. Shulman and Gary Sykes, 42–80. New York: Longman, 1983.

Goodlad, John I. *A Place Called School: Prospects for the Future.* New York: McGraw-Hill, 1984.

Graham, Patricia Albjerg. "Black Teachers: A Drastically Scarce Resource." *Phi Delta Kappan* 68 no. 8 (April 1987):598–605.

Grant, Gerald. *The World We Created at Hamilton High.* Cambridge: Harvard University Press, 1985.

Grissmer, David W., and Kirby, Sheila Naturaz. *Teacher Attrition: The Uphill Climb to Staff the Nation's Schools.* R-3512-CSTP. Santa Monica, CA: RAND Corporation, August 1987.

Gyllenhammer, Pehr G. *People at Work.* Reading, MA: Addison-Wesley, 1977.

Hackman, John, and Oldham, G. R. *Work Redesign.* Reading, MA: Addison-Wesley, 1983.

Hannaway, Jane, and Crowson, Robert, editors. *The Politics of Reforming School Administration.* New York: The Falmer Press, 1989.

Harrington, Alan. "A Day at the Crystal Palace." In *Life in Organizations: Workplaces As People Experience Them,* edited by Rosabeth Moss Kanter and Barry A. Stein, 105–16. New York: Basic Books, 1979.

Harris, Louis, and Associates. *The American Teacher 1986: Restructuring the Teaching Profession.* New York: Metropolitan Life Insurance Company, 1987.

———. *1988 Survey of the American Teacher,* New York: Metropolitan Life Insurance Company, 1988.

Hatry, H. P., and Greiner, J. M. *Issues in Teacher Incentive Plans.* Washington, D.C.: The Urban Institute, 1984.

Hemmings, Annette. *"Real" Teaching: How Teachers Negotiate National, Community, and Student Pressures When They Define Their Work.* Madison, WI: National Center on Effective Secondary Schools, 1988.

Herrick, Neal Q., and Macoby, Michael, "Humanizing Work: A Priority Goal of the 1970s." In *The Quality of Working Life.* Vol. 1, *Problems, Prospects, and the State of the Art,* edited by Louis E. Davis and Albert B. Cherns, 63–77. New York: The Free Press, 1975.

Hirschman, Albert O. *Exit, Voice, and Loyalty: Responses to Decline in Firms, Organizations, and States.* Cambridge: Harvard University Press, 1970.

Hoffman, Nancy. *Women's "True" Profession: Voices from the History of Teaching.* Old Westbury, NY: The Feminist Press, 1981.

Holmes Group. *Tomorrow's Teachers.* East Lansing, MI: Holmes Group, 1986.

Houston, Holly. "Restructuring Secondary Schools." In *Building a Professional Culture in Schools,* edited by Ann Lieberman, 109–28. New York: Teachers College Press, 1988.

Jackson, Philip W. *Life in Classrooms.* New York: Holt, Rinehart and Winston, 1968.

———. "Facing Our Ignorance." *Teachers College Record* 88 (Spring 1987):384–89.

———. *The Practice of Teaching.* New York: Teachers College Press, 1986.

Jennings, John F. "The Sputnik of the Eighties." *Phi Delta Kappan* 69 no. 2 (October 1987), 104–9.

Johnson, Susan Moore. *Teacher Unions in Schools.* Philadelphia: Temple University Press, 1983.

———. "Can Schools Be Reformed at the Bargaining Table?" *Teachers College Record* 89 no. 2 (Winter 1987):269–80.

———. "Incentives for Teachers: What Motivates, What Matters." *Educational Administration Quarterly* 22 (Summer 1986):54–79.

———. "Merit Pay for Teachers: A Poor Prescription for Reform." *Harvard Educational Review* 54 no. 2 (May 1984):175–85.

———. "Performance-Based Layoffs in the Public Schools: Implementation and Outcomes." *Harvard Educational Review* 50 no. 2 (May 1980):214–33.

———. "Pursuing Professional Reform in Cincinnati." *Phi Delta Kappan* 69 no. 10 (June 1988):746–51.

———. "Schoolwork and Its Reform." In *The Politics of Reforming School Administration,* edited by Jane Hannaway and Robert Crowson, 95–112. New York: The Falmer Press, 1989.

Johnson, Susan Moore, and Nelson, Niall C. W. "Conflict and Compatibility in Visions of Reform." *Educational Policy* 1 no. 1 (Winter 1987):67–80.

Kahn, Robert. "The Meaning of Work: Interpretation and Proposals for Measurement." In *The Human Meaning of Social Change,* edited by Angus Campbell and Philip E. Converse. 159–203. New York: Russell Sage, 1972.

Kane, Pearl R. *The Teachers College New Jersey Survey: A Comparative Study of Public and Independent School Teachers.* New York: Teachers College, Columbia University, 1986.

Kanter, Rosabeth Moss. *The Change Masters: Innovation for Productivity in the American Corporation.* New York: Simon & Schuster, 1983.

Kanter, Rosabeth Moss, and Stein, Barry A., editors. *Life in Organizations: Workplaces As People Experience Them.* New York: Basic Books, 1979.

Kean, Elizabeth B. "Left Behind." *Teacher Magazine* 1 no. 1 (October 1989):8–9.

Kearns, David T. "An Education Recovery Plan for America." *Phi Delta Kappan* 69 no. 8 (April 1988):565–70.

Kerr, Donna H. "Teaching Competence and Teacher Education in the United States." *Teachers College Record,* 84 (Spring 1983):525–52.

Kidder, Tracy. *Among Schoolchildren.* Boston: Houghton Mifflin, 1989.

Koppich, Julia E., and Kerchner, Charles T. *The Trust Agreement Project: Broadening the Vision of School Labor-Management Relations: A First-Year Progress Report.* Berkeley, CA: Policy Analysis for California Education, September 1988.

Lampert, Magdelene. "How Do Teachers Manage to Teach? Perspectives on Problems in Practice." *Harvard Educational Review* 55 (May 1985):178–94.

Lawler, Edward E., III. *Pay and Organization Development.* Reading, MA: Addison-Wesley, 1983.

Lawrence, Paul R., and Lorsch, Jay W. *Organization and Environment: Managing Differentiation and Integration.* Boston: Graduate School of Business Administration, Harvard University, 1967.

Lesko, Nancy. *Symbolizing Society: Stories, Rites, and Structure in a Catholic High School.* New York: The Falmer Press, 1988.

Levine, Sarah L. *Promoting Adult Growth in Schools: The Promise of Professional Development.* Boston: Allyn and Bacon, 1989.

Lewis, Anne. *Wolves at the Schoolhouse Door: An Investigation of the Condition of Public School Buildings.* Washington, D.C.: Education Writers Association, 1989.

Lieberman, Ann, editor. *Building a Professional Culture in Schools.* New York: Teachers College Press, 1988.

Lieberman, Myron. *Beyond Public Education.* New York: Praeger, 1986.

Lightfoot, Sara Lawrence. *The Good High School: Portraits of Character and Culture.* New York: Basic Books, 1983.

———. *Worlds Apart: Relationships Between Families and Schools.* New York: Basic Books, 1978.

———. "The Lives of Teachers." In *Handbook of Teaching Policy,* edited by Lee S. Shulman and Gary Sykes, 241–60. New York: Longman, 1983.

Lipsitz, Joan. *Successful Schools for Young Adolescents.* New Brunswick, NJ: Transaction Books, 1984.

Lipsky, Michael. *Street-Level Bureaucracy.* New York: Russell Sage, 1980.

Little, Judith Warren. "Norms of Collegiality and Experimentation: Workplace Conditions of School Success." *American Educational Research Journal* 19 no. 3 (1982):325–40.

———. "Teachers As Colleagues." *Educators' Handbook: A Research Perspective,* edited by Virginia Richardson-Koehler, 491–518. New York: Longman, 1987.

Lohr, Steve. "Making Cars the Volvo Way." *New York Times,* 23 June 1987, D1, D5.

Lortie, Dan C. *Schoolteacher: A Sociological Study.* Chicago: University of Chicago Press, 1975.

Lovin, Robin. "The School and the Articulation of Values." *American Journal of Education* 96 no. 2 (February 1988):143–61.

Loving, Rush, Jr. "W. T. Grant's Last Days." In *Life in Organizations: Workplaces As People Experience Them,* edited by Rosabeth Moss Kanter and Barry A. Stein, 400–412. New York: Basic Books, 1979.

Madaus, George. "The Influence of Testing on the Curriculum." In *Critical Issues in Curriculum: 87th Yearbook of the NSSE, Part I,* 83–121. Chicago: University of Chicago Press, 1988.

Maeroff, Gene. *The Empowerment of Teachers: Overcoming the Crisis of Confidence.* New York: Teachers College Press, 1988.

Mann, Dale. "Authority and School Improvement: An Essay on 'Little King' Leadership." *Teachers College Record* 88 no. 1 (Fall 1986):41–52.

Massachusetts Institute of Technology Commission on Industrial Productivity. *Made in America.* Cambridge: Massachusetts Institute of Technology, 1989.

McDonnell, Lorraine M., and Pascal, Anthony. *Teacher Unions and Educational Reform.* Santa Monica, CA: RAND Corporation, 1988.

McLaughlin, Milbrey Wallin, and Pfeifer, R. Scott. *Teacher Evaluation: Improvement, Accountability, and Effective Learning.* New York: Teachers College Press, 1988.

McLaughlin, Milbrey Wallin, and Yee, Sylvia Mei-ling. "School As a Place to Have a Career." In *Building a Professional Culture in Schools,* edited by Ann Lieberman, 23–44. New York: Teachers College Press, 1988.

McNeil, Linda M. *Contradictions of Control: School Structure and School Knowledge,* New York: Routledge and Kegan Paul, 1986.

———. "Contradictions of Control, Part 3: Contradictions of Reform." *Phi Delta Kappan* 69 no. 7 (March 1988):478–85.

———. "Exit, Voice, and Community: Magnet Teachers' Responses to Standardization." *Educational Policy* 1 no. 1 (Winter 1987):93–113.

McPherson, Gertrude. *Small Town Teacher.* Cambridge: Harvard University Press, 1972.

Metz, Mary Haywood. *"The American High School": A Universal Drama Amid Disparate Experience.* Madison, WI: National Center on Effective Secondary Schools, 1988.

———. *Classrooms and Corridors: The Crisis of Authority in Desegregated Secondary Schools.* Berkeley: University of California Press, 1978.

———. *Different By Design: The Context and Character of Three Magnet Schools.* New York: Routledge and Kegan Paul, 1986.

———. *Teachers' Ultimate Dependence on Their Students: Implications for Teachers' Responses to Student Bodies of Differing Social Class.* Madison, WI: National Center on Effective Secondary Schools, 1988.

Meyer, John W., and Rowan, Brian. "Institutionalized Organizations: Formal Structure As Myth and Ceremony." *American Journal of Sociology* 83 no. 2 (1977):340–63.

———. "The Structure of Educational Organizations." In *Environments and Organizations: Theoretical and Empirical Perspectives,* edited by M. Meyer and Associates. 78–109. San Francisco: Jossey-Bass, 1978.

Mintzberg, Henry. *The Structuring of Organizations.* Englewood Cliffs, NJ: Prentice-Hall, 1979.

Mitchell, Douglas E., and Kerchner, Charles T. "Labor Relations and Teacher Policy." In *Handbook of Teaching and Policy,* edited by Lee S. Shulman and Gary Sykes, 214–38. New York: Longman, 1983.

Moore, Donald R., and Hyde, Arthur A. *Making Sense of Staff Development: An Analysis of School District Programs and Their Costs in Three Urban School Districts.* Chicago: Designs for Change, 1981.

Moore, Donald R., and Davenport, Suzanne. *The New Improved Sorting Machine.* Madison, WI: National Center on Effective Secondary Schools, December 1988.

Murnane, Richard J., and Cohen, David K. "Merit Pay and the Evaluation Problem: Why Some Merit Pay Plans Fail and a Few Survive." *Harvard Educational Review* 56 no. 1 (1986):1–17.

Murnane, Richard J.; Singer, Judith D.; and Willett, John B. "The Influences of Salaries and 'Opportunity Costs' on Teachers' Career Choices: Evidence from North Carolina." *Harvard Educational Review* 59 no. 3 (1989):325–46.

National Assessment of Education Progress. *The Nation's Report Card.* Princeton, NJ: National Assessment of Education Progress, 1988.

National Commission on Excellence in Education. *A Nation at Risk: The Imperative for Educational Reform.* Washington, D.C.: U.S. Government Printing Office, 1983.

Neufeld, Barbara. "Evaluating the Effective Teaching Research." *Harvard Education Letter* 1 no. 5 (November 1985):5.

Neufeld, Barbara, and Haavind, Sarah. *Professional Development Schools in Massachusetts: Beginning the Process.* Cambridge, MA: Education Matters, 1988.

Noddings, Nel. "An Ethics of Caring and Its Implications for Instructional Arrangements." *American Journal of Education* 96 no. 2 (February 1988):215–30.

Oakes, Jeannie. *Keeping Track: How Schools Structure Inequality.* New Haven: Yale University Press, 1985.

Ogbu, John. "Variability in Minority School Performance: A Problem in Search of an Explanation." *Anthropology and Education Quarterly* 18 no. 4 (December 1987):312–34.

Olson, Lynn. "Teaching's 'Knowledge Base' Seen Still Elusive." *Education Week* 7 no. 23 (2 March 1988):7.

Olson, Lynn, and Rodman, Blake. "Growing Need, Fewer Teachers: Everybody Is Out There Bidding." *Education Week* 5 no. 39 (June 18, 1986):1.

———. "Is There a Teacher Shortage? It's Anyone's Guess." *Education Week* 6 no. 39 (24 June 1987):1, 14.

Pascale, Richard T., and Athos, Anthony G. *The Art of Japanese Management.* New York: Simon & Schuster, 1981.

Perrow, Charles. "Three Types of Effectiveness Studies." In *New Perspectives on Organizational Effectiveness*, edited by Paul S. Goodman, Johannes M. Pennings, and Associates, 96–105. San Francisco: Jossey-Bass, 1977.

Peters, Thomas J., and Waterman, Robert H., Jr. *In Search of Excellence: Lessons from America's Best-Run Companies.* New York: Warner, 1982.

Powell, Arthur G. "The Conditions of Teachers' Work in Independent Schools: Some Preliminary Observations." In *The Secondary School Workplace,* edited by Milbrey Wallin McLaughlin and Joan Talbert. New York: Teachers College Press, 1990.

Powell, Arthur G.; Farrar, Eleanor; and Cohen, David K. *The Shopping Mall High School: Winners and Losers in the Educational Marketplace.* Boston: Houghton Mifflin, 1985.

Richardson, Elliot. *Work in America.* Cambridge: MIT Press, 1975.

Ritchie, John McGee. "Experiments in Promoting Teacher Collegiality: A Qualitative Study of Three Schools." Ph.D. diss., Harvard University, 1989.

Robinson, John P. "Some Approaches to Examining Quality of Employment Indicators for Disaggregated Segments of the Work Force." In *Measuring Work Quality for Social Reporting,* edited by Albert D. Biderman and Thomas F. Drury, 44–59. New York: Wiley, 1976.

Rosenholtz, Susan J. *Teachers' Workplace: The Social Organization of Schools.* New York: Longman, 1989.

———. "Effective Schools: Interpreting the Evidence." *American Journal of Education* 93 no. 3 (May 1985):352–88.

Rosow, Jerome, and Zager, Robert. *Allies in Educational Reform: How Teachers, Unions, and Administrators Can Join Forces for Better Schools.* San Francisco: Jossey-Bass, 1989.

Rothman, Robert. "Teachers Vs. Curriculum in Philadelphia." *Education Week* 7 no. 26 (23 March 1988):1.

Rutter, Michael; Maughan, B.; Mortimore, P.; and Outston, J. *Fifteen Thousand Hours: Secondary Schools and Their Effects on Children.* Cambridge: Harvard University Press, 1979.

Ryan, Kevin. "The Wrong Report at the Right Time." *Teachers College Record* 88 (Spring 1987):419–22.

Sarason, Seymour. *The Culture of School and the Problem of Change.* Boston: Allyn and Bacon, 1971.

Schein, Edgar H. *Organizational Culture and Leadership: A Dynamic View.* San Francisco: Jossey-Bass, 1985.

Schlechty, Philip C., and Vance, V. S. "Do Academically Able Teachers

Leave Education? The North Carolina Case." *Phi Delta Kappan* 63 (October 1981):106–12.

Schön, Donald A. *The Reflective Practitioner: How Professionals Think in Action.* New York: Basic Books, 1983.

Schorr, Lisbeth. *Within Our Reach: Breaking the Cycle of Disadvantage.* New York: Anchor Press/Doubleday, 1988.

Schrank, Robert. *Ten Thousand Working Days.* Cambridge: MIT Press, 1978.

Scott, W. Richard. "Effectiveness of Organizational Effectiveness Studies." In *New Perspectives on Organizational Effectiveness,* edited by Paul S. Goodman, Johannes M. Pennings, and Associates, 63–95. San Francisco: Jossey-Bass, 1977.

Seashore, Stanley. "Defining and Measuring the Quality of Working Life." In *The Quality of Working Life,* Vol. 1, edited by Louis E. Davis and Albert B. Cherns, 105–18. New York: The Free Press, 1975.

Sedlak, Michael; Wheeler, Christopher W.; Pullin, Diana C.; and Cusick, Philip A. *Selling Students Short: Classroom Bargains and Academic Reform in the American High School.* New York: Teachers College Press, 1986.

See, Carolyn. "A Veterinarian." *Atlantic Monthly,* October 1971, 95–102.

Serrin, William. "The Assembly Line." *Atlantic Monthly,* October 1971, 62–73.

Sizer, Theodore R. *Horace's Compromise: The Dilemma of the American High School.* Boston: Houghton Mifflin, 1984.

Spradley, James P., and Mann, Brenda J. *The Cocktail Waitress: Woman's Work in a Man's World.* New York: Wiley, 1975.

Steers, R. M. *Organizational Effectiveness: A Behavioral View.* Pacific Palisades, CA: Goodyear, 1977.

Terkel, Studs. *Working.* New York: Avon, 1972.

Tonnies, Ferdinand. *Gemeinschaft und Gesellschaft.* Leipzig: Fues's Verlag, 1887.

Tyack, David B. *The One Best System: A History of American Urban Education.* Cambridge: Harvard University Press, 1974.

Tyack, David B., and Stroher, M. "Jobs and Gender: A History of the Structuring of Educational Employment by Sex." In *Educational Policy and Management: Sex Differentials,* edited by Patricia A. Schmuck, W. W. Charters, and Richard O. Carlson, 131–52. New York: Academic Press, 1981.

U.S. Department of Education. *The Nation Responds: Recent Efforts to Improve Education.* Washington, D.C.: U.S. Government Printing Office, 1984.

———. *Class Size and Public Policy: Politics and Panaceas.* Washington, D.C.: U.S. Government Printing Office, 1986.

Vance, V. S., and Schlechty, Philip C. "The Distribution of Academic Ability in the Teaching Force: Policy Implications." *Phi Delta Kappan* 64 (September 1982):22–27.

Van Maanen, J. "The Self, the Situation, and the Rules of Interpersonal Dynamics," in *Essays in Interpersonal Dynamics*, edited by W. Bennis, and Associates. Homewood, IL: Dorsey Press, 1979.

Vroom, V. *Work and Motivation.* New York: Wiley, 1964.

Waller, Willard. *The Sociology of Teaching.* 1932. Reprint. New York: Wiley, 1972.

Walton, Richard E. "Criteria for Quality of Working Life," in *The Quality of Working Life* Vol. 1, edited by Louis E. Davis and Albert B. Cherns, 91–104. New York: The Free Press, 1975.

Ward, B., and Tikunoff, W. *Conditions of Schooling in the Los Angeles Unified School District: A Survey of the Experiences and Perceptions of the Teachers in the Los Angeles School District.* San Francisco: Center for Interactive Research and Development, 1984.

Weaver, W. Timothy. "Solving the Problem of Teacher Quality." *Phi Delta Kappan* 66 (October 1984):108–15.

Weber, Max. *The Theory of Social and Economic Organization.* Edited by Talcott Parsons. New York: The Free Press, 1947.

Weick, Karl E. "Educational Organizations As Loosely Coupled Systems." *Administrative Science Quarterly* 21 (1976):1–19.

Wiggins, Grant. "10 'Radical' Suggestions for School Reform." *Education Week* 7 no. 24 (9 March 1988):28.

Wise, Arthur E. *Legislated Learning: The Bureaucratization of the American Classroom.* Berkeley: The University of California Press, 1979.

Wise, Arthur E., Linda Darling-Hammond, Milbrey W. McLaughlin, and Harriet T. Bernstein, *Case Studies for Teacher Evaluation: A Study of Effective Practices.* Santa Monica, CA: RAND Corporation, 1984.

Zimpel, Lloyd, editor. *Man Against Work.* Grand Rapids, MI: Eerdmans, 1974.

Zwerdling, Daniel. "At IGP, It's Not Business As Usual." In *Life in Organizations: Workplaces As People Experience Them,* edited by Rosabeth Moss Kanter and Barry A. Stein, 349–63. New York: Basic Books, 1979.

Index

INDEX

INDEX

INDEX

INDEX